MW00415153

Between Specters of War and Visions of Peace

Between Specters of War and Visions of Peace

DIALOGIC POLITICAL THEORY AND THE
CHALLENGES OF POLITICS

GERALD M. MARA

OXFORD
UNIVERSITY PRESS

OXFORD
UNIVERSITY PRESS

Oxford University Press is a department of the University of Oxford. It furthers
the University's objective of excellence in research, scholarship, and education
by publishing worldwide. Oxford is a registered trade mark of Oxford University
Press in the UK and certain other countries.

Published in the United States of America by Oxford University Press
198 Madison Avenue, New York, NY 10016, United States of America.

© Oxford University Press 2019

CIP data is on file at the Library of Congress
ISBN 978–0–19–090391–6

9 8 7 6 5 4 3 2 1

Printed by Sheridan Books, Inc., United States of America

To Peter Euben, *In Memoriam*

CONTENTS

Acknowledgments   ix

Political Philosophy in War and Peace   1

1 Enmity or Friendship?   11

2 War and Order   37

3 Perpetual Peace   85

4 War Is History   128

5 Political Philosophy Between Peace and War   177

Notes   205
References   237
Index   255

ACKNOWLEDGMENTS

This book has been in preparation for many years and I have accumulated more debts than I acknowledge; a failure of memory, not of gratitude. Some debts do stand out. Roslyn Weiss read much longer drafts of chapters 1 through 3. The revised and shortened versions were improved significantly by her questions and criticisms. As an entry in *The Oxford Handbook of Thucydides*, an earlier version of chapter 5 was strengthened thanks to Ryan Balot, Jill Frank, Melissa Lane, Paul Ludwig, and Rachel Templer. Jill Frank's insightful comments on the introduction made it much better than it otherwise would have been. The project as a whole profited from the specific challenges and suggestions, including advice on the title, offered by Bruce Douglass, Jill Frank, Joel Alden Schlosser and Stephen Salkever, and was generally enriched by conversations with Christine Lee, Clifford Orwin, Arlene Saxonhouse, Catherine Zuckert, and the late Peter Euben. I am particularly grateful to Oxford's two readers for their critical responses, to editor Angela Chnapko and assistant editor Alexcee Bechthold for their guidance throughout the submission and review process, and to Asish Krishna and colleagues for shepherding this through production.

More long-standing debts are to various (some former) colleagues at Georgetown: Harley Balzer, Richard Boyd, James Collins, Patrick Deneen, Bruce Douglass, Andrzej Kaminski, Catherine Keesling, Thomas Kerch, Julia Lamm, David Lightfoot, Charles McNelis, Joshua Mitchell, James O'Donnell, Josiah Osgood, Victoria Pedrick, Terry Pinkard, Henry Richardson, Alex Sens, Nancy Sherman, and Mark Warren; and to former students, now young(er) colleagues Richard Avramenko, Aspen

Brinton, John Buschman, Eric Cheng, Mihaela Czobor-Lupp, Siobhan Doucette, Suzanne Dovi, Craig French, Farah Godrej, Christian Golden, William Gould, Emily Hoechst, Guy Lurie, Christopher McClure, Catherine McKenna, Curtis Murphy, Felicia Rosu, Jonathan Silver, Maureen Steinbruner, Luke Swiderski, Matthew Taylor, Rachel Templer, Christopher Utter, and Gregory Weiner. More generally, I thank the numerous undergraduate and graduate students who patiently listened to and actively challenged so many of the interpretations offered here. Yet when speaking of supportive patience, the deepest thanks must always be given to Joy Roff Mara.

The Oxford Handbook, noted above, is edited by Sara Forsdyke, Ryan Balot, and Edith Foster (2017). A version of chapter 3's Kant section was given at the 2010 annual meeting of the Northeast Political Science Association and eventually appeared as "Possessions Forever: Thucydides and Kant on Peace, War and Politics," *Polity*, 45, 2013 (318–346). A much earlier version of a portion of the Hobbes section, also in chapter 3, was published as "Hobbes's Counsel to Sovereigns," *Journal of Politics*, 50, 1988 (390–411). This material appears with permission.

| Political Philosophy in War and Peace

T HIS BOOK EXAMINES HOW SIGNIFICANT authors in the history of
Western political philosophy have written and thought about
war and peace. Its purposes are both theoretical and practical.
Significant political events have generally prompted redirections in political philosophy. Waves of democratization in the late 1980s generated not
only widespread confidence in democracy's global prospects, but also vigorous extensions of democratic political theory. Indeed, for all of its cre-
ativity and texture, political theory essentially became democratic theory
(Shapiro, 2003, 1–2; Warren, 2001, 226). Its theoretical forays began with
questions about internal governance. They soon migrated into international
politics, as in John Rawls's effort in *The Law of Peoples* to map "the extension of a general social contract idea into a Society of Peoples" (1999,
4). In that work, Rawls envisaged a future wherein motivations for war
diminished, perhaps even disappeared (1999, 19), replaced by peaceful
means of resolving conflicts within reasonable international institutions.
Whatever war powers individual governments retained would need to
function within and be limited by this law of peoples (1999, 26).

Since the beginning of the twenty-first century, however, recurring political violence and instability have tempered practical optimism and unsettled the parameters of political thought. Following al-Qaeda's attacks
against the United States in 2001, the classicist Victor Davis Hanson
detected a "fault line in American thinking: the great divide between a
tragic appreciation of the universe and a confidence that all humanity's
problems of the age are solvable through the proper therapeutic and enlightened response" (2002, xiv–xv). As corrective, Hanson urged recourse to the "glum" ancient Greeks. Nearly ten years later, in the wake

of wars whose frequency and intensity have not abated, the philosopher Judith Butler wrote a scathing critique of American world views allegedly dominated by "frames of war," arguing not for revisiting the ancients, but for advancing toward the future of "an interdependent world . . . within the terms of a more radical and effective egalitarianism" (2010, xxii).

Hanson's and Butler's dramatically different assessments of modern political life indicate that the trajectory of political theory remains controversial. While both of their statements focused on US policy, they could easily describe fundamental alternatives informing a broader spectrum of political thought, contextualizing the questions we ask about politics, the descriptions of the pragmatic and moral choices we face, and the concepts and metaphors we employ. While such frames of reference can vary, the alternatives of cruel or tragic war, on the one side, and humane or enlightened peace, on the other, are not unique to Hanson's and Butler's formulations. They have recurred across time as thoughtful writers and agents have attempted to make pragmatic sense of political life. The persistence of these alternatives does not imply that they are transhistorical or cross-culturally unchanging, but it does suggest that their concerns may, in striking ways, be permanent. While this philosophical history may parallel shifting political events, exploring how its frames of reference have functioned historically is not simply a historical exercise.

Yet a number of influential voices disagree, arguing that studies of the history of Western political philosophy must *remain* historical, confined to clarifying how earlier modes of political thinking were epistemologically structured or culturally situated. Often such arguments are analytic, emphasizing the distances between premodern modes of thought and modern national and international societies (Habermas, 1998, 249–252; Warren, 2001, 5–6) or celebrating the maturation of philosophy into postmetaphysical thinking (Habermas, 1992, 34–39; Benhabib, 2004, 129–132). Other arguments are pragmatic, maintaining that theorizations offered by so-called canonical works threaten to displace real politics (Geuss, 2008, 100–101; Honig, 1993, 2) or that its ideologies foment conflict or abet domination (Rawls, 2005, 13; Connolly, 1995, 106). Whatever the bases of these different judgments, the shared conclusion is that most of the works inhabiting this (broad, deep, and contentious) history of thought are generally unsatisfactory intellectual resources for meeting the political challenges of a turbulent and precarious world. I will say more about these critiques in the pages that follow. It must immediately be noted, however, that all of those who urge moving on from the history of Western thought trace their own intellectual ancestries to different, often opposing, voices within the tradition itself, presuming their own contro- versial frames of reference and demonstrating that their own theoretical and practical legibility depends upon *not* moving totally away from this history. Additionally, as I will argue, modern theoretical attempts to cope with the pragmatic realities of war and peace do not avoid the roadblocks and frustrations that confounded their predecessors. Insofar as the dangers and damages so heavily emphasized by Hanson and Butler are not new, barriers between premodernity, modernity, and postmodernity will turn out to be permeable.

Beyond theory, Hanson and Butler, like other contemporary thinkers, are responding to practical challenges confronting democratic citizens in the twenty-first century. At least in principle, such citizens are if not authors at least judges of public policy. They face the need for and the responsibility of thinking about policies their governments may adopt, enabling democratic accountability. Often this thinking is chastened by stern warnings (like Hanson's) against the dangers of a hostile world or instructed by civilized lectures (like Rawls's) about the trajectory of progressive history. While such positions can be offered from multiple ideological standpoints, they similarly threaten to discourage the critical thinking that healthy democratic politics presumes. Resources for such critical thinking are numerous and varied. I argue that one of these re- sources should be the history of Western political thought, that the lines between politics and political philosophy should be continuous.

Yet while arguing for an attention to political philosophy's history, the book is not a strictly historical study in either of two currently influential senses. It offers no linear narrative of either the philosophical progress (Habermas, 1996; Benhabib, 2004; Pinkard, 1994; Korsgaard, 1996) or the intellectual disarray (Arendt, 1958; Wolin, 1960; Strauss, 1964, 1989; Smith, 2016) of Western modernity. Neither does it try to construct a series of particular histories that "surround these classic texts with their appro- priate ideological context, [so that] we may be able to build up a more re- alistic picture of how political thinking . . . was in fact conducted in earlier periods" (Skinner, 1978, 11). Instead, I present readings of the history of Western political thought that are more dialogic and multivocal, offering mutually interrogating interpretations that invite critical inquiries. The book engages multiple conversation partners across the tradition without situating them—as refuted, corrected, absorbed, or redeemed—within any synoptic theorization. It avoids categories (such as "metaphysical" or "premodern") that peremptorily marginalize or constrict voices. Sensitive to historical influences, these readings attend to how such contexts are inscribed and transformed within texts. Yet they also take seriously, in ways that more local contextualizing may not, explicit authorial intentions to offer contributions of lasting import.

The book's central substantive claim is that the persistence of *both* war and peace must be acknowledged as framing conditions for a political philosophy capable of assisting the critical judgments that citizens need to exercise, particularly in times of intense regime stress or disturbing human precarity. Though this claim may seem modest to the point of being obvious, the interpretations offered in these chapters suggest that one or the other of these two frames has often predominated within philosophical attempts to engage politics' most pressing questions. Sometimes these alternatives are represented along an idealist/realist axis. Consider the striking differences between Rawls and Raymond Geuss over philosophy's relation to political reality. For Rawls, ideal theory is indispensable. Any nonideal theory able to guide well-ordered peoples inhabiting a flawed world must presuppose an ideal theory already on hand (1999, 89–90). For Geuss, ideal theory too often disregards the historical, psychological, and sociological realities that comprise actual politics (2008, 8, 38, 98–99). Though I will argue that the realist/idealist bifurcation encounters numerous descriptive and normative problems, the divide can often be traced to the conflicting philosophical understandings of politics offered by the authors interpreted here with the resulting binary reinforcing oversimplified readings of the originating texts.

I argue that presenting the alternatives of peace and war in this dichotomizing way offers a false choice and that awarding priority to either perspective distorts historical texts, diminishes their capacity for informing actual politics, and weakens important contemporary statements that draw upon these works as resources. As an alternative I encourage a political thinking practiced between war and peace which, I argue, can serve as a resource for political choices as we continue to engage a dangerous and complex world. This does not mean, for example, asking how Thucydides would diagnose the challenges to the West posed by Putin's Russia or Xi's China or how Machiavelli or Hobbes would interpret the ongoing (as of 2018) Syrian catastrophe. It means considering how both the insights and blind spots of the authors explored here can assist our thinking about pressing current questions. On the interpretive approach followed here, these historical works become most politically and educationally relevant when questions about their immediate applicability are bracketed.

I pursue this inquiry by partnering selected authors in five thematic chapters that examine how polemical and pacific frames of reference have functioned within some of Western political theory's most frequently read works. The sequence (beginning in the twentieth century, moving back to medieval and early modern thinkers, then forward through modernity and early postmodernity, and ending with the classical Greeks) reflects the book's departure from linear histories of ideas. In one sense, these chapters comprise a series of essays linked by thematic filaments. While pointing to problems of general significance, I direct my attention to particular texts, never moving very far away from them even when making broader claims.

Yet there are also continuities that, I believe, add up to something. The most obvious of these is the claim that while the alternative framings of war and peace have played essential roles in the history of Western political theory, the philosophical and practical complexities of the most ambitious works within that history frustrate efforts to establish either frame as dominant, revealing instead the overlapping byplays and tensions between them. These themes are examined across multiple registers. Though my point of entry is political conflict, the authors interpreted in this book also represent war and peace as existential conditions, epistemological structures, and rhetorical strategies. My goal is not to integrate these perspectives into some overarching metatheory but to appreciate how their textures deepen political philosophy's various inquiries, while always returning to my problem-oriented beginning, political relations of peace and war.

A second—and related—continuity is the book's ongoing re-examination of how theory connects with practice. Across the thinkers interpreted, textual representations of politics often unsettle or outstrip surrounding philosophical frameworks. While this complication is particularly striking in works aiming at theoretical resolution (Schmitt, Aquinas, Hobbes, Kant, Hegel), authors theorizing disjuncture (Derrida, Machiavelli, Nietzsche) acknowledge elements of politics that they, too, leave underappreciated. We are therefore cautioned against expecting political theory to organize or cohere political phenomena in ways that eliminate puzzles, discontinuities and disruptions. However, the absence of philosophical resolution does not mean giving up on efforts to situate political practices within rigorous understandings of human beings, human knowledge, and human society, the concerns of epistemology, psychology, sociology and anthropology, or of political theory broadly understood. At the same time, however the texts themselves are more than theories. They are also political, not just because they are practically elicited by very real political dilemmas but because they are practically constituted within obstructive, resistant and even threatening political environments.

A third continuity broadens the examination of theory and practice into reflections on the complex linkages between texts, readers, and citizens. While the depth and structure of these philosophical texts should discipline interpretive efforts, the activity of reading requires an openness to different modes of interpretation and a suspicion of intellectual resolutions, a sensitivity to multivocality that this plurality of authors and texts should encourage. In one sense, this blend of structured responsibility and interpretive openness parallels the critical activity of democratic citizens (Harpham, 2017). Yet these texts also remind us that reading and acting are different practices. The interpretation of these texts also discloses the limits of interpretation and the risks and liabilities of a politics that always stretches beyond it. This mutually complicating byplay both associates and distinguishes our activities as readers on the one hand and as citizens on the other. Bearing these initial orientations in mind, the outline of the book is as follows.

Chapter 1 ("Enmity or Friendship?") introduces the problem of political theory's relation to the framing categories of war and peace by considering the influential statements of Carl Schmitt, in *The Concept of the Political*, and Jacques Derrida in *The Politics of Friendship*. While both works make the importance of political philosophy's frame of reference explicit, they offer nearly opposite judgments on its character, whether enmity (Schmitt) or friendship (Derrida) should be constitutive of political practice and thought. Moreover, though both authors acknowledge the importance of this question within Western political thought's history, each argues that the right answer (and for these thinkers there is one) demands a radical reordering if not rejection of what has gone before. In different ways, each monitors prior contributions to political thought in light of settled political/theoretical conclusions.

Chapter 1 is introductory in two ways. First, I engage the substantive positions of Schmitt and Derrida to unsettle the question of how political thought should be framed. I show that Schmitt's focus on enmity as the foundational political concept obscures how activities that he recognizes as political imply more peaceful mutuality. Analogously, I argue that the flourishing of Derrida's political friendship eventually requires the persistence of a certain kind of enmity. Second, I challenge both authors' treatments of the history of political philosophy. By suspecting or rejecting any form of philosophy not regulated by a theoretically privileged kind of politics, they eliminate one of the most important political functions of philosophy, namely its capacity to comment reflectively and critically on the challenging possibilities facing human beings, especially within communities of meaning whose priorities seem settled. In response to these substantive and methodological concerns, I open reconsideration of how the competing perspectives of war and peace have been treated within Western political philosophy's history, following this path in the succeeding chapters.

Chapter 2 ("War and Order") examines how Thomas Aquinas (Part Two of the *Summa Theologiae*) and Niccolo Machiavelli (*Prince* and *Discourses on Livy*) relate war to political order. This partnering of authors seems odd. Aquinas's contributions to modern just war theory, both religious and secular, contrast sharply with a Machiavellian realism that allegedly discounts justice. Aquinas grounds political theory in a philosophical and theological teleology, while Machiavelli embraces an anti-teleological politics of *virtu*. Consequently, they offer strikingly different accounts of how war relates to political order. For Aquinas, politics is set within a comprehensive natural order that human beings should recognize and respect. Just wars restore political order when it is threatened. By contrast, Machiavelli's politics are constructed by an aggressive praxis that seeks to harness human passions, even as it is constantly unsettled by them. Yet in spite of these oppositions there are important reasons to interpret these texts comparatively. It is not simply that each author identifies dimensions of politics that the other marginalizes or overlooks. Their individual representations of practice show the limitations of their own theoretical frameworks. Methodologically, this comparative reading helps not only to reveal tensions between political philosophy's two partners but also to show why such tensions cannot be addressed by giving either one of these—philosophy or politics—pride of place. In different ways, both Aquinas and Machiavelli frustrate that more discursive attention.

These readings can help us appreciate questions about the relationship between political order and war that are muted in more contemporary efforts to understand this problem. Is contemporary political philosophy less attentive than it should be to the origins of the constitutional orders that both require and constrain political violence? Yet if we acknowledge political order's violent conditions, does politics itself become completely polemicized? How should we understand the relation between philosophy and politics once we uncover problems in alternative prioritizations of one or the other?

Stepping back from theorizations of war, chapter 3 ("Perpetual Peace") considers two authors aiming to establish stable political peace, Thomas Hobbes (*Leviathan*) and Immanuel Kant (*Toward Perpetual Peace*). While their statements differ significantly in both practical focus (domestic versus international politics) and metaethical form (prudential versus moral rationality), they converge in seeing peace as achievable under institutional conditions that are discovered and justified by a privileged form of philosophy. These perspectives have significant presences in contemporary treatments of political institutions, with Hobbes a key source for rational choice theory's approach to political cooperation and Kant for deliberative democracy's support for human rights and moral equality.

I argue that reading these authors in tandem complicates the apparently binary categories of war and peace. Hobbes's peace is not just relief from his polemical state of nature's terrifying fear of violent death. It fundamentally structures analytic and evaluative categories that are both revealing and incomplete. While Kant resolutely affirms the imperative of peace, he is also disturbingly frank about war's civilizational and even moral benefits, both enriching and problematizing his pacific imperative. Complications also beset each individual perspective. Hobbes's institutional ambitions are frustrated by aspects of politics that he recognizes as less susceptible to structural control. Though Kant aspires to provide rational guidance for "moral politicians," his rigid divide between heroic morality and the all too human flaws of politics frustrates prospects for moral influence. We are left wondering whether political conflict can be either controlled by Hobbes's political science or regulated by Kant's rational morality. I suggest that similar challenges afflict their different intellectual descendants, for both rational choice theory and global democratic theory find their projected reforms continually challenged by politics itself.

While Hobbes and Kant depend upon a stable scientific or moral rationality persisting across times and spaces, both also gesture toward how human beings change their worlds through their own historical activities. Chapter 4 ("War Is History") examines two different treatments of war, understood historically. At first glance, G. W. F. Hegel (*Phenomenology of Spirit, Philosophy of History*, and *Elements of the Philosophy of Right*) and Friedrich Nietzsche (*Beyond Good and Evil*) see historical human activity through nearly opposite lenses. Hegel traces how the creation of modernity's social order has actualized free rationality, overcoming primitive impulses to war-making within the structures of a modern ethical state. Nietzsche reasserts the value of aggression, not merely as the sign of robust politics but as the core of a psychic energy continually expended in self-overcoming. Read less confrontationally, however, there are significant and complicating parallels. Though both thinkers recognize the influences of historical or genealogical violence on the emergence of modernity, they both eventually diminish the pragmatic importance of political conflict for philosophy. Instead, such conflicts are institutionalized within the practices of the ethical state (Hegel) or transformed into active self-disruption and re-creation (Nietzsche).

Yet both narratives leave spaces for the continuation or re-emergence of wars that their philosophical perspectives cannot critically engage. Though Hegel's synoptic statements interpret practices and languages of war as flawed gestures within a spiritual movement toward mature freedom, his eventual treatment of war and the courage that war demands reveals the limits of his synoptic philosophy amidst the persistent challenges of turbulent contingency. Though Nietzsche's developing narrative in *Beyond Good and Evil* may redirect polemical energy from society to psyche and reimagine politics as personal self-overcoming, it remains connected to a politics whose darker sides are sidestepped.

I contend that similar questions can be asked about the treatments of politics offered by Hegel's and Nietzsche's contemporary descendants. One set (drawing on Hegel's theorization of the modern state as the condition for ethical life) focuses too much on rational institutions and practices; the other (politicizing Nietzsche's will to power as a resource for contestative democracy) too much on agonistics, both treating the alternatives of peace and war as binaries. As we will see, neither gives due recognition to the spaces between these alternatives or to the kind of political philosophy capable of engaging them.

Acknowledging that these selective but significant texts are interestingly problematic, the final chapter ("Political Philosophy Between War and Peace") revisits the classical Greeks but does so in a way that is very different from Hanson's. I argue that while Thucydides's *War Between the Peloponnesians and the Athenians* and Plato's *Republic* appear to answer the question "enmity or friendship?" in completely different ways, their texts frustrate attempts to see either perspective as dominant, thus reminding us of the persistence of both war and peace and the need for a political philosophy that takes both prospects seriously.

I interpret Thucydides's description (1.22) of his book a possession forever, *ktēma te es aiei*, not as establishing a conclusive last word, but as marking his text as a resource to be discursively consulted amidst ongoing practical challenges. While his book is not explicitly philosophical, it gestures toward philosophical concerns and invites philosophical reflection. In parallel, the *Republic* represents a kind of conversation able to take Thucydides's book seriously. While the dialogue's philosophical core can seem universal and distant, its dramatic setting situates its participants in a particularity constituted by both external and internal wars. I proceed to investigate two common relevant themes in the *Peloponnesian War* and the *Republic*, the epistemic question of the role of extremes in political theorizing and the practical question of the necessity of war.

These thematic convergences suggest that the selection of either war or peace as the dominant frame of reference for political theory is inadequate. Appreciating the need for attention to both makes a dialogic interpretive approach to Western political philosophy attractive, stimulating a critical thinking neither driven by nor disconnected from politics. Though I argue that this kind of political theory emerges with particular clarity in the conversation I stage between Thucydides and Plato, I do not claim that these authors offer a separate theoretical perspective that is superior to other paradigms. I recommend reading the philosophical statements considered throughout the book not as systematic arguments to be proven or refuted but as diverse voices to be taken seriously and critically interpreted. In keeping with these texts' pragmatic characteristics, this dialogic space must be constructed politically, which is to say it must involve an interpretive practice significant for citizens in democracies, a practice that points toward the complex relationship between textual interpretation and civic activity and reconnects the last chapter with the theoretical and practical aspirations referenced at the beginning of this introduction. What this book offers, in short, is a nontraditional defense of a tradition and a democratic justification for moving beyond democratic theory.

1 | Enmity or Friendship?

CARL SCHMITT, *The Concept of the Political*
JACQUES DERRIDA, *The Politics of Friendship*

Democratic Political Theory's Gentle Wars and Schmitt's Politics of Enmity

This chapter introduces the book's themes by interpreting statements offered by two twentieth-century philosophers, Carl Schmitt, principally in *The Concept of the Political* and Jacques Derrida, in his critique of Schmitt in *The Politics of Friendship*. Why these texts? I have noted two reasons. First, unlike many other current formulations, both works make the importance of political philosophy's frame of reference explicit, though they offer opposed characterizations of its content. Second, while both authors acknowledge the role of historical textual interpretation within the assessment of these competing frames, each judges those historical contributions from a theoretical vantage point that privileges a certain kind of politics. In this chapter I will try to justify these readings, then move to more critical observations. I first suggest that the substantive positions taken in the two works share more characteristics than are initially apparent. Schmitt's characterization of enmity as the essence of politics must accommodate a kind of mutuality. And Derrida's political friendship eventually constructs its own distinctive enemy. Those complicating parallels diminish confidence in either author's ability to settle the question of how political thought should be framed. Second, I contend that these criticisms should prompt a reconsideration of how allegedly overarching imperatives of war and peace have been treated within the history of Western political philosophy, not simply to retrieve the voices of the tradition from musty archives but to revisit ways of practicing political philosophy, treating historical texts as a plurality of critical resources.

I begin by considering how Schmitt might critically engage more congenial or more accessible forms of political thought. If contemporary political theory must, in significant ways, be democratic theory (Shapiro, 2003, 1; Warren, 2001, 226), we can identify its two most influential current perspectives: that of the deliberative democrats, most prominently John Rawls and Jurgen Habermas, and that of the democratic agonists, represented in the work of Judith Butler, William Connolly, Bonnie Honig, and Chantal Mouffe. Though there are significant differences both within and between each position, both expressly reject foundational frames of reference for political thought, beginning instead from more sociologically or politically contextualized assumptions (as in Rawls, 1999, 34; 2005, 97–98; Connolly, 1995, xv–xix, 109–122). Yet both the significance and the characterization of these contexts implicitly depend upon more general framing assumptions that make such descriptions persuasive. For both perspectives, this framing is a reliable stability that allows political agents to function in reasonable or civilized ways.

Important differences aside, both Rawls and Habermas affirm procedural understandings of democracy that allow all who are potentially affected by public policies to contribute meaningfully to their determination through communicative discourse (Rawls, 1999, 6; 2005, 67–68; Habermas, 1993, 49–50; 1996, 108; 1998, 230–231). What protects these decisions from being manipulated by power or money or driven by anger or fear are the partners' general reasonableness (Rawls) or their commitments to the normative practices implicit in communicative action (Habermas). Consequently, a constructive political analysis should identify the institutional and sociological conditions that reinforce deliberative practices and motivations. The most important political outcome is not the flourishing or survival of a particular ethic, but institutional fairness and respect for moral equality (Benhabib, 2004; Habermas, 1993, 130–131; 1998, 112; Rawls, 1999, 78–79, 111; 2005, 455–456; Richardson, 2002, 17–18; Warren, 2001, 62–69).

While Rawls and Habermas focus primarily on how deliberative democracy can function within domestic political arrangements, they both project its structural replication within international politics. Though neither envisages the disappearance of individual state sovereignty, both argue for international institutions capable of fostering deliberation across political communities under conditions of basic fairness. Rawls's "law of peoples" (1999, 9, 15–19) envisages an expanding coalition of liberal and decent nonliberal regimes that will encourage, through both example and soft power, decent but nonliberal societies to develop into more liberal communities. Extending further, this coalition will assist "burdened societies" struggling against deprivation to become more well-ordered and reform "outlaw states" into relatively more decent regimes that can potentially follow the same path (1999, 36, 59–61, 93, 106, 110, 118, 162). When this society of peoples' member communities must wage war, they will do so only to protect human rights threatened by predatory states and only under deliberative conditions that prevent abuse or bad faith (Rawls, 1999, 91–92). While rejecting a liberal universalism that would justify coerced regime change, these perspectives are guided by respect for the universal value of autonomy and human rights (Habermas, 1998, 193, 199; 2006, 163–166).

Agonistic democrats criticize concentrations on procedural deliberation, fairness, and universalism for ignoring both the reality and the importance of contestation, identity formation, and particularity, those existential features most *politically* significant. The model of domestic politics informing these statements emphasizes the continued significance of conflict among fluid and contingent life experiments (Butler, 1997a, 15; Connolly, 1995, xix; Honig, 1993, 208; Mouffe, 2000, 101–103). The healthiest political institutions are active and vigorous democracies fostering spirited interactions among political agents (Connolly, 1995, xix; Mouffe, 2000, 101–103). To the extent that these politics extend into the international sphere, they should multiply forms of democratic engagement across communities, encouraging contestations where identities can be formed, revised, and protected (Butler, 2010, 145–150). Yet in spite of its agonistic focus, this perspective presumes civilizing conditions under which its wars are, in Connolly's language, gentle (1995, 194; 1993, 155–157). This is why Butler's proposals both point toward and presuppose conditions making the recognition and remediation of precarity the most important human priority.

For all of their differences, then, both forms of democratic theory presuppose a stable and civilized frame of reference for political practice. Schmitt intrudes. Yet why should we take this man seriously as a critical resource, given his own politics? Though the degree and duration of his influence within the Nazi party may be uncertain, his more than nominal affiliation is clear.[1] However, this cannot settle things. A number of thinkers with strong democratic allegiances insist that Schmitt offers challenges and insights not easily ignored. While rejecting Schmitt's understanding of the political as abstruse and dangerous, Habermas acknowledges his influence on serious criticisms of liberal institutionalist theories of constitutional governance and international law.[2] Mouffe (1998, 163–165; 1999,

39–49) reluctantly appreciates Schmitt's diagnosis of some of the limitations of deliberative democracy. Beyond its place within these particular conversations, Schmitt's *Concept of the Political* (*CP*) is important not because of any simplistic observation that politics is conflictual but because it challenges how contemporary democratic theorists of all sorts construe political thinking's frame of reference. Rejecting *CP*'s ideas simply because of their author's execrable politics limits abilities to respond critically when such ideas return in other guises.

CP is structured around controversial methodological and substantive claims. Formally, Schmitt insists that politics be theorized separately from other forms of social interaction, religious, ethical, aesthetic, or economic (*CP*, 25–26). He does not offer an explicit argument for why this distinctiveness is necessary but the tone and direction of his analysis indicate that his concerns go beyond conceptual clarity (*CP*, 20). Though he sometimes claims to construct a representation of politics faithful to "realism" (*CP*, 28, 65),[3] his overriding objective is pragmatic, opposing what he sees as accelerating and dangerous historical challenges to the political, particularly those posed by economics and technology, leading to a condition he characterizes as neutralization and depoliticization.[4]

Substantively understood, "the concept of the political" telescopes the ongoing possibility of a struggle to the death between collective ways of life. "The enemy is solely the public enemy (*offentliche Feind*), because everything that has a relationship to such a collectivity (*Gesamtheit*) of human beings, particularly to a whole nation, becomes public by virtue of such a relationship" (*CP*, 28).[5] This identification of politics with collective enmity goes beyond emphasizing defense as the first political responsibility.[6] The continued possibility of war is essential to theorizing political relationships as such. "The specific political distinction to which political actions and motives can be reduced is the distinction between friend and enemy" (*CP*, 26). More than competitions for power and not just expressions of the love of one's own, political conflicts are struggles over the survival or disappearance of ways of life (*CP*, 27, 32–33). *Political* agents are individuated by memberships in existential communities, not simply by socialization into community norms. Fellow citizens are political friends because they may wage wars against common enemies; a truly *political* conflict among citizens is civil war (*CP*, 32, 47).[7] Though not all conflicts begin or end with stakes so frighteningly high, the distinctive mark of a political struggle is that it can become a fight to the death over collective existence. What is essential to political interaction is therefore disclosed by its most extreme potential, not by its more ordinary constitutional processes or political behaviors (*CP*, 29–30, 35, 39; *PT*, 15). Indeed, the extreme possibility makes such normality coherent. So, it oversimplifies to say that Schmitt's politics gives foreign policy primacy (Aron, 2003, 293; Slomp, 2009, 54). If conflicts between collectivities are archetypically political, domestic politics must forge a collectivity prepared for such a struggle. Peaceful agonism between political communities is an oxymoron.[8]

Initially, defining the political according to its own exclusive criterion would appear, bizarrely, to place Schmitt alongside Rawls, who also separates politics from more comprehensive philosophical or religious commitments (1999, 34, 55; 2005, 144–145; 170–171; cf. Habermas, 1996, xli; 2006, 116). For both, isolating politics from other realms of interaction should temper political conflicts. Schmitt rejects moral or aesthetic characterizations of the enemy—as evil or hideous—because they intensify collective violence (*CP*, 30, 35–37). He particularly condemns wars allegedly fought for humanity itself. Sometimes such appeals mask sinister agendas; "when a state fights its political enemy in the name of humanity, it is no war for the sake of humanity, but a war wherein a particular state seeks to usurp (*okkupieren*) a universal concept against its polemic opponent" (*CP*, 54). Yet such hypocrisies pale in comparison with wars sincerely fought against those demonized as inhuman. "Such a war is a necessarily intense and inhuman war because, by surpassing the political, it at the very same time degrades the enemy into moral and other categories and must make him into an inhuman monster who must be not only defeated but completely destroyed" (*CP*, 36). From this point of view, separating the political from other modes of life imposes restraint on political agents. Though polemical, this frame of reference insists on *limited* war.[9]

Yet in reality Schmitt gives politics pride of place, generating an evaluative position fundamentally opposed to Rawls's, focusing not on reasonableness, but on commitment. The political cannot be adequately explained or justified simply because it safeguards or enables other social functions. Providing this nurturing context may be one task of normal politics—"the normal state consists above all in assuring total peace within the state and its territory" (*CP*, 46).[10] However, because normality does not represent the most intense (*CP*, 26–27), and therefore the most "serious" (*CP*, 48) politics, its priority would demote (Schmitt's) political activity to subordinate or instrumental status and deprive normality of the very condition that enables it. We should note parenthetically that while Schmitt's particular target is modern liberalism, a broader range of theoretical perspectives make the peaceful activities that war protects more important than war itself. This is clearly the position taken, for example, within Aristotelian political philosophy (*Nicomachean Ethics*, 10.7; *Politics*, 7.14.). In such cases, peacefulness provides a critical safeguard against political excesses. Here, Schmitt is the outlier. For him, subordinating politics to these other forms of life is the neutralization that depoliticizes. In stark contrast with Rawls, Schmitt makes it highly uncertain whether any social practices, let alone moral standards, can impose independent normative limits on political intensity.

Schmitt initially defends his position by arguing that deadly political conflict is an ever present possibility into which all other forms of competition may be transformed. Though he traces fundamental changes in what he calls the central domains of society over the course of Western history (from the religious through the technological—*AND*, 81–89), he denies that any have permanently eliminated possibilities of war with political enemies.[11] While these metacultural shifts may (or may not) be stable as historical sequences (within modernity, technology appears to have supplanted metaphysics), all domains are potentially unstable in themselves because of the polemical possibility existing alongside or underneath their varying (religious, ethical, or economic) forms of association. However peaceful such communities may be within or among themselves, the resilience of politics is confirmed by the possibility that any competition may become political once ways of life are seen as existentially threatened, defendable only by deadly wars (*CP*, 45). Nations can remain friends and even allies for decades but their political character is shown not by their structural relation within an international legal order, but by the ineradicable possibility of their reverting to the deadliest enmity. No transformation of nonpolitical into political conflict is ever strictly necessary because determinations of when ways of life are existentially threatened are historically contingent (*CP*, 26–27, 36). However, the continuous possibility of such transformations proves the resilience of a politicality that might be characterized as transhistorical (Slomp, 2003, 25–26).

Presented this way, Schmitt's political science seems more fluid than John McCormick's (1997, 245) designation, "existential positivism," suggests. There is no permanent typology of the different associations that may become political adversaries. Shapes of nations change dramatically and subnational or supranational communities can always be formed by regional, ethnic, religious, or economic affiliations. Any of these can become political once the preservation of its way of life is seen to be at stake. "The political can derive its strength (*Kraft*) from the most varied range of human practices, from the religious, economic, moral and other oppositions; [the political] does not mark (*bezeichnet*) its own substance (*eigenes Sachgebiet*), but only the intensity of an association or dissociation of human beings whose motives can be religious, national (in the ethnic or cultural sense), economic, or of another kind" (*CP*, 38). Consequently, politics is not indefinite space needing to be defined by more substantial human projects. If this were true, the intensification of politics as such could be condemned as a pathological distortion. Instead, Schmitt draws the altogether different—extreme—conclusion that politics is a distinctive activity that transforms the character of any first level interactions within which conflicts might arise. Though conflicts may originate from religious difference or economic competition, "the real friend-enemy grouping is existentially so strong and decisive that the nonpolitical opposition, at precisely the instant at which it leads to this grouping, pushes aside its hitherto 'purely' religious, 'purely' economic, 'purely' cultural criteria and motives, which are subordinated to the altogether new and unique conditions and conclusions of the immediate political situation, which seem often very inconsequential and 'irrational' if seen from the vantage of the 'purely' religious, 'purely' economic and the other 'purities'" (*CP*, 38). In representing this transformative possibility as a human enhancement and its possible disappearance as a threat, Schmitt's political theory goes beyond claims to realistic objectivity to become aggressively evaluative.[12]

Why does Schmitt prize this politics so highly? Habermas and Richard Wolin point to the influence of an irrational and emotional vitalism.[13] As such, his work parallels and legitimates intense nationalisms that threaten to undermine the international rule of law.[14] So assessed, however, Schmitt becomes less interesting theoretically. Though Habermas and Wolin welcome the dismissal of Schmitt's theoretical position as civilizational progress, the need to examine its intellectual structure persists not only because nationalist atavisms are recalcitrant but also because the political perspectives of Habermas and Wolin are precisely those challenged by Schmitt's deeper critique of a politics of stable normality.

Alternatively, Heinrich Meier (1995, 54–56; 1998, 66–69) rejects claims that Schmitt obsesses over "pure politics," arguing instead that his conception of the political is directed by the demands of revealed theology. Meier sees this foundation made explicit in the transition from the second (1932) to the third (1933) editions of *CP* as Schmitt responds to Leo Strauss's critique of the second edition.[15] For Meier, the conceptual centrality of enmity is not Schmitt's idiosyncrasy but an imperative essential to any purported revelation. Revealed faith "cannot avoid seeing in unfaith its enemy from the very beginning. . . .The distinction between friend and enemy would not only find its theoretical justification in revelation, but simultaneously would prove its practical unavoidability in such a faith" (Meier, 1998, 66–67; 1995, 80). "Political" is attached to revealed theology as a matter of necessity, embracing "political theologians whose basic attitude is conservative or liberal, who have revolutionary or counterrevolutionary convictions, who profess Christianity, Judaism or Islam" (1998, 171; 1995, xv). Against (such a) political theology, Meier sets a political philosophy that interrogates revealed claims appreciatively but critically, moving beyond the binary of loyalists/rebels.

Meier may be correct to attribute this understanding of revelation to Schmitt. Yet perhaps this judgment about revealed theology, whether offered by Schmitt, Meier or both, still presumes an intensely polemicized politics as its theoretical core. While revealed theology as divine law anticipates both possibilities of disobedience and means of enforcement, arguing that punishing disobedient enemies is *the* decisive aspect of revelation's structure is itself excessive.[16] Appreciating differences among revealed theologies, both as historically written and as historically read, seems essential. Strauss notes—in a not altogether distinct context—that Hebrew orthodoxy privileges itself precisely because of a superior rationality.[17] The relation between authoritative command and rational obedience becomes a question that authoritative command cannot itself answer. Nietzsche's second essay of the *Genealogy of Morals* (2.10–14) argues that the punitive enforcement of religious and cultural values varies inversely with social confidence. There is much more to what both Strauss and Nietzsche say, of course, and their interpretations of religious orthodoxies are controversial, but they do call essentialist (Müller's "totalized"—2003, 204) readings of revealed theology into question. Whatever Schmitt's direction in the third edition of *CP*, he frames it in the second by sketching a theology read though a political anthropology (*CP*, 65). "It is a fact that the entire life of a human being is a struggle and every human being symbolically a combatant" (*CP*, 33). Revealed theology may acquire a distinctively punitive character within an anthropology radicalized by polemical politics (*CP*, 57–58, 60).[18]

Tracy Strong sharpens the anthropological focus, arguing that Schmitt's politics is grounded in the centrality of struggle for the construction of human meaning and identity.[19] "A world in which the possibility of war is utterly eliminated . . . would be a world without the distinction of friend and enemy and so a world without politics. It is possible that such a world might contain many very interesting oppositions and contrasts, competitions and intrigues of all kinds, but there would not be a meaningful opposition (*sinnvollerweise Gegensatz*) upon which human beings would be required (*verlangt*) to sacrifice their lives, empowered (*ermächtigt*) to shed blood and kill other human beings" (*CP*, 35, 38, 53, 59). Meaningfulness is not established through Clifford Geertz's semiotic cultural forms, distinctive ways of "imagining the real" (1973, 5; 1983, 173). It is constituted by the discovered commitment to obey requirements or follow authorizations to fight and kill.

The directive influence of this polemical anthropology within *CP* is striking. "One could test all theories of state and political ideas according to their anthropology and thereby classify these as to whether they consciously or unconsciously presuppose human beings to be by nature good or by nature evil" (*CP*, 58). Designations of goodness or evil (which are— allegedly—treated "in summary fashion" and not in "any specifically moral or ethical sense") follow from determinations of whether humans are harmless or dangerous (*gefährliches*), with genuine political anthropologies falling on the side of dangerousness. Applied politically, this determination reinforces the need for an authoritarian politics that can resist anarchic chaos (*CP*, 60). This goes beyond endorsing strong state power; it demands vesting a truly political leader (*Political Theology*, 6) with autocratic authority to identify and to respond to political emergencies. Initially, this resonates with Gabriella Slomp's reading (2003, 38, 132) of Schmitt's critical but appreciative engagement with Hobbes. Both emphasize politics' capacity to protect (Slomp, 2009, 38, 46, 65–66, 114, 131). However, Strauss comments that Schmitt's acceptance of "man's dangerousness, revealed as a need for dominion" poses the very problem that (Hobbesian) politics addresses (2007, 115), dangerousness as the enemy of politics. Discrepancies are both explained and sharpened if we interpret Schmitt's dangerousness not as a source of disruption needing remedy (as for Hobbes), but as a condition under which meaningful existences can be constructed, a rich dangerousness compelling human beings to identify the commitments that might justify an aggressive embrace of the possibilities of suffering or inflicting violent death. A third synonym for "evil" and "dangerous" is "problematic" (*problematische*) (*CP*, 58).[20]

War thus becomes significant not for its surfaces, however frightening, but for its depth, what it compels (through requirements) and reveals (through empowerments) pychoculturally. From one perspective, presenting readiness to fight enemies to the death as the field where meaning is constituted might paradoxically reveal the importance of a biological life whose value is clearest only on the brink of sacrifice. But instead, Schmitt radically revises assessments of life itself. A collective life (or culture) of comfortable security, lacking depth, is a much more disturbing form of human death. "Whoever knows no other enemy than death and recognizes in his enemy nothing more than an empty mechanism is nearer to death than [to] life" (AND, 95). The capacities to kill and to die in the name of the collectivity and not merely for the sake of private aggression or defense (both presuming continued attachment to personal or familial survival) disclose a deeper, more estimable need than those for security or leisure. Hobbes and Schmitt have very different senses of what politics protects.

If Schmitt connects political fights to the death with the creation of deeply significant human meanings, Strauss's critique that "the affirmation of the political as such is the affirmation of fighting as such, wholly irrespective of *what* is being fought *for*" seems too simple.[21] Yet how do such polemics work to construct meanings? Any rejoinder from Schmitt is, to say the least, elusive. But there are clues. Political wars are not treated as instruments serving the collective agendas of other realms. "It would be senseless (*sinnwidrig*) to wage war for purely religious, purely moral, purely juristic or purely economic motives" (CP, 36). Yet since the political "does not mark its own substance, but only the intensity of an association or dissociation of human beings" (CP, 38), a focus on political intensity altogether separated from its origins is dangerously vacuous. Perhaps it is that a politics defined as the deadly confrontation with public enemies supervenes any collective form of life for which it fights.[22] While political conflict is not the condition for collective projects or identities becoming religiously, ethically, or economically more meaningful, it may drive these different forms of life toward deeper human meaningfulness once they are implicated in political fights to the death, as trade or culture wars become clashes of civilizations.[23] Thus, while Geertz delves beneath "intense but indeterminate" conflicts among political ideologies to discover "search[es] for a new symbolic framework in terms of which to formulate, think about, and react to political problems" (1973, 221), Schmitt insists that symbolic frameworks only become existentially meaningful when informed by political intensity (CP, 48). Schmitt comments in his later work, *Theory of the Partisan*, "the enemy is our very own question as formation (*Der Feind ist unser eigene Frage als Gestalt*)" (TP, 85).[24] If this dynamic explains the character of polemical meaningfulness, we might read Strauss's critique more sympathetically. On the surface, Strauss simply misunderstands Schmitt as an agonist, but what may matter more is the recognition that a focus on intensity as politics' definitive mark marginalizes attention to what elicits intensity in the first place.

Problems of meaning go on to inform Schmitt's diagnosis of the threats to humanity originating from modernity, condensed in the symbol of technicity (*Technizität*), the strategically rational ordering of the world where securing material comfort becomes politics' most important task.[25] Strauss (2007, 115–117) calls Schmitt's response to the prospects of a depoliticized world comprised of "culture, civilization, economics, morality, law, art, entertainment, etc." (*CP*, 53) a kind of "nausea." Pushing back, Schmitt embraces the political as rescuing the "seriousness of human life" from the trivialities of amusement. While McCormick has nothing good to say about Strauss, he agrees (1997, 18, 109–112) about the reactivity of Schmitt's project, pointing to an obsessive fear of technology that both reflected and radicalized cultural anxieties within early twentieth-century Europe. Echoing Max Weber's dark projections at the end of the *Protestant Ethic*, Schmitt observes that "the irresistible power of technology appears here as the domination of spiritlessness over spirit, or, perhaps, as an intelligent but soulless mechanism" (*AND*, 93).[26] Yet while Weber simply acknowledges indeterminacy ("no one knows who will live in this cage in the future"—2001, 124; cf. Douglass, 2018, 133), Schmitt envisages resistance. "The spirit of technicity, which has led to a mass belief in an anti-religious activism, is still spirit; perhaps an evil and demonic spirit, but not one which can be dismissed as mechanistic and attributed to technology. . . . We see through the mood of that generation which saw only spiritual death or a soulless mechanism in the age of technicity" (*AND*, 94–95). As an expression of spirit, however debilitating, technicity may be opposed by other spiritual activities. McCormick seems right (1997, 93–95) that Schmitt's political response is a mythology structured around enmity toward the other, then seen as the Soviet Union (*AND*, 81). Such a political mythology must be crafted by charismatic leaders and supported by what Schmitt calls "democracy" (*CP*, 23) but what is, in reality, a radicalized populism driven by fear and hatred.

However, this is not the only possible outcome. Understood less pathologically, Schmitt's appeal to the political can be recharacterized as a response to a significant but addressable pragmatic problem. Once we decline to accompany Schmitt on an inexorable path toward deadly enmity, we might interpret his focus on the persistent or inescapable (Strauss's term) character of the political as identifying a set of resources for change, leading to a rejection of his position in light of other possibilities toward which he unintentionally gestures. Building on McCormick, we might

argue that Schmitt's pragmatic counter to technicity works against his express definition of the political, pointing to a politics where shared senses
of erroneous misdirections and appropriate redirections of common life
are deliberatively considered and not, or not decisively, infused by a
readiness to fight enemies to the death. In discovering shared needs and
concerns, Schmitt performatively acknowledges the prospect of a friendship not simply dependent upon the identification of the enemy and the
possibility of a kind of democracy that counters rather than reinforces pop-
ulist emotionalism. McCormick thus grounds (1997, 75, 80, 114–115) appropriate responses to the problems posed by instrumental rationality and
the technologization of human life not in attempts to construct a political
mythology vitalized by the invention of the enemy but in a democratic discourse enriched by the contributions of critical theory.

Yet this alternative still faces the nagging problems posed by Schmitt's
focus on aspects of politics that are undeniably real. McCormick looks
forward to conversations involving traditional liberal pluralists and
"advocates of identity and difference via concrete otherness" that will be
conducted through "commonality and mutual rational exchange" (1997,
306). However, we need not go as far as Schmitt to acknowledge the violent character of politics as it is all too often practiced. Those attentive
to such politics cannot ignore the violence into which the most political
of conflicts may sink. Schmitt may distort the character of a politics seen
through this extremity but he also may make this characteristic of politics
more difficult to avoid. Hanson hardly valorizes war for its construction
of identities but he is closer to a position recognizing human dangerousness. Though thoroughly critical of Schmitt, Jan-Werner Müller (2003,
242) acknowledges that his "ultimate challenge to philosophical liberals
[is whether] new, supranational identities [can exist] without enmity."

Those who would counter Schmitt need to confront him on philosophical terms that do more than reject his position as conservative. This does
not mean, as McCormick (1997, 15) warns, "drawing [ourselves] into
adopting Schmitt's own pathological methodology in order to criticize
him," but, instead, engaging his work on the appropriate theoretical plane,
a moral discourse that I have argued is anthropologically rooted. For this
purpose, foreclosing serious access to authors within the broader historical archive of Western political thought may be a liability, not an advance.
Dismissing the importance of that archive as hopelessly premodern may be
another way in which contemporary opponents of Schmitt adopt problematic features of his approach.[27] Schmitt's constrained vision of the archive
of Western political theory therefore distorts that resource in a way that

parallels his distortion of politics. In characterizing human beings as essentially dangerous Schmitt claims to rely heavily on the weight of evidence provided by a variety of figures within the history of political philosophy. Yet his own reading of that history is transparently selective, applying a prior standard that purports to distinguish true or genuine (*echten*) political theories from those that are false or misdirected. Genuinely *political* theories speak with one voice about the evil, dangerous, and problematic character of human beings (*CP*, 61). Those who do not see dangerousness as *the* central human characteristic (for example, the Socrates of the *Republic* who sees politics as originating in need or the Aristotle of the *Politics* who traces human politicality to the capacity for *logos*) are not allowed to give serious evidence. Schmitt's version of the tradition is not supportive of but directed by his controversial interpretation of the political. His anthropology identifies the existential condition of human beings that must be true if his understanding of the political is to be accepted. Nothing within the tradition can effectively challenge Schmitt's concept of the political because a departure from his framework disqualifies a philosophy from being genuinely political.

Yet by gesturing toward a political practice that is not simply polemical, Schmitt undercuts his own criterion for determining the genuineness or truthfulness of works of political theory. In *Theory of the Partisan* (*TP*) he hints why he refuses to see philosophical arguments not controlled by his conception of the political as genuine contributions to political thought. Here, philosophy is interpreted as an intellectual imperative to reorder the world according to the scientific priorities of the Enlightenment (*TP*, 53–54), an "alliance of philosophy with the elemental forces of an insurrection" that creates an absolute enemy who must be opposed by absolute war. In ways that partially echo the warnings of Martin Heidegger and Hannah Arendt, Schmitt sees the impulse toward total control transforming itself into wars of total annihilation. The prospectively devastating consequences of attempting to place politics under the control of this sort of philosophy may reinforce Schmitt's commitment to proceed according to the requirements of politics itself. Yet once Schmitt effectively admits the possibility of a politics not centered around the deadly opposition of enemies and friends, he introduces both the need for and the possibility of employing the broader resources of Western political philosophy for more comprehensively serious thinking about political practice. The political dominance of enmity and dangerousness could be challenged and not confirmed by a more varying range of voices. However, this proposal is far from being generally accepted. Indeed, there is a powerful argument that Schmitt's distorted and dangerous representation of politics can only be countered by an even more thorough critique of the historical tradition.

The Politics of Friendship and Its Deconstructions

This is Jacques Derrida's stand in *The Politics of Friendship* as he argues that deep instabilities within Schmitt's theorizations compel rejection of the politics of enmity and its transformation into a politics of friendship. However, Derrida's alternative does not draw positively on the history of political thought's resources. Read deconstructively, that history is indicted for an androcentrism that contributes directly to the deficiencies of Schmitt's perspective. Derrida's critique is not simply an undermining of Schmitt's position, but a deconstruction of the tradition itself. Yet in executing this attack, Derrida may deprive himself of valuable allies for moving beyond polemics.

While there is more to *The Politics of Friendship* (*PF*) than a critique of Schmitt, that argument is central to Derrida's overall project. By deconstructing Schmitt's formulations Derrida opens possibilities for a very different kind of politics, called a democracy that could be (*peut-etre*) (*PF*, 37, 42, 104–105, 163, 245, 250, 306), democratizing, rather than politicizing, political philosophy's frame of reference.

Derrida's reading of Schmitt is dense and allusive. Let me try to provide structure by outlining what I believe are *PF*'s three central critiques: disputing Schmitt's conceptual demarcation between enemy and friend; challenging the structure of Schmitt's theoretical framework, especially its alleged realism; and exposing the instability of Schmitt's conception of the political, particularly its linkages between politics and the state.

First, enemies and friends. In seeing the divide between *public* enemies and friends as central to politics (*PF*, 84–85), Schmitt's analytic depends on two intersecting categories, friend/enemy and public/private. Here, Derrida reads Schmitt as offering not simply a theory but a discourse (*PF*, 117–118)[28] whose categories draw upon the linguistic practices of a definite historical context, "structures of ethnic, social and political organization" that are distinctively European (*PF*, 89). Not surprisingly, Derrida finds these categories to be both less neutral and less stable than their originators and defenders believe.

Schmitt draws upon Greek and Latin vocabularies to clarify the distinction between a public enemy (a *polemios* or a *hostis*) and a private or personal one (an *ekhthros* or an *inimicus*). As primary illustration, he refers to

Socrates's differentiation in the *Republic* between wars (*polemoi*) fought between Greeks and barbarians and internal conflicts (*staseis*) within Greek cities. "For Plato, it is only the war between Greeks and barbarians (who are 'by nature enemies') that is real war (*wirklich Krieg*), as set against conflicts among the Greeks which are for him *staseis*" (*CP*, 28–29, n9). Derrida's sustained interrogation of the Platonic narrative (drawing on both the *Republic* and the *Menexenus*) makes two points about the linguistic/conceptual basis of the political enemy/friend distinction. One challenges Schmitt on the basis of a more acute reading of the *Republic*. The other attacks the Platonic categories themselves.

Initially, Derrida contends that because Schmitt explicitly builds upon the *Republic*'s separation of wars from factional conflicts, we must examine the full structure of Socrates's comparison. When we do, we find that Socrates implicitly undermines any permanent separation between these two forms of fighting. Both occur within nature (*stasis* is cognate to a certain kind of disease—*nosos*), making it difficult for Schmitt to characterize the conflict between Greeks and barbarians as the only "real war," fought by those who are "by nature enemies" (*PF*, 90–92, 113–114). Moreover, Socrates reinforces fluidity, not permanence when he envisages circumstances wherein Greeks no longer fight one another as they now fight barbarians, but instead do battle as those who will sometime be reconciled, coming to fight barbarians as they now fight among themselves. Though he might do so, Derrida does not address a further transition where Greeks would fight barbarians in ways that look toward eventual peace, perhaps contributing to a potential "erasure" of the Greek/barbarian distinction altogether (*PF*, 90, 114).[29]

The encounter with Plato becomes more deeply critical within an interpretation of the fictive Socratic/Aspasian funeral speech of the *Menexenus*. Derrida's deconstructive reading reveals that all of the oration's linguistic categories point to cultural origins (*PF*, 92–93, 119), signaling the dependence of allegedly natural classifications on political structures. Derrida confines his attention to nature as process physiology (*PF*, 114), extrapolated to a population genetics that appeals to an alleged ethnic homogeneity (*Menexenus*, 245d). He does not (here) address the more challenging language of natural teleology, though his response to that perspective is not difficult to imagine (*PF*, 198–199). However this may be, the implications for the critique of Schmitt are clear. Since identities are culturally constructed and continuously revisable, the particular form of enmity/friendship upon which Schmitt's concept of the political relies is not essential to politicality, but one contingent possibility among many.

Derrida's second challenge confronts Schmitt's theoretical structure which collapses all forms of social reality into one possibility. Schmitt grounds his practical agenda in what he represents as conclusive science, a mode of discovery that corrects sloppy categories and erroneous opinions (*PF*, 117–118; cf. *CP*, 20–21). This science is not positivism's arrangement of lawlike statements confirmed by empirically observed regularities. Instead, it penetrates empirical variations in group competitions (triggered by differences of religious belief, ethical commitment or economic interest) to discover the ever present possibility of a deadly conflict into which any or all may eventually fall. Science detects the extreme prospect which empirical variances obscure. For Schmitt, "the enemy is only an eventual possibility in which a collectivity of human beings stands against a collectivity of the same sort with the real possibility (*realen Moglichkeit*) of fighting" (*CP*, 28). Derrida acutely comments, "this last sentence points up in fact . . . the innermost spring of this logic: the passage from possibility to eventuality . . . and from eventuality to effective actuality. . . . As soon as war is possible, it is effectively taking place. . . . The concept of the enemy is thereby deduced or constructed a priori" (*PF*, 86, 113, 121). Because the politically real is seen as what may be eventually possible, its reality is discovered through the detection of an extreme but remote condition rather than through more empirically sensitive inquiries that take normal political practices and meanings seriously.[30] By equating the possible extreme with the continuously real Schmitt tries to prove that the possibility of enmity is the *only* possibility in the most precise sense; descriptions of alternative forms of political interaction are superficial (*CP*, 28, 30–32). However, this attempt to bind the necessary to the possible can also be quite literally deconstructed; if reality and possibility are linked by contestable linguistic or rhetorical moves, they could also be interpreted as potentially disjunctive. If the immediately real is decoupled from the remotely possible, varied political experiences may be examined on their own terms and may pragmatically falsify the conclusion that they *must* be read in light of possible transformations into deep enmity, now only one (not the strongest) possibility among several.

Finally, Derrida contends that Schmitt's critical analysis points not to the looming depoliticization that he fears, but to a hyperpoliticization that disconnects politics from the state (*PF*, 129–130). The primary text here is not *The Concept of the Political*, but *Theory of the Partisan*. In that work, Schmitt traces how the emergence of partisan fighting challenges classical theories of both war and politics (*TP*, 36, 61). From its inception in the early nineteenth century, partisan warfare served not only to collapse the distinction between combatants and noncombatants (*TP*, 9) but also to erode the structure of state centered conflicts (*TP*, 88). Initially, the irregularity of partisan fighting could only be understood against the regularity of interstate wars. Lenin's theory of revolution dissolved this pattern in two respects. First, radical revolutionary partisan fighting introduced a "new type of war, whose meaning and goal was destruction of the existing social order" (*TP*, 72) and therefore the elimination of the context making normal politicality possible. Second, in calling for global class warfare against the bourgeoisie, Lenin laid the basis for a war waged for the sake of humanity against an absolute enemy (*TP*, 93). Consequently, the limitations on war fighting embedded in the state system eroded and partisan war became not simply another political transformation but the most radical depoliticization, intensified by the technological nightmare of nuclear weapons. "Men who use these weapons against other human beings feel compelled morally to destroy these others. . . . They must declare their opponents to be totally criminal and inhuman, to be a total non-value" (*TP*, 94). Since the identity of the self is dialectically tied to the valued identity of the other as enemy (*TP*, 85), seeing the other as a creature so completely without value suicidally devalues the self as well. In this respect, the depoliticization induced by the creation of absolute enmity shatters the entire context in which the construction of human meaningfulness is possible. Thus far, *Theory of the Partisan*.

For Derrida, however, the apparent shift in focus from *CP* to *TP* is *only* apparent and the connections between the two works actually demonstrate the instability of Schmitt's attempt to establish a coherent definition of the political as such. "The salute to Lenin forms the link between the two texts . . . [so that] the second [*TP*] confirms the first [*CP*] precisely at that point where the former seems to contradict the latter" (*PF*, 141). Derrida's argument in support of this claim is also dense but it seems to rely on two contentions. The first is that although Schmitt intends to define the essence of the political by going beyond the empirical presence of the state (*CP*, 19), his analysis is far more state-centered than is represented.[31] The state is the authority with the right to determine the exception and thus to set the structural conditions for the continuity of the norm (*CP*, 45; cf. *PT*, 13). For Derrida, "[Schmitt's] State presupposes the political to be sure, hence it is logically distinguished from it; but the analysis of the political, strictly speaking, and its irreducible core, the friend/enemy configuration, can only privilege from the beginning and as its sole guiding thread, the State form of this configuration—in other words, the friend or enemy *qua* citizen" (*PF*, 120). Second, since the essence of the political is allegedly rooted in the friend/enemy distinction, one must see Lenin's theoretical move as intensifying rather than eliminating this distinction "by carrying hostility to its absolute limit" (*PF*, 147). Like the most dedicated suicide bomber, the partisan acts in the name of some collectivity. At the same time, this radicalized consistency unravels the stable fabric of the state that informs Schmitt's analysis. Indeed, from the perspective of this intensified enmity, the state seems not quintessentially political, but regressively anti-political, for it blocks carrying the friend/enemy distinction to its most intense conclusion. Thus, the proliferation of partisan and revolutionary causes in the late twentieth century and beyond provide "just so many forms of the abyss for Schmitt's 'clear cut distinctions' and his nostalgia" (*PF*, 144; cf. 133, 149, 151).

Though Derrida deconstructs, his challenges to Schmitt make three significant contributions to his own positive statement. Because Schmitt's attempt to separate friends from enemies is unstable, Derrida can envisage enemies becoming friends (*PF*, 122–123, 151). Because Schmitt's project depends on a possibility that is not simply replicated by empirical reality, Derrida can project a different politics which is, while remote, no less possible. Finally, because Schmitt's understanding of the political eventually destabilizes the state, Derrida can offer a politicality that is not state centered. These three positive threads are interwoven within a vision of politics that takes a very different stand from Schmitt's on the nature and significance of the enemy.

In one sense, Derrida's project starts with extended reflections on the strengths and limitations of a politics centered around fraternity. If politics enables the creation of meaning, we need to take the dynamics of that creation seriously, starting from Schmitt's statement, "the enemy is our very own question as figure [or form] (*als Gestalt*)" (*TP*, 85; *PF*, 162–163). G. L. Ulmen comments that calling this question our own (*unsere eigene Frage*), images political conflict as a war between brothers, in the ways that "Hobbes and the Roman Church" are brothers.[32] Derrida expands upon this parallel, finding the image of the brother central not only for Schmitt, but for the entire Western political tradition, notably in the assimilation of citizens and brothers (*PF*, 94–96). Returning to the *Republic's staseis* (not *polemoi*) among the Greeks (470d –471a), Derrida finds possibilities for reconciliation among cultural kin. Since brothers can be intimate friends as well as threatening enemies, the figure of the citizen/brother anticipates an affirmative politics of friendship. Yet however reconciled, the figure of citizen/brother still denies political recognition to the sister (*PF*, 96, 149, 202). While this exclusion is allegedly justified by natural differences, that argument collapses once we recognize (as in the reading of *Menexenus*) that allegedly decisive natural differences really originate in contestable cultural discourses. Consequently, the image of the excluded sister indicts rather than reinforces (as in *Republic*, 454b) any natural imperatives. "Everything in political discourse that appeals to birth, to nature or to the nation—indeed to nations or to the universal notion of human brotherhood—this entire familialism consists in a renaturalization of the 'fiction.' What we are calling here 'fraternization,' is what produces symbolically, conventionally, through authorized engagement a *determined politics*, which . . . alleges a real fraternity . . . on a symbolic projection" (*PF*, 93).

Initially, the recovery of the sister or the woman gestures toward a politics not constrained by aggressive androcentrism (*PF*, iii, 13, 148, 156). But its deeper revelation is that fraternal politics however generously expanded (from the limited *hetairoi* of the Athenians through the supposedly universal brotherhood of the French Revolution—237) depends on damaging exclusions calling for remedy. Once reimagined, the other will not erect closed borders of hostility but invite enriching encounters nourished by openness (*PF*, 37, 42, 163, 222, 224, 245, 250, 306). Derrida thus envisages friendships inclusive not only of genders (180, 277, 279) but indeed of generations, linking authors to texts and readers, binding the living to the dead and the yet unborn (32, 70, 294–295, 305).

But are these expansive linkages political? Derrida answers affirmatively (*PF*, 43, 277, 294, 305) but only on condition of a revolution of the political itself (6, 27, 43, 67), the emergence of a certain kind of democracy. Though this democracy is clearly a projection (a "could be" and not a program—*PF* 218; cf. 38, 128, 155) its functions are politically intelligible (196), depending on two seemingly opposed but equally essential requirements, that its members relate to one another both as heterogeneously distinct individuals and as identically equal citizens (22). One of the cohering conditions of this democracy is, paradoxically, a deep incoherence; characteristics that threaten to fly apart are kept together. Thus understood, democracy's openness and deconstruction's interrogations overlap. This democracy does not simply withstand but is nourished by deconstruction's challenges precisely because its political framework is enrichingly unstable. In democracies "one keeps this indefinite right to question, to criticism, to deconstruction" (105; cf. 38–39; 42–43; 103–104; 199; 216; 214, 306). Indeed, there is "no deconstruction without democracy, no democracy without deconstruction" (105).

By imagining a democracy that could be, Derrida neither projects its realization in definite historical time nor permanently forecloses its possibility in the face of depressingly resilient barriers (272).[33] Its prospects are elaborated more fully in a comment in the subsequent book, *Rogues*. "The *to* of the 'to come' wavers between imperative injunction (call or performative) and the patient *perhaps* of messianicity, nonperformative exposure to what comes, to what can always not come or has already come" (*R*, 90–92). From one point of view, this positioning between activism and patience classifies Derrida's deconstructive readings as political exercises, forms of irony or criticism that open democratic spaces to tones that challenge strategic control or mythologizing rhetoric (*R*, 92; *PF*, 19, 28, 43, 100). This understanding of democracy confronts the power politics implied by Schmitt's focus on enmity and offers a broad alternative frame of reference that interprets both politics and the tradition of political philosophy in ways fundamentally different from Schmitt.

Building on a deconstructive reading of an alleged Aristotelian statement, "O my friends, there is no friend," Derrida interprets a parallel (similarly deconstructible) Nietzschean reply (in *Human, All Too Human*), "O my enemies, there is no enemy" (*PF*, 50, 59, 112). The frame of reference for understanding politics now becomes pervasively yet dynamically peaceful (*R*, 157–158), not a serenity that ignores historical time but a fluidity in which alterity and fluctuation stimulate continued revisions of identity without any urge to overcome or to reinvent the other (*PF*, 222, 224). From this perspective, Schmitt's theorizing of conditions under which meaning and identity are established distorts both the dynamics of the process (by engaging the other as deadly enemy not as enriching friend) and the stability of the outcome (by presuming state-centered politics not the prospect of a deconstructing democracy). Yet this mobile but pacific frame of reference also reveals that the domestic and international proposals of Rawls and Habermas are, while far preferable to Schmitt's intractable enmity, halfway houses, still too focused on separation and coercion (*R*, 141). Any insistence on the importance of communicative agreement imposes artificial and damaging closure on identity formation, creating relations of equality or proportion that threaten to flatten or regulate difference. Within the democracy to come, "whether or not the other answers, in one way or another, no mutuality, no harmony, no agreement can or must reduce the infinite disproportion" (*PF*, 220). Within international politics, the conception "rogue states" can be read as yet another symptom of the misguided influence of enmity (*R*, 2–3). And while the agonistic democrats' commitment to the priority of contestative engagement more fully recognizes the unstable character of meanings, their insistence on the continued need for exclusion as a condition for politics (Mouffe, 1999, 46) reproduces the androcentrism that infected previous Western political discourses.[34]

The harshness and instability of Schmitt's language is, therefore, not a distortion but a clarification of the character of Western political philosophy, generally (*PF*, 67, 218, 262–263, 277), explaining why Derrida devotes four full chapters of *PF* to its critique. Interpreted in light of Schmitt's androcentrism, none of the tradition's representatives offer their own positive resources for constructing alternatives to Schmitt. Their value emerges against their own constructed frameworks, from Derrida's deconstructions (*PF*, 28, 199, 263, 277, 278, 306). Yet Derrida's position encounters difficulties that render his alternative to Schmitt problematic. What are these?

While Derrida does not ignore modernity's political violence (*PF*, 272–273), his projected politics of friendship emerges from the deconstruction of written texts (*PF*, 242–243, 250). Reading texts as discourses (*PF*, 82) has both advantages and limitations. By expanding textual criticism to confront the "structures of ethnic, social and political organization" underlying a text's intellectual structure, Derrida is able to expose theories of political realism (including but not limited to Schmitt's) as polemical creations of fields allegedly analyzed by objective science (*PF*, 115, 117). Yet by absorbing political structures and impacts into discursive texts this framework misleadingly condenses all politics into language (*PF*, 71, 82), drawing attention to sentences, semantics, words, letters, and breathings (208–210, 234) while potentially marginalizing the material forces and coercive instruments of political control that the critique is intended to challenge. The darkest recognition of political damages in *PF* (272–273) represents them parenthetically as illustrations drawn from "the most spectacular 'news' on political scenes."

Certainly, even the cruelest *political* violence can be understood fully only in light of its meaning.[35] Yet disclosing political meanings through the interpretation of textual representations is different from theorizing those politics as forms of language. When Thucydides writes about Athens' war with the Peloponnesians he distinguishes (1.22) his treatment of events or deeds (*erga*) from his representation of thoughts or speeches (*logoi*). Though *erga* can only be engaged through *logoi* (the entire book is itself a *logos*), Thucydides keeps the categories separate, depending simultaneously on distinction and connection, but avoiding the binaries of sameness and otherness. By contrast, Derrida's convergence of texts/discourses/

politics collapses these realms of practice and thought into a single field that is dominated by and not simply accessible to language. This perspective surprisingly resembles that of a different Greek, Plato's Gorgias, who also sees political interactions exclusively through their speeches (*Gorgias*, 456a –c).

How does this convergence afflict attempts to understand the democracy that might come? If there is "no deconstruction without democracy, no democracy without deconstruction" (*PF*, 105; *R*, 142), deconstruction becomes the functional equivalent to the concept of the political. Yet though they may be conceptually disruptive, deconstruction's forays remain not simply peaceful but playful. Insofar as deconstruction and the appropriate frame of reference for political thought are linked, this framing becomes playful as well, a continuous and mutual stimulation between texts/readings and countertexts/contested readings. While this play is serious in giving even the most hostile or frightening discourses (Schmitt) voice, its seriousness is playful in its explicit denial of the possibility or desirability of resolution (*PF*, 216, 221, 229). Derrida's "public" is not simply open to irony and criticism, but is redefined in light of those linguistic possibilities.

Political decision interrupts this playful fluidity. Decisive answers to questions about what is to be done may now seem counterdemocratic. Yet such decisions must be made and it is not clear how Derrida's democracy to come accommodates them. In *PF* he acknowledges that when the indeterminacy of identity formation is converted into the political language of decision, there is the unavoidable possibility of abuse. "Without the possibility of radical evil, of perjury, and of absolute crime, there is no responsibility, no freedom, no decision" (219). There is no remedy to this abuse in any form of theory. "The instant of decision must remain heterogeneous to all knowledge as such, to all theoretical or reportive determination." Resources for resisting evils and exposing perjuries are found in the continued possibility of deconstruction itself (305–306). However, this remedy works only so long as deconstruction engages its own appropriate partners, texts/discourses that misrepresent dynamic processes as static forms or heterogeneous experimentations as homogeneous communities. The deeper analysis of decision (68) sees it not as a determinative political move creating winners and losers (waging war or not) but as an existential event decentering the subject. Deconstruction challenges abuses within linguistic contexts, but the peaceful character of those collisions is ensured by the persistence of linguistic or logographic forms of interaction. In a sense, this transformative move is opposite to the construction of a discourse that embeds speech in patterns of domination. Instead of language becoming politics, politics becomes language.

From this vantage point, the relation between democracy and deconstruction converges less than Derrida suggests and deconstruction's critical project is compromised from two somewhat different directions. Yes, deconstruction interrogates the social and historical contexts that construct linguistic categories and texts. Yet such texts can also migrate, stimulating unpredictable experiments in performative speech and critical thought. In commenting on the meaning of the statement—"O my friends, there is no friend."—that grounds the long exegesis in *PF* Derrida underscores the fluid journeys and transformations of texts. The accepted version of this text "will have lined the library shelves of this tradition with illustrious variants. . . . like a capital with bottomless surplus value. . . . Yet without any value of orthodoxy, without a call to order, without discrediting the canonical version, this one might well engage, on other paths, sometimes at the intersection of the original one, with new adventures of thought" (*PF*, 208). This migratory perspective elicits Butler's critique (1997a, 150) of one of Derrida's earlier essays. For her, the contention that performative speech can break dramatically from its contexts frustrates attempts to understand more localized political forces impacting and fostered by performance, "paralyzing the social analysis of forceful utterance." If Butler is right, Derrida's deconstruction is less equipped to offer immediate political critique than he suggests. The second, more serious, compromising influence emerges once more persistent functions of politics are restored to the democracy to come, for these would seem to implicate deconstruction/ democracy in a set of power relations that require confronting some other who is a kind of public enemy. The more expressly political understanding of democracy, elaborated in *Rogues*, cannot dispense with the presence of a rule, *kratia*, of some sort (*R*, 100–101), thus re-establishing the ordering and hierarchy that deconstruction aims at dissolving. Insofar as Derrida wishes to take politics seriously, he cannot, any more than Gorgias (471a ff.), simply exclude material and coercive power. Seen as a form of *kratia*, Derrida's democracy must recognize some enemies as hostile others, specifically those who assert and follow the oppressive agendas of oligarchies and dogmatisms. If Schmitt's politics must include more than willingness to fight the enemy to the death, Derrida's cannot avoid an enmity protective of political friendship. The democracy perhaps to come is theoretically compromised not simply because its character is ill defined and ever-elusive (Müller, 2003, 241) but because its possibility intersects with practices that it, in principle, opposes.

Once the necessity of *kratia* and the persistence of political enmity are acknowledged, Derrida's position seems vulnerable to two further critiques, the first stemming from a prospective rejoinder by Schmitt, the second from recognition of a problematic—rather than enriching—instability that continues within this prospective democracy. For Schmitt, resistance to enemies who threaten the democracy to come may resemble a war fought for the sake of humanity itself, a war to end all wars. Though the rhetoric is playful, the trajectory of Derrida's argument also establishes an extreme condition as the standard for characterizing and evaluating political practice. Further, in light of the instability that deconstruction must expose even within democracy's *kratia*, there is no reason to see the unraveling that occurs between *The Concept of the Political* and *Theory of the Partisan* as terminating in Derrida's hyperpoliticization. Carried through consistently, this hyperpoliticization may be transformed into a depoliticization different from that which Schmitt fears. This possibility may be illustrated concretely within Thucydides's narrative of the politically destructive *stasis* in Corcyra. At first, the party allegiances of the Athenian-leaning democrats and the Spartan-inclined oligarchs overwhelm kinship relations, pious reverence, and civic membership. Brother citizens kill one another in the name of a party loyalty (*philetairos*) now all-consuming (3.82). Yet as the narrative of the *stasis* progresses, Thucydides moves from hostility among parties (still organized politically) to deadly clashes whose participants are described in increasingly individualistic terms, strengths, and weaknesses, whose own meanings become increasingly unstable (3.83).[36] Derrida's formulations seem unable to protect the hyperpoliticization that should foster his alternative democracy from further disruption.

These concerns make Derrida's project, too, vulnerable to extremism and instability. Because his proposals depend upon deconstructive readings of Schmitt's texts, his alternative may acquire some of those texts' essential features, particularly a continued reliance on a problematic form of enmity and an ongoing liability to dissolution. Once transferred from the world of texts to the harsher realities of politics, we may find troubling parallels between the two seemingly opposing visions of the political. While Schmitt sees through all forms of historically variable human interactions to discover the intense politicality at their core, Derrida may set conditions for an enmity that is constructed in the name of humanity while originating for reasons that deconstruction must, by its own logic, see as contingent, threatening a fragmentation of collectivities that is more hyperpolemical than hyperpolitical.

Such difficulties are exacerbated by the narrow ways in which both Derrida and Schmitt construe political philosophy. Schmitt insists that only those philosophical anthropologies validating the politics of enmity deserve serious hearing (*CP*, 61)—Derrida effectively categorizes all previous attempts at political theory as expressions of the aggressive androcentrism that culminates in Schmitt (*PF*, ix, 28, 199, 263, 278, 306).[37] However, neither successfully argues why these very different voices within the Western tradition need to be understood in such reductive ways. Failures to address this question are traceable to the shared insistence that the intellectual activities of political philosophy be politically driven (*CP*, 61; *PF*, 81–82). Though Schmitt and Derrida disagree about both the content and stability of a concept (Schmitt) or discourse (Derrida) of the political, both performatively acknowledge that political thought must be controlled by the language of politics itself. Schmitt's framework controls philosophy in the name of a politics of enmity validated before the fact. Derrida's claim that there is "no deconstruction without democracy" (*PF*, 105) is on the surface knowingly incorrect, for his deconstructive readings are offered within a democracy still shackled by exclusions (*PF*, 159, 263, 295). Yet the deconstructions that advance the text of *PF* all presume the revolutionary democracy to come. At a deeper level, "no deconstruction without democracy" acknowledges subordination of critical philosophy to the imperatives of this politics (*PF*, 196). Derrida's verdict on Plato's *Republic*, that "the perfectly rigorous description of these pure structures of the ideal State . . . give meaning . . . to every concept, and hence to every term, of political philosophy" (*PF*, 91), might be applied to *The Politics of Friendship* itself. Both Schmitt and Derrida offer extremes not only by focusing on polarities of behavior but also by insisting on the epistemic dominance of the sharpest images.

The danger of this move is that political philosophy will be distorted by understandings of politics not themselves subjected to philosophical examination. Any philosophy not constituted in light of such political demands will be discounted, either because it naively presumes a nondangerous humanity (*CP*, 58) or because it masks and sustains androcentric exclusion (*PF*, 28, 218, 263; *R*, 40–41). Consequently, neither Schmitt nor Derrida takes seriously the possibility of a philosophy related to political practice in more constructively nuanced yet still critical ways. Both the politics of enmity and the politics of friendship silence too much of political philosophy's history and frustrate political thought's most important tasks, reflecting on the advantages and hazards of different political arrangements and critically commenting on the directions of public choice.

Such assistance is particularly essential in times of political stress. While political communities should avoid seeing their most basic commitments in light of immediately compelling events, the circumstances to which Hanson's earlier reflections respond are real and continuing, reminding us (not simply as Americans but as political human beings) of the seriousness of the political and moral challenges we face. That powerful societies can initiate as well as respond to conditions of war reinforce Butler's emphasis on the need to attend to human precarity and her insistence that an appreciation of the complexities of the basic alternatives of war and peace must inform the judgments of democratic citizens in ways that go beyond grieving (2010, 98). Can the history of Western political philosophy be of any help?

In attempting to identify such resources, I revisit important voices within that history to examine how their frames of reference are situated with respect to questions of war or peace. The first inquiry concentrates on a fundamental problem identified by Schmitt and Derrida and initiates the reconsideration of the tradition for which I argue.

2 | War and Order

THOMAS AQUINAS, *Summa Theologiae; De Regno*
NICCOLO MACHIAVELLI, *The Prince; Discourses on Livy*

Political Order as a Problem

Though doing so in very different ways, both Schmitt and Derrida challenge the broadly peaceful international order that underlies the liberalisms of Rawls and Habermas. In spite of the significant conceptual and pragmatic problems afflicting each position, both Schmitt and Derrida draw attention to the ambiguities of political order and to alternative ways in which that order may relate to practices of war.

In this chapter I explore this question more fully by interpreting how the relationship of war to order is understood by Thomas Aquinas and Niccolo Machiavelli. On first view, the substantive conclusions and intellectual approaches of these two authors are nearly opposite. For Aquinas, just and unjust wars are understood within an order validated by a series of hierarchical laws, both human and divine. Unjust aggressions violate that order, just wars restore it. For Machiavelli, political orders must be forged by practices that harness human passions even while remaining vulnerable to their disruptive influence. Within a political world where fortunes always ascend or decline, the powers required for constructing political order continually threaten to destroy it. Order is dynamically linked to ongoing war. This substantive difference reflects strikingly divergent philosophical orientations. Aquinas's political theory is offered within an intellectual framework that broadly parallels the hierarchical ordering of the world, a perspective designated (controversially) as metaphysical (Rawls, 2005, 134–135; Owens, 1993). Within this ordering, political languages and categories do not stand on their own but require the reinforcement and supervision of a philosophical and theological teleology. By contrast,

Machiavelli insists that political life be understood and evaluated through its own distinctive language, constructing what Sheldon Wolin calls a political metaphysic without philosophy (1960, 211; cf. Arendt, 158, 77–78; 1968, 136–141; Honig, 1993, 2–3; Pitkin, 1999, 324).

Yet in spite of these differences, there is considerable value in reading these thinkers in juxtaposition. At one level, such comparisons require each to take the other's perspective more seriously. Reading Aquinas more politically, we can investigate just wars in ways that are more critical and less conclusive, making politics not so much more "realistic" as more problematic and more interesting. I will argue that such a political reading identifies both potentials and liabilities that Aquinas's philosophical perspective does not adequately consider. Reading Machiavelli more philosophically, we can discover a deeper grounding to his project than many commentators acknowledge, a political metaphysic more metaphysical than Wolin suggests. This philosophical framework is itself informed by a deeply polemical conception of politics that Machiavelli's own political interpretations expose as partial and distorting. This extended appreciation of politics allows a continuity between political *virtu* and political philosophy that can encourage a more critical interrogation of Machiavelli's contributions.

More theoretically, comparative readings of Aquinas and Machiavelli help not only to identify tensions between political philosophy's two partners but also to show why such tensions cannot be resolved by giving either philosophy or politics pride of place. What is needed, instead, is a critical attention to each of these practices. However, the texts of Aquinas and Machiavelli frustrate that attention even as they show why it is needed.

I argue that these critical readings underscore persisting questions about the relationship between political order and war that are muted in more contemporary engagements with this problem. Are modern theorizations of international constitutionalism (such as those of Rawls and Habermas) less attentive than they should be to the coercive character of such orders? Yet if we acknowledge the ongoing presence of coercion, do we altogether polemicize politics' "realism"? Methodologically, do the modern heirs of either the philosophical Aquinas or the political Machiavelli give adequate recognition to the intellectual space within which political philosophy must occur? Does the first set of heirs sequester philosophical reasoning too far away from turbulent political practice? Does the second infuse political thought with an aggressive turbulence that blocks critical distance?

Aquinas and the Order of the World

Aquinas's teaching on war has exerted significant influence on modern just war theory, extending beyond thinkers informed by a Roman Catholic or religious perspective.[1] Because his examination of this issue in the *Summa Theologiae* (*ST*) occupies only one question (Q. 40) within the Second Part of Part Two (II–II),[2] this inquiry requires consideration of *ST*'s broader context. However, it is this very framing that seems to place Aquinas in a completely different world not only from Machiavelli but also from a modern political philosophy that has become resolutely secular.[3] Aquinas's practical philosophy is informed by a theology ultimately dependent on the truths of revelation. "Where human reason is defective, it is necessary to have recourse to eternal reason" (19. 4; I.1.1).[4] This framework supports a practical reasoning capable of providing normative assessments of political practices, including questions of war and peace. Yet by endorsing practical philosophy only insofar as it is consistent with and subordinate to a sacred doctrine that reveals providential order (I. 1.5, 8; 103.1), Aquinas may constrict or undercut intellectual resources that become necessary once the presence of that alleged order is questioned. Can those skeptical of Aquinas's revealed order engage him productively about questions of war and peace?

Two considerations recommend an affirmative answer. First, though Aquinas's political theory is theologically grounded, it does not ignore the tensions and even the agonies of politics. Indeed, his theological commitments often draw him much closer than many of modernity's foundational thinkers to flawed human realities. His recourse to faith as a necessary extension of natural reason (I.1.1, 7) makes him more modest than Hegel about the achievements of purely human wisdom. His acknowledgment of the inevitable presence of sinfulness (73, 1; 94.6; II–II, 60.2) makes him more forgiving than Kant of human moral failings. Second, Aquinas's position complicates as much as it reinforces modern secular statements.[5] This is not simply a complication via difference, because Aquinas relies on a perspective that is substantively ethical rather than formally procedural (cf. MacIntyre, 2016). It is also a complication via similarity because modern liberal constitutionalism's theorizations about war and peace face challenges that have instructive parallels with those encountered by Thomistic just war theory.

Instead of beginning with *ST*'s theological structure and working back to politics, I start with its more obvious political and rhetorical character, its engagements with questions and objections arising from a variety of sources. This format leads commentators such as Alasdair MacIntyre (1988, 164; 2016, 88–89, 207) and John Finnis (1998a, 10–14), to argue that *ST* is interrogative and multivocal, dialogic rather than demonstrative. Aquinas does not limit his resources to voices within Catholicism or Christianity; he seriously consults both Jewish law (the Hebrew Bible) and Gentile traditions of philosophy (Aristotle) and rhetoric (Cicero).[6] Yet at least three considerations qualify *ST*'s dialogic character.

First, the conversation partners are authorities who offer structured intellectual positions (I.1.8). While Aquinas takes cultural influences seriously, he does so either because their legitimacy is validated by reasoning informed by sacred doctrine (91.4) or because they are psychologically important for political stability (97.2). In neither case are the cultural opinions of common sense morality valuable because of any distinctive insights (100.1, 4). No voice in *ST* is comparable to the political cultural *endoxa* examined within Aristotle's practical inquiries or Socrates's interrogations in the Platonic dialogues.[7]

Second, the contributions of even the most influential of *ST*'s authorities undergo significant translations within Aquinas's text. The Jewish tradition, as the Old Law, is read as a partial, even immature statement of commands and insights given fuller and more adult refinements within Christian revelation (91.5; 98.1, 4–6). Though Aristotle's philosophical voice seems especially privileged, *ST*'s treatment of the most significant philosophical and moral issues often departs noticeably from Aristotle's own.[8]

Third, Aquinas resolves. While *ST* may not foreclose the introduction of additional questions (MacIntyre, 1988, 171–172; 2016, 88–89), the work anticipates settling them, not deepening their puzzles. In spite of its questioning tone and multivocal archive, *ST* offers a definitive series of statements by one authoritative voice (I.1.8).

Structurally, *ST*'s political theorizations are constituted by hierarchically intersecting laws, elaborated in what has been called the *Treatise on Law*, occupying Qs 90–97 of *ST* I–II. The forms of law regulating practice, natural law and human or positive law, are informed by the eternal law of the cosmos and ultimately by divine law set at creation (93.1; I.103.4–6). Human understanding of and obedience to nature's laws is enabled by a rationality and free will distinguishing humans from other created beings and by a conscience rooted in the inclination to do good and avoid evil (19.5; 92.2; 93.1; II–II, 58.4, 12). Nonetheless, full moral guidance is only provided by revealed truth grasped through infused faith (91.4; 93.1, 3; 95.3; 100.1, 3, 12; I. II–II, 6.1).

This ordering hierarchy provides a broad but distinctive teleological frame of reference for human practice; some action choices are according to, others against, nature (91.2; 94.2; I.103.5–6; *DR*, I.1).[9] Naturally ordered ends are themselves hierarchical. Plants and animals can be legitimately used for (higher) human purposes (II–II, 64.1). Within moral psychology's infrastructure, intellect should rule passion; a well-ordered life is guided by the intellect exercising appropriate (reasonable, not despotic) control (91.6; 94.25; II–II, 58. 2; 104.1; *DR*, I, 1). Yet while the Aristotelian teleology that Aquinas frequently cites construes the ends of animals, generally, as flourishings appropriate to natural species (*NE*, 1.7, 10. 6–7; *Politics*, 1.2, 7.1–3), Aquinas's reliance on divine law traces species perfections to purposes set by God (90.4; 91.1; 93.1; 100.12; I.103. 5–6).[10]

The political order violated by injustice and restored by just war is intelligible within this hierarchy. In both *ST* and the more provisional and fragmentary *De Regno*, political rule parallels the divine governance of the world (93.3; I.103. 3; *DR*, I.2). The principal value of politics lies in its contributions to the common good (90.2; 92.2; 96.1; 100.8; II–II. 9, 12; *DR*, I.1). Like Aristotle's common advantage, Aquinas's common good emphasizes relations of ruling and being ruled, not collective allegiances forged by external enmity. Adhering to the foundational significance of divine law, Aquinas's common good goes beyond Aristotle's political *koinon sympheron* (*Pol*, 3.6–7) to embrace the most complete good of a human community held together by charity within the love of God (I.103.3; II–II.58.6; 59.4), privileging not physical, psychological, or even ethical well being, but salvation (100.6). By preparing humans for a life of perfect beatitude, the Church, not the *civitas*, is the partnership enabling the highest, though still imperfect, happiness possible on earth (91.5; II–II, 39.1; *DR*, II. 3). Aquinas seconds Isidore of Seville's characterization of the purposes of human law as curbing audacity and protecting innocence by instilling fear of punishment (95.1; 90.3; 96.5; 100.9; I.103.5). More than this, however, though it is not the highest human partnership, the properly ordered *civitas* provides its own good by fostering conditions of peaceful cooperation and allowing partnerships such as the family and the Church to function appropriately.

Two consequences of Aquinas's teleology are notable. First, the ends set for human beings by God's providence significantly alter the ways in which human inclinations and perfections are ultimately understood. Since nothing is created in vain (3.8; *DR*, I.8), the human desire for perfect happiness confirms the accessibility of perfect beatitude within the community of the saved (65.5; *DR*, II.3). There is a parallel recentering of the character of the virtues. From a human perspective unassisted by faith, the virtues are (broadly) political (61.5), enabling constructive societal interactions in peaceful comity. However, once understood in revelation's light these excellences move away from the world. The political prudence that properly governs worldly things is radically transformed once comprehended in light of a purifying and purified virtue that ultimately scorns (*despiciat*) worldly things (61.5; I.1.4).[11]

Second, Aquinas's teleology makes all moral and political problems *intellectually* resolvable. Just as there can be no frustrated human inclinations, there are no truly tragic human dilemmas. The conflict between the justice of the sovereign administering capital punishment and the familial piety of those who resist and grieve at the criminal's death is situated within a broader perspective that sees why punishment is needed to safeguard the common good (19.10), wrenching effects on individuals notwithstanding. This does not mean that good rulers cannot make mistakes (defining crimes inadequately or punishing them inappropriately) or that partial views are morally defective (supporting a condemned murderer who is a beloved father is not sinful). However, fully adequate practical narratives will not disrupt the coherence of the moral world. The response of the criminal's family does not signal the inevitable ugliness of executions or the cruelties of necessity, but instead reflect the understandable but limited pain of a partial perspective (94.5; 100.8).[12]

Read within the context of Aquinas's fully articulated position, these outcomes limit spaces for critical politics. However, once we engage the human world on its own terms, a move encouraged both by Aquinas and by modern Thomists and natural law theorists (Finnis, 1998b, 15), the political and moral problems that emerge become increasingly problematic, particularly with respect to the initiation and waging of war.

Just and Unjust Wars

In *ST* II–II, Q.40, war (*bellum*) is one of the vices against peace involving deeds, grouped with schism (*schisma*) (Q.39), brawling (*rixa*) (Q. 41), and sedition (*seditio*) (Q. 42). Only war is not condemned categorically. For wars to be not sinful, therefore just, three conditions must hold. They must be initiated by competent authorities, not by private persons; they must be fought for just causes, understood as defense against criminal aggression, recovery of goods unlawfully taken, or punishment imposed on those deserving it; and they must be guided by the right intention (*intentio recta*) of restoring peace. Even if justly begun, wars with evil intentions—certainly including Schmitt's commitment to kill the political enemy—may damage the common good in at least two ways. They can pollute the society waging war by perverting or brutalizing its practices. Or they can violate the broader civilizational good of peace by spawning continuous fighting (cycles of revenge). Victory in a just war must restore the order that unjust aggression violates. Yet even if the unjust prevail on earth, they will not escape the just punishment suffered eternally.[13]

These conditions are intended to guide human beings confronting the wrenching problems of war. Yet by situating politics, including the politics of war, within a broader moral, natural, eternal, and divine order, Aquinas may also obscure the importance and complexity of political problems as they are understood and confronted by human beings and not, or not simply, as they are situated within a natural order disclosed by revelation's authoritative teachings (91.4; II–II, 40.2). Were human affairs seen as more problematic, there would be a greater need for political philosophy to consider them on their own terms, employing its own resources, exhibiting less confidence in the adequacy or finality (91.4) of resolutions. Pragmatic complications do not arise simply within religious alternatives to Aquinas's theological paradigm or as a part of reasserted secularism.[14] By insisting on the need to take the human condition seriously on its own terms (II–II.57.2), Aquinas may pose more challenging questions than those he explicitly considers, pointing to philosophical needs and possibilities different from those that he expressly validates. We should reconsider the three conditions that must be satisfied for wars to be just: competent authority, just cause, and right intention.

First, how should we judge the appropriate location, meaning and status of authority? Aquinas's theory of political institutions is not systematically developed (Finnis, 1998a, 219–220). Yet this does not mean that he casually accepts existing power structures. His best regime of constitutional monarchy requires civic consent (105.1; *DR*, I.6). Freedom to oppose some commands given by those in authority makes this form of rule political rather than despotic (58.2). We are not bound to obey unjust laws and in some cases are compelled by conscience to disobey (96.4; II–II, 57.2; 60.5; 104.5). Extreme cases may call for a tyrannical ruler's forcible removal (*DR*, I.6; II.3), a justificatory argument going even beyond Aristotle's condemnation of tyranny (*Pol*, 5.10). Yet these judgments are qualified significantly by Aquinas's adoption of a model of political rule strongly informed by the teleologies of natural and crafted orders (*DR*,

I.2; II.1–2; *ST*, I.103.1, 3, 6; 105.6). Because it parallels these ordered hierarchies, political rule is implicitly legitimate even when furthering the rulers' interests, not the common good (93.3; 96.4). The analogy with natural order creates presumption of approximate (*similitudine*) legality even for unjust laws, since obedience to earthly authority is sanctioned by eternal law (96.4–5).

General deference to authority is implied within Aquinas's under-standing of politics' contributions to society's common good (II–II.5; *DR*, I.1–2). Because salvation relies more on familial or church memberships, the *civitas* contributes only secondarily to ultimate happiness or perfection (91.4; 95.1; 96.2; 100.2, 9; *DR*, II.4). Human law should not punish eve-rything forbidden by natural law (96.2) and should "not prescribe all acts of virtue, but only those ordered [with a view toward] the common good" (96.3; II–II.7). While this acknowledgment makes Aquinas less vulnerable to charges that his politics are coercively illiberal,[15] it also means that he instructs citizens to accept even heavily flawed legal structures or political cultures as imperfect but tolerable responses to purely human needs.

Aquinas's characterizations of political virtues and practices under-score this posture (92.2; 96.6; II–II, 64.6; 104.1). His cautious endorse-ment of political dissent is limited by two considerations. First, its most appropriate focus concerns the general legitimacy of those who rule, indexed by their contributions to the common good, however approximate. Challenges to particular policies, including decisions to wage war, is given less leeway; the possibility that those in authority might lose claims to le-gitimacy or competence because of irresponsible or deceptive decisions is not broached. Moreover, even if authority is abused to the point of tyranny, there is a strong presumption that it should be endured. Intense political resistance may cause more harm than good and the aims and motives of rebels are often deeply suspect (*DR*, I.6). Such dissent borders closely on sedition with no justifications or extenuations (II–II, 42.1; II–II, 104.6). If resistance to the most vicious tyranny is unavoidable, it is the tyrant who is seditious, for he fosters a discord among the subjects (II–II, 42.2). Even when necessary, resistance may scandalize others (II–II, 42.2) and scandal is a greater sin against charity than war because it occasions ever more serious sins. Moreover, intense political dissent gives human affairs an outsized importance in light of the prospect of perfect beatitude. At the extremes, a more edifying response to earthly tyranny is Christian mar-tyrdom (*DR*, I.6).[16]

Second, the appropriate site of dissent is an established corporate body, the Church or, more vaguely, the people (*multitudine*) as a whole (*DR*,

I.6). While the latter possibility could be developed into a fuller discussion of spaces for civic activity, perhaps even approaching MacIntyre's (2016, 89) "prologue to radical social critique," other elements of Aquinas's perspective frustrate that potential. Where a people is not empowered to make its own laws, deference to authority is presumed if custom has been continually followed (97.3). Aquinas's extended response to the objection that war is always sinful (citing Matthew, 26.52, "all those who draw the sword shall perish by the sword"), thus condemns only private persons acting without authority, but absolves "that private person who uses the sword on the authority of the prince or the laws, or that public person [who acts] out of a zeal for justice, almost on the authority of God; he does not take up the sword himself, but uses it by the commission of another" (II–II, 40, a.1; cf. I–II, 100.8; II–II, 64.3, 7). At some level, this conclusion simply acknowledges the factual reality that Michael Walzer (1977, 39–42) calls the tyranny of war. Yet it also largely insulates what just war theorists call the war decision from active civic criticism, let alone dissent.[17]

Questions surrounding the meaning of competent authority also complicate assumptions about political sequences. In insisting that just wars be authorized by the prince (or the sovereign), Aquinas may give incomplete attention to wars fought over the location of authority, often presuming a context of stable legitimacy that is underinterrogated. Two of the four articles of *ST*'s question on war consider how war fighting intersects with the offices (may clerics and bishops wage war?) and practices (may wars be fought on feast days?) of institutionalized Roman Catholicism. Far from being simply historical idiosyncrasies,[18] these concerns display general acceptance of the character and origins of the order that just war theory presupposes and legitimates.

Requirements for consent notwithstanding, this perspective discourages forms of politics that would be more active practically and more critical intellectually. Yet though the first condition for just war may largely protect the decisions of those in authority from extensive scrutiny on the part of citizens, acknowledging the possibility of tyranny and insisting that the appropriate site of resistance is the people introduce political potentials extending beyond the boundaries of Aquinas's framework. Appreciating these possibilities allows us to read the second and third conditions, just cause and right intention, as inviting more critical challenges to those authorized to initiate war.

In *ST*, II–II, 40.1, a just cause arises when "those who are attacked deserve so due to some crime (*aliquam culpam*). As Augustine says: 'A just war is customarily defined as one that avenges injuries, as when a country or a city is punished because of disregarding just claims against wrongs done by its subjects or to restore that which is taken unjustly.' "[19] As stated, this proviso imposes significant restrictions on justifications for war and sets standards allowing challenges to those in power. Yet the meanings of these standards and the contexts in which they can be applied raise questions. Just wars are not exclusively defensive. In response to three scriptural passages that seem to oppose violence categorically (*Matthew*, 26.52; 5.39; *Romans*, 12.19), Aquinas cites Augustine to validate not only defense against aggressors but also punitive violence undertaken to improve souls. "For he who is liberated (*eripitur*) from the licentiousness of iniquity is defeated beneficially (*vincitur utiliter*): nothing is unhappier than the happiness of sinners" (II–II, 39.3; 40.1). Punishment through just war can be corrective, opening possibilities for initiating wars that might well be called aggressive. There are obvious dangers that self-serving justifications will mask naked greed or hatred (II–II, 34.4) or, even worse, that wars will be waged out of a sincere "benign severity" (*invitis benigna*). Consequently, Aquinas's standard for identifying just causes may fail precisely because it does not limit such causes to defense (thus, Finnis, 1998b, 33). While such concerns are serious, there are more complicated possibilities, identifying additional insights within, while raising more questions about, Aquinas's framework.

The refusal to limit just causes to defense may simply recognize that lines between defensive and aggressive wars are often blurred. Such blurring can be traced in part to the regime-specific character of threats, particularly in cases where the continuation of the regime as a way of life is at issue, Walzer's (1977, 251–255) supreme emergency. Aquinas does not confront this question directly, yet he prompts it indirectly by recognizing that regimes may be compared in terms of their moral qualities not just their structural characteristics (97.1; *DR*, I.1, II–7). The worst regimes foster ways of life that are perverse or predatory. What, then, constitutes a regime-threatening emergency that can justify war? The clearest threat is an attack on physical integrity (Rawls, 1999, 91). Yet even here, ambiguities arise. An example from Book Two of Plato's *Republic* may help. When Socrates constructs a city in speech as an analogic image for seeing justice in the soul, he initially populates it with craftsmen who satisfy moderate needs by production and exchange. Responding to his interlocutor Glaucon's objection that the city is primitive, Socrates turns it toward luxury. This invites conflicts with other societies. While such disputes seem straightforward quarrels over scarce resources, regime-specific interpretations become central. Once the original city turns luxurious, it can no longer support its population with its own resources. "Then we shall have to cut off a portion of our neighbor's land if we are to have enough for growing and grazing" (373d).[20] While this expansion is presented as necessary, it emerges only after a change in the regime's character. Soon, this luxurious city believes itself to be threatened by aggressive neighbors who "abandon themselves to the pursuit of wealth without limit, exceeding the boundaries of necessity" (373d). Yet perhaps those "greedy" neighbors see themselves driven by necessity, while interpreting the supposedly needful expansion of the (now luxurious) first city as unlimited greed. What seems compelled or unavoidable is largely triggered by regime priorities and what seems desperation to the one looks like overreaching aggression to the other.

Threats to regime existence become more controversial once they are extended beyond safeguarding physical boundaries. In Thucydides's Melian dialogue, the Athenians explain their aggression toward Melos as necessary to preserve Athens' identity as an empire whose goods are not merely material but reputational (5.91, 97, 99). The Melians are urged to protect their safety by becoming subject to Athens, but they resist in the name of political independence and honor, goods whose loss is more terrifying than physical destruction (5.92, 112). Therefore, though the need to confront threats seems essential for distinguishing between aggressive and defensive wars, threats may be as various and contestable as regimes themselves. After its most devastating battle, Abraham Lincoln characterized the American Civil War as one waged so "that government of the people, by the people, for the people shall not perish from the earth." Are economic or technological threats to the United States in the twenty-first century existential threats to its way of life? Read in this context, Aquinas's extension of just causes beyond defense is not simply a reflection of the limitations of his times (as for Finnis, 1998b, 23–24) but an acknowledgment of the complex character of political conflicts and the controversies attached to assessments of their justice.

In defending wars originating from a zeal for justice (II–II, 34.4; 40.1), Aquinas introduces the possibility of just war as crusade (cf. II–II, 10.8; II–II, 64.2).[21] While such zealotry should be tempered by the overriding concern for salvation (II–II, 36.2), the correction of sinners, however harsh, could be seen as beneficence, even charity (II–II, 34.3). Critics are legitimately disturbed not merely by possibilities of deception but also by more frightening prospects of sincerity. More wars over salvation.[22] Yet this focus may also communicate something uncomfortably important. Confrontations with political ways of life, judged on secular grounds and avoiding languages of sinfulness and punishment, may inevitably be part of wars against particularly heinous regimes. Can the war against Nazi Germany be fully understood without appreciating it, even if retrospectively, as a war against a political ethic?[23] Less dramatically, Rawls's version of just wars against rogue states envisages not simply the defense of liberal or decent nonliberal states from predators, but the eventual initiation of internal reform (1999, 91–92). While contemporary liberal internationalism does not justify wars waged solely for this purpose, the correction of rogue states' political cultures, for example their oppression of women or their violent abuse of racial or religious minorities, could plausibly be seen as one justification for confronting them militarily. Here, an assessment of war's justice is not disconnected from evaluative judgments about regime quality. In this respect, the Thomistic perspective shows the limits of Walzer's (1977, 61–63, 108) allegedly neutral legalist paradigm and underscores the importance of questions of substance as well as process in judging the justice of military interventions. Yet it also points to the practical and moral uncertainties that arise once neutralism is seen as illusory.

Complications persist in the movement to right intention. In its absence, even wars initiated by competent authorities for just causes are morally compromised. This imperative regulates both dimensions of war distinguished by later just war theorists, *jus ad bellum*, whether to fight and *jus in bello*, how to do so.[24] For Aquinas, right intention wages war for the sake of peace, supporting the most important political common good and opposing the evils that threaten it. On the testimony of Augustine, he provides two examples of wrong intentions, cupidity and cruelty, further differentiated into desire for injury, cruelty of revenge, unappeased and implacable spirit, savageness of fighting, and lust for domination. Other potential examples are hinted by Augustine's adding "and those things that are similar" (*et si qua sunt similia*).

Aquinas's theorization of intention reflects an ethical psychology (1.1; 8.1; 17.3; 18.6), which both presumes and revises Aristotle's statements in the *Nicomachean Ethics*. Intention (*intentio*) identifies ends in view while choice (*electio*) selects appropriate means to reach them (12, a.4; 13, a1). Though conceptually distinct, ends and means are closely integrated pragmatically (Finnis, 1998a, 62–71; 1998b, 17–18; Langan, 1977, 185). Like Aristotle, Aquinas would reject modern rational choice theory's treatment of ends as preferences, limiting rationality to efficient calculation.[25] Instead, the character of ends must be subjected to a rationality that extends beyond strategic thinking (15.3; 19.3). Intention and choice thus implicate one another within continuous judgments and evaluations. Actions chosen as means are intellectually and morally coherent only in light of the rightness of the intended end (8.2; 12.4; 19.3). Effective means toward sinful ends are badly chosen (II–II, 64.5). And the dependence of an intended end on sinful means must prompt reassessment of the end itself (18.4; 19.8). Because certain means are unredeemably irrational and wrong (2.4; 8.2; 19.7; 58.4), choosing them undermines or perverts the goodness of the intended end. This complex psychological dynamic implies that Aquinas's judgments about the conduct of war should become ever more complex once we appreciate the imperfect textures of the human world (63.4; 91.4).

Yet his approach often resists the fuller implications of this practical complexity. Yes, by insisting on right intention Aquinas refuses to validate every war authorized by legitimate authorities acting on just cause. At the same time, he may make it too easy to justify problematic acts of war in light of their underlying intentions, especially when partnered with a deference to authority. While right intention is insufficient by itself to make an act good (20.2), Aquinas's account of moral structure of action choices gives a strongly constitutive and normative role to ends in view (18.4; 19.7; II–II. 39.1), especially in circumstances where the protection of the common good is at stake and where public authority legitimately speaks.

This difficulty is especially pronounced within attempts by modern just war theorists to judge violence against noncombatants. Though wars have always put civilians at risk,[26] modern warfare is extreme (Burkhardt, 2017, 4, 50). Absent an ability to cope with this reality, a theory of just and limited war may not be possible at all.[27] One consequence might be admission that war is immoral in itself (making just war contradictory). Yet another might be the removal of all moral prohibitions on wars that will, nonetheless, be fought.[28] Refusing to go in either of these directions, systematic just war theory after Aquinas has responded with a series of distinctions, the most important of which seem to be discrimination, proportionality, and double effect.

The requirement for discrimination demands serious efforts to protect noncombatants, even if this means increasing risks for soldiers.[29] Discrimination has presumptive force as a moral restriction (II–II, 64.6–7), but its effectiveness in practice, certainly within modern warfare, is circumstantially limited. Precision weapons allow concentration on well-defined targets, but the integration of civilian and military sites (often done deliberately) means that even precision campaigns may cause significant civilian casualties. Deadly harm to civilians through the destruction of food, water, and health care infrastructures can also result indirectly but inevitably from attacks against military targets (Burkhardt, 2017, 24, 65–68;

Satkunanandan, 2015, 193). Finally, guerilla or terrorist strategies often depend on an intentional embedding of combatants with noncombatants. In recognition, the tendency of many modern just war theorists has been to insist that damages be proportionate to rightly intentioned ends (Walzer, 1977, 119–120; Elshtain, 2003, 65). Civilian casualties should be limited by sincere, not cosmetic, attempts at discrimination and their occurrence should be worth it in light of the larger goals at stake, not only within individual military engagements but within the broader context of a particular war itself. Disproportionate force may pollute any guiding right intention. The obvious difficulty here is the prospect of what Walzer calls the sliding scale (1977, 246), where levels of justifiable violence escalate as the importance of objectives ratchets higher. Like the content and significance of just causes, claims of importance are always situated and are impacted significantly by the priorities of involved regimes. Such judgments are also usually made by those in control. Even the peace at which right intention aims can be controversial, with the restoration of humane relations only a nebulous baseline. One response to such complications within just war theory (noticeably though not exclusively among its Catholic representatives)[30] has been the idea of double effect, where the foreseen is distinguished from the intended. This starts from Aquinas's judgment about homicides committed in self-defense (II–II, 64.7); one may foresee that protecting oneself or one's family will result in the death of an attacker without intending that the assailant die. Similarly, though military actions may foreseeably cause civilian deaths, those outcomes are not intentional but accidental (in colder terms, collateral). Thus, war fighting that causes civilian casualties is morally permissible, so long as the effects are not intended and if serious efforts are made to respect discrimination and proportion (II–II. 64.7).

Any reasonable practical psychology recognizes that not everything foreseen is intended (Anscombe, 1961, 57). How much this distinction assists in justifying or even excusing (Mapel, 1998, 72–73) wartime violence against noncombatants (in circumstances not remotely anticipated by Aquinas) is a different question. When considering the massive allied firebombings of German and Japanese cities and the use of nuclear weapons against Japan at the end of World War II, critics have rejected this framework as a dangerous sophistry generating moral blindness.[31] Related concerns about civilian deaths underlie more recent criticisms of the United States' invasion of Iraq and the accompanying bombing of Baghdad in 2003; Israel's military campaigns in Gaza in 2008, 2014, and 2018; and Iraq's Western-supported retaking of Mosul from the Islamic

State in 2017. At some point, devastating consequences become so predictable that all claims they are nonetheless unintended collapse. In the World War Two examples, massive civilian casualties were intended as proportional means to ending the conflict with less overall loss of life.

Raising these concerns may seem disturbingly close to Schmitt's aggressive critique in *The Nomos of the Earth* that faults searches for "just cause" as ending in the demonization of the enemy and condemns appeals to "right intention" as legitimating whatever means are necessary for victory (1983, 121, 124, 159, 324). Both moves are assailed as justifications intensifying wars (246), undercutting the alleged purposes of just war *theory* generally. It is predictable that Schmitt overlooks any potential attention to just war *considerations* on the part of critical citizens. We can, however, reinvolve such concerns within forms of civic questioning that could be both more democratic and more philosophical.

Two Approaches to Just War Theory

One political way of life that just wars should protect worries sincerely about the justice of its own wars. The Iraq and Gaza cases are troubling for the United States and Israel because, for all of their flaws, they are regimes (unlike Bashar al-Assad's Syria or Vladimir Putin's Russia, both of which have unleashed sickening violence against civilians in the Syrian civil war) that should take the justice of war seriously.[32] Democratic institutions (the United States is not Donald Trump's and Israel is not Benjamin Netanyahu's) make this seriousness possible though they do not guarantee it. How might just war theory, both as understood by Aquinas and as reconstructed by modern thinkers, serve as a resource for such seriousness in a democracy?

One approach, which might be called programmatic, sets the moral conditions that need to be met for wars to be considered just. A related but different perspective, that might be called critical, sees that framework as identifying complex problems about politics: the location and legitimacy of authority, the character and complexity of just causes, and the content and moral significance of political intentions. The two perspectives can be complementary (O'Driscoll, 2015, 374–375) but they can also clash if emphasis on one limits attention to the other. Considering the first approach in light of questions raised by the second, three concerns emerge.

First, there is a risk that just war's standards may be applied too formally, as items on a checklist rather than as substantive problems that need to be thoughtfully examined.[33] This prospect is reinforced by the creation of a specialized vocabulary (proportionality, double effect, collateral damage) that often conceals moral problems by appearing to resolve them. Questions asked about the justice of wars and the intentions behind them should also evolve with historical experience and there is no reason why the questions themselves cannot be expanded. Todd Burkhardt (2017, 41–42, 154) argues that the established categories of just war theory need expansion to cover transition periods between war and peace, setting standards for the just treatment of defeated civilian populations. Insisting that war decisions, broadly understood, be proportional to justifiable ends also imposes responsibilities on political leaders to commit soldiers to combat only after careful reflection and to provide responsible support for their welfare both during their terms of service and afterward. Violations of these responsibilities intensify questions about leadership competence. Second, both the questions asked about decisions and practices of political agents and the responses given to them may defer too readily to authorities whose perspectives and disclosures often need more critical scrutiny than they receive. Finally, there is the attraction of comfortable closure. This is not a matter of the political misapplication of just war principles but of an epistemic presumption within just war theory itself.[34] While the need for an intellectual resource distinguishing between just and unjust wars is essential, the Thomistic contention that dilemmas arising in these circumstances are always capable of morally satisfactory resolutions seems too comfortable. Some moral choices leave immoral residues, some political hands are unavoidably dirty.[35] At one level, continued awareness of these possibilities is a cautionary warning that favors moderation. Yet moderation can also at times counsel, perhaps even require, a restraint courting tragedies of its own.

For all of his insistence on confronting the complexities of the world (II–II. 57.2), then, Aquinas's hierarchical order may obscure particularity.[36] All of the pathologies marking wars as depraved—desiring injury, inflicting cruel revenge, unappeased and implacable spirit, savagery of fighting, lust for domination, "and all things that might be similar"— are clustered as opposites to right intention, with binary moral categories (made easier by the association of wrong intentions with savagery) replacing political specifics. For Aquinas, an excessive attention to these specifics may reflect the error of taking worldly things too seriously. The just war theorizations of his successors surely attempt to respect both the requirements of moral truth (Boyle, 1998, 42) and the complexities of politics (Finnis, 1998b, 15). Yet this often means that the second imperative defers to the first, preventing practical complexities from intruding too disruptively on truth claims. If we pay more attention to the details of politics, Aquinas's moral examination of war and its circumstances seems too compressed, suggesting a need to consider not only the justice of wars but also the origins of political order and the goods of political communities more fully, engaging particularities more carefully.

This is Walzer's approach in *Just and Unjust Wars* (1977, 20) as he provides moral inquiries that never move too far beyond historical cases. Still, he cannot avoid recourses to theoretical positions that are not always cohesive. His guiding template for understanding both the goods of politics and the circumstances of war focuses on the importance of rights (53), whose defense is war's only justification (72).[37] Yet he also defers to a more vaguely communitarian template in his respect for national self-determination (which sets strict limits on interventions—108) and his recognition of the compelling reality of supreme emergencies (responses to which may override the welfare of innocents—262, 268).[38] His notion of supreme emergency attempts to bridge the gap between rights-based and communitarian political theory by insisting that rights-based side constraints should apply to all justifications of wars except in cases where the very survival of the community is at stake. Yet as I have suggested, conceptions of existential threats are not easily disconnected from the characters of the regimes involved and the designation, supreme emergency, is not simply neutral (cf. Geuss, 2008, 83). Acknowledging that Walzer may be trying to have things both ways theoretically may offer one more reason to avoid overtheorization but it also reminds us of the problems of ignoring philosophy when it is most needed, not as a network of theoretical concepts capable of more precise specification, but as a rationality that engages particularity with a philosophically informed critical distance, *theōria* less as structure than as attention.

However, this is not the kind of political philosophy encouraged by Aquinas. At the broadest level, he claims to have completed philosophy, not simply by doing better philosophy but by discovering philosophy's limits in light of the higher truths of revelation (I, 1.1, 5; II–II.1.1). Commentators differ over the consequences of this claim for Thomistic philosophy. Joseph Owens (1993, 46, 48, 51) interprets the priority given to divinely revealed truths as improving Aristotle's philosophical efforts to articulate a science of being. For Mark Jordan (1993, 248), however, such appeals convert philosophy into theology. Either way, the outcome is a closure that treats deep philosophical challenges as correctible errors, through either better philosophical analysis or foundational revelatory guidance.

The immediate secular response is that Aquinas's theological claims are not rationally provable, a judgment with which Aquinas would not disagree (II–II. 6.1). But a more modest question asks how Aquinas conceives of philosophical practice. The engagement with Aristotle is emblematic.[39] If Aristotle's practical philosophy aims at resolving moral and political problems (sharing a continuous natural law tradition with Aquinas), we can see why its anomalies and puzzles might demand more definitive grounding in revealed truth.[40] Yet this conclusion presumes a reading of Aristotelian philosophy that some commentators (often sympathetic to Aquinas) question.[41] The issue is not whether Aquinas gets Aristotle right, but whether a different reading of Aristotle can sketch a philosophy offering an alternative to Aquinas's. Harry Jaffa claims that it can, focusing on Aristotle's continued engagement with political or cultural opinions on their own terms (1979, 143). In Jaffa's reading, Aristotle's practical philosophy is not an implicit but imperfect system but a sequence of performative representations of the moral point of view from the perspective of morality's own flawed and developing experiences (1979, 65–66). One could go further and argue that Aristotle's approach is dialogic and multivocal, pointing to the provisionality even of the strictly philosophical point of view that is overtly embraced in *NE* (10, 6–7).[42] Thus interpreted, the puzzles arising within Aristotle's examinations of the moral life are problematic for reasons that Aristotle's philosophical practice not simply acknowledges but embraces. While Aquinas makes apparently similar moves in *ST*, Aristotle's approach differs in two respects. Aristotle's philosophical puzzles (*aporiai*) can only be addressed by more philosophy, not by anything beyond. And this philosophy proceeds not through foundational conclusions resolving our *aporiai*, but through conversations that continually revise them.

Aquinas and Modern International Constitutionalism

If political philosophy's historical texts are resources for understanding the political challenges of war and peace, how should we interpret Aquinas's texts? Finnis argues that they should have pride of place, offering an approach to moral and political theory that is superior to those of both classical predecessors and modern or postmodern critics (1998a, vii). Given Finnis's important work in natural law theory (1980; 1998a),[43] his assessment deserves both respect and scrutiny. Confining myself to a reading of Aquinas's treatment of just war, I have suggested that his perspective is both constructive and limiting. He forces us to question the distinction between defensive and aggressive wars more carefully and insists that regime character has to matter for judgments about war's justice. Neither contribution is insignificant in a fractious world where political distortions are harder to detect, yet moral abuses harder to ignore. Both insights also offer friendly amendments to those who see a deliberatively grounded law of peoples as setting the boundaries that separate just from unjust wars. That said, Aquinas's constrained vision of philosophy also frustrates the deeper political critique that such a context requires.

An appreciative but skeptical reading of Aquinas can also inform critical appraisals of liberal constitutionalism's treatment of the relation between war and order. Obviously, there are major historical and philosophical differences between these perspectives (though noting Rawls, 1999, 77). Rawls and Habermas address the historical condition of modernity, not the place of human beings within a broader natural order and they offer a political theory grounded in human reasonableness alone with no connection to metaphysics or theology (Rawls, 1999, 34). Yet there are also important parallels. Both Thomistic just war theory and liberal constitutionalism's law of peoples interpret just wars as defending or restoring political orders threatened by aggressive violence. Both perspectives set moral boundaries around exercises of political power and both endorse some form of constitutionalism as the best political way of doing so. Finally, both projects offer moral resolutions. Aquinas's confidence in the ability to unpack practical dilemmas without leaving disordering moral residues is roughly paralleled by Habermas's confidence in the forceless force of the stronger argument (Habermas, 1996, 541, n. 58) and Rawls's articulation of a reasonable law of peoples that only needs to expand its scope beyond domestic political liberalism (1999, 9, 15–19, 23). These parallels mean that questions raised about Aquinas's approach may resonate even when assessing a paradigm that seems so different. There are at least three concerns.

First, Aquinas may not adequately theorize political order's origins. We should appreciate Nietzsche's warning (*Genealogy of Morals*, 2.12) against confusing origin (*Ursprung*) with purpose (*Zweck*), yet also note that *Genealogy* aims to correct misunderstandings of morality's purposes by clarifying its origins (*GM, Vor* 2). To this end, there can be two initial, rough distinctions. The first separates origins initiating political associations from those sustaining them. While necessary at one point, initiating origins are followed by a functionality which, while preserving some of initiation's traces, can be both historically distant and conceptually separable. Sustaining origins are ongoing, relating to political functionality continuously. A second distinction asks if origins, whether initiating or sustaining, relate to functionality in commensurate or disjunctive ways. Initiating origins may be violent, and therefore disjunctive with civilized governance, yet they may eventually give way to sustaining constitutional forms commensurate with healthy political functionality. Yet if sustaining origins wear out or break down, new initiations may be necessary with no assurances about their commensurability with the healthy society they are designed to restore. Moreover, even sustaining origins may be disjunctively situated with the functionality they enable. War and punishment may be continually needed to sustain a healthy *civitas* but there is something undeniably disjunctive between such forms of violence and a functioning rational governance. By insisting on moral coherence, Aquinas denies that either initiating or sustaining origins can ultimately be disjunctive with a politics supportive of the common good. The (admittedly incomplete) treatment of political founding in *De Regno* (II.5–8) focuses nearly exclusively on technical dimensions, location, environment, and resources, and very little on conflictual dynamics, let alone on necessary violence. This in spite of the fact that its two named examples of founders are Romulus and Alexander. *DR*'s earlier extensive consideration of tyranny (I.6, 9) represents it as the deterioration of a healthy kingship, an unjust domestic war to be corrected through just violence, human or divine. Within *ST*, a suitably expanded vantage point shows that the violence needed to resist aggression or punish criminals is fully commensurate with the functioning of a healthy *civitas*. However, treating political origins as inevitably continuous with healthy political purposes disregards Nietzsche's caution against equating them and disables recognition of more troubling disjunctures. Instead of highlighting such pragmatic problems, however, Aquinas's approach threatens to conceal them A more critical attention to Aquinas's own treatments of politics would unsettle such comfortable conclusions and admit the ongoing, disturbing possibility of dirty hands.

How do things stand with Rawls and Habermas, both of whom also understand just war as preserving or enhancing legitimate political order? Their common perspective sustains that order not through a politics practiced according to nature but in the agreements of rational persons engaged in ethical communicative action. Extended internationally as the law of peoples, the sustaining origin of these agreements is a postnational state system whose members draw on their own constitutional potentials to strengthen institutions supporting autonomy and human rights (Rawls, 1999, 37). The history leading to this condition is recognized as bloody, the wars of religion and modernity's greatest war. Yet such bloodshed seems understood as an initiating origin that civilizational progress will outgrow (Rawls, 1999, expressly at 19, 26, 79). Under nearly ideal conditions, the initiation of liberal societies first among decent but nonliberal peoples, then within burdened societies and eventually accommodating reformed rogue states would resemble the sustaining origins of political liberalism (Rawls, 1999, 35, 106, 118, 122). Otherwise, "these are not matters on which political philosophy has much to add" (93). Any aggression threatening this progressive advance should be resisted by wars and punishments that would, for that very reason, be just. Political practices according to or against nature are replaced by those situated on the right or the wrong side of moral progress. Yet an overconfident reliance on this narrative can downplay or misrepresent power's role in sustaining deliberative politics. As many critics of the domestic side of deliberative democratic theory have noted, this perspective presumes rational and decent partners without focusing enough on how their presence and influence can be continually secured.[44] To this extent, deliberative democracy remains uncomfortable with international political environments characterized by turbulence and hostility, where its institutions must sometimes be sustained by a power not always commensurate with reasonableness or justice. Current (as of 2018) unease over the West's embrace of drone warfare (Satkunanandan, 2015, 193–194) is only one example. The Rawlsian implication (1999, 7, 26) that such an order cannot be truly peaceful does not so much address this uncertainty as ignore it.

Second, my reading of Aquinas's treatment of war finds his perspective complicated by questions arising within, but too easily obscured by, his own framework. When does an established authority lose competence? Are all causes of war either just or unjust? How much violence does right intention justify? We should ask if modern international constitutionalism encounters similar dilemmas and if so why. One source of distorting overconfidence might be the status afforded to liberalism's political culture. In *Political Liberalism* Rawls abandons *A Theory of Justice*'s attempt to speak *sub specie aeternitatis* in favor of outlining the political justice most compatible with a constitutional democratic society (1999, 179; 2005, 223). Interpreting that constitutional culture, Rawls gives reasonable pluralism pride of place (2005, 36). However, this judgment is one sided. Where do unreasonable pluralities come in and what separates one from the other? Rawls's cultural turn calls for more complex cultural analyses than he provides. More seriously, the selectivity of this cultural reading raises concerns that Rawlsian liberalism is as much politicized as political, a sociological characterization directed by a pragmatic agenda.[45] This concern is only elevated as Rawls returns to more universalist proposals in *The Law of Peoples*. Do the articulated categories of liberal, nonliberal but decent, and burdened societies versus aggressor or rogue states, map *Political Liberalism*'s self-consciously localized constitutional democracy onto a wider world? Here, we might reinvolve Habermas. His institutional schematic for constitutional governance comprises overlapping and hierarchical institutional spheres framed by a cultural context that he calls a lifeworld (*Lebenswelt*) (1996, 22, 354). Is the spread of that cultural lifeworld one of liberalism's political tasks? If concerns remain about the deployment of political power in service to this goal, continued recourse to a political philosophy able to judge that power, practiced not so much outside ethics (a la Geuss, 2005) as critically distant from globalized liberal political culture, would be salutary.

Yet neither Rawls nor Habermas makes such a critical philosophy available. For all of their secularism, their philosophical potentials seem constrained in ways whose outcomes parallel Aquinas's, introducing a third point of comparison. Both modern statements reject foundational understandings of the human good as intellectually inadequate (because they are metaphysical) and politically dangerous (because they are controversially comprehensive).[46] Both face the problem of justifying and limiting applications of political power in a way that is universally obligatory but not metaphysically foundational or politically threatening. Their frames of reference, Habermas's theory of communicative action and Rawls's reasonable law of peoples, are presented as solutions. Yet are these formulations really functional equivalents to comprehensive doctrines, indeed to metaphysics, avoiding such problems by surreptitiously resolving them?[47] From very different directions, Aquinas (on the one hand) and Rawls and Habermas (on the other) may obscure the problem of articulating the foundational bases for political evaluation and judgment: Aquinas by definitively answering it, Rawls and Habermas by alleging its obsolescence or impossibility. Read against one another, the Thomistic and liberal constitutional perspectives suggest two more complicated conclusions about the role of so-called foundational questions in political philosophy. First, difficulties involved in attempts to answer such questions do not justify dismissing them as unintelligible. Second, the importance of such questions does not imply the necessity of final, nonproblematic answers. What both positions call for, against their own explicit pronouncements, is the continued practice of a more critical kind of political philosophy.

I have argued that Aquinas undercuts the possibility of the sort of philosophy that his own problematics elicit. One unintended consequence is that his understanding of political goods does not take politics' support for critical rationality—the *logos* that considers the problematic character of justice and injustice—seriously enough. This sort of good, performatively displayed, for example, in both the Platonic dialogues and Aristotle's practical investigations, is not fully captured by Finnis's schema of the political alternatives that Aquinas confronts, protecting the peace or legislating morality (1998a, 245–252). Ultimately, Aquinas's political philosophy is not an activity continuous with that of the citizen, but an inquiry belonging within the bounded and disciplined scholarly community (100.1; II–II, 2.6). Aquinas groups moral precepts into three categories: self-evident even to the uneducated, easily grasped upon promulgation, or in need of instruction at the hands of the wise (100.11). Any potential tensions between politics and a philosophy that politics enables but does not control are minimized by the appropriate separation of political from philosophical spheres.

Rawls and Habermas, too, constrain the kind of philosophical criticism that the problematics of their positions demand. The dismissal of certain sorts of arguments as meaningless in a postmetaphysical age can be as stipulative as appeals to revelation. But while Aquinas limits philosophy for theological reasons, Rawls and Habermas do so for broadly political ones; the kind of philosophy they recognize must be compatible with political priorities taken as settled, Rawls's broadly constitutional context or Habermas's democratic theorems derived from discourse ethics. While Habermas may be more welcoming than Rawls to the consideration of controversial proposals within the public sphere,[48] both see irresolvable tensions between a politics that establishes and manages power through democratic institutions and a political philosophy that refuses to surrender its comprehensive or metaphysical pretensions (Rawls, 1999, 148). In so doing, Rawls and Habermas may also come to resemble Aquinas, for none seems fully to acknowledge either the problematic characteristics of politics that make critical rationality necessary or the character of a *political philosophy* that takes both parts of its identity seriously.

Given such controversies, why not take a much more radical turn toward a world understood not philosophically but politically? This is apparently Machiavelli's approach.

Machiavelli's Turbulent Orders

While Aquinas treats war as a sporadic necessity justified and limited by the need to restore healthy political order, Machiavellian war is a continuous struggle for stability in a world where human affairs always ascend or decline (*Discourses*, 1.37, 2. Pr; *Florentine Histories*, 5.1). In terms introduced earlier, Machiavelli posits no sharp distinction between initiating and sustaining origins because both involve polemical responses to a turbulent world. War is not disjunctive with, but is, in fact, dynamically related to politics itself.

This political framing departs significantly from Aquinas's in both form and content. To be sure, neither thinker conceives of political order simply as the absence of conflict; it is a pattern of civic life whose functions, when effective, transform multitudes into citizens.[49] However, Machiavelli's political orders are not reflections of nature's coherence, but tenuous constructions for which there are no fully intelligible natural standards or completely successful historical examples (*FH*, 2.1). Where Aquinas insists that orders be just, Machiavelli demands that they be good, fostering virtue and countering corruption (*Disc*, 1.16–18). Within such orders peace is not the most important common good (as in *DR*, I.2); the principal political virtue is neither justice nor charity.[50] Rather, good orders enable successful collective responses to ongoing conflicts (*Disc*, 1, 37), fostering the courage and discipline that allow political communities to cohere and prevail (*Disc*, 1.6, 2.2, 2.19).[51] Political corruption is vulnerability to softness and dissension (*Disc*, 1. 10), though the extreme deterioration of a corrupt regime may initiate regeneration.[52] Machiavelli thus rejects Aquinas's peaceful *civitas* as fostering an idleness (*ozio*) that will eventually give way to either effeminacy (*Disc*, 1.18; 2.2; 2.25) or collapse (compare *DR*, 2.3 and *Disc*, 1.6, 37). Whether good or bad orders emerge depends on how well or badly conflict is managed (*Disc*, 1.4, 7; *FH*, 2.1; 7.1).[53] Regarding international politics, Machiavelli concurs that wars must be limited but he offers no just war theory.[54] Indeed, a healthy political community organizes desires not only to control debilitating passions that prompt softness or fearfulness but also to resist misguided inclinations toward mercy or humanity (*Disc*, 1.26; 3.41).

Wars are permanent not only because decent communities can never presume the reform or disappearance of rogue states, but also because human appetites are aggressively insatiable (*Disc*, 1.37). This means that war is not simply external to order, either as sinful threat or as controlled instrument. In one sense, war is the source of order, for political groups are consolidated only under some necessity or coercion (*Disc*, 1.1). Yet coercion's materials (matters, *Disc*, 1.18, subjects, *Disc*, 3. 8) are the very desires for gain and recognition that make coercion necessary (*FH*, 3.11; 4.18). Conflicting ambitions persist even after material necessities disappear (*Disc*, 1.37; *FH*, 4.18). The health of a political community requires that oppositional ambitions guard against one another (*Disc*, 1.2), fostering not peaceful cooperation but disciplined competition (*Disc*, 1.4). "There is nothing that makes a republic more stable and firm than to order it in a mode that the alteration of those humors (*umori*) agitating it have a way of venting themselves as ordered by the laws" (*Disc*, 1.7).[55]

Consequently, the same turbulent energies that can be forged into order limit or threaten any resulting stability. Though founders are advised "to presuppose that all men are bad, and that they always have to use the malignity of their spirit at whatever time they have free occasion" (*Disc*, 1.3; cf. *Pr*, 15, 17, 18), the rhetorical progression of the *Discourses* (Strauss, 1969, 91–107) might imply that such malignity can be corrected by right order (*Disc*, 3. 29; cf. *FH*, 3.5; *AW*, 2.167). However, the final chapter of the book associates political health with the repeated application of (and thus the continued need for) executions (*Disc*, 3.49; cf. *Disc*, 1.4, 19.42; 3.11; *AW*, 6.112–113). And while the virtue of republican politics is its greater capacity to achieve the common good (*Disc*, 2.2; *FH*, 7.33; *AW*, 1.33, 64; 2.293), this good is represented as the aggregated desires of a majority, established politically when those profiting from the regime's expansion are able to suppress (*oppressire*) those who lose (cf. *FH*, 7.1).[56] If the competing *umori* that agitate a political community can only be cohered by necessities arising from threats, political identities are never stable.[57] And it is too simple to suggest that Machiavelli's only consideration in waging war is success (one reading of *Prince* 3 and *Disc* 3.41),[58] for he cannot envisage conditions under which complete success, construed as either domination or pacification, is possible.

The limits to forging order out of the materials of disorder are shown most clearly in the experiences of Machiavelli's ancient Romans (Coby, 1999, 11; Sullivan 1996, 99). Though the Roman republic prospered because of its organized expansion (*Disc*, 1.60), its successes led to disputes over the Agrarian Law (*Disc*, 1. 37) and extensions of the consular terms (*Disc*, 3.24) that eventually ruined it.[59] This irony is communicated powerfully in the first sentence of *Disc* 1.1. "Those who read of what the beginning (*principio*) of the city of Rome was, and by what givers of laws and how it was ordered, will not marvel that so much virtue was maintained for so many centuries in that city; and that afterwards there was born such an empire as was acquired by that republic." Though it destroyed the republic (*Disc*, 1.10), empire seems embedded in the Roman regime from its beginnings.[60] Still, this threat of recurring instability does not counsel political caution.[61] Instead, Machiavelli demands more radical innovations that will surpass Roman achievements and the ancient orders generally (cf. *Pr*, 26; *Disc*, 2. Pr).[62] Even corrupt cities can stay free if their governing orders (*Disc*, 1.18) manage embedded dangers more effectively (cf. *Disc*, 1.18; 3.31, 49). Yet no task is more difficult and dangerous than introducing such new orders (*Prince*, 6), a project compared to the exploration of "unknown waters and lands" (*Disc*, 1, Pr). Accomplishing this "difficult," "doubtful" and "dangerous" work requires various forms of war; the prince "should have no other object, nor any other thought, nor take anything as his art outside of war and its orders and discipline" (*Prince*, 14).[63]

Foundational War

It would be understandable to interpret this statement as strategic advice to ambitious and beleaguered political agents. Mikael Hornqvist (2004, 98) and Michael Mallett (1991, 174–177) trace Machiavelli's concentration on war to the pressures of contemporary Florentine politics. Yet his texts are political in deeper ways. First, initiating new modes and orders depends on agents whose capacities and identities are not settled, requiring construction and testing through practice.[64] Such tests pose risks that no science—or prudence—can eliminate.[65] These are not simply risks of failure, for the success of the Roman republic destroyed civic liberty in Italy (*Disc*, 2.2; Zuckert, 2017, 82). Second, the motivational appeals of the *Prince* and the *Discourses* valorize the honor available to the "heads and orderers" of religions, republics, or kingdoms (*Disc*, 1.10).[66] Insofar as the embrace of honor clashes with the undifferentiated urgings and passive gratifications of material need (*Disc*, 1.5, 37), it is a distinctively political good achievable only under conditions of differentiation and agency. Successful regimes may keep their states rich and their citizens poor by offsetting love of gain with love of honor as the most powerful civic motivation (*Disc*, 3.25). Even if Machiavelli intends to elevate literary men (*Disc*, 1.10)—perhaps including a kind of philosopher—above politicians and thus to reposition the site of reputation from regimes to texts or from action to thought (Strauss, 1969, 233, 288), he still politicizes literature and philosophy, commensurating them with the more striking achievements of political founders.

The speech acts that are Machiavelli's texts intensify the polemical character of his project.[67] The prospect of honor draws readers toward the greatest risks. Such risks are both obscured and elevated when Machiavelli downplays anxiety about success while emphasizing nobility of effort. The last portion of the Preface to *Discourses* Book One surely deceives in claiming that after Machiavelli's exploration only "a short road will remain for another to bring it to its destined place."[68] Even if this statement performatively acknowledges fraud as a necessary part of war (*Disc*, 1.40), the inducement presumes readers who are daringly ambitious, not cautiously thoughtful. While a balanced regime might be the true political life (*il vero vivere politico, Disc*, 1.6), the turbulence of desire renders that condition unattainable, so "in ordering a republic there is a need to think of the more honorable part (*ale parte piu onorevole*)" that longs for expansion. Yet thinking of the more honorable part also redoubles uncertainties, for honor is subject to the changing standards of ethical cultures. The re-recreation of meaning may be the most daunting challenge faced by Machiavelli's indefinite princes.[69]

Consequently, I believe that the call for princes to study war is more than strategic. It discloses the philosophical frame of reference that informs Machiavelli's project, generally. This assessment challenges judgments that Machiavelli avoids serious philosophical entanglements.[70] Though most scholars making this claim fully acknowledge Machiavelli's engagements with his contemporaries' treatments of providence, fortune, or nature, they often read them as secondary or fragmented. These judgments oversimplify, in part because of the assumption that authentically philosophical statements must be systematic.[71] However, the absence of systematization does not mean the absence of philosophical seriousness and coherence. When Anthony Parel disputes Machiavelli's reliance on Lucretius's natural philosophy, he asks (2013, 600), "granted that Machiavelli knew the theory of the swerve well, does it follow that he also subscribed to it?" The question is right, but it should be posed to all of Machiavelli's encounters with concerns extending beyond the immediate political world. Here, the assessment of Harvey Mansfield and Nathan Tarcov that "philosophy lurks everywhere in [Machiavelli's] work behind the scenes in which politics plays out its lessons" (Machiavelli, 1996, xxxvi–xxxvii) seems correct. Yet I want to develop this more explicitly. I argue that Machiavelli's philosophical backstory, his consideration of the roles of providence, fortune, and nature within human affairs, is itself informed by an understanding of politics that emphasizes its polemical character above all else, pointing toward an agency defined by aggressive daring. If Machiavelli dispenses with a need for any systematic or conventional philosophical framing, he does so in ways that challenge rather than ignore how human practice is framed by philosophical inquiry.[72] Yet this philosophical privileging of polemical agency marginalizes other political functions toward which Machiavelli also gestures, showing the distortions of the call for princes to subordinate everything to the study of war.

Politicized Providence

Machiavelli's most obvious departure from Aquinas is his dismissal of the substantive questions of theology. Yet we should not stop there. His well-known criticisms of the pernicious influences of the Roman church, institutionally or historically understood, are scathing (*Prince*, 11, 17; *Discourses*, 1.12). But how deeply do these assaults touch religious traditions that look to providence as the essential framing for human practice? While John Pocock argues (2003, 191, 214) that Machiavelli's healthy civic life is fully secular, Sebastian De Grazia and Maurizio Viroli read his political program as responding to providential guidance on how fallen man can be redeemed,[73] aiming to reform politics through a truer interpretation of Christianity.[74] In contrast, while denying that Machiavelli is guided by Christian providence, Miguel Vatter (2013, 612–618) interprets his respect for armed prophets (Moses, not Savonarola) as drawing on the providential messianism of the Hebrew tradition. For these commentators, regard for some form of providential care is central to Machiavelli's political thinking.

Differences aside, these judgments presume the cohesiveness of originating religious traditions or revealed sources. At times, Machiavelli seems to agree. As liberator of the Hebrews, Moses was "a mere executor of things that were ordered (*erano ordinate*) for him by God" though "he should be admired if only for that grace (*grazia*) that made him worthy of speaking with God" (*Pr*, 6). The inspiring lives of Francis and Dominic saved Christianity when the abuses of the prelates threatened to consign it to ignominy. By following "the example of the life of Christ . . . they brought [this faith] back into the minds of human beings" (*Disc*, 3.1).[75] Yet both of these originary traditions are radically revised in Machiavelli's hands. Restoring Christianity through the example of its founder (the only reference to Christ in the *Discourses*) turns out to have been politically ruinous, "giving [the people] to understand that is evil to speak evil of the evil, and that it is good to live under obedience to them, and, if they make an error, to leave their punishment to God: and thus they do the worst they can, because they do not fear that punishment they do not see or believe" (3.1).[76] Though this outcome seems to block reconciliation between Christianity and country, *Discourses* 2.2 imagines that even though "the world appears to be made effeminate and heaven disarmed," "our religion" could allow "the exaltation and defense of the *patria*" if it were interpreted in accordance with *virtu* and not out of laziness (*ozio*). This is read by Viroli (2010) as expressing Machiavelli's appreciation of the political potentials of Christianity (the disarming and effeminate interpretation is said to be false).[77] Yet we might just as easily concur with Vatter that this statement imagines a ferocious, decisively non-Christian, politics (2013, 608). However, even deeper questions emerge when we consult Machiavelli's elusive consideration of the origins of religious traditions themselves. What would make any of them *true*?

In envisaging his alternative interpretation of "our religion," Machiavelli sees religious forms through the prism of political need. This change in perspective does not simply discount all beyond the here and now. It is, instead, justified by a challenge to the cosmic principle upon which Aquinas's perspective in particular (*ST*, I.103.1, 4–5; I–II 93.2–3) and Judeo-Christian theology in general are based, the divine creation of the world. In *Discourses* 2.5, Machiavelli confronts those attempting to refute "those philosophers who have had it that the world may have been [in existence] from eternity," on the evidence that there are no memories of events beyond five thousand years. Challenging the refutation, he points to what should be inferred cosmically from history and experience (or what is "seen"). "Memories of times are scattered (*spengano*) by diverse causes, of which some come from human beings, some from heaven."[78] Human causes operate through political mechanisms, the obliteration of the old through persecutions, and originate from political motives, desires for power and reputation. Paradigmatic examples are religious changes, the replacement of the gentile religions by Christianity, following the gentiles' destruction of their predecessors' beliefs. Religions themselves (now called sects—*sette*) are cultural constructions, paralleling linguistic traditions (cf. *FH*, 1.5). As contingent communities, sects cannot control their futures perfectly. Because the Christians retained the Latin language, they failed to erase memories of classical antiquity completely.[79] Within the fluid horizon of cultural change, Christianity may also be reinvented, perhaps using Latin's preserved memory of what was done by antiquity's "excellent men" (*uomini eccellenti*) as a resource. *Discourses* 2.5 thus makes the reinterpretation of Christianity envisaged in 2.2 anthropologically and, therefore, theologically plausible. The reinterpretation of "our religion" may end in non-Christian patriotism only if there is something that can be originally identified as true Christianity (De Grazia, 1989, 89).

Similarly, the basis for admiring Moses in the *Prince* shifts from God's grace (*Pr*, 6) to Moses's virtue (*Pr*, 26); he is no longer mere executor of higher orders. If the readers of the *Discourses* consider the Bible judiciously (*sensatamente*), they "will see that since he wished his laws and his orders (*le sue legge e . . . li suoi ordini*) to go forward, Moses was forced to kill infinite men" (3.30).[80] In this reading, Hebrew law originated not from God's commandments (as for Aquinas, *ST*, I–II, 100.3, 11) but from Moses's virtues. To the extent that the Hebrew tradition interprets providence through images of generals and armies (Vatter, 2013, 615), it may offer a vision of divine rule compatible at first glance with Machiavelli's. Ralph Lerner (1972, 218) comments that Maimonides's "Messiah is a successful Bar Kokhba or, more precisely, a son of David, a general rather than a prophet." Yet Lerner also underscores Maimonides's insistence that political success must be "in the service of something higher," a world to come linked to the immortality of the soul. By contrast, the requirements of political practice dictate Machiavelli's reconstructions of originary scriptural sources. Facing hardships that allegedly parallel those of the enslaved Hebrews, modern Italians are promised a *redentore* in *Prince* 26. A radical revision of the *Magnificat* of Luke's Gospel in *Discourses* 1.26 represents David not as God's executor but as his own originator, who "filled the hungry with good things and sent the rich away empty," all in the name of an aggressive political agency aspiring to make everything new in a very different vision of a world to come, reinventing providential past and salvational future.[81]

Wars Against Fortuna

In considering Machiavelli's framing alternatives to providence, commentators have focused on two broad possibilities, fortune and nature. For Parel, Machiavelli's political science is subordinate to an astrological science that discloses the influences of heavens (*i cieli*) and humors (*i umori*) on human affairs. While noting ambiguities in Machiavelli's formulations, Parel is clear about the consequences. *Fortuna*, whether directed by the heavens or infused within the humors, constrains human agency significantly (1992, 65). Machiavelli's acceptance of this reality means that efforts, like those of Leo Strauss, to interpret him as a foundational figure within modernity are wrong.[82]

However, for two of Strauss's students, Mansfield and Roger Masters, Machiavelli's engagement with fortune acknowledges a rhetorical context that it goes on to challenge,[83] confronting defeatism about the transformative possibilities open to free will or agency. For these commentators, Machiavelli redescribes fortune's alleged power as a series of natural forces, explicable and controllable through a science of power (Masters, 1996, 209) capable of forging a more "perfect republic" (Machiavelli, 1996, xl; Zuckert, 2017, 238).[84] I will not offer comprehensive assessments of the questions raised within this debate. Instead, I make two extended observations relevant to Machiavelli's political framing, one (this section) concerning fortune, the other (the next), nature.

In interpreting Machiavelli's cosmos, it is important to note how much that world invites rather than constrains agency, envisaging fortune confronted by a *virtu* waging certain kinds of war.[85] The thematic treatment in *Prince* 25 is central. The chapter's title raises the question of fortune's power; how much can *fortuna* do in human affairs and in what way (*quomodo*) may it be opposed, immediately implying skepticism about the force and permanence of its influence. Envisaging opposition, it is not merely "how much?," and certainly not "whether?," but "in what way?." The chapter examines two modes of understanding and confronting *fortuna*, intriguingly marked by philosophical terms, universal and particular.[86] Each inquiry employs a distinctive image of *fortuna* and identifies a cognate model of oppositional *virtu*. Interpreted universally, fortune is a river (a part of nature) whose inundations threaten destruction (Parel, 1992, 68; Masters, 1996, 56–67). River fortune wages war, when, becoming enraged (*adirano*), it floods plains, ruins trees and buildings, and causes all to flee before its power. Interpreted particularly, fortune is a woman, recalling both gendered cultural symbol and goddess (Pitkin, 1999, 120–130, 154–155; Parel, 1992, 65–66). To the degree that woman fortune threatens disruption, through either volatility or deception (Pitkin, 1999, 228), her power is less predictable and perhaps more dangerous than river fortune's.

Machiavelli's images of oppositional *virtu* imply that human beings may control both predictable and unpredictable fortune through different forms of controlled violence. The first confronts river fortune through prudent anticipation and physical exertion, constructing dikes and dams that violate natural contours of earth and water.[87] The second meets woman fortune with the emotional aggressions of impetuosity, recklessness, and youth. "I judge indeed [that] it would be better to be impetuous than respectful, because fortune is a woman and it is necessary if one wishes to have her submit, to beat her and strike her down. And one sees that she lets herself be conquered (*vincere*) more by these than by those who proceed coldly. And so always like a woman, she is a friend of the young, because they are less respectful, more ferocious, and with greater audacity, they command her." Notably, neither response is simply repressive. River fortune's forces can be turned to useful purposes (Masters, 1996, chapter 7). Woman fortune's favors are courted, not just conquered; though beaten, she must also become friend (*amica*).[88] Yet the two responding virtues are potentially incompatible, for the experience and maturity that channel the river fit uneasily with the impetuosity and youthfulness that win the woman.

Prince 25 examines these images in structurally analogous ways. In each inquiry, Machiavelli represents positions skeptical of agency, but follows with reasons energizing confidence. The counsels of despair have different origins. Those intimidated by river fortune are driven by a confused fearfulness of powers that seem overwhelming (the heavens?). Those undone by woman fortune are hamstrung by their own emotional profiles (the humors?). If Machiavelli resolves only objections from general ignorance, he may be more confident in scientific calculation than in impetuous daring. Yet the aggressiveness needed to overcome woman fortune reveals the inadequacy of a virtue relying exclusively on science.[89]

Machiavelli begins by referencing the opinion that "many have held and still hold . . . that worldly things (*le cose del mondo*) being so governed by fortune and by God that human beings are not able to correct them with their prudence, indeed that they have no remedy whatever; and, because of this, one might judge that he should not sweat much about things, but leave himself to be governed by chance." Disagreement has already been hinted in the chapter title. In rejecting these opinions, Machiavelli may recall the position taken at the beginning of *Prince* 15, where he departed from the "orders" of others to disclose the effectual truth (*verita effetuale*) of things. There, the "others" were political writers who have "imagined republics and principalities which have never been seen or known to exist in truth."[90] In 25, the disputed opinion arises from a variety of sources, ranging from Christian and pagan religious traditions to an atheistic materialism which sees the world governed (*governare*) entirely by chance (*sorte*). The casual shift from fortune's decrees and God's oversight—coupled, whether distinguished or equated[91]—to chance generally, may reveal Machiavelli's own position (comparing with Aquinas, *ST* I.103.1, 7). Or the progression may simply mirror popular confusion. Either way, the standard from which all of these influences are characterized is that of intensely challenged agency. While Aquinas opposes the ancient philosophers' claims that everything originates from chance (*omnia fortuito agi*) with a defense of God's providential care (*ST*, I. 103.1), Machiavelli speaks "so that our free will may not be exhausted (*el nostro libero arbitrio non sia spento*)." If the appropriate criterion for truth is the *verita effetuale* of *Prince* 15, there may be no *effectual* difference between fortune, God and chance. If 15 ironically points toward Machiavelli's own imagination of a republic/ principality that has never been seen or known (so far?) to exist, 25 may reposition the broadest concerns of philosophy, universals and particulars, in light of the agency's *verita effetuale*.

Yet no prospective redemption of agency can give free will complete autonomy; Machiavelli judges (*iudicare*) that "it might be true that fortune is the arbiter of half of our actions but she leaves governing the other half or close to it to us." Parel finds this vagueness unhelpful, as either motivation or measure (1992, 81). Yet uncertainty may also energize. If (only) half of our actions are ours to govern, we may (still) never be sure which half. The motivational payoff is communicated in the concluding exhortation of another thematic consideration of fortune, the reflections on Roman *virtu* in *Discourses*, 2.29. After confessing that "human beings can second fortune but not oppose it, they can weave its warp but not break it," Machiavelli adds: "They should indeed never abandon themselves, because not knowing her [fortune's] aim and [since] it travels through oblique and unknown ways, they must always hope and, hoping, not abandon themselves in whatever fortune or in whatever travail they find themselves."[92] Ambiguities about fortune's power should attract ambitious agents, for they may hope not only for pragmatic success but also for reputational renown. All of this implies a psychological, rather than a material model of agency, explored more fully in the second half of *Prince* 25.

Parel interprets Machiavelli's examination of fortune's particulars as moving from impacts on countries to influences on individuals (1992, 67–84). This is insightful, but preliminary. Countries either surrendering to or in control of river fortune are benefitted/ damaged by the foolishness/prudence of their leaders. And the individuals whose psychological characters are diagnosed are political figures. One implication of the move to particulars is that abstract speculations concerning free will are insufficient; agency is always situated. Yet though Machiavelli's contexts vary—Florence, Italy, worldly things generally—they are always interpreted politically. What *governs* worldly things?[93] The problem of governance recalls the concern for good order (looking toward *Pr* 26's image of an Italy freed from the barbarians) amidst continued threats of disorder (26's conditions of enslavement, servility and dispersal). *Prince* 25's moral psychology is cued by this political challenge. So far, this seems a restatement of the need to control river fortune through intelligence, but Machiavelli now insists that the prudence capable of foresight and control requires a personality defined in emotional terms, with impetuosity (*impetuoso*) and respect (*respetto*) as polar alternatives. This model of psychological individuation moves Machiavelli away from Aquinas's will as a rational appetite toward a willing whose success depends on affective responses to fluidity, how the impetuous or cautious character of agents comports with the times.[94] This redescription of agency revises understandings of such Thomistic moral concepts as virtue, sin and scandal to give pride of place to how impetuous agents deal with the promises and dangers of politics (*Pr*, 12, 15, 16; *Disc*, 1.7; 1.8; 1.29; 1.37; 2.23; 3.29).

However, the emotionally driven character of situated action may undercut agency for more intractable reasons than those traceable to intellectual errors about the cosmos. Because the emotions are so powerful, it seems that no "man [can] be found so prudent (*sí prudente*) as to know (*si sappi*) when to accommodate himself to this, whether because he cannot deviate from what nature inclines him to or also because, when having always prospered by following one path, he cannot be persuaded to depart from it." While Machiavelli seems to affirm impetuosity over caution, impetuous responses to woman fortune are successful only when the temper of the times allows.[95]

Yet Machiavelli presses on to rescue an agency capable of emotional reconstruction. Unpacking the barriers against pragmatic change, one possibility is that prudent agency is hopelessly constrained by natural inclinations, but another is that it is difficult to persuade anyone to abandon ways that have proven successful. What seems emotional necessity may be overreliance on experience with an inadequate attention to practical causality coupled with limited imagination (cf. *AW*, 2.313). Machiavelli thus follows his identification of impediments to change with a vision of what change would mean. "If he could change his nature with the times and with affairs [things] (*se si mutassi di natura con li tempi e con le* cose) his fortune would not change." Fortune's constraints look different to those envisaging agency's possibilities than to those lamenting its frustrations. Because this change in nature is accomplished not by science, but by will (staying forever young) it cannot be taught as much as encouraged and tested. Energized recognition of agency's potentials is the indeterminate outcome of the interaction between Machiavelli as author and his indefinite readership. The institutional parallel is represented in *Discourses* 3.9 when Machiavelli suggests that the diverse presence of excellent men in republics makes those regimes particularly suitable not merely for coping with but for initiating political change.[96]

Nature's Polemics

If *Prince* 25 collapses God and fortune into chance, *Discourses* 2.5 gives priority to nature, exploring both human and heavenly causes of civilizational change. Parel (2013, 290) sees no significant difference between fortune and heaven, but Viroli (2010, 31) finds heaven's patterns more regular and less arbitrary. In 2.5, Machiavelli contends that the purging of the world by periodic plagues, famines and inundations "from heaven" (*dal cielo*) is verifiable not only because "all of the histories are full of them" but also because "this effect of the oblivion of things is seen [and because] it seems reasonable (*e pare ragionevole*) that it be so." Such reasoning is anticipated in the preface to Book One, where dynamics influencing human beings are compared with "heaven, sun, elements," all accessible through their "motion, order and power," anticipating connections between political explanations and changes afflicting "mixed bodies" (*Disc*, 3.1). Since the examination of the human causes (*dagli uomini*) of such purges relies also on judging the reasonableness of things seen, both sets of causes might be construed as natural.

These explanations reject both the natural teleologies of Aristotle or Aquinas and the natural cycles of Polybius.[97] Initially, this seems a surrender to accidents. In *Discourses* 1.2 Machiavelli redescribes regime changes that (an uncredited) Polybius explains as occurring "by nature" (*kata phusin*) as arising from chance (*nacquono questo variazioni de' governi a caso*) and doubts that any projected circle (*cerchio*) of regimes can be completed.[98] Next (1.3), the disputes (*inimicizie*) between nobles and populace that enabled the Roman republic's liberty are called *accidenti*, attributable to chance (*fece il caso*). For Strauss, recourse to accidents excludes attention to substance, eliminating the central ontological category of Machiavelli's classical or scholastic rivals. While this judgment resonates, seeing "chance . . . as the cause of simply unforeseeable accidents" (Strauss, 1969, 223) says too little. Sequences of accidents have orders. In *Prince* 3, internal sequences within mixed principalities acquired by new princes follow "natural and ordinary necessity." Within the *Discourses*, Machiavelli eventually revises his verdict on the power of chance by explaining political motions in a way that relies on natural human tendencies. "Nature has created (*la natura ha creato*) human beings in such a way that they are capable of desiring every thing but unable to attain every thing." What results is "discontent (*mala contentezza*) with what one possesses and little satisfaction (*poca sodifazione*) with it; from this is born (*nasce*) the variation of fortune,[99] because some human beings desiring to have more, some fearing to lose what they have acquired, they come to enmities and to wars, from which is born (*nasce*) the ruin of one province and the exaltation of another" (1.37). Though desires to dominate and to resist seem to differentiate motivations of the great and the people, respectively (*Pr*, 9; *Disc*, 1. 5, 58), there is ultimately no difference between those seeking to acquire and those determined to retain (*Disc*, 1.5; *FH*, 3.1, 11). Human beings (*umani*) esteem material possessions over honor or reputation; the self-glorification of the great is pretense (1.37).[100] These underlying processes ground a more general science of accidents that examines how behavior patterns function within orders of causality. In *Discourses* 1.46, "the order of these accidents (*l'ordine di questi accidenti*) is that when men seek not to fear, they begin to make others fear." The appropriate units of analysis are not simply *Prince* 25's cautious or impetuous individuals but collective behaviors clustered by group. "It appears then that not only does one city have certain diverse modes and institutions and procreates human beings harder or more effeminate, but one sees such a difference to exist from one family to another" (*Disc*, 3.46). Such causal knowledge enables prediction. If accidents threaten disorder (*Disc*, 3.14), the prudent knowledge of other orders may remediate (*AW*, 3.174; 5. 107–108). Changes from princely to popular rule are often caused by "plots and conspiracies" (*Disc,* 1.2); the longest concentrated discussion in either the *Prince* or the *Discourses* is a systematic assessment of conspiracies, including how their failures or successes might be foreseen (*Disc*, 3.6; *Pr* 19; cf. *FH*, 8.1).

In proposing a human science explaining the motions of mixed bodies Machiavelli invites Paul Rahe's and Alison Brown's judgments that his political theory is significantly informed by Lucretius's natural philosophy.[101] There are striking parallels (both reject natural teleology and the soul's immorality)[102] and intriguing puzzles (Does Machiavelli believe in the eternity of the world? Does Lucretius?).[103] Yet while Lucretius's science of nature corrects anthropocentric obsessions (*DRN*, 1. 455–458),[104] Machiavelli's is aggressively anthropomorphized. Within 2.5's tracing of the causes of obliteration wrought by heaven—plagues, famines, and inundations—Machiavelli comments that when "human astuteness and malignity have gone as far as they can go, it happens by necessity (*conviene di necessità*) that the world is purged by one of the three [above] modes, so that men, having become few and beaten, may live more commodiously and become better." Of these disruptions, inundation is the "more important . . . because more universal" with its cataclysmic effects leaving humans "few" and "beaten". Such purges are not divinely imposed punishments but the consequences of natural forces.[105] Yet they are also not traced to a nature that is simply indifferent, for they are (somehow) triggered by human astuteness and malignity.[106] This connection implies that the chapter's initial separation of human from heavenly causes was provisional and that human and heavenly causes of civilizational change may interpenetrate. Plagues, famine, and inundation may originate from microbial or climatological causes but their catastrophic consequences are intensified within if not triggered by overpopulation, the social analogue to an accretion of superfluous matter in simple bodies. Such population crises may well arise from a nonsustainable fecundity driven by natural urges, only temporarily protected by a social stability that will eventually be overwhelmed. Yet the consequences of stable civilization, including greater population densities, may themselves destabilize. How are extremes of human astuteness and malignity to be understood?

Within a cosmic diagnosis that converges the heavenly and the human, does politics become epiphenomenal? First, yes, then no. Initially, 2.5's causal sequence replaces narrowly political or linguistic with broadly natural explanations of civilizational upheavals. In this way, 2.5 retrospectively revises and clarifies the trajectory of the *Discourses'* introductory analysis of political change. In 1.1, when examining the beginnings of cities universally and of Rome particularly, Machiavelli comments on the origins of those built by free foreigners, "when some peoples either under a prince or by themselves have been compelled by disease, famine or war to abandon their fatherland and search for a new seat." Here, war occupies the position that 2.5 will give to inundation by water and is simply one— the most political—of dislocation's three causes, not its more important and more universal. Yet 1.1 presumes cohesive peoples and stable political forms (those migrating may be "under some prince") while 2.5 envisages more radical upheavals, especially those caused by inundations that leave the survivors few and beaten. This more cosmic disruption may explain the transition from the organized migrations of 1.1 to the starker precarity of 1.2, which imagines the construction of societies by those who "were sparse in the beginning of the world [and] lived dispersed for a time like beasts." Yet though 2.5 seems to eclipse war and politics with heavenly or natural purges, war and politics reappear in 2.8 where inundation becomes a metaphor for a "war . . . most cruel and most feared," revising 1.1 in a different way. In 1.1, Moses is one of those leading a free but stable people able to re-establish itself in a new seat. In 2.8 this re-establishment becomes an example of the most destructive inundation as the Hebrew invasion of Syria led by Moses and Joshua displaced the Maurusians who in turn "went from there into Africa" and though they "had not been able to defend their own country, were able to occupy that of others." Are the most destructive inundations really the necessary movements of mixed political bodies? Is the inundation of 2.5 heaven's war against the human race?[107]

Machiavelli's response to violent civilizational upheavals also departs from Lucretius's serene philosophy[108] in favor of "the more honorable course" attractive to the distinctively political (*Disc*, 1.6). Among inundation's few and beaten survivors, "if among them someone is saved who has knowledge of [antiquity], to make a reputation and a name for himself he conceals it and perverts it in his way (*a suo modo*), so that what remains for his successors is only what he has wished to write, and nothing else." Though physical survival is accidental, the love of reputation, which replaces wonder as the origin of past knowledge, may be deeply rooted in human nature. Does the survival of humanity depend on the resilience of this love, driving those seeking a "name" whose memory will always be precarious and, however resilient, will eventually be obliterated by human astuteness and malignity?[109]

Yet the crucial role given to love of reputation also exposes the incompleteness of Machiavelli's human science. The gap is not created by a vain attempt at value neutrality, for good and evil are embedded in accounts of the most global societal changes. In "thinking about how [ascents or declines of communities] proceed, I judge the world always to have been in the same mode (*sempre essere stato ad uno medesimo modo*) and there to have been as much good as evil (*tanto do buono quanto di cattivo*) in it" (*Disc*, 2. Pr). If the world has eternally existed, this evaluative language is neither providential ordering nor cultural construction. Fluctuating distributions of worldly goods or evils instead reflect the successes or failures of societies competing for satisfactions that human beings naturally pursue (1.37). Changes can be mapped across both space (east and west) and time (ancient and modern)—"the evil and the good vary from province to province . . . where it had first placed its virtue in Assyria, it put it in Media, then in Persia, until it came to be in Italy and Rome" (*Disc*, 2. Pr). Since successes and declines are interdependent, communities that ascend must do so at others' expense. Yet the persistence of an unchanging balance of good and evil in the world means that no universal science of motion can instruct any particular political community at any determinate historical time. Its policies may alter particular fortunes but not general equilibrium.[110]

Yet though distributions of good and evil shift, their meanings do not. However inspiring, the examples of Francis and Dominic cannot make the endurance of abuse into a virtue. By creating (so to speak) human beings so that they desire everything, nature may, after all, provide a benchmark for evaluation, how well or badly human practices enable desire's satisfaction. All desires are not, however, created equal. What distinguishes humans from other animals is that in desiring *ogni cosa* they long for goods extending beyond physical gratification or replenishment. Achievements worthy of "names" endure longer than the consolidation of security or the accumulation of luxury, both disappearing with death.[111] Far from claiming, as Hobbes will, that the desire for fame is ruinous, Machiavelli ennobles extraordinary ambition by positioning it within its only intelligible context, urging achievements that will merit indefinite praise. Though successes and failures vary across clashes of civilizations and though languages of praise and blame violently supplant one another, Machiavelli's synoptic vision recognizes the accomplishments of founders across cultures and ages (cf. *Pr*, Ep Ded; *Disc*, 1.10).

But how can a science of the motions and orders common to mixed bodies conclude that love of fame is the most fully human desire?[112] The nature disclosed by that science may call for a revision that recognizes the most distinctively human desire. But what kind of revision is possible if this estimation requires seeing human motions not just dynamically but qualitatively? By acknowledging that a physico-political science cannot fully accommodate agency's motivations, Machiavelli returns to questions of practical philosophy that his natural science cannot fully engage.

Prince 15's commitment to effectual truth opens two directions for practical philosophy that potentially stand in tension. If truth is framed by effectuality, the possibility of agency becomes the condition for truth.[113] Machiavelli's practical objective is to convince readers to accept the valorization of the highest political ambition as something that must be true if those "think[ing] of the more honorable part" (*Disc*, 1.6) are to be regarded as praiseworthy and not crazy. While this move might seem rhetorical or pragmatic rather than logical or epistemic, the constitutive influence of effectuality on truth challenges strict separations of rhetoric or agency from science or wisdom. Notably, philosophy is mentioned three time in the *Discourses*: 1.56 imagines, "as some philosopher wishes," that the air is full of compassionate intelligences that warn human beings of future events through signs;[114] 2.5 defends "those philosophers" affirming the eternal existence of the world; 3.12 approvingly recognizes "certain moral philosophers" who have written that the hands and tongues of human beings would not have operated perfectly and conducted human beings to noble heights unless spurred by necessity. Read sequentially, Book One's philosophy defers to natural or cosmic signs; Book Two's establishes foundations for a more rigorous science of mixed bodies; and Book Three's recognizes the power of necessity while celebrating aggressive and ennobling human responses. The moves from compassion to necessity and from the deferential interpretation of signs to the noble control of events restructure the understanding of philosophy generally and moral philosophy particularly. Philosophy's last appearance in 3.12 thus offers a philosophical basis for privileging effectual truth in *Prince* 15, even as it frames philosophy by its level of effectuality.

Yet while effectuality structures truth, it does not displace it. Machiavelli denies he is imagining things. Seen from this vantage point, truth must be understood as well as effected. The truth to be understood cannot simply be a science of mixed bodies blind to the pursuit of the noblest goals. Yet this admission undercuts Machiavelli's rejection of teleology. By presenting one way of life as distinctively best for human beings he effectively offers a functional equivalent, restoring a pragmatic concern for questions earlier dismissed, especially the question of how we ought to live.[115] Taken together, complications besetting *Prince* 15's truth standard encourage a reconsideration of Machiavelli's political philosophy that takes its concerns seriously but does not accept its resolutions as decisive.

Politics' Ambiguities and Philosophy's Possibilities

Machiavelli challenges stable conceptual boundaries: principalities and republics, nobles and peoples, individual and common goods, politics and religion.[116] These crossings converge within politics itself, in byplays between the functions of making (*poiesis*), the institutional control of river fortune aiming at stabilization, and practice (*praxis*), the agonistic confrontation with woman fortune courting both nobility and failure. Each function informs alternative Machiavellian legacies within modern and postmodern political thought. While Masters's Machiavelli is committed to "harnessing science and technology to the goals of human action" (1996, 209), he is no thoughtless technocrat. In denying that institutions can create permanent conditions of order, he recognizes the need to direct science by the judgment of prudent elites (Masters, 1996, 226; cf. Zuckert,

2017, 262–263). For Hannah Pitkin, Machiavelli's politics at its best opens "the possibility of an active intentional membership enabling us jointly to take responsibility for our objective interconnections, the large scale consequences for each other of what we are actually doing" (1999, 299). The intellectual resource for coping with the problems of membership is not a science discovering causes or a statesmanlike prudence directing from above but a judgment negotiating connections and differences. Not the sole prerogative of elites, this judgment requires discursive, mutual citizenship.[117]

Interpreting Machiavelli's politics with a primary attention to either *poiesis* or *praxis* is frustrated by his continual recourse to both templates. While healthy politics requires institutions able to accomplish intelligently and effectively what the Romans did accidentally and inadequately, those institutions must be continuously reinvigorated by daring, risky civic activity (*Disc*, 3.1). Neither the science of power nor the mutual engagement of citizens captures Machiavelli politics exactly. What may be particularly interesting in this context is how Machiavelli's political inquiries call for a form of political thought that he discourages. We can begin to appreciate this disconnection by revisiting his understandings, first, of politics and then, of philosophy.

As noted earlier, Machiavelli's political theory is often interpreted as privileging the common good.[118] Pitkin sees "Machiavelli's best understanding of politics [as] reminiscent of Aristotle's teaching that man is a political animal."[119] However, Machiavelli's theorizations of the common good and citizenship are less straightforward, for he turns the common good and civic virtue into problems. These are not simply questions of whether common and individual goods are compatible or which has priority; they extend to deeper problems concerning how human beings are individuated and how collective goods are constructed and judged. In *Discourses* 2.2 Machiavelli praises republics as regimes most capable of securing the common good, but this good is the collective achievement of riches and dominion, the ascension of one community at the expense of others, a civic liberty constructing political empire.[120] Internally, this political common good is the agreement of a majority of individual egoists to unite in the aggressive pursuit of material and status goods. Those disadvantaged by or disagreeing with that vision are suppressed or excluded. Here, Machiavelli does not so much ennoble as analyze the common good, seeing through its civic rhetoric to discover individuals collaborating for self-advancement. If the common good is nothing more than this, it is dubious whether there is any human good beyond that which classical political philosophy rejects as *pleonexia* (*Republic*, 344a; *Gorgias*, 508a).

Before condemning Machiavelli's cynicism we should recognize that sincere and intense attachments to communal goods can extend in multiple directions, including Schmitt's willingness to fight political enemies to the death in the name of constructed meaningfulness. But beyond this, Machiavelli's analytic of the common good is decisive only if we discount the relevance of other political functions recognized in his texts. When he compares civilizational to linguistic change in *Discourses* 2.5 he also acknowledges that cultures construct meanings. Yet while such changes are overtly described as persecutions and power moves, the introduction of language as a condition for meaning exposes that perspective as one sided. Since human beings are constituted by an education that draws upon linguistic memberships (*Disc*, 3. 47), they can be individuated in ways that may correct or limit obsessions with material or status goods. Linguistic communities may foster criticism, not simply reproduction, of the *pleonexia* that competing political memberships intensify. This may be one implication of Aristotle's claim that human beings are political animals because their *logos* allows perception of the just and the unjust (*Politics*, 1.2). If so, the common good becomes a problem to be examined, not just a symbol to be deconstructed. By rejecting the rhetoric of the common good in favor of an analytic that decodes it as cooperative selfishness, Machiavelli ignores the deeper complexities of the social functions revealed in his images of cultural change.

In spite of its apparent dissolution, ambiguities about the status of the common good persist both in Machiavelli's interpretations of civic practices and in the rhetoric of his texts. To compete successfully with other societies, communities must strengthen civic commitments, offsetting or limiting the universal love of wealth (1.37) with the civic love of honor, imaged in the Roman narrative of Cincinnatus's heroism (*Disc*, 3.25).[121] Yet by seeing through the ennoblement of the common good in 2.2, Machiavelli calls the intelligibility of any valorized public symbol into question. In the *Florentine Histories* Machiavelli often writes— either explicitly or in the speeches of his characters—in the persona of the good Florentine, yet analyses of political motivations made in his own name often call that persona's judgments into serious question (*FH*, 3.5, 11; 7.1). Are citizens inspired by "Cincinnatus" just dupes? Are public honors anything other than a satisfied crowd's approbations? These difficulties are only exacerbated when Machiavelli delves more deeply into civic motivations. One candidate for model citizenship in *Discourses*

Book Three is Titus Manlius, called Torquatus. Known for his intense severity, he practiced a civic virtue "harmful in a prince [but] useful in a citizen" (3.22). His disciplined harshness eventually demanded the execution of his own son, whose victory in combat originated in disobedience to his consul father. Livy presents this execution as a committed citizen's faithfulness to the republic's laws and discipline (8. 7. 15–19). However, as the *Discourses* proceeds, Machiavelli reimagines Manlius's behaviors as ambitious not devotional.[122] Assessing his spectacular history—terrorizing a tribune who tried to prosecute his own imperious father (cf. *Disc*, 1.11),[123] defeating a formidable Gaul in single combat, and executing his disobedient son—Machiavelli comments, "these three actions, then, gave [Manlius] more name and made him more celebrated (*piu celebre*) for all centuries than did any triumph or any other victory for which he was decorated (3.34)."[124] By redescribing these actions as vehicles for ambition, Machiavelli undermines the legitimacy of the common good as public symbol.

Yet even though exposing the selfishness behind civic virtue, Machiavelli embraces the public symbols that such exposures should discredit. Prior to commending the strategies of citizens seeking fame, Machiavelli warns that "the reputation of citizens is the cause of the tyranny of republics" (3. 28; cf. 1.46).[125] Later, in 3.41, defending the *patria* by whatever means is a pragmatic imperative in circumstances of emergency. "Where one deliberates entirely on the safety of the *patria*, there should be no other consideration, neither of justice nor injustice, nor mercy nor cruelty, nor nobility nor ignominy" (*Disc*, 3, 41; *FH*, 5.8).[126] Are individual motivations, whether rooted in passion or calculation, endorsed only when they elicit patriotic devotion? In confronting the analytic dissection of the common good with the rhetoric of the *patria*, Machiavelli restores the civic community that his analysis dissolves.[127] Yet the byplay of analytics and rhetoric also discloses each side's potential abuses. The analysis of the common good implies that images of fatherland can be manipulated to suppress dissent or to justify crimes committed in the nation's name.[128] Valorizing a rhetoric of the fatherland introduces threats of disintegration when politics becomes only the contingent clustering of selfish interests.

Machiavelli's exploration of political motives also raises questions about how healthy politics relates to morality. Wolin argues that violence infuses only Machiavelli's public ethics and does so to good purpose; effective politics, sometimes necessarily harsh, enables a more decent private ethics to function safely. Consequently, order's reliance on war is narrowly political; its penetration into moral character is prevented by the separation of the spheres.[129] Even if successful, this claim could be criticized by thinkers ranging from Aquinas to Rawls and Habermas for grounding moral constitutional orders on underworlds of violence.[130] Yet Machiavelli's presentation raises doubts about whether political harshness can be so easily sequestered. To reorient citizens away from eternal beatitude and toward the well being of the *patria*, Machiavelli's redefined Christianity must reach into the souls (spirits?) of Christian citizens. For them, charity cannot be the highest virtue,[131] but must be replaced by a (Manlian?) harshness which subordinates even family affections to the demands of politics.

The same ambiguities within Machiavelli's texts also remind readers of what is lost or threatened by his vision. The Christian examples of Francis and Dominic, even as read by Machiavelli, affirm a selflessness that cannot be redescribed simply as ambition's instrument. Manlius's relentless severity is most striking in the context of a familial nurturing whose destruction remains deeply disturbing.[132] The exhortation to defend the fatherland without any consideration of what is just or unjust, merciful or cruel, praiseworthy or ignominious acknowledges powerful counters to that imperative. The needs of the *patria* do not simply erase distinctions between and among these alternatives.[133]

Machiavelli's treatment of politics therefore introduces a series of problems that need to be taken seriously within the turbulent practices of common life, raising the question of how a political community prepares its members to do so. By conceiving of politics as an arrangement forging order amidst disorder through the violent control imposed by war, Machiavelli eliminates the critically educative functions supportive of citizens able to take these problems seriously. While aware of the need to understand political orders as formative influences, Machiavelli's projects, sketched *in* his texts and represented *by* his texts, ignore questions that his textual treatments of politics raise. This outcome eventually afflicts the stability of his own program. Can institutions displace the love of gain with the love of honor if regime success is indexed by riches and dominion? [134]

Pitkin's observation that such questions demand the exercise of political judgment is surely right.[135] She argues that Machiavelli's best insights support such judgments through an implicit respect for autonomy and mutuality that is tragically misdirected by a misogynistic fear of and aggression against the feminine.[136] She then reconstructs the peaceful struggles of Machiavellian political thought at its best.[137] Yet in explaining the more disturbing elements of Machiavelli's theorizations as psychological immaturities, Pitkin risks simply explaining them away. Machiavelli's most important contributions, as well as his most serious shortcomings, may be discovered in his focus on questions that readers would prefer to avoid.[138] His own version of political judgment is driven by the paramount need to study war in a world where states and parties are always ascending and declining due to the incessant motion of desire. Consequently, the judgment he praises as a resource for public life is expressed through decisive verdicts in circumstances of contention, pointedly avoiding middle ways, punishing or liberating, not considering and reflecting (*Disc*, 2.23).[139] In this respect, Machiavelli both anticipates and challenges the judgments of Derrida and Schmitt. Like Derrida, he traces the establishment of a manly common good to coercion, yet he offers no prospect for its transformation into a politics of friendship. Here, he seems more like one of Schmitt's real (in multiple senses) political theorists, tracing an inevitable connection between politics and hostility. Yet by recognizing that politics has functions beyond organizing political communities into oppositional cohorts of deadly enemies, he unsettles both Schmitt's binary characterization of political theory and Derrida's binary alternatives of domination or deconstruction.

Consequently, if we give the residual political possibilities that Machiavelli both acknowledges and marginalizes a fuller hearing, we discover questions emerging from his representations of politics that call for judgments going beyond the judicial or the punitive to include practical, and therefore moral, clarifications and criticisms. The need for such judgments is elicited by dilemmas about the coherence and the character of the common good, uncertainties regarding the value of different ways of life, and the limitations of attempts to explain human action through the motions and powers of mixed bodies. This extended treatment of politics indicts Machiavelli's political critique of a lazy and vulnerable peacefulness as cramped and partial. If war is an inadequate template for characterizing politics, peace can be something other than inactive *ozio*. Taking this possibility seriously would not mean denying violent political realities or ignoring the limits of perspectives that fail to recognize them. It would, however, mean acknowledging that peace is more important than war and proposing that war be seen principally in terms of its contributions to a worthwhile peace supportive, in turn, of activities not indexed by power alone.

Machiavelli's effort to provide a philosophical framework for political thought from within political life itself reflects our need to start such thinking from where we are. Absent a Thomistic recourse to revealed light, all political writing is what Hornqvist (2004, 241) calls sublunar. Yet we can challenge Machiavelli's sublunar narrative from a philosophical perspective which, while no less situated, is more critically distant. Machiavelli's framework is constructed around a theory of agency that telescopes influence or power, neither heir to Aristotelian *energeia* nor forerunner to Kantian autonomy.[140] His theorization of action as power underwrites the rejection of providence (memories of religions are constantly disappearing because of aggressive political changes) and informs his treatments of both fortune (in what way can *fortuna* be opposed?) and nature (which has created human beings so that they are always testing limited powers against desires for everything). Thought or intelligence is understood strategically (like the hands and tongues of human beings), as a resource that enables groups (seeking riches and dominion) or individuals (pursuing deathless glory) to prevail. From one point of view, this network of concepts is highly integrated and we can understand why war would condense this form of action. Yet from another perspective, this framework is structured around conceptions of action and politics whose compelling character is presumed or affirmed rather than examined or defended.

The kind of judgment invited by a more extended account of where we are presumes an intelligence beyond the strategic. We should appreciate but expand Pitkin's expectations (1999, 287–288) of the best politics that might emerge from the Machiavellian paradigm to recognize the needed contributions of philosophy. Once the character and outcomes of that philosophy are clarified, however, it becomes more difficult to see it embraced in any simple sense by Machiavelli at his best. The importance of political judgment informed by critical philosophy may be a potential within Machiavelli's political thought that is not merely unpursued but actively blocked. His express treatment of political order ignores a richer politics that is only discernible in light of readings that begin with but go beyond his texts. To the extent that writers such as Arendt and Honig (hardly aggressive warriors)[141] endorse a performative or agonistic politics suspicious of theory as an impediment to action,[142] they, too, may exclude a resource that their own understandings of politics demand.

Up to a point, then, one may accept Strauss's conclusion that Machiavelli's most significant shortcoming is failing to recognize that his own philosophy is pragmatic evidence against "his own narrow view of the nature of man" (1969, 294). Yet there is no need to concur with Strauss's further claim that a full appreciation of philosophy reinforces a radical separation of philosophers from nonphilosophers (296), distancing philosophy from political judgment. The philosophy that Machiavelli's assessments of politics requires is not edification appreciated by a gifted few, but serious conversation among citizens, suggesting continuities between politics and political thought.[143] To the degree that politics is a space where significant meanings intersect, the participation of different voices is called for within the conversational determination of collective action. This prospect may be appreciated more fully if we recognize both the politics that Machiavelli marginalizes and the philosophical reasons for seeing that marginalization as unsatisfactory.

The Continuing Dilemmas of War and Order

In spite of their many divergences, these texts of Aquinas and Machiavelli can be intriguingly juxtaposed at both political and philosophical levels. Politically, Aquinas's perspective might be challenged as being too forgetful of the role of violence within the construction of what I have called initiating and sustaining political origins. This is not to assail him for being insufficiently tough-minded but rather to note the limited scope of his inquiry into war. By contrast, Machiavelli makes the disturbing origins of political order all too clear. Yet by infusing war into his politics so thoroughly, he distorts political functions and practices that his broader inquiry acknowledges. By reading them in tandem, we may find that both Aquinas and Machiavelli leave important questions about the relation between political order and war not simply unresolved (an inappropriate expectation), but unconsidered.

These political questions are not disconnected from concerns about their broader theoretical frameworks. In one sense, these framing perspectives can be interpreted as two rival foundational commitments—to a moral philosophy discoverable by reason versus a pragmatic politics driven by agency. This is not a confrontation between faith and secularism. For all of their skepticism about metaphysics, Rawls and Habermas aspire to regulate political institutions and practices under the scrutiny of ideal theory (Rawls, 1999, 89–90). And Machiavelli's opposition to philosophy's attempted hegemony over politics in *Prince* 15 targets not simply philosophical statements informed by theology, but rather the imaginaries of *all* of those who have previously written on politics.

The critical readings that I have offered in this chapter suggest that both of these commitments are one-sided and self-undermining. Aquinas's political theorizing acknowledges both possibilities (the critical scrutiny of public policy exercised by active citizens) and hazards (irresolvable tensions between different human commitments) that challenge not only the completeness of his engagement with politics but also the adequacy of his philosophical analysis. Yet any expansion of that analysis is discouraged by the limited way in which he characterizes philosophy. While these particular limitations may be traceable to Aquinas's ultimate recourse to revealed theology, there are modern secular parallels. A similar restriction of philosophy by fiat afflicts Rawls's and Habermas's theorizations of deliberative democratic autonomy. They do not so much overcome Aquinas's difficulties as reenact them. Likewise, Machiavelli's dismissal of imaginings paradoxically precedes his own political imaginary, a new world of modes and orders discovered through aggressive rereadings of the old. In this respect, Machiavelli's politics is grounded in a commitment (declared, not revealed) to effectual truth that nonetheless invites challenges. By demanding a respect for an effectuality that is also truthful, Machiavelli implies that the criteria for identifying and evaluating effectuality should be subjected to judgments about their truthfulness that effectuality alone cannot dictate.

More broadly stated, these critical engagements suggest that attempts to prioritize either side of the philosophy/politics binary threaten to distort our understandings of both practices and thus to constrict the ways in which we might practice political philosophy. As readers, we should attempt to articulate what a fuller and more fruitful political philosophy might look like, interpreting Aquinas's and Machiavelli's competing commitments not as binary affirmations but as disagreements stimulating critical inquiry. One direction of this inquiry draws our attention away from war to examine the fuller character and possibility of a political peace identified and enabled by secular philosophy.

3 | Perpetual Peace

THOMAS HOBBES, *Leviathan*
IMMANUEL KANT, *Toward Perpetual Peace*

Imperatives of Peace

Instead of advising political leaders to study war, Hobbes and Kant set
the establishment of peace as the fundamental problem of politics. Their
perspectives differ significantly. Hobbes's principal concern is domestic
politics; Kant's is international. And while Hobbes argues that peace is the
prudentially rational foundation for commodious living, Kant insists that
creating political peace is commanded by moral rationality. Differences
aside, both see peace as achievable under institutional conditions that are
explained and justified philosophically and both envisage a peace that can
be enduring, even, in Kant's word, perpetual (*ewigen*). These perspectives
have influenced different contemporary treatments of political institutions.
Hobbes is a key source for rational choice theory's structural approach to
political cooperation,[1] Kant for deliberative democracy's moral commitment to human rights and moral equality.[2] Any difficulties within their
positions highlight problems that modern successors must take seriously.

Questions arise not just when we compare the two perspectives with
one another,[3] in part because they share more priorities than is sometimes recognized.[4] Concerns also emerge out of critical readings of their
individual texts, interpreted both as structured arguments and as rhetorical presentations. In spite of his ambitions for institutions "designed to
live as long as mankind, or as the laws of nature, or as justice itself"
(*Leviathan*, 29.1), Hobbes acknowledges elements of politics that make
those ambitions impossible and perhaps even dangerous to fulfill. Though
Kant wishes to guide moral politicians, his distinctions between the
demands of morality and the practical dynamics and dilemmas of politics

significantly diminishes the support he can provide. Consequently, it becomes uncertain whether the passions and competitions of political life can be either controlled by a foundational political science or disciplined by a compelling moral imperative. Their intellectual descendants may encounter similar roadblocks as their institutional designs are often unsettled by politics itself.

Hobbes: Peace's Seminal Presence in Leviathan

For some, Hobbes's political theory presumes that human beings are evil or aggressive. Schmitt places him among those who see humans as essentially dangerous (*CP*, 7 [58]). Rousseau contrasts his own peaceful natural man with Hobbes's who "is naturally intrepid and seeks only to attack and fight" (*Discourse on Inequality*, 107). Following these readings, we would expect Hobbes's dominant frame of reference to be war.[5] His state of nature is a disordered condition with no "common power to keep . . . all in awe" (*Lev*, 13.8). Natural freedom (natural right unvarnished) descriptively measures power and natural equality is the chilling reality that anyone can be killed (13.1).[6] Peace may only be an interval within the ongoing threat of a war of all against all (13.8). Even the first of the so-called laws of nature, "to seek peace and follow it," includes as its "second branch," that "when [one] cannot obtain [peace], that he may seek and use all helps and advantages of war" (14. 4).

Such impressions mislead. Hobbes's conception of war is only coherent and persuasive in light of a theoretically prior understanding of the helps and advantages of peace. Hobbesian war is neither Schmitt's stress test compelling humans to discover their most meaningful commitments nor Machiavelli's forging of a vigorous, if continually threatened, order. In arguing that violent death rather than damnation is the greatest human evil, Hobbes goes beyond Aquinas's attempt to set conditions for war's limited justifiability. War is peace's violent and disruptive other.

In *Leviathan* peace offers more than a respite from the devastating state of nature.[7] It exerts a formative influence throughout the work, constructing the terms of Hobbes's anthropology, moral psychology, institutional political theory, and scriptural interpretation. Each of these elements of his practical philosophy both derives its stability from and generates a recognition of stable peacefulness as the dominant human priority. The safety that the sovereign is charged to ensure is no "bare preservation, but also all other contentments of life, which every man by lawful industry . . . shall acquire to himself" (30.1), arts, sciences, letters, society (13.30). Without the achievements of peace, the human condition in all of its expressions and aspirations is practically and intellectually incoherent. This reading agrees with those of Michael Williams (2006, 254–259) and Gabriella Slomp (2000, 141–142), who interpret Hobbes's political project as an epistemic construction. Yet the epistemological influence of peace may also distort, for it eliminates or misrepresents aspects of human practice that Hobbes cannot avoid recognizing.

As a text, *Leviathan* itself relies on a complex partnership between demonstrative science and sobering narrative. Writing within the turbulence of the English Civil War, Hobbes is only too aware of how "the disorders of the present time" (*Review and Conclusion*, 17) have been intensified by incendiary political and religious rhetorics.[8] At one level, he responds by attempting to replace disordered, destructive speech with a clearly articulated, conclusive science, Thomas Spragens's theorized politics of motion.[9] As a branch of philosophy (*De Corpore*, 1.9), political science both requires and bolsters systematic inquiry's stable leisure (46. 6). Yet since humans are also appetitive, Hobbes cannot simply prove the truth of his political maxims deductively; he must speak persuasively through rhetorical narratives. Such a rhetoric goes beyond immediate satire and ridicule (Skinner, 1996, 395–425) to attempt a more comprehensive reconstruction of the emotions.[10]

The scientific and rhetorical components of *Leviathan* are neither straightforwardly sequential (Parts One and Two, followed by Three and Four)[11] nor seamlessly parallel (appeals to audiences with different capabilities). Instead, science and rhetoric (or narrative) are employed throughout as both mutual reinforcements and simultaneous corrections. Their interactions are signaled in the *Preface* where Hobbes urges the reader to confirm the truths of science through introspection, asking oneself where one's priorities truly lie and answering in coldly honest ways (*Author's Introduction*, 3). Yet introspection is reliable only when cued by a prior sense that survival (rather than honor or eternal salvation) is the most important human good. This outcome is not logically demanded by the scientific materialism that Hobbes represents as the most fundamental ontological truth (46. 15), for Machiavelli projects an altogether different response to the discovery that humans are mixed bodies in motion. To this extent, awareness of the priority of survival is pre- or extra-scientific. Yet this awareness can be reinforced by the scientific proof that physical existence is all there is.[12] In subordinating prudence to sapience, "both useful, but the latter infallible," (5. 21; 46. 2), Hobbes employs science not simply as method but as trope. *Leviathan* paradoxically exerts authority by appealing to a scientific framework that allegedly dismisses rhetoric within a narrative that rhetorically conditions receptivity to science.[13] Scientific and narrative appeals converge in Hobbes's image of the state of nature.[14]

Pacifying Pride

Though Hobbes's biological materialism rejects any fundamental privileging of humans over other animals ("beasts also deliberate"—6. 51), his examination of the benefits of and dangers to peace suggest that humans experience distinctive problems and possibilities within nature's chaos.[15] Human problems originate in pridefulness and human possibilities are enabled by confidence. The psychological resource that supplants pridefulness with confidence is also particularly human, a fearfulness that does not engender paralysis or superstition but eventually stimulates the creation of a peaceable kingdom anchoring progress.[16]

Hobbes's treatment of pride is counter-Machiavellian.[17] Machiavelli's explanation of conflict also begins with acquisitive designs spawning quarrels over scarce resources (*Prince*, 3; *Discourses*, 1.37); just like Hobbes, he shows how managing such conflicts through bargained cooperation is frustrated by pursuits of honor. However, Machiavelli does not simply accept the love of honor as a permanent, though regrettable, human drive. Instead, the achievement of a "name" most fully satisfies the desire for everything that makes humans distinctive. Consequently, discovering how quests for honor can be politically satisfied is not only necessary and useful but also constructive and ennobling.

Hobbes stridently disagrees, seeking not to replace the love of gain with the love of honor but to replace the love of honor with the desire for commodious living. For Hobbes, as for Machiavelli, human conflicts have multiple origins. "In the nature of man we find three principal sources of quarrel: first competition, secondly, diffidence; thirdly, glory" (13.6). Yet while Hobbes sees the first two as rational within contexts of uncertainty, he argues that fighting over glory is madness. Indeed, the reckless pursuit of honor polemicizes those who might be otherwise content. "Also because there be some that taking pleasure in contemplating their own power in the acts of conquest, which they pursue further than their own security requires, if others (that otherwise would be glad to be at ease within modest bounds) should not by invasion increase their power, they would not be able long time, by standing only on their defense, to subsist" (13.4).[18]

Yet how can Hobbes condemn such ambitions in light of his foundational claim that objects are good or evil only "with relation to the person that useth [the terms], there being nothing simply and absolutely so" (6.7)? Designations of good and evil seem simply to reflect preferences, varying with different individuals' physiological configurations that themselves change over time (6.6). Why privilege Hobbes's preference for security over those of Pericles's Athenians' for reputation or the English Commonwealth's Puritans' for salvation? The salutary social consequences of accommodation over aggression are not decisive absent a prior standard for measuring consequences. And Hobbes cannot test conceptions of the good against a Kantian/Rawlsian priority of right grounded in a deontological social contract, for all covenants are instrumental, made to secure good consequences (14.8).[19]

Peace offers an epistemic normative resource by theorizing a psychic health that can serve as a standard for comparing individual perceptions about the good. Good and evil may exist only in relation to persons, but persons vary according to the healthy or diseased configurations of their bodies and health and disease are not just preferences. The treatment of madness is emblematic. Initially, madness is behavior departing from what is normally or ordinarily seen (8.16).[20] Yet this cannot be the last word since the burning curiosity that drives science is an outlier when compared with ordinary passivity or gullibility (11.17–23). Consequently, diagnoses of psychic well being and distress must ultimately appeal to an evaluative norm beyond observable frequencies.[21] Pathological intensity is all too common. "Whereof there be almost as many kinds [of madness] as of the passions themselves. Sometimes the extraordinary and extravagant passion proceedeth from the evil constitution of the organs of the body as harm done them; and sometimes the hurt and indisposition of the organs is caused by the vehemence or long continuance of the passion" (8.17). Hobbes underscores how such vehemence can distort self-images. "The passion whose violence or continuance maketh madness is either great *vain-glory*, which is commonly called *pride* and *self-conceit*, or great *dejection* of mind" (8.18). While the pridefulness that causes quarrels is distinctively human (bees and ants do not fight over perceived insults—17.11), it should be suppressed, not ennobled. "Pride subjecteth a man to anger, the excess whereof is the madness of rage and fury" (8.19). In contrast, both "fear of death; [and] desire of such things as are necessary for commodious living and a hope by their industry to obtain them" (13.14) allow discovery of an architecture of healthy passions. "By manners I mean not here decency of behavior . . . but those qualities of mankind that concern their living together in peace and unity" (11.1). While such psychic health is not satiation, "the repose of a mind satisfied," it is the condition for reliable progress. When Hobbes defines felicity as "a continual progress of the desire, from one object to another, the attaining of the former being still the way to the latter" (11.1), grounding "a perpetual and relentless desire of power after power" (11.2), he might seem to offer a neutral account of how we pursue whatever we want, seeing power as a primary good (Kavka, 1986, 93). Going deeper, however, this statement presumes a particular vision of both emotional health (where progressive satisfactions are not threatened by irrational outbursts) and practical stability (where secure possession of one object enables planning for the next). Indeed, desire itself "is not to enjoy once only, and for one instant of time, but to assure forever the way of . . . future desire (11.1)." By limiting himself to the felicity of this life, Hobbes dispenses with Aquinas's perfect happiness. "There is no such *Finis ultimus* (utmost aim) nor *Summum Bonum* (greatest good) as is spoken of in the books of the old moral philosophers" (11. 1). Yet though prospects for human happiness are bounded by the recognition of mortality (Ahrensdorf, 2000, 585–586), they are extended indefinitely by the prospect of a secure infrastructure for commodious living. We want to assure our felicity, including the felicity of our descendants, "forever." From one point of view, then, Hobbesian action is not simply a relentless drive for primary power but a flourishing activity wherein the intellect is exercised and the emotions fulfilled as they create and enjoy the goods of society.[22] The state of nature makes all of this impossible.

The pre-eminence of peace also structures Hobbes's incipient escape strategy, the natural laws articulated in chapters 14 and 15, whose first and fundamental imperative is to seek peace (14.4). These are not Aquinas's natural laws, for Hobbesian nature exerts no normative authority.[23] Instead, the state of nature constitutes the circumstances in which humans may discover those "conclusions and theorems" necessary for their own preservation (15.41). Initially, the intellectual sequence of Hobbes's argument (14.4–15.41) seems straightforward. The impossibility of achieving secure control over others within nature is premised on a natural equality (13. 1) that reinforces fear of violent death, one of the passions compelling men to peace. Yet what does this equality mean? It is difficult to identify any particular characteristics of natural individuals supporting the radical equality that Hobbes posits. The distinctive capacity for science shows that human intelligence is unequally distributed (13.2). Though variations in intellect may be explained by differences in the passions (8.3), this simply reinforces the reality of natural inequality rather than offering any basis for disputing it.[24] Neither can Hobbes point to an underlying human worth allowing us to challenge unequal outcomes of the natural lottery, since once we abstract from the varying passions and diverse motions of individuals, what individuality would remain beyond generic vital and specific voluntary motions (6.1)?[25] The conception of equality at work here is therefore a kind of relational equality of power that eventually secretes the simple but compelling conclusion that humans cannot be confident in individual self-help.

This outcome depends less on rigorous demonstration than on concurring responses from those persuaded to a risk aversion that suspects all individual attempts to establish personal security as dangerously unstable. "For as to strength of body, the weakest has strength enough to kill the strongest, either by secret machinations or by confederacy with others. . . . And as to the faculties of the mind. . . . I find yet a greater equality amongst men than that of strength" (13.1–2). Read from the perspective of such vulnerability, pretensions to intelligence that dismiss competitors as stupid are fatal self-deceptions. "Men that distrust their own subtlety are, in tumult and sedition, better disposed for victory than those that suppose themselves wise or crafty" (11.10).

Eventually, the imperative of peace is so overwhelming that it rearranges not only the description of the state of nature but also the structure of Hobbes's argument. As the laws of nature extend beyond their first and fundamental imperative, recognition of equality is not a premise entailing the "need to seek peace and follow it" but a consequence of the compelling need to keep the peace. In condemning pride as a breach of nature's ninth law, against arrogance, Hobbes notes "if nature therefore have made men equal, that equality is to be acknowledged; or if nature have made men unequal, yet because men that think themselves equal will not enter into conditions of peace but upon equal terms, such equality must be admitted" (15.21). Joshua Mitchell (1993, 52) even suggests that Hobbesian equality is a kind of noble lie. At the very least, acknowledging equality follows the priority of peace, not the other way around.

This priority influences Hobbes's political theory in both obvious and subtle ways. Critics always note problems within Hobbes's argument for the rationality of obeying an absolute (20.18) sovereign, preferably, though not necessarily, monarchical (19.4–9).[26] As long as the sovereign physically protects, it is irrational to threaten its authority (cf. 21.21; 29.6–13). Hobbes explicitly extends this conclusion beyond his thought experiment to ordinary political experience when he insists on the necessity of obeying all established governments (20.3, 14;26.8–10, 16, 41).[27] This outcome is driven by both the logic and the rhetoric of the state of nature narrative. If the natural condition is worse than anything, continued obedience to existing powers, whatever their deficiencies or pathologies, is the only rational choice. Yet this outcome compels only the audience that this narrative both presumes and constructs. That sovereign authority must be absolute is entailed by a reasoning that acknowledges protection as the dominant priority and fears any resistance to authority as posing intolerable risks. In his well-known criticism, Locke objects (*Second Treatise*, 2.13) that subjection to absolute power is irrational and that vulnerable individuals are better off taking their chances in a condition where there is no common power.[28] However, the internal structure of Hobbes's argument is unsteady in itself, discounting complications of which the text is all too aware.

First, the meaning of security is less straightforward than the terrifying state of nature image implies. The need for peace is prompted not just by fear of violent death, but by the attractive goods of commodious living "and a hope by . . . industry to attain them" (13.14).[29] Emphasizing fear as the principal psychological force in mere nature is one sided and distorting, as is the survivalist politics that such a fear supports (cf. 18.20). This inadequacy is reinforced by the terms of exit from the state of nature both immediately and over time. In narrating the rational construction of a commonwealth that guarantees the covenants (demanded by the second law of nature; 14.5–23) that can terminate vulnerability, Hobbes claims that the need for sovereign as enforcer follows the realization that "covenants without the sword are but words and of no strength to secure a man at all" (17.2). Yet the initial agreement "to confer all . . . strength and power upon one man or upon one assembly of men, that may reduce all their wills, by plurality of voices, unto one will" (17.13) itself seems a covenant without the sword. Hobbes's response might be that this concord is unique in immediately creating its own enforcement mechanism (cf. 17.13).[30] Yet this response flounders more than persuades.[31] Read more critically, Hobbes points to the need for rational interactions extending beyond the fearful but prudential bargaining of masterless men. Even absent a common power to coerce, there must be cooperation involving mutuality,[32] underlying a society whose security goes beyond bare preservation (30.1). This richer security informs chapter 30's treatment of the "office of the sovereign representative" and opens the door to criticisms of political mismanagement that the image of security *as* bare preservation (18.20) was intended to suppress.

Second, Hobbes eventually acknowledges the limits of his attempt to persuade readers of a logic of obedience that confines rational terms of political exit to times when the sovereign's ability to protect collapses (29.23). We should consider the remarks on natural punishments in chapter 31, near the conclusion of *Leviathan*'s Second Part. "Having thus briefly spoken of the natural kingdom of God and his natural laws, I will only add to this chapter a short declaration of his natural punishments. There is no action of man in this life that is not the beginning of so long a chain of consequences as no human providence is high enough to give a man a prospect to the end. And in this chain there are linked together both pleasing and unpleasing events, in such manner as that he who will do anything for his pleasure must engage himself to suffer all the pains annexed to it; and these pains are the natural punishments of those actions, which are the beginning of more harm than good. And hereby it comes to pass that intemperance is naturally punished with diseases; rashness, with mischances; injustice with the violence of enemies; pride, with ruin; cowardice, with oppression; negligent government of princes, with rebellion; and rebellion, with slaughter. For seeing punishments are consequent to the breach of laws, natural punishments must be naturally consequent to the breach of the laws of nature, and therefore, follow them as their natural, not arbitrary effects" (31.40).

Epistemologically, these comments juxtapose indeterminacy and inevitability. In one sense, chains of consequence are uncertain; "no human providence is high enough to give a man a prospect to the end." Hobbes does not confront this uncertainty with a Machiavellian call for a daring that challenges fortune. The impossibility of managing this chain is reinforced by ascribing its sequence not to randomness or bad luck but to the causal dynamics of the natural kingdom of God. Impressions of uncertainty morph into realizations of inevitability, linked rhetorically in a way designed to both heighten anxiety and quell impulses toward radical change. Yet the links in this determined chain are just those irrationalities that Hobbes's logic of obedience had been intended to suppress, notably pride and rebellion. Nature's punitive sequence is further revised to move away from what Ioannis Evrigenis (2014) calls images of anarchy toward more familiar conflicts between internally coordinated groups. By enabling senses of belonging and empowerment, providing exhilarating visions of success and terrifying depictions of failure, and exerting coercive control over membership and loyalty (Hardin, 1995), this logic of group action counters the isolation and hopelessness deliberately emphasized in chapter 13's state of nature narrative. Chapter 31's wars may be more immediately recognizable (especially by those whose peace has degenerated into civil war—13.11), yet they are also more violently intractable. Natural punishments do not simply reinforce political lessons that all should learn; they also reveal why they are so hard to absorb.[33]

Among its many implications, this "short declaration" casts doubts upon the success of any prior argument for the rationality of virtually uncontested compliance. The anticipated weaknesses of Hobbes's theorems are suggested by the eventual inadequacy of his attempt to debunk intellectual justifications for challenging the sovereign's legitimacy. In chapter 19, he insists that condemnations of regimes as tyrannies, oligarchies, or anarchies, often found "in the histories and books of policy," have no rational standing. Scientific distinctions among "the several kinds of commonwealth" only classify empirical differences in the numbers of those governing: one, few, or many (19.1). The power exercised by them must be equally absolute, though they differ in their "aptitude to produce the peace" (19.4). Tyranny and oligarchy "are not the names of other forms of government [than the monarchical or aristocratic], but of the same forms misliked" (19.2). More than ignorant tantrums, these expressions are reckless threats to social peace. Yet while denying that the name of tyranny has any intellectual weight, Hobbes's summary of natural punishments acknowledges the reality of negligence, an accusation reinforced by the importance of a security beyond bare preservation. Logics and rhetorics of obedience notwithstanding, such negligence will be seen and resented as tyranny, met predictably with rebellion, followed predictably by slaughter.

Rational Counsel

This dark recognition invites us to reconsider *Leviathan*'s intended audience. If demonstrating the imperative of obedience is primary, the principal audience should comprise those subjects—or the opinion leaders among them—whose acceptance of sovereign authority is essential to the commonwealth's stability.[34] However, if that argument does not counter the negligent governance that triggers rebellion, Hobbes must confront such negligence at its source. The aspiration for the book imagined at the end of chapter 31 identifies the most important addressee as some (indefinite) sovereign (31. 41).[35] In one respect, this possibility reinforces *Leviathan*'s focus on civic obedience, since those in power are asked to protect its "public teaching."[36] Yet in urging this sovereign also to "consider [the work] himself . . . without the help of any interested or envious interpreter," Hobbes potentially initiates a more private conversation with those in authority, a cautious attempt to speak truth to power. The hope "that men may learn thereby both how to govern and how to obey" (3.41) places the learning of governance first. While condemning passionate calls for rebellion against tyranny as incoherent and irresponsible, Hobbes nonetheless points to the catastrophic consequences of negligence. Yet how can Hobbes propose such a conversation when he is acutely sensitive to how easily any political criticisms can turn subversive?

One answer may be chapter 25's comments on counsel.[37] Unlike command, counsel does not speak authoritatively, for its influence depends not on force or status but on persuasion. The performative basis of counsel is "that he that giveth counsel pretendeth (whatever he intendeth) the good of he to whom he giveth it" (25.3). This relation acknowledges both hierarchy and equality. While those in power cannot be challenged by competing claims to authority, they can relate to those who would offer advice in ways presuming more equality, enabling limited degrees of frankness, as well as encouraging healthy degrees of caution (whose good does the counsellor really seek?). This is not an equality of interests, since the good of the one counseled is (allegedly) primary. At the same time, since the good of the sovereign, particularly a monarch, is said to be identical with the common good (19. 4), counselling the sovereign's good can also encourage good governance, living up to the responsibility implied in chapter 30's focus on the sovereign representative's office. Such counsel is not purely strategic, accepting a sovereign's vision of its own good, whatever it may be, without reflection, for one aspect of counsel potentially urges reconsideration of what the sovereign's good means. Hobbes's claim that a monarch is more apt to secure the peace because "in monarchy the private interest is the same with the public" (19. 4) may be pragmatically reconstructive and not naively descriptive or basely subservient.[38] If so, Hobbes's provision of counsel marks a hierarchy of wisdom different from the hierarchy of command.[39]

As he concludes Part Two, Hobbes counsels sovereigns to create and maintain a political infrastructure supportive of a peace beyond bare preservation.[40] Fundamentally, this advice counsels sovereigns to reject any arguments or institutions that would limit their power, for example, claims that individuals may privately interpret the laws, that property rights limit sovereign power, or that sovereign power can be divided.[41] Yet just as importantly, sovereigns are urged to adopt policies reinforcing the effectiveness of the laws of nature, reminding any ruler that he is "as much subject [to these laws] as the meanest of his people" (30. 15). Though the sovereign's obedience to natural laws is enforceable by God alone (30.1), such enforcement does not rely on rewards and punishments in an afterlife.[42] The natural punishment for negligence is rebellion followed by slaughter, perhaps giving a more political cast to the punishment of pride with ruin. Prudential respect for the laws of nature can thus counter the more dangerously absolutist tendencies of rulers on Hobbesian grounds, making both alleged tyranny and real negligence less likely. Key to this project is the distinction between just laws and good ones. Though no law can be unjust because any law established by sovereign command is just by definition, laws will differ in quality.[43] "To the care of the sovereign belongeth the making of good laws. But what is a good law? By a good law I mean not a just law, for no law can be unjust. The law is made by sovereign power, and all that is done by such power is warranted and owned by every one of the people; and that which every man will have so, no man can say in unjust. . . . A good law is that which is needful for the good of the people and withal perspicuous" (30.20). While a precise understanding of justice exposes attacks on supposedly "unjust" laws as incoherent, sovereigns can be counseled on how laws can be better, more responsive to societal needs and more generally comprehensible. "For the laws of nature, which consist in equity, justice, gratitude, and other moral virtues on these depending, in the condition of mere nature . . . are not properly laws, but qualities that dispose men to peace and obedience. When a commonwealth is once settled, then they are actually laws and not before; as being then the commands of the commonwealth; and therefore also civil laws" (26.8).

If taken seriously by sovereigns, the laws of nature should also affect how civil laws are applied. The eleventh natural law, regard for equity, requires that "justice be administered to all degrees of people: that is, that as well the rich and mighty, as poor and obscure persons may be righted of the injuries done them; so as the great may have no greater hope of immunity, when they do violence, dishonor, or any injury to the meaner sort, than when one of these does the like to one of them" (30.15; cf. 15.23). The seventh, "that in revenges, men respect only the future good," places Hobbes firmly on the side of deterrence not retribution. (15.19). At the same time, the sixth, "facility to pardon," affirms "that upon condition of a future time, a man ought to pardon the offenses past of them that repenting, desire it" (15.18). An entire chapter (27) considers "crimes, excuses and extenuations," outlining conditions under which punishments may be adjusted upward or downward. While laws should be applied equitably, the sovereign should recognize how different societal positions impact appropriate degrees of both offense and punishment. Power and high status aggravate offenses that poverty and powerlessness may mitigate (27.30; 30.23).[44] Equitable criminal law is not blind legalism. Most significantly, the imposition of punishment should allow the natural law enjoining pardon to be observed whenever possible, for "there is place many times for lenity, without prejudice to the commonwealth; and lenity, where there is much place for it, is required by the law of nature" (30.23).

The well-counseled sovereign's policies should also go beyond regulatory and punitive applications of the law. In particular, Hobbes focuses on civic education, for "the grounds of these rights [of sovereigns] have the rather need to be diligently and truly taught, because they cannot be maintained by any civil law or terror of legal punishment" (30.4). The "instruction of the people in the essential rights which are the natural and fundamental laws of sovereignty" (30.6) is one sovereign *duty* mentioned explicitly in *Leviathan*. This aim of this instruction is not simply outward conformity, but a deeper restructuring of character. Both Strauss and Gauthier may therefore underappreciate Hobbes's educative goals. What Strauss (1963, 120–121) calls a privileging of bourgeois over aristocratic virtue could be more generously characterized as the replacement of a valorization of warlike virtue with an appreciation of achievements contributing to peaceful social progress.[45] The sovereign's establishing the "laws of honor and a public rate of worth" should thus encourage pacific virtues by downplaying qualities historically associated with warriors.[46] Vainglorious egoists who attribute their supposed pre-eminence to personal distinction rather than to the "will of those that have the sovereign authority" (27.13) need to be chastened. Honors given to those serving the commonwealth should be moderate in scope and offered only to those who act out of a loyal public spirit rather than from a dangerous public ambition (30.24).[47] Gauthier may therefore also underestimate Hobbes's aspirations for human improvement. One broad outcome of Hobbes's institutional reforms is a strengthened sense of fellowship impossible for the suspicious inhabitants of the state of nature. Institutions preventing us from doing to others as we would *not* be done by may create an environment where doing to others as we *would* be done by is more possible (15.35; 30.13).[48]

Moreover, though Hobbes's political theory is often criticized for excessive deference to existing political structures, its full implications point to significant social transformation.[49] Recommendations for educational and economic policies, the administration of justice, and the crafting of manners and morals aim at a greater social equality, which should not be confused with social leveling.[50] All citizens should receive a common education explaining the nature and grounds of their political duties (30.4–6). Economic structures should discourage wasteful and flamboyant consumption among the wealthy, reward the efficient and stable accumulations of the middle class, and protect the blamelessly poor from destitution (30.15–19). All of this suggests that the sovereign's office is responsibly fulfilled when its power encourages widespread and substantial peaceableness. This is the vision of society imaged in the provocative frontispiece of the Head edition (1651) of *Leviathan*,[51] where a peaceful and civilized town and country landscape is supervised by a crowned sovereign whose body is composed of his individual subjects, the authorizing agents of all he does.[52] This sovereign wields the sword in his right hand and the crozier in his left.

Peaceful Faith

The crozier images ecclesiastical authority. Though the sovereign's educational responsibilities that end the first half of *Leviathan* amount to a secular decalogue (30.7–13) grounded in proven moral theorems (31.41), the second half of the book offers extensive treatments of religious questions. Commentators are divided over the sequencing. Some see Hobbes's political theory as essentially completed in Part Two and treat the subsequent discussion of religion as rhetorical, confronting confessional differences that inflamed the civil war.[53] Others read the second half as an acknowledgment that political theory cannot stand on reason alone and that it requires theological support.[54] While a full exploration is not attempted here, it should be noted that sharp distinctions between secular and religious portions of *Leviathan* are complicated by the text.[55] Parts One and Two posit God as ultimate origin of the world's causes (11. 25; 12.6; 21.4).[56] The most complete definition of philosophy appears in Part Four (46.1). Here, I argue that Hobbes's engagement with religion attempts to pacify conflicts, both between reason and scripture and among scriptural interpretations, continuing the political theory of the first half in a different context and voice. Parts One and Two argue that accepting *Leviathan*'s political principles does not require membership in any particular religious tradition.[57] Part Three contends that such acceptance does not demand rejection of Christian faith.[58] Part Four frighteningly redescribes the alternative to political and religious peace as a condition of pervasive darkness.[59] *Leviathan* both argues for and performatively represents religious peace.

Whatever Hobbes's beliefs about personal salvation, *Leviathan* focuses on the political impacts of religious conflicts. Chapter 43 (Part Three's final chapter) is introduced by the statement that the "most frequent pretext of sedition and civil war, in Christian commonwealths hath proceeded from a difficulty, not yet sufficiently resolved, of obeying at once both God and man when their commandments are one contrary to the other." The ensuing reflection seems less a presentation of Hobbes's own argument than a representation of widespread anxiety.[60] "For if the command of the civil sovereign be such as that it may be obeyed without the forfeiture of life eternal, not to obey it is unjust. . . . But if the command be such as cannot be obeyed without being damned to eternal death, then it were madness to obey it, and the counsel of our Saviour takes place (Matt. 10.28): 'Fear not those that kill the body, but cannot kill the soul'" (43.2). Hobbes will reject the second prospect as a false choice. Its intractability as a salvational either/or would mean no end to civil disruption. Consequently, when he engages theological disputes over the independent existence of the soul from the body (44.15, 32; 46.21), the meaning of eternal life and torment (37.11, 14; 38.1; 42.26),[61] the comparative importance of faith and works for salvation (43.3–4, 20), or the significance and site of the kingdom of God (38.5; 44.4), he does so only to the extent that such controversies threaten civil peace.[62] Thus, "seeing eternal life is a greater reward than the life present, and eternal torment a greater punishment than the death of nature, it is a thing worthy to be well considered, of all men that desire (by obeying authority) to avoid the calamities of confusion and civil war, what is meant in Holy Scripture by life eternal and torment eternal" (38.1).

Hobbes's interpretive strategy is summarized at the end of Part Three. "It is not the bare words, but the scope of the writer that giveth the true light by which any writing is to be interpreted; and they that insist upon single texts without considering the main design, can derive nothing from them clearly, but rather by casting atoms of scripture, as dust before men's eyes, make everything more obscure than it is—an ordinary artifice of those that seek not the truth, but their own advantage" (43.24). In employing an approach suitable to "any writing," Hobbes implicitly deprives scripture of any unique authority. Yet he also claims there is a (scriptural) text to be read and that the text's teaching, as presented through Hobbes's readings and as confirmed by his reasoning, establishes civil peace as scripture's truest interpretive light. In a sense, Part Three's scriptural readings stand opposite to Part One's state of nature narrative. While the latter images chaos and uncertainty, the former offers order and reassurance.[63] Does Part Four reinforce this need for order by reintroducing anxiety, presenting disorders of the mind that recall and reposition the physical disorders of nature?

However this may be, the substance of Part Three offers a scriptural narrative tracing God's covenant with human beings, beginning with the politically specific Hebrew covenant and leading to the more universal covenant signaled by Christ's promise of redemption and the coming reality of a kingdom of God following the final judgment (42.43; 44.4). Within this narrative, the interdependence of salvation and political peace is supported from two directions. First, Hobbes makes a scriptural case for vesting authority over religious matters in the secular power (42.71). At one level, this requirement follows analytically from the definition of law offered earlier. "Seeing therefore I have already proved that sovereigns in their own dominions are sole legislators, those books only are canonical (that is, law) in every nation which are established for such by the sovereign authority" (33.1). In Part Three, this theoretical conclusion is reinforced by scriptural readings arguing that the Old Testament's imperatives only became binding as laws under Hebrew civil authority (42.41) just as the doctrines of the New Testament do not become such "until obedience to them [is] commanded by them that God had given power to on earth to be legislators" (42.43). What holds rationally for all commonwealths is also commanded scripturally for Christian commonwealths.

Second, Hobbes's scriptural account of "what is necessary for a man's reception into the kingdom of heaven" undercuts any "pretext[s] of sedition and civil war" that might arise from alleged conflicts between divine and sovereign commands. His indefinite consideration of the alternatives of faith and works (43.21; cf. Lessay, 2007; Farneti, 2007, 302) suggests that salvific works are enabled by a sovereign authority with which faith cannot conflict. The specific works identified are reducible to civil obedience, following laws of nature that can be securely obeyed only when sovereigns (Christian or otherwise) establish civil law (43.3). "Having thus shown what is necessary to salvation, it is not hard to reconcile our obedience to God with our obedience to the civil sovereign, who is either Christian or infidel" (43.22–3). And since faith is a matter of inner assent, it cannot be affected by external commands or coercions. "Faith is a gift of God, which man can neither give nor take away by promises of rewards or menace of torture" (42.11; cf. 43.23).[64] Salvific works are enabled by civil laws and civil laws pose no threat to faith. The future tense of the promise of the kingdom of God on earth ("Thy Kingdom come") undercuts divisive claims to temporal authority asserted by any existing church (35.13–14; 38, 23; 39.5; 44.4).[65]

Within Hobbes's scriptural reading, Old and New Testaments are pacifically integrated.[66] While Moses is central to forging the Hebrew covenant, his political leadership is read retrospectively within the broader story of God's universal covenant and Christ's redemption of mankind (33.20; 40.14; 41.1–3, 7–9; 42.3).[67] Hobbes's Moses is the representative and steward of his people (40.6) and the loyal servant and fiduciary of God (30.5). His delivery of God's laws to the Hebrews is continuous with the rational discovery of the laws of nature (42.37; 43.5). The punishments inflicted under his stewardship were administered by God and limited in number (40.7).[68] By contrast, though there are no grounds for believing that Hobbes has this comparison in mind, Machiavelli's Moses is a daring political innovator whose Hebrew god was his own invention and whose foundational acts of violence were sweeping in scope and ruthless in intensity (*Disc*, 3.30). The pacific character of Hobbes's New Testament narrative is clearest in his treatment of martyrdom (42.12). Instead of being willing to die for faith in defiance of civil authority, the martyr becomes a witness to the truth of a faith whose illumination shines within.

Yet Hobbes's scriptural interpretations do not simply parallel the earlier science of good governance and civic obedience; they are informed by a prior commitment to rationality. Part Three's introduction emphasizes that the treatment of the nature and rights of a Christian Commonwealth is a specific discourse within the broader theorization of the nature and rights of sovereign power "derived . . . hitherto from the principles of nature only" (32.1). While this exposition requires attention to the prophetical as well as the natural word of God, it does not demand renunciation of "our senses and experience, nor . . . our natural reason" (32.2). The claims of individual prophets to speak the revealed word must be subjected to critical scrutiny, in part because prophetic claims are often contradictory (32.7). Prophecy opposing natural reason should be rejected as ignorant or fraudulent. Since the scriptures themselves show the word of God to be "consonant to reason and equity" (36.5), reason communicates God's word even through the (reasonable) words of idolaters (36.5–6). The bad faith of prophets opposing reason (and peace) is exposed by a natural understanding of human motives. "For he that pretends to teach men the way of so great felicity pretends to govern them . . . which is a thing that all men naturally desire" (36.19).

In subjecting the prophetical word of God to the scrutiny of reason Hobbes continues and complicates Part One's ontological treatment of God as ultimate cause. When "the love of knowledge of causes, draws a man from the consideration of the effect to seek the cause, and again the cause of that cause, till of necessity he must come to the thought at last: that there is some cause, whereof there is no former cause, but is eternal," he is led to that "which is it men call God" (11.25).[69] From one perspective, this sequence of discoveries reinforces the belief that "there is one God eternal, though [men] cannot have any idea of him in their mind answerable to his nature." This intellectual program implies that expanding and indeterminate boundaries of science will disclose ever more remote and sophisticated causes in natural bodies and motions. Such discoveries may provide more reasons for awe of a divinity that we can honor but not understand or explain.[70] Yet such a progression through the chain of causes also gives (that which men call) God much less work to do within explanations of the wonders and possibilities of the world.[71]

Peace's Epistemic Distortions

I have argued that Hobbes's project in *Leviathan* is intellectually structured by a commitment to peace as the most important human priority. This commitment does not depend, as it does for Aquinas, on a cosmic order that humans need to understand and respect. Rather, it represents a pragmatic agenda for emotionally mature and intellectually responsible individuals whose decisions and practices can establish a commonwealth "designed to live as long as mankind, or as the laws of nature, or as justice itself" (29.1). Consequently, the book outlines a program for "men [not] as they are the matter, but as they are the makers and orderers" of political and social institutions. Yet this capacity for making conditions of peace into realities also complicates and challenges Hobbes's project.

In one sense, political institutions enable philosophy by creating conditions for leisure (46.6). Absent leisure, there is no space for systematic methods of inquiry that separate conclusive science and stable progress from random experience and tenuous survival. Epistemically, such institutions construct the fields theorized by the human sciences. The turbulent state of nature forecloses possibilities for intellectual advance not simply because it offers no secure leisure but also because the coherent identities and relations that science presupposes cannot emerge.[72] A natural equality enabling the weakest to kill the strongest shatters reliable conceptions of strength and weakness (13.1). If natural freedom is limited only by external constraints, human powers are constantly unsettled as they encounter physical accommodations or resistances. Even the particular motions individuating bodies can be radically enhanced or diminished by experiences whose fundamental character is turbulence. Alternating senses of vain glory and dejection become endless. Diagnosing these self-understandings as forms of madness is impossible absent normalcy. But what behavior ordinarily seen in nature is a benchmark for sanity? And since the sciences of man presuppose the ability to read "not simply oneself but mankind" (*Author's Introduction*), such readings must be distorted when fearful aggression and persistent suspicion infect all encounters.

Yet political stability and epistemic order may also obscure the most important causal discoveries and pragmatic imperatives of Hobbes's political and moral science.[73] Widespread social peace can diminish the anxiety for future time that prompts attention to political stability's foundations (11.24). Moreover, complete acceptance of the imperatives of peace may distort moral psychology by misconstruing or ignoring human characteristics whose persistence and significance should remain matters of concern. Fear is not unambiguously beneficial and Strauss's judgment that Hobbes eventually omits courage from *Leviathan* altogether (1963, 49–50) oversimplifies. While strict Hobbesian logic may deny that personal sacrifice for the community is rational,[74] the chain of natural punishments mapped at the end of chapter 31 predicts that "cowardice" will be followed by "oppression" (31.40). Here, the condemnation of governmental abuse may go further than indictments of negligence, approaching accusations of tyranny previously rejected as senseless (19.2). Oppression now seems an objective or rational rather than a prejudicial or emotional judgment. Within the sequence of natural causes, the appropriate response is not prudent compliance (because "covenants extorted by fear are valid"—14.27), but determined resistance (yet what of the rebellion followed by slaughter?). The praise of the slain Sydney Godolphin's valor in the passages beginning and ending *Leviathan* may be more than expressions of personal respect.[75] Resisting the imprecations of aggressive divines may require courage from ordinary people facing extraordinary times.[76]

If fear is not always to be appreciated, pride is not always to be demonized, for what would motivate a sovereign willing to receive and follow Hobbes's counsel? Perhaps the practice of sovereign leadership is one place where the seemingly irrational love of a seemingly irrational good actually makes sense. "Though after death there be no sense of the praise given us on earth, as being joys that are either swallowed up in the unspeakable joys of Heaven or extinguished in the extreme torments of hell, yet is not such fame vain, because they have a present delight therein from the foresight of it and of the benefit that may redound thereby to their posterity, which though they now see not, yet they imagine" (11.6).[77]

Complications within Hobbes's own projected frame of reference also suggest that his political theory must involve more than either building a firm intellectual edifice upon established definitions or fostering general enlightenment through attacks on magical thinking.[78] Political intelligence must also critically engage or interrogate the pacific frame of reference that simultaneously enables and clouds its own discoveries. Yet doing so would seem to require a kind of philosophy different from either "the knowledge acquired by reasoning from the manner of the generation of anything to the properties, or from the properties to some possible way of generation of the same" (46.1), or the deepest introspection that searches hearts (*Author's Introduction*). This alternative philosophy might resemble a counsel that is more bidirectional or mutual, a less strategic and more purposive form of deliberation.[79]

What makes such deliberation both necessary and problematic within Hobbes's framework? Enlightened (absolute) monarchy is not politically recognizable now, but a more familiar form of Hobbesian governance may be a just and efficient bureaucracy, performing the broad and beneficial offices of a sovereign representative. However, this arrangement leaves questions of the ultimate sources of political direction open. What keeps bureaucracies, however efficient, just? Reinterpretations of Hobbesian politics along more currently approachable lines include Flathman's and Martel's democratic activism, Gauthier's representative constitutionalism, and Kavka's welfare state liberalism. All ground political authority— and place political responsibility—in the agreements or promises of individuals, not in machines that would run of themselves. Yet none of the intellectual resources available for such agreements and promises— Flathman's skepticism, Martel's subversive decenterings, Gauthier's logic of authorization, or Kavka's prudently restrained egoism—seem fully adequate to meet the political challenges that Hobbes recognizes all too well, perhaps especially political questions about war and peace. Don Herzog's judgment (1989, 90–95) that Hobbes produces bad philosophy for the sake of good politics may be right, but we should add that Hobbes's politics are, while hardly bad, overly narrow.

This narrowness becomes apparent if we reconsider the implications of separating human beings as "the matter" of society from humans as "the makers" of political institutions.[80] In focusing on political making,

Hobbes's project resembles Machiavelli's. But this parallel raises questions about the eventual stability of Hobbes's separation of peace from war and therefore about his ability to affirm peace as the most compelling priority. Machiavelli's politics attempt to control the impacts of desires for material goods and honors through their constructive channeling but it continually faces resistance from the passions on which it depends. In accepting permanent turbulence, he cautions against illusions of closure. Though Hobbes might see "men as they are matter" as malleable to pacification through the redirection of the passions or as receptive to enlightenment through the elimination of magical thinking, it is more difficult to see where the limits of "men as they are . . . makers and orderers" might lie. Are the activities of men as makers in principle unlimited? Does Hobbes's image of a society capable of existing as long as "mankind" introduce the possibility of more aggressively ambitious forms of making whose limits are set only by the projected outcome's perceived advantages and the makers' capabilities?[81] Seen from this perspective, the transformative prospect of a domestic peace lasting as long as justice itself may overcome reservations about enlisting political coercion—either within domestic police powers or toward "rogue states"—when such coercion is needed to achieve making's best purposes. Hobbes's wars may be limited by imperatives of peace in ways very different from the bounds set by Aquinas. The concern may be not when wars are not sinful but when are they are not pointless or bungled. And if human beings as makers have the ability to re-create social bonds by enlisting the advances of an open-ended science, there may be no principled reason to take Hobbes's sincerely humane societal aspirations as the last word.

Hobbes does not strive to empower unbounded technical rationality. His denial that human beings are passionless calculators (8.3) recognizes that emotions drive all human projects. While this recognition may prevent him from lapsing into technocracy, it may also reveal forms of pride and fear not so easily managed by institutional design or reformed by rhetorical power. Such intense expressions persist in the text of Hobbes's most respected classical author. In representing Pericles's anticipation of an Athens whose name will shine in eternal memory, Thucydides discloses the hubris of unbounded pridefulness. Pride shines forth in Pericles's boast that Athens "has abidden the greatest wars against [the Grecians], both universally and singly" (2.64; Hobbes, trans. 1975, 147), envisaging that his own criteria for praise and blame will extend indefinitely into the future.[82] When Hobbes counsels a sovereign to allow the public teaching of *Leviathan* so as to turn "this truth of speculation into the utility of practice" (31.41), he imagines that the outcome of this practical utility may also be timeless, institutions "designed to live as long as mankind, or as the laws of nature, or as justice itself" (29.1). Cautioned by the admired Thucydides, can we detect a dangerous pridefulness in *Leviathan* itself?[83]

Exposures to such prideful ambition may trigger a fearfulness not conducive to peace. For Thucydides, the "truest quarrel" (1.23; Hobbes, trans, 1975, 42) behind the calamitous Peloponnesian war was the confrontation of Athenian power by Lacedaemonian fear. Does Hobbes's appeal to healthy fear in *Leviathan* give inadequate attention to conditions under which confidence is shaken to the core and fear lashes out against existential threats? A more Thucydidean reading of fear and pride may interpret them not as opposing (healthy versus diseased) political psychologies but as mutually destructive codependents. The resolution of the ill-fated Melian leaders in Thucydides's fifth book can be another cautionary tale about the disasters that follow from discounting fear in the name of pride.[84] Yet the Athenian voices in this exchange reveal the pathologies of a fearfulness become more dangerous owing to nourishments of pride and instruments of power. Pride in the achievements and power of the Athenian empire paradoxically intensify fears that its reputation may collapse.[85]

Not surprisingly, Hobbes's framework for pacified politics becomes less stable as political contexts shift from domestic to international, even though the relations among nations most clearly image the state of nature.[86] "In all times kings and persons of sovereign authority, because of their independency, are in continual jealousies and in the state and posture of gladiators, having their weapons pointing and their eyes fixed on one another, that is, their forts, garrisons, and guns upon the frontiers of their kingdoms, and continual spies upon their neighbors, which is a posture of war" (13.12). Though prospects for conflict among states might be continuous, Hobbes treats such clashes as less devastating than civil war. Warlike external stances reinforce internal peace by "uphold[ing] thereby the industry of their subjects." Yet the peaceful continuity of a political industry that facilitates and enhances commodious living may also mask the destructiveness of foreign wars whose consequences do not recoil at home. In this context, the pervasiveness of peace may do worse than cloud an appreciation of the bases of internal power. Since rational Hobbesian populations will only reject wars against other societies if they see prospects of harm to themselves, how will they respond to the opportunities and threats of international politics, where the restraining equality of an imagined state of nature is absent, allowing more integrated and sophisticated societies to compete against less advantaged cultures, some "other"?[87] Inequalities within international politics may reinforce the relations described by the Athenian participants in the Melian dialogue (as translated by Hobbes): "they that have odds of power exact as much as they can, and the weak yield to such conditions as they can get" (5.89; 1975, 379). Because inequalities unbalance the international state of nature, a powerful regime's pridefulness may not be simply delusional. Yet such confidence may be resisted by the intensified emotions of other men as makers, who see themselves either as transformative change agents or as desperate characters with nothing to lose.[88] The deep seated fear experienced by the "weakest" may become a passion that inclines to war, with the fear of violent death that should terrify natural individuals becoming a potential equalizer in the politics among nations.[89] Is powerlessness one root cause of terrorism? Are threats to obliterate civilian populations in response to such terror themselves generated by unstable mixtures of power and fear? In this context, the temptations of a peace lasting as long as mankind, but inevitably situated within flawed civilizational narratives, may be as dangerous as Schmitt's wars fought for the sake of humanity. That these difficulties require an altogether different philosophical framework, grounds Kant's proposals for achieving a truly perpetual peace.

Kant: The Philosophy and Politics of Peace

Kant's statement on the imperative of peace in *Toward Perpetual Peace* (*TPP*) is clear and uncompromising. "From the throne of the highest moral lawmaking (*höchsten moralisch gesetzgebenden*), reason absolutely condemns war as rights-determining and makes the seeking of peace an unmitigated duty" (116)[90] (cf. *Metaphysical Elements of the Theory of Right*, Conclusion, 174–175; *Theory and Practice*, 86; *Idea of a Universal History with a Cosmopolitan Intent*, 34). This conclusion emerges not from Hobbes's prudential natural laws but from the moral imperatives of free rationality. Kantian peace presumes but extends Hobbes's vision of how the infrastructure of civilization (called cultures of skill and discipline in *Critique of Judgment*) can be stabilized and prospects for delightful living secured. Its achievement will enable human beings to treat one another as ends in themselves (*Groundwork for the Metaphysics of Morals* 40–41; *METR*, 166–167), not simply within individual communities but also globally. Indeed, "the problem of establishing a perfect civil constitution depends on the problem of law governed external relations among states (*gesetzmässigen äusseren Staatenverhältnisses*) and cannot be resolved without [resolving] the latter as well" (*UH*, 34; cf. *CJ*, 83. 299–301; *METR*, 136–137, 171).

TPP's "philosophical sketch" (*philosophischer entwurf*) strongly impacts current theory. It is read as both the culminating statement of Kant's political philosophy (Ellis, 2005, 87; Korsgaard, 1996, 33; Bohman and Lutz-Bachmann, 1997, 2) and the most important intellectual resource for political theorists envisaging the democratic reconstruction of international politics (Benhabib, 2004, 25–26; Rawls, 1999, 10, 22, 36, 56, 126; Habermas, 1998, 165–166; Lutz-Bachmann, 59–60; Bohman, 1997, 28; Ellis, 2005 71–72, 184; Smith, 2016, 132). While Kant's formulations cannot play this latter role without undergoing significant revision, particularly with respect to what Habermas (1998, 170–171) criticizes as its deference to the "classical-modern world of nation states,"[91] his projected constitutional global order can guide the construction of postnation state governance in the late twentieth century and beyond, a global constitutionalism whose institutional supports strongly parallel the structures of deliberative democracy.[92]

In spite of the compelling character and cosmic scope of this ideal, Kant's sketch for its achievement is in various ways both ambiguous and problematic, hinted even in the structure of *Toward Perpetual Peace*. As is well known, the initial case is built around six preliminary and three definitive articles. The preliminary articles resemble items in a treaty.[93] The definitive articles call for three structural transformations within domestic and international politics. The first insists that all constitutions respectful of right be republican (*TPP*, 112–115). The second identifies a federation of free states as the international governance structure fully consistent with autonomous rationality (115–116; *CJ*, 83.299–301; *METR*, 171; *TP*, 87–88). The third extends cosmopolitan right "to conditions of universal hospitality" (118), though not to universal citizenship.[94] Modern proposals for establishing an effective law of peoples treat one or more of these provisions as key resources.[95]

However, the articles do not exhaust Kant's sketch. They are followed first, by two supplements, then, by two appendices. The *First Supplement* guarantees the eventual achievement of perpetual peace in historical time. The *Second Supplement* insists on consulting the maxims of philosophers as the "secret article" for the establishment of peace. These are followed by a *First Appendix* that outlines the contributions of philosophy's moral maxims to politics, underscoring differences between figures called the moral politician (who regulates her practices according to the priority of right) and the political moralist (who uses moral language as a smokescreen for the pursuit of interest) and a *Second Appendix* that reaffirms the need for a kind of public reason. It is tempting to read *TPP* sequentially, moving from traditional and limited political formulations to a philosophical argument (Ellis, 2005, 79). However, the full text complicates Kant's presentation and does so in at least three ways.

First, the *First Supplement*'s acknowledgment that the end of peace can only be guaranteed by the continued experience of war introduces a verdict on war more conflicted than Hobbes's outright condemnation. While Kant calls the pursuit of peace an unmitigated duty, his account of human progress depends on the continued, even intensified presence of war. Second, Kant's treatment of historical time is embedded within a metaphysical structure that his project both requires and problematizes. This creates a series of structural problems in the treatment of war and peace traceable not simply to the historical and intellectual circumstances of his time,[96] but to conflicts intrinsic to his philosophical framework. Third, Kant's eventual separation of rational morality from historical pragmatics limits the extent to which his moral philosophy can usefully inform the activities of the moral politician. The problems of politics as he represents them require a more expansive understanding of politics than he provides and his competing, binary images of political agents do not capture possibilities that a constructive political theory needs to recognize.

The Sites and the Goods of Kantian Peace

Kant's initial critique of Hobbes's inattention to international peace is internal. The benefits of a security "more than bare preservation" are undercut by war preparations made by nations comprising the (still) hostile international state of nature. "For since the advancing culture of states . . . will multiply the number of wars . . . costs must continuously go higher. Meanwhile, the price of all necessities constantly grows. . . . No peace extends so long for the savings accumulated during it to equal the costs of the next war" (*TP*, 88; cf, *UH*, 34, 37; *TPP*, 108–109, 125; *SB*, 58). Hobbes's confidence that states having "their weapons pointing and their eyes fixed on one another" will "uphold thereby the industry of their subjects" is misguided.

More generally, Hobbesian aspirations to foster commodious living and civilizational progress are regarded as worthwhile but incomplete (*SB*, 56–57). Kant is as firmly supportive of commercial republics as any of the classical liberals.[97] Within *TPP*, the growth of commerce leads to more

peaceful interactions. "The spirit of trade (*Handelsgeist*) cannot stand together with war and earlier or later this [spirit] seizes control of every
people. For under all those powers or means ordered by the state, the power
of money (*Geldmacht*) might well be the most dependable for pressing the
state to promote the noble cause of peace (though [not] . . . through the mo-
tive of morality)" (*TPP*, 125). Kant thus reinforces and amplifies Hobbes's
attempt to replace warlike with peaceful virtues within an international
context. Yet additionally (and going well beyond Hobbes's concerns), the
protection of individual economic activity provides a more stable basis for
political autonomy, where free citizens can be (in some sense) the sources
of the laws that bind them (*TP*, 72–73; *TPP*, 111–112; *Gr*, 53–54; *CPrR*,
30–31; *CJ*, 83: 299–300; *Contest of Faculties*, 182–183). Autonomous
citizenship requires the material independence that property confers (*TP*,
75–77; *METR*, 139). These prospects play forward into *TPP*'s principal
concern, for a constitutional order respecting autonomy makes aggressive
wars less likely. "If . . . the consent of the citizenry (*die Bestimmung der
Staatsbürger*) is required in order to determine whether or not there will be
war, it is natural that [the citizens] consider all the calamities of war before
deciding . . . By contrast, under a constitution where subjects are not citizens and which is therefore not republican, the easiest thing in the world
to do is to declare war" (*TPP*, 113; cf. *CF*, 186–187, note).

Likewise, when Kant examines the contributions of civilization or
culture (*CJ*, 83. 297–301) to human development, he both builds upon
and goes beyond Hobbes. For Kant, a society dedicated to "delightful
living" is only a culture of skill (*Kultur der Geschicklichkeit*) "not adequate to promoting the will in its determination and choice of ends"
(*CJ*, 83, 299). Without an enhanced function informing such choices, the
culture of skill's achievements are vulnerable not just to instability but
to perversion. "As this culture goes forth (the height of which is called
luxury . . .), . . . plagues grow equally great on both sides, on the one
hand through violence from outside, and on the other hand through internal discontent" (*CJ*, 83. 299; cf. *UH*, 35–36).[98] Kant therefore adds
the need for a more educative function, a "culture of training (discipline)
(*Kultur der Disziplin*) [which] is negative and consists in the freeing of
the will from the despotism of the desires" (*CJ*, 83, 299). In pointing to
this possibility, Kant is not embracing the habituating but (to him) pater-
nalistic functions of culture that are emphasized by Plato and Aristotle.[99]
Rather, in contributing to the liberation of the will from desire, the culture
of discipline allows human beings to set their own purposes in accordance
with man's position "as the only being on earth that has an understanding

(*Verstand*) and, consequently, a capacity of setting willful ends (*willkürlich Zwecke*)" (*CJ*, 83, 298; *SB*, 52–53).

Kant's goals thus extend beyond producing and protecting "such effects as human life requireth" (*Lev*, 46. 1). Peace is also a *moral* imperative because it allows human beings to interact as creatures who respect one another as ends in themselves owing to their common capacity for rationality (*SB*, 55–57).[100] Absent culture's moral dimension, the achievements praised by Hobbes mark the advance only of "mere [naked] civilization" (*Bloss die Zivilisierung—UH*, 36). War is rejected not only as the threat to civilization's material progress but also as a moral crime that violates human dignity (*CF*, 187; *SB*, 57–58). Consequently, striving for international peace is an unmitigated duty.

In offering a philosophical sketch that advances this goal, Kant also presents a more sophisticated assessment of the problem of order confronted in different, but problematic, ways by Aquinas and Machiavelli. While Aquinas presumes an empirical and normative natural order among nations, Kant treats order's origin and character as historical problems. Yet while Machiavelli traces the creation of order to an energetic agency unleashed by desire, Kant's philosophical assessment commands a rational moral agency. "All politics must bend the knee before right" (*TPP*, 135). Yet even within Kant's own presentation, these commitments are complicated by the continuing presence and influence of war.[101]

War's Creative Destruction

Elisabeth Ellis suggests (2005, 100) that *TPP*'s *First Supplement* could easily be excluded from the text because it offers a natural teleology discordant with the guidance of moral willing. Identifying this inconsistency makes sense, but perhaps the *Supplement* is more provocative complication than dispensable appendage. It jarringly situates war as the *Garantie* of perpetual peace. "What provides this [guarantee] . . . is that great artist nature . . . whose mechanical course (*mechanischem Laufe*) makes her purposiveness visibly displayed, letting concord among human beings emerge through their discord (*Zwietracht*), even against their own wills" (*TPP*, 120; cf. *TP*, 87; *UH*, 15). This claim is embedded within a more comprehensive vision of the dynamics and outcomes of historical conflicts (*TPP*, 120–125). To the extent that war is the mechanism allowing emergence of the moral condition commanded by autonomous rationality, it may not be an unambiguous evil. Thus, in *CJ*, external and internal violence arising from inequalities created within cultures of skill forge a "splendid [or 'shining,' Shell's translation] misery (*glänzende Elend*) which is bound up with the development of the natural capacities of the human race" (*CJ*, 83, 299; cf. *SB*, 121).[102] Three constructive functions of conflict seem relevant.

First, the dynamics and outcomes of war create infrastructures for society and culture, which, while not sufficient, are necessary for the eventual emergence of the kingdom of ends.[103] "All the culture and art that adorn mankind, as well as the most beautiful social order, are fruits of unsociableness (*Ungeselligkeit*) that is forced to discipline itself and thus through an imposed art to develop nature's seed completely" (*UH*, 33; cf. *SB*, 57–58). Concerning the spread of human populations, "through war [nature] has driven [human beings] in all directions, even to the most inhospitable regions so they might inhabit them" (*TPP*, 121 cf. *UH*, 38, note). The natural environments to which humans are dispersed are harsh; "in [nature's] destructive operations—plague, hunger, perils of waters, frost, assaults of other animals, great and small, etc—in these she has spared [the human] as little as any other animal" (*CJ*, 83: 298; cf. 67, 249). Making these sites habitable often demands recurring and perhaps even escalating violence. When prompted by their "war against the animals (*Kriege gegen die Tiere*) . . . [humans must] live in peace among themselves" (*TPP*, 121; *UH*, 33). But progress is always threatened by turbulent desire; victory over the animals is followed by wars against other humans. "The conflict in the natural predispositions of the human being reduces him and others of his own species, by means of self-devised plagues such as the oppression of domination (*Herrschaft*), the barbarism of war, and so forth" (*CJ*, 83, 298). However, though this aggression "works so hard for the destruction of [the human] species," it is also "one more incentive . . . for developing to their highest degree all the talents that serve for culture" (*CJ*, 83, 298, 300; cf. *UH*, 32).

Second, wars reveal the complex dynamics of political self-determination (*TPP*, 108, 112–113, note; cf. *UH*, 33), as Kant's narrative tacks between aggression and independence. The promise of political freedom may be most clearly recognized, if not decisively constructed, when independence is threatened. Yet independence is most sharply asserted through aggression, "by which sometimes states subdivide and resolve themselves into smaller states, sometimes a state annexes smaller states and strives to form a greater whole" (*CJ*, 83. 300). From a moral point of view, this condition is devoid of right altogether, resembling the relations of lawless savages. In *METR* Kant emphasizes that adjacent states finding themselves in such a condition of "injustice" are "bound" to move toward a more rational condition through the establishment of a league of peace among themselves (*METR*, 165). Here, lawless nature and the metaphysics of right are binaries. *TPP*'s judgment is more nuanced. The need to confront aggressors has substantial positive consequences for freedom, internal and external. "Every people finds itself neighbor to another people that threatens it, and it must form itself into a state so as to be able to stand against this threat with its power" (124), reinforcing an internal cooperation that requires politics, perhaps even an incipient republicanism. Though no moral motivation grounds these bonds, "man, even though he is not morally good, is forced to be a good citizen" (124). Externally considered, such conflicts are far "preferable to [these states] being overrun by a superior power that melds them into a universal monarchy" (*TPP*, 125; *SB*, 57–58). In this context, the cultural systems that frustrate the cosmopolitanism demanded by morality, "differences in language and religion, which do indeed dispose men to mutual hatred and to pretexts for war" (*TPP*, 125) also serve however imperfectly as resources for resisting tyranny.

Third, war engenders esteem for nobility. Though often originating in quarrels over resources, "war itself needs no particular motivation, but appears to be ingrained in human nature and is even valued as something noble (*etwas Edles*); indeed, the drive for glory inspires human beings to [wage war], even without selfish motives" and "often war is begun only to display courage" (*TPP*, 123). Within this vaguely anthropological focus on "what nature does to further its own ends in respect to the human species as a class of animal," Kant comments on the ubiquity of the praise assigned to warlike courage in cultures ranging from the Native American to the European, even though he has earlier condemned both for their savage wars (*TPP*, 116, 123). Philosophical statements recognizing war's psychological outcomes likewise praise it as having an ennobling influence on human beings.[104] At one level, this assessment may be a psychologically realistic acknowledgment of the commitments needed to resist despotism. Yet the affirmation of nobility can be elevated beyond the love of honor into a respect for moral heroism. "To see a virtuous man struggling with tribulations and temptations toward evil and still standing firm against them is a sight worthy of a deity" (*TP*, 86; cf. *TP*, 70; *UH*, 39; though see qualifications at *CPrR*, 88).[105]

If the experiences and possibilities of war strengthen the infrastructure of culture, sharpen recognitions of and commitments to freedom, and develop senses of nobility, they cannot be seen simply as signs of human nature's depravity (*TPP* 116). "Thus, thanks to nature for the quarrelsomeness, for the distasteful competitive vanity, for the insatiable desire to possess and also to rule" (*UH*, 32). Here, Kant seems to depart significantly from Hobbes's categorical condemnation of war.[106] Yet while this recognition of war's benefits initially unsettles, it is eventually transformed by trajectories that move human beings toward the kingdom of ends.

Nature, History, Providence

The *First Supplement* maps three routes toward perpetual peace, the sequences of nature, the course of history and the plan of providence. Each is rooted in a distinctively modern tradition of thought: Enlightenment science, rational historicism, and Protestant theology. Together, they cohere within a metaphysics of human progress.[107] While Kant's project depends on the convergence of these trajectories, incongruities prompt reservations about the sufficiency of each direction and the eventual stability of their convergence.

Kant's purpose is to foster confidence in prospects for human improvement. Though the empirical possibility of positive change is not necessary to make the pursuit of peace morally obligatory, there is anxiety that witnessing an "empty activity where good and evil continually interchange moving forward and backward would mean that the whole interplay of members of our species on earth must be seen as pure farce that can have no greater worth in the eyes of reason than those of the other animal species" (*CF*, 180; cf. *UH*, 30, 35, 39). Oddly, this concern about the prospect of meaninglessness resembles Schmitt's. Yet while Schmitt discovers resources for creating meaning in the possibility of war, Kant fears that endless repetitions of conflict will reinforce the nihilistic (or "Abderitic"[108]) conclusion that attempts to make things better are simply pointless.[109]

Responses to needs for reassurance vary in scope and ambition. In *Theory and Practice*, "the anticipation of a better future" is a hope whose "futility cannot be shown to be completely certain," a prospect "not demonstrably impossible" (*TP*, 86–87; cf. *METR*, 173–174; *CPuR*, 473). Comments in *UH, CF*, and *TPP* are more confident.[110] *TPP*'s guarantee is the "mechanism" of natural sequences that stands as an alternative to both providential care and practical agency. "The use of the word nature is the thing to do . . . , in light of the limits of human reason (for in reflecting on the relations of effects to their causes, it must remain within the bounds of possible experience); this is more modest than a phrase connoting a providence of which we can have no cognitive knowledge, and on which we take flight as on Icarus's wings in order to come nearer to the secrets of some unfathomable intention" (120; *UH*,129). Concord arises from nature's hand against the wills of human beings. The pacific influences of republican politics and the spirit of trade are enabled by physical and psychological infrastructures initiated and nourished by conflict. "Nature guarantees perpetual peace by virtue of the mechanisms of human inclinations themselves" (*TPP*, 125).

This recourse to natural (mechanistic) causality inevitably raises questions. How can determinism explain transformative change (*SB*, 51)? A scientific account of human motion focuses only on behaviors "subject to the same mechanism of nature as [those of] the other animal species" (*METR*, 174; *CPuR*, 332, 464–467), seeming to ignore the distinctive capability of humans to act in accordance with their own purposes (*CJ*, 83. 298–301; *SB*, 49–50). In the first sections of *CF*, Kant denies that a predictive science of human society is "discoverable from known laws of nature (as with eclipses of the sun and moon, which can be foretold by natural means)" (*CF*, 177).[111] The only alternative seems some form of prophecy. Yet prophecies cannot be validated by "cognitive knowledge" and history is rife with false prophets. What both determinism and prophecy ignore, however, is human agency. "How is it possible to have history a priori? The answer is that it is possible if the prophet himself makes and organizes the occurrences he predicts" (*CF*, 177). What might be seen as sequences of natural motions and countermotions may need to be reinterpreted as outcomes of historical or cultural practice (*SB*, 50–51).[112] Potentially, this has a critical edge. Kant assails conservative or opportunistic thinkers who retreat to agenda-driven appeals to the way things are, often ignoring or concealing damages inflicted by social practices, "by unjust coercion, by treachery" (*CF*, 178).

However, replacing determined nature with historical practice encounters its own challenges.[113] How can historical agency produce a definite or irreversible end (*SB*, 112–113)? Are the "willful ends" that human beings set for themselves not endlessly revisable? "Reason in a creature is a capability of widening the rules and intentions of the use of its powers (*Kräfte*) far beyond natural instinct, and it knows no limits to its designs" (*UH*, 30). On what basis can a reflective philosophy of history predict progress rather than the reverse? Indeed, how can progress or reversal be distinguished from a neutrally tracked linear change?[114]

Kant's responds by embedding historical agency within providential care. This move has parallels and differences with his projection of teleology's ability to make natural sequences intelligible in light of their outcomes or functions. Within the study of nature, purposes are heuristic and not ontological, "pertain[ing] entirely to the combinations of our concepts and not to the constitution of things" (*CJ*, 68, 255). Consequently, natural teleology regulates, without replacing or transcending, a science of natural causes (*CJ*, 76, 273–274), revealing "how nature must be judged in accordance with the principle of final causes" (*CJ*, 79, 286; 84, 301–303). Its value is shown in the progressive and useful discoveries of a natural science so informed.

Like natural teleology, historical purpose is a human imaginary, not illusion or fantasy but a humanly constructed condition for possibility. While natural teleology and history's purposefulness are not altogether separable in construction or application (*TPP*, 120), the historical imaginary is far more ambitious and controversial.[115] Though the "idea of a [purposive] world history that is in a way guided a priori is [not intended] to revise history as such, whose composition is wholly empirical," it nonetheless offers "a reflection of what a philosophical mind (which must above all be well versed in history) could attempt to do from another perspective" (*UH*, 39), one which proceeds from a cosmopolitan, practical intent.

At times Kant implies that historical purposiveness can be confirmed by experience. Sympathetic responses to the French Revolution are said to prove (*Beweisen*) the presence "of a moral disposition within the human race" (*CF*, 182) and to reinforce the belief that human progress is a reasonable hope.[116] Yet in *TPP*, detecting this moral purpose in history eventually requires the more powerful support of a directing providence.[117] Providential influence cannot be a theoretical discovery, for the existence of God cannot be rationally proven or disproven (*CJ*, 90, 330–331; *CpuR*, 525–531). However, it is pragmatically necessary to posit providential care if the moral aspiration for societal improvement is not to be dismissed as a tragic illusion and societal improvement not to be exposed as fragile and accidental (cf. *CJ*, 87, 313–318; *CPrR*, 128–130). "From a morally practical point of view . . . e.g., the belief that God will compensate for our own deficiencies in justice if only our dispositions are pure, though by means that are wholly inconceivable to us, and that we should not, therefore give up our striving to do good—the concept of a divine *concursus* is entirely fitting and even necessary" (*TPP*, 122, note; cf. *CJ*, 87, 316; 91, 334–335; *CPrR*, 126–130, 132; *CpuR*, 640). The core of this imaginary is not an appreciative confidence validated by useful science but a resilient hope refusing surrender to moral despair (cf. Smith, 2016, 142).

Yet because the historical guidance of providence is grounded in hope, Kant's framework inevitably requires that its influence be dispensable if moral rationality is to be truly autonomous and unconditioned. Just as questions about the existence of God cannot be rationally resolved, moral imperatives compel unconditionally even without God (*CJ*, 87, 316; *CpuR*, 498–499). Kant defends both of these claims through deep epistemological investigations into the powers and limitations of rationality (*CJ*, 89–90, 323–331; *CpuR*, 297–300, 601). However, on the basis of this analysis the cohering role of historical providence dissipates; the relation between nature and history becomes less certain; and the standing of moral agents becomes more problematic and more interesting.

If seemingly permanent patterns of human behavior can be revised by a historical agency knowing no limits to its designs (as in *CF*, 177; *UH*, 29–30; *SB*, 51) and if the guiding influence of providence is a matter of hope, the conclusion that any permanent historical outcome is guaranteed is unjustified. Now, war and peace are not radically alternative destinations for the human species but indeterminate possibilities surrounding human practice.[118] A similar indeterminacy undermines the projects of modern Kantians such as Karl-Otto Apel, Elisabeth Ellis, and Martha Nussbaum. Though they exclude teleological or providential architectonics (Ellis's shedding of "teleological blinders," 2005, 42), confidence in secular progress is undiminished. Apel's revision of Kant (1997, 94–96) replaces a single constitutional imperative with "heterogeneous possibilities," which might extend in frightening as well as inspiring directions. Nussbaum's sense that we can dispense with Kant's providential resource and rely only on ourselves (1997, 42–43; cf. Ellis, 2005, 182) presumes a particular understanding of our situation and a moral confidence in ourselves. Can the Kantian moral narrative be sustained in the presence of ongoing contingency and an autonomy bounded only by what we construct for and expect from ourselves? Does Kant's secular treatment of the possibility of human agency provide the best resource for understanding ourselves as *political* beings responding to dramatically heterogeneous possibilities?

Morality's Aloofness and the Dilemmas of Politics

In *TPP*, practical uncertainties about historical guarantees are ultimately overridden by the moral imperatives of autonomous practical rationality.[119] Kant offers these resources to a moral politician who will limit what she decides, advises, or accepts as public policy according to reason's norms.

However, the introduction of this figure also problematizes how surrounding political circumstances and challenges are engaged by Kantian rationality, implicitly calling for a more expansive characterization of politics, needing a different kind of philosophical attention.

Within *TPP*, the insight that morality has an integrity beyond expedience emerges initially within Kant's critical interpretation of political speeches. Even the most calculating politicians cannot "openly dare to base their politics on the devices of cleverness alone, and consequently they cannot altogether refuse obedience to the concept of public right. . . . Instead, they let this concept enjoy all appropriate honor, even if they also may invent a hundred excuses and deceptions to escape observing it in practice" (*TPP*, 131). This assessment goes beyond Machiavelli's acknowledgments of morality's stubborn cultural persistence in *Prince* 18. Respecting justice does not merely soothe convention; it points to a fundamental reality revealed by political justifications. Even the language of the hypocritical political moralist performatively validates the moral politician's seriousness about justice.[120]

Though stimulated by political critique, however, the force of Kant's morality is ultimately grounded in rational necessities discoverable a priori. This claim is condensed in *TPP*'s *First Appendix*, "act so that you can will that your maxim ought to become a universal law (making the end whatever one wants). Without any doubt [this] principle must take precedence [over the prudential pursuit of ends] because as a principle of right (*Rechtsprinzip*) it has unconditioned necessity (*unbedingte Notwendigkeit*)" (*TPP*, 132; *Gr*, 26). This imperative controls what may be consistently endorsed as public policy once political judgments are universalized, demanding not only a formal argumentative consistency but also a substantive moral consistency that supports the emergence of the kingdom of ends.[121] Policies rooted in "the self seeking inclinations of human beings, which . . . are not grounded on maxims of reason" (*PP*, 134) are exposed as at best nonmoral even though their disputes and aggressions are steps in the species' progress toward pacification.

Morality's imperatives therefore set limits on human practices from a vantage point different from either the natural or the providential. Absent regulative boundaries, the distinctive human capacity to set arbitrary purposes for itself can mislead and endanger. When such purposes respond to external objects of desire or fear, they bespeak contingent fluidity and heteronomous causality (*TP*, 71; *Gr*, 45–46). From this perspective, the damages inflicted by assertive republican communities are not traceable simply to an emerging nationalism that Kant failed to recognize. Instead, they reflect the predictable collective aggressions of regimes attracted by riches and dominion. And though providence's limits and assurances are hopeful, perhaps even practically necessary (*TPP* 122), they cannot be intellectually confirmed. Therefore, rational or autonomous self-direction provides the only firm grounding for moral commitment or restraint, the only true site of human agency (*TP*, 67–68; *CPrR*, 28–32, 95, 109). Since the possibility of acting morally belongs to human beings because of their free rationality, its validity is transhistorical, not requiring the constitutive validation supplied by particular cultural forms (differing from Rawls, 1999, 31–32).

The reasons behind Kant's strictness are located in the deep structure of his moral philosophy, including his contention that questions of happiness are irresolvably subjective (*CPrR*, 20–24, 66–67, 121–122; cf. *CpuR*, 638–9; *Gr* 27–28; *TP*,69; *AnP*, 149–150) and his decisive separations of the rational from the empirical will, autonomy from heteronomy, freedom from constraint (*TPP*, 379; cf. *Gr*, 45–48; *CPR*, 33–33, 94–96; *CpuR*, 312–313, 464–479, 659–660). The rigidity of these divides means that disputes over different possibilities for human happiness, ways of life that would contribute or detract from human well being, are seen as disagreements between varying empirical wills (*CPrR*, 24–25), individually or collectively expressed. The philosopher can intervene only by reiterating the priority of right, insisting that conceptions of happiness be judged regulatively (*CPrR*, 115). Politically, the appropriate response is to devise procedures that manage external conflicts while respecting rights.

Epistemological critiques of this structure have been offered by many others.[122] Here, I suggest that Kant's representation of moral rationality discounts important features of politics and therefore cannot provide the resources needed by the moral politician. This critique is primarily political, though its directions suggest accompanying problems in Kant's epistemology.[123] Insofar as that epistemology aspires to identify transcendental conditions making practical experiences possible and pragmatic descriptions coherent, distorting or incoherent descriptions of practice reflexively compromise attempts to articulate conditions of possibility.[124] Raising such questions goes beyond asking whether Kant's political philosophy accommodates realism (O'Neill, 2015, 210–213) to consider more seriously what political realism involves. And even if Kant's treatment of politics is centered around Ellis's "provisional right" or the prudential recognition of what is needed practically to progress incrementally toward a more completely just state (2005, 70, 86, 110, 150–151), judgments about those politics may be seriously constrained by limits within Kant's own argument. When we confront Kant more directly with politics, we can identify three interrelated political problems marginalized by his framework: the political relevance of the emotions, the influence of ways of life on the quality of choices, and the unpredictable and potentially tragic character of political action.

Rationality and Emotion

When introducing the moral politician in *TPP*'s *First Appendix*, Kant claims to overcome the "conflict (*Misshelligkeit*) between morality and politics (*TPP*, 134). This section follows the *Second Supplement*'s statement that "the maxims of philosophers concerning the conditions of possibility for public peace ought to be consulted by nations armed for war" (126). Though Kant calls the *Second Supplement* a "Secret Article," he admits that giving "secret" advice in a published essay paradoxically makes its contents open (126). At one level, philosophical maxims can remain in some sense secret because a public policy of openness does not expressly privilege philosophical advice. Nonetheless, philosophy's counsel has particular weight because "this class is by nature incapable of sedition and of forming cliques, therefore it cannot be slanderously suspected of propagandizing" (126). Though insisting on the need to open political speech to all (Ellis, 2005, 152), Kant privileges the philosopher's maxims (Garsten, 2006, 86–87, 91).

In one sense, then, the *Second Supplement* points back to the entire essay. Yet because the *First Appendix* explicitly represents the situation of the moral politician, it can be read as this consultation's principal site. Consistent with his reliance on free rationality, Kant's very conception of the moral politician emerges not simply from an engagement with political practice, but as the product of constructive reason. "I can indeed think of a moral politician, one who so interprets the principles of political prudence that they can stand together with morality, but I cannot think (*aber nicht . . . denken*) of a political moralist, one who forges a morality as he finds it beneficial to statesman's advantage" (128). How politics must be shaped according to a respect for right can be conceived without contradiction, while any move to argue for the subordination of right to political advantage would end in making any notion of right absurd (128–129). In a sense, Kant's image of the moral politician is constructed a priori and the agreement of morals and politics according to the priority of right is a premise rather than an outcome of his thinking.

Yet even though the moral politician is conceptually produced by abstract reasoning, this figure's situation is presented in more psychologically and historically complex ways. In *TPP*, Kant follows his condemnation of those whose maxims are instruments for self-advancement by praising the moral politician's heroism. The maxims of reason provide "the whetstone of virtue, whose true courage (according to the principle 'do not give in to evil, but dare to stand against it') in the present case consists not so much in resolutely confronting evils and sacrifices that must be taken on; rather it consists in seeing and overcoming the cunning of an evil principle in ourselves (*bösen Prinzip in uns selbst*), something more dangerous, devious and treacherous that rationalizes all of our transgressions through a justification that speaks of human nature's weakness" (134). This praise builds upon and transforms the earlier recognition of how challenges of war elicit nobility (123; in spite of *CPR*, 158–159). While employing the language of Virgil's *Aeneid* (6.86–95), Kant resituates conflict from the battlefield to the will and recharacterizes enemy, victory and heroism in moral terms, a rational exhortation to peace, not a sybilline prophecy of war.

Yet this esteem for nobility also suggests that the separation of morality from inclination or rationality from emotion cannot be as sharp as Kant's moral theory demands.[125] By recognizing the need to counter despondencies afflicting even the most dutiful (*TPP*, 127–128), Kant gestures toward psychological interactions that embed the emotions in moral practice.[126] Once this possibility is introduced, it is not clear either that emotional influences must be morally irrelevant or derivative or that their trajectory be unidirectional. When Kant separates philanthropy from rational duty (*TPP*, 118), he may underappreciate both the degree to which philanthropy can emerge in light of reason's discoveries and the ways in which respect for right can be deepened by philanthropy. To this extent, we may need to reconsider the infrastructure of Kant's moral psychology.[127] Yet there are political implications as well. By treating philanthropy as an affective response linked to individual particularity, Kant downplays the significance of emotional intersubjectivity,[128] obscuring political resources that a moral politician needs. If she is to respond to the possible emergence of evil principles within, the moral politician must understand the processes through which deeply held emotional attachments can lead either to the rationalization of selfishness or to the flourishing of moral generosity. Can republican institutions and the spirit of trade guarantee a peaceful world without a greater degree of attention to the possibilities and dangers of the continuing emotional attachments that they inevitably foster? While the moral politician may (or may not) be adequately instructed by the philosopher's maxims, she must also depend on a more emotionally grounded rhetoric to communicate with and to influence the practices of her fellow citizens.

Procedures and Purposes

Kant's characterization of political problems is both challenging and limiting. From one perspective, the moral politician's practical task is, while daunting, simply stated. She must respect constraints set by principles of right that impose "an obligation on those having power not to deny or diminish anyone else's rights through either dislike or sympathy" (*TPP*, 133). Proceduralism based on the priority of right refuses to define moral politics by particular outcomes or purposes. "The less . . . conduct depends on a proposed end, be it a physical or a moral advantage, the more conduct will in general harmonize with morality" (*TPP*, 133). One immediately relevant consequence of this position is that Kant's just war theory is far more restrictive than Aquinas's. For Kant, it is difficult to see any war as just other than one fought in defense against aggression or as protection of those threatened by predatory states (*METR*, 168–169). Even here, Kant counsels restraint for fear of partiality or abuse. " 'Let justice rule even though all the rogues in the world would therefore perish' is a sound principle of right that cuts across all the bent paths of cunning and force; only it must not be misunderstood nor, perhaps, be taken as permission simply to press for one's own right with the greatest strength" (*TPP*, 133).[129] While Aquinas justifies some punitive wars (*ST*, II–II, 40. a.1), Kant explicitly forbids them (*TPP*, 109–110; *METR*, 168), envisaging a time when even defensive wars will be unnecessary. The integrity of the moral politician, particularly acting within an international context, is most apparent in what she cannot do. "All the evil that stands in the way of perpetual peace arises from the fact that the political moralist begins where the moral politician rightly stops" (*TPP*, 132).[130]

However, Kant's framework implies that politics involves functions and challenges extending beyond respecting rights, suggesting that the contributions of political theory to politics must do more than map fair procedures. An ambiguous posture toward procedures informs the structure of *TPP* as a whole; the preliminary and definitive articles require (alternative) supplementations (Ellis, 2005, 79, 100–101). Could a focus on procedures be at once too superficial, ignoring the substantive resources on which adequate procedures must depend, and too glib, disregarding political vulnerabilities and risks?[131]

One of TPP's signature statements is that it is possible to create a sustainable political structure "even for a nation of devils as long as they are intelligent" (124). This conclusion sits uneasily with the demand that politics be guided by moral imperatives, not least because a political science focused exclusively on identifying how barriers and incentives influence behavior would treat human beings only as sensuous creatures who can be heteronomously influenced. To the extent that aspirations for domestic political institutions go beyond the prudential creation of security structures for egoists, they may require the educative functions of a political culture and the support of a political rationality that both influences and limits public policy by reflecting on the quality of civic purposes.[132] The citizens of Kant's commercial republic practice virtues and exhibit capacities that characterize them as particular kinds of human beings; the practical emergence of peace depends on certain ways of life. How these are understood, valued, and enhanced by those who share them would seem to constitute one essential concern of the moral politician. Absent the focus on social worthiness, the political structures required by procedural imperatives may differ very little from those managing the interactions of smart devils able to do significant damage. Moreover, to the extent that Kant embraces the priorities of both republicanism and commercialism, he provokes the contributions of a critical intelligence that can judge these sometimes competing cultures. Kant's most important political philosophical predecessor, Rousseau, emphasizes that the way of life encouraged within a republic of energetic citizens differs substantially from that supported by a commercial ethos (*Social Contract*, 3.15).[133]

The moral politician's concern with how shared ways of life are embedded in policy choices is particularly important in contexts of war, where reminders of what one is defending are continually implicated within, even as they are obscured by, the press of seeming necessity. This is not to move closer to Schmitt's contention that the possibility of war preserves cultural meanings but rather to underscore that all occasions for war demand that citizens be more critically attuned to fuller dimensions of meaning that might be otherwise ignored or assumed. Who or what is being fought for? Both a concern for the priority of right inattentive to the goods of different ways of life and the privileging of fair procedures inattentive to questions of substance gives an illusion of settling things while leaving recurring questions unaddressed.[134]

Contingency and Moral Uncertainty

Still, Kant's moral politician is no "despotic moralist" (cf. *TPP*, 129) who ignores circumstances in the pursuit of justice. She must also exercise permissive reason, "for permissions arise only circumstantially, not according to a principle, that is, they arise only in considering specific situations" (*TPP*, 111, note; cf. Ellis, 2005, 80; O'Neill, 2015, 212–213). However, while this comment acknowledges the injustices and imperfections of empirical politics and recognizes that premature or overreactive responses can create more injustice, the moral politician recognizes contingency only to a point.[135] The pulls of circumstance, ranging from attractions of wealth and power to sympathy for the desperate, cannot justify disregarding principles of right. When this distortion is cynical, the political moralist disguises himself as the moral politician (*TPP*, 130). When sincere, citizens or statesmen can fall victim to evil—or at least misguided—principles within themselves, for example, being tempted out of philanthropy to violate the fifth preliminary article's respect for political self-determination.[136] More fundamentally, Kant's perspective implies that the moral politician can successfully direct her practices without compromising the moral character of her decisions (*TPP*, 127; *CPR*, 87–88), making the agent secure in her fulfillment of moral duty (*UH*, 38–39). This is not confidence in a pragmatic success dependent on the contingencies of an uncertain world, but an assurance of moral rationality's ultimate rectitude.[137] While permissive reason counsels moderation and recognizes imperfections, morality's coherence implies that its pursuit cannot be morally tragic (*CPR*, 164–165).[138]

Yet this assurance encounters obstacles in Kant's own treatments of political time and space. *TPP*'s time horizon is in one respect immediate, for moral duties stand as constant imperatives (128). At the same time, the trajectory of history's guarantee stretches indefinitely into the future (120–122, 124–125), and its scope is the human race itself (120). The fluctuating and contestable perspectives of individual political agents or communities are thus supplanted by the immediate imperatives of moral duty and by the ultimate progress of the species, both in a way timeless.[139] Yet Kant needs to explain how the limited vantage point of any single political agent can engage visions of a cosmopolitan and perpetual peace guaranteed only ultimately.[140] In projecting how individual human action-choices may serve species progress, Kant comments on uncertainties and errors, requiring the resources not of moral imperatives but of "trial, practice and instruction" (*UH*, 30). This implies that the moral politician is situated within a condition of partial ignorance where her perspective is confined by immediate historical circumstances, her choices reliant on prudential calculations informed by inclination or need, and her commitments rooted in heroic faith.[141] Within this more clouded vision, however, Kant's distinction between the moral politician and the political moralist seems too binary and reductive to recognize ranges of variation among both political agents and political actions. Within this horizon, the eventual emergence of peace is not guaranteed and the indefinite persistence of war must be continually presumed. A resolute commitment to the priority of right cannot assure the moral politician that she will be protected from the commission of wrongs.

Perpetual Questions

Both Hobbes and Kant envisage conditions under which a peace lasting "as long as justice itself" or "perpetually" is possible. Those aspirations remain historically unfulfilled and it is difficult to see how they could be fully met by adherence to either Hobbesian or Kantian proposals. By stopping at the borders of the nation state, Hobbes's domestic stability is not only incomplete but also potentially threatening, as power supportive of the nation's industry or competitiveness is strategically deployed. In a globalized context, we should be able to see the limits and dangers of political arrangements that are exclusively inward looking and purely expedient. Yet Kant's sketch for a cosmopolitan peace achieved through the intersection of predictable historical trajectories and dutiful moral agency seems equally unsteady. Absent providential care, both natural and historical outcomes are morally indeterminate. In the face of unpredictable practical challenges, Kant's radical divide between the duties of the moral politician and the passions and interests of political moralists paradoxically threatens to deprive statesmen or citizens of resources for judgment when they are most needed.

Here, Hobbes and Kant may both be susceptible to the illusion that the emotions and clashes of political life can be ultimately controlled by science or disciplined by duty. Though each offers representations of politics that complicate their philosophical programs, both of their arguments are compromised by epistemological commitments to proving moral outcomes in ways that are intellectually certain (*Lev*, 5. 21; *CPuR*, 394–395, 607–608, 617–618, 646–647, 668–669). When such promises are unfulfilled, those needing to cope with the challenges of political life are left to face the demoralizing return of endless wars in their own conditions of precarity. These dire prospects are not accidental disturbances within particular historical experiences, but theoretical fissures within the structures of Hobbesian science and Kantian morality. Absent the successful construction and implementation of a Hobbesian science of politics, political society must be a project undertaken "without the help of a very able architect . . . [constructing] a crazy building, such as hardly lasting out [the builders'] own time, [that] must assuredly fall upon the heads of their posterity" (*Lev*, 29.1). If Kant's projection of a moral certainty reinforced by a cohering providence is rejected, human life turns purposeless and vain (*UH*, 30; *SB* 58–59). Science/chaos and rational agency/pointless violence are mutually constituting binaries within Hobbes's and Kant's political theories.

Though this prospect can only be hinted here, Hobbes's and Kant's intellectual descendants face similar challenges. For all of their differences, both rational choice theory and deliberative global democracy aspire to manage the passions and turbulence of political life through institutional designs that are continually frustrated by politics itself. Though rational choice theory is hardly monolithic, its proponents must eventually take one or the other of two unattractive intellectual paths: either relying on one particular and controversial conception of rationality,[142] or characterizing all self-interested behavior as rational.[143] Relying on institutional solutions that can remediate social problems (including the problem of collective violence) by appealing to the calculative rationality of self-interested individuals only works if political phenomena can be reconstructed as rational in light of rational choice's problematic theoretical structures. While clearly distant from rational choice theory, Kantian moral rationality encounters oddly parallel challenges. Rawls's and Habermas's proposals for international democratic governance presume communities of reasonable pluralists (Rawls, 1999, 35, 37) or lifeworlds where differences are respected (Habermas, 1998, 229–230). Political sociology's attention to how such societies function assume their presence. What can political philosophy say when those circumstances are absent (noting, for example, Rawls's—1999, 93 skepticism)?

However, perhaps both approaches suffer from paying too little attention to history, each privileging a stable rationality, scientific or moral, that is timelessly valid. Hobbesian science may depend on the historical establishment of the commonwealth, but science's capacity to prove moral theorems is a permanent human possibility. Though embedded in a historical trajectory, Kantian duty transcends its circumstances; a culturally specific morality is as absurd as a culturally specific religion (*TPP*, 131, note). Yet each of these philosophers also gestures toward a more historically informed understanding of human practice. Hobbes's science of behavior may only explain how men "as they are the matter" of political orders are susceptible to external stimuli, liberating the creative activities of men "as they are the makers and orderers" (*Lev*, 29. 1). Kant's separation of historical freedom from natural necessity (*CF*, 177) and his eventual bracketing of any providential direction of history (*TPP*, 120–121) end by relying on a transformative human agency. How would the frames of reference for political theory be reinterpreted if human historical activity were central?

4 | War Is History

G. W. F. HEGEL, *Phenomenology of Spirit, "Lordship and Bondage"; Lectures on the Philosophy of History; Elements of the Philosophy of Right*

FRIEDRICH NIETZSCHE, *Beyond Good and Evil*

History as Spiritual Activity

Hegel and Nietzsche critically reconstruct Kant's focus on humans as spiritual (*geistliche*) beings (*GR*, 26–27, 34–35, 49; *CPrR*, 5, 27, 29; *CJ*, 49). In acknowledging that both rational autonomy and sensuous or material heteronomy influence practice, Kant effectively offers two perspectives for human science (*GR*, 45; *CPrR*, 6, 21, 98). Hegel and Nietzsche, on the other hand, treat spiritual activity as defining humanness. Hegel's introduction to his *Lectures on the Philosophy of History* (*PhH*) identifies the essence of spirit (*Geist*) as freedom that is conscious of its own presence in the world, forged through its own historically created institutions and socially enabled practices (*PhH*, 20, 22, 42, 66, 74; *Philosophy of Right* (*PhR*), 23, 142, 257–258, 268, 270). This achievement is most fully actualized in the state, "which first presents a content that is not only entirely appropriate to the prose of history, it also generates (*erzeugen*) itself as such" (*PhH*, 50; 64–65; *PhR*, 257–258).[1] This designates not the Prussian state of Hegel's time[2] but the universally significant, though concretely realized, institutions of Western modernity. By contrast, Nietzsche represents spirit—and humanness—through metaphors of struggle and overcoming, contests not only between societies but also within individual psyches (*Beyond Good and Evil*, 260; *Genealogy of Morals*, 2. 24). For him, spirit's most important struggle and most necessary overcoming must be directed against modernity's politics and culture.

On first view, these perspectives repeatedly clash. While Hegel's spiritual activities are rationally differentiated social practices established within an intelligible historical sequence (*PhH*, 13, 82; *PhR*, 141; *Phen*, 808), Nietzsche's are destabilizing discharges that shatter or overcome rather than preserve or retain (*BGE*, 13). Politics is not cleanly embedded within an overarching history but disruptively contested within what Nietzsche will call genealogies. Hegel's spirit eventually achieves its own coherent completion (*PhH*, 82: *PhR*, Preface, 129, 360), whereas Nietzsche's is unendingly restless (*BGE*, 296). Hegel's units of analyses are peoples and nations (*PhH*, 82; cf. 41, 56, 71). Nietzsche's are exemplary individuals who organize their own psychological chaos to revalue values (*Uses and Disadvantages of History for Life*, 10; *BGE*, 203). Hegel eventually moves beyond contingency to a comprehensive vision which "as concerning itself with the true, has to do with the eternal present" (*PhH*, 82; *PhR*, Preface, 23; sec. 360). Nietzsche preserves contingency and accident as resources for combatting threats to energetic freedom. These differences all culminate in divergent representations of philosophy. Comprehending the social totality that makes it possible, Hegel's philosophy is intellectually serene (*PHG*, 808; *PhH*, 457). The continuous overcoming tasked to Nietzsche's philosophers of the future (*BGE*, 42, 43, 44, 203, 205, 212) makes philosophy itself into a certain kind of war (188, 200, 209, 242, 262).

Yet though these perspectives are opposed in many respects, both diminish the problematics of war for political philosophy. By absorbing war within the historical emergence of spirit, Hegel theorizes a politics of rational stability and order. By redirecting metaphors of war toward the psyche, Nietzsche deemphasizes societal aggression in favor of ongoing self-transformation. For both thinkers, political war *is* history in two related senses. First, it is eclipsed not by permanent natural laws or transcendent moral duties but by the activities of human beings situated within or contending against their political cultural horizons (Church, 2012, 3, 23, 56). Second, in spite of frequent references to historical or genealogical violence, political conflict ceases to be a central pragmatic challenge for the highest or deepest forms of philosophy. However, because both thinkers leave spaces for its continuation or re-emergence, war persists as a problem that political philosophy needs to engage, even if its resources for doing so are compromised.

Similar questions beset important statements in contemporary political theory. For those who understand political communities as self-constituting ethical partnerships, reflecting the Hegelian focus on the state as conditioning ethical life (*PhH*, 5; *PhR*, 257), challenges to Hegel's theorizations raise the question of how such communities will deal intellectually with disruptive contingency, a challenge made especially pressing by threats of war. For those who theorize politics as democratic agonistics, politicizing Nietzsche's psychology of will to power, this framework leaves unconsidered the question of how political contestation can differentiate between and set limits upon agonistic practices. Because Hegel and Nietzsche contribute seminally to modern and postmodern efforts to displace traditional metaphysics,[3] their frustrations may initiate challenges to those forms of political thought.

Hegelian Geist as Freedom

Hegel's narrative of freedom's actualization simultaneously elevates and diminishes politics and political theory. The elevation begins with revisions to Kant. While Kant critically scrutinizes politics in light of the moral imperatives discovered by free rationality, Hegel's rational freedom is fully achievable only within the social memberships and ethical intersubjectivities of modernity. *Sittlichkeit* (ethical life) enables *Moralität*.[4] The same institutions condition the emergence of Hegelian philosophy itself. When introducing his philosophical analysis of modern political life in *PhR* Hegel's well-known comment is that philosophy cannot "[issue] instructions on how the world ought to be," appearing to defer completely to politics, broadly understood. It is not simply that fully developed self-consciousness can only be realized in a culture that has constructed its freedom historically. That project has been sufficiently completed to allow, for the first time, its comprehensive philosophical exposition. Philosophy cannot change the world because the spiritual activities of human beings in history have already done so.

Yet this elevation of politics goes only so far and political theory eventually gives way to a transformative philosophical vocabulary. The emergence of rational modernity culminates a sequence of immanent critiques across the cultures comprising fully developed Western consciousness. The social practices constituting this sequence failed to achieve their own ethical purposes because of internal contradictions, pointing to new arrangements surpassing, even while preserving, what was previously in place (*PhH*, 60, 67–68, 81; *PhR*, 342).[5] Yet while this dialectical narrative reveals how spiritual achievements and frustrations have been understood by historical agents, including Western history's philosophers (not just Antigone and Socrates but Sophocles and Plato, not just Robespierre and

Napoleon but Rousseau and Kant), it can only be adequately written by the philosopher able to see spirit's full self-realization. Spirit's actualization is "not to be regarded as a presupposition of our science, but to be taken as an overview of the totality . . . a result that is known to me because I already know the whole" (*PhH*, 13). While Hegel's historical presentation is both embedded and synoptic, ultimately synopticism prevails.[6] This overview eventually absorbs theological aspirations, rejecting Kant's caution (*CJ*, 90, 327; *CpuR*, 525–531) against attempting to resolve the question of God's existence rationally (*PhH*, 18–19). The *Phenomenology* traces how developed consciousness conceptualizes religious expressions which have begun imagistically; the *Lectures* claim to have comprehended and justified God's presence in the world (*PhH*, 457).

Consequently, the vocabulary of Hegel's philosophical narrative supersedes and transforms those of any situated historical agents. This separation holds regardless of how actualized *Geist* is interpreted. For Charles Taylor (1979, 23), Hegelian spirit is a cosmic subject existing beyond culturally limited forms of subjectivity; Terry Pinkard (1994, 264–265), Robert Pippin (1989, 39, 147, 168; 2008, 220, 239), and Robert Williams (1997, 102) treat actualized *Geist* as the socialized structure of self-consciousness that allows human beings to function epistemically and pragmatically.[7] Either way, however, Hegel's philosophical narrative departs significantly from how even the most modern nonphilosophical agents understand themselves. Pinkard (1994, 338–339) hypothesizes that "future Hegelian philosophers" might conclude that "the institutions and practices developed by the European community in the postrevolutionary era did not fully realize the norm of freedom," inviting appreciation of the contributions of non-Western cultures to freedom's actualization. Yet such advances would still need to be articulated through Hegel's philosophical categories. What consciousness thinks it is doing is interpreted as something different from what Hegel's philosopher knows it is doing (and has done) and the pragmatic problems confronted by situated political actors are eventually recast as moments in the development or extension of objective freedom (*PhH*, 28, 30, 33: *PhR*, 268).[8]

Experiences of political war and peace are situated within this narrative. Though its historical movements may be warlike and destructive (*PhH*, 256; *Phen*, 187; cf. Rosen, 1974, 136, n18), spirit's mature activity is orderly and rational (*PhH*, 82). Practices and languages of war are partial or surface intervals within a deeper spiritual progression toward freedom. I will argue, however, that Hegel's treatment of war—and the courage that war demands—reveal the limits of synopticism as against the persistent challenges of particular embeddedness. I develop this claim through sequential and necessarily selective readings of portions of three works: the lordship and bondage narrative of the *Phenomenology*, the treatment of Greek culture in the *Lectures*, and the waging of war by an "estate of courage" in the *Philosophy of Right*. The lordship/bondage narrative projects the need to move beyond warlike recklessness in the name of spiritual maturity. However, the historical and political philosophies of the *Lectures* and *PhR* challenge this prospect, reintroducing an attention to war—and politics— that Hegel's philosophical framework cannot fully accommodate.

Spirit's Overcoming of Spiritedness: Lord and Bondsman

The lord/bondsman narrative, chapter 4 of the *Phenomenology*, remains controversial. Hegel's purpose is to represent human consciousness' experiences as it comes to self-knowledge as wisdom and self-determination as freedom; the lord/bondsman struggle images the primordial experience of intersubjectivity. Consciousness cannot recognize itself as free simply by confronting and consuming external objects. This would mean dependence on contingent influences, identity only a network of sensuous desires (*Phen*, 175), what Pippin calls mere sunkenness in life.[9] To recognize itself as an autonomous agent whose activities have noncontingent, nondependent, and spiritually free significance, consciousness must be recognized as such by another consciousness. This recognition cannot occur simply through strategic cooperation where partners treat one another as means for achieving practical objectives. Instead, self-conscious autonomy requires recognition of the self as free by another consciousness similarly recognized, true mutuality (*Phen*, 177; cf. Williams, 1997, 27, 60, 81–83; Cortella, 2015, 151; Pippin, 2008, 190. 198). However, these two consciousnesses do not interact peacefully. To have its own freedom recognized by another who is equally free, each consciousness must show "that it is not attached to any determinate existence, not to the individuality common to existence generally, that it is not attached to life" (187). This disregard for (mere) survival leads to a life and death struggle (*Kampf auf Leben und Tod*) that is eventually resolved by one party's surrender to the other and the establishment of a structured relationship of lordship (*Herrschaft*) and bondage (*Knechtschaft*) (189). However this narrative is read, it offers a good starting place for interpreting Hegel's understanding of the significance of war.

But how *should* the narrative be read? Alexandre Kojeve's (1969, 43–44; 56–57) well-known claim that this primordial conflict anticipates the political struggles of the West is too single mindedly political, disconnecting chapter 4 from the *Phenomenology*'s earlier representations of how consciousness experiences itself.[10] On the other hand, John McDowell's (2006, 43–45) epistemic reading, emphasizing different moments of development within a single consciousness, threatens to eliminate sociality and to treat the struggle's life and death character as an overwrought metaphor.[11] Both the insights and the incompletenesses of these readings recommend that the social narrative should be neither hyperpoliticized nor discounted.[12] Moreover, while Hegel does not provide "any account of the specific institutions that would provide the reciprocal recognition that arises" (Pippin, 1989, 155; cf. Williams, 1997, 49), interpretations of his story are not politically neutral. Kojeve may be the most explicit (1969, 23, 51–52), but his critics have their own political edges. H. S. Harris (1997, 351–353) interprets the conflict as revealing competitions between two assertions of pure self-will. Pippin (2011, 52, 77) identifies a dispute over normative authority where there are no established standards for judgment. Anton Barba-Kay (2017, 54) diagnoses a display of commitments ready, if necessary, to sacrifice life. Patchen Markell (2003, 108) traces how the dynamics of the conflict reveal the need to acknowledge human plurality and the consequences of failing to do so. While all insist that the struggle presumes no explicit social context, they seem to offer alternative political readings, rather than alternatives to them.[13] Harris sees pure willfulness spiritualized in a Greek warrior culture valorizing honor, eventually challenged by a Socratic narrative of education wherein a different kind of struggle leads to alternative recognitions (1997, 345, 348).[14] Pippin's affirmation of normative autonomy is most fully at home within a society structured by the moral and political priorities of deliberative democracy.[15] Barba-Kay represents the forceful commitments of the competing consciousnesses as revising Habermas's communicatively grounded forceless force of the stronger argument.[16] Markell's emphasis on the inescapability of plurality (2003, 64, 107, 113) gestures toward the praxis of Hannah Arendt.

Taking the political implications seriously, we might compare Hegel's narrative with Hobbes's image of the transition from nature to commonwealth. In validating a struggle for *recognition* as central to aspirations for freedom, Hegel rejects Hobbes's dismissal of the value of the love of honor. Yet the honorable risk of death cannot simply be unyielding. *Mutual recognition implies mutual survival* (*Phen*, 188). And though the lord's victory appears to redeem his contempt for life, the bondsman's surrender supports Hobbes's insight that fear is the condition for politics (*Leviathan*, 13.14).[17] Moreover, while Hobbes's narrative offers closure (*Leviathan*, 29.1), Hegel's is unstable. At the struggle's end, the parties stand not as Hobbesian equals before the fear of death but as radical unequals within a power structure that resembles not politicality but despotism.[18] However, this structure of domination is eventually undercut by the activities of both parties and the relationship eventually becomes the opposite of that originally established (*Phen*, 192–193). Though seeking free recognition, the victorious lord is acknowledged only by a dependent consciousness submitting out of fear and his experience of superiority is limited to material gratifications produced by another (190). By contrast, the bondsman's oppression initiates his progress toward freedom. The deep fear underlying his submission disconnects him from all material attractions beyond life itself, eventually becoming the wellspring of free subjectivity expressed through the continuous negations or transformations resulting from his active work (194–196). As producer of the goods consumed by the lord, he is both forced and enabled to objectify his activity in the world by shaping the things of nature for another's use (196). Conversely, the nobility of the lord's risk ceases with victory; he cannot regain free recognition through a renewed struggle that would be undone by the same internal contradictions, escapable only through violent death. While the narrative may initially ennoble spiritedness (Berns, 1984, 336; Kalkavage, 2007, 117), its *thymos* must eventually be subsumed within a society achieved by a perfected *Geist*.

This only begins the *Phenomenology's* narrative of the emergence of rational consciousness within modernity; the bondsman's liberating work is not in itself the actualization of freedom (196).[19] Yet even provisionally, the story initiates a developing series of political and cultural changes. One reason why the original encounter must be a life and death struggle is that there are no resources enabling mutual recognition on other terms.[20] Constructing those resources—not simply devising security structures for cooperating egoists—is the most important task confronting humans as historical agents. As these changes progress, partners interact under conditions of a more equal freedom, structured and mediated through modern political and social forms. Both conflict and spiritedness are subsumed and contextualized by structures of peace and the spiritual activities that they enable.[21]

Eventually, this subordination transforms how Western culture synoptically understands itself, first within consciousness's imagistic construction of religion (*Phen*, chapter 7) and then in religion's conceptual transformation into an absolute wisdom (chapter 8) that exists alongside, even as it outshines, political cultural understandings within the actualized state.[22] The end of the *Phenomenology* sketches the philosophical perspective that oversees the *Lectures* and the *Philosophy of Right*, a projection implied in the *Phenomenology*'s final section. "The realm of spirit (*das Geisterreich*) which forms (*gebildet*) itself in this way in existence (*Dasein*) constitutes a sequence wherein one [form of spirit] superseded another and each assumed the empire of the world (*das Reich der Welt*) from the one that had gone before. Their goal is the disclosure of depth and this is the absolute concept (*der absolute Begriff*)" (*Phen*, 808). Philosophical completeness and the actualization of human freedom within the institutions of modernity coincide. Yet complicating disconnects persist between how this spiritual narrative is understood by philosophy and how it is established by political agency. In a way, this judgment resembles Markell's reading of the persistence and "impropriety" of action within Hegel's phenomenological narrative (2003, 92–94), but I want to suggest that Hegel's story of modernity takes a different and more unsettled direction when it recognizes the continued significance of war.

Spirit and War in History: The Overcoming and the Persistence of the Greeks

The subordination of war to peace in the lord/bondsman narrative seems extended in Hegel's broader account of the actualization of spirit across historical cultures.[23] According to the *Lectures*,[24] while spirit's progressive self-actualization must be understood philosophically, its political dynamics are violent cultural conflicts (*PhH*, 22, 25–26). "A people is ethical (*sittlich*), virtuous, strong, insofar as it brings forth that which it wills, and defends what it accomplishes against external force (*äussere Gewalt*) in its work (*Arbeit*) of objectifying itself" (*PhH*, 78). Effective political assertion does not simply reap the Machiavellian rewards of riches and dominion; it constructs spiritual/cultural identities. While this claim seems disturbingly close to Schmitt's, Hegel reverses the byplay between conflict and meaning, seeing wars as meaningful not because of their existential political intensity but because of their deeper civilizational, therefore rational, outcomes. Recalling Kant, Hegel worries that "when we look upon this spectacle of the passions and at all that arises from their violence, seeing the unreason that follows not only from them but also, perhaps especially, from [those things done] out of good intentions . . . we can only be filled with sorrow over all of this transitoriness. . . we might well end up with a sense of moral grief, with the indignation of our good spirit" (*PhH*, 23–24; 76). His response is neither a faith based appeal to supervisory providence (*PhH*, 16, 27, 39; *PhR*, 343) nor a tragic resignation to the impotence of reason (*PhH*, 24). Instead, he discloses how "the events that have produced such a picture for our distressed feelings and our thoughtful reflection, at once also establish a field, where we might see [in suffering] only the means for that which we claim is . . . the true result of world history. . . . containing the essential determinations for answering the questions arising from the preceding picture [of misery]" (*PhH*, 24; 75–76).

This is different from Machiavelli's excusing violence for its politically constructive results (*Disc*, 1.9). While Machiavelli never deviates from engaging politics on (his version of) its own terms and never flinches from seeing its harshness for what it is (*Disc*, 1.26), Hegel interprets such historical bloodlettings as surface events whose deeper significance is discovered by philosophy (*PhH*, 28, 30, 40, 71). "Philosophy has only to do with the glory of the idea, which mirrors itself in world history. . . .its interest is to recognize the ongoing development of the idea as it makes itself real; and this to be sure is the idea of freedom, which [is real] only as consciousness of freedom" (*PhH*, 457). Absorption in history's wars may signal an intellectual immaturity that sees only local histories, not world history (*PhH*, 71). And any political science theorizing war's sequential causes and consequences falls far short of philosophical wisdom, "which concerns itself with the true . . . with what is eternally present" (*PhH*, 82: *Phen*, 679).

Yet Hegel's narratives continue to recognize the complexities of human conflicts as they are both encountered on the surface and theorized in their depth. The stubborn resiliencies of particular wars and individual voices within this universal narrative implicitly question whether the human experience of war can be overcome by spiritual maturity or conceptualized by synoptic philosophy (*PhH*, 13). Guided by Steven Smith's claim (1989, 162) that Hegel sees war as coeval with politics, war/politics poses a series of ongoing challenges that may call for a different kind of philosophy than that which Hegel offers. Persisting surface and depth complexities emerge within the interpretation of classical Greek culture (*die griechischen Welt*).

Commentators note Greece's distinctive place within Hegel's framework. While this attention may reflect the classical idealizations of early nineteenth-century German scholarship (Shklar, 1976, 74), Greek ethical life (*Sittlichkeit*) plays a more complicated role within Hegel's narrative of spirit's progression to freedom. "Among the Greeks we feel ourselves immediately at home (*sogleich heimatlich*), for we are in the region of spirit . . . so that the actual coming forth, the true rebirth of spirit must be sought in Greece first" (*PhH*, 223). In both the *Phenomenology* and the *Lectures*, the self-interpretation of the Greek *polis* is represented as a cohesive context for public morality. "An Athenian citizen did what was fitting for him as it were by instinct" (*PhH*, 42). Hegel will eventually challenge this feeling of being immediately at home and suggest that the Greek self-interpretation was self-deceptive. Yet while Greece's *Sittlichkeit* was not sustainable on its own terms, its central cultural functions have been preserved and elevated within modernity where individual choice and rational autonomy are actualized in the constitutional state's ethical life (*PhH*, 77–78; *PhR*, 70).[25]

In the *Lectures*, Hegel introduces Greece by noting its youthful energy, a dynamism so vibrant that it outshone any definite goals and valorized the transformative negation that lay at the heart of spirit's actualization. Still, youthfulness unconstrained by defining projects falls short of adulthood, where man "lives in the service [or working] (*Arbeit*) of an objective goal (*eines objektiven Zwecks*)" (*PhH*, 223). For all its energy, Greek culture was incomplete (*PhH*, 238–239). Its journey into maturity may parallel the overcoming of spiritedness by spirit that provisionally closes the lord/bondsman narrative (*Phen*, 196).

This youthfulness was also aggressive; the flourishing of Greece's culture was framed temporally by the exploits of the young warriors, Achilles and Alexander (*PhH*, 223–224, 273). Its spiritual achievements were therefore embodied in its wars. Greek freedom's primordial origin is represented by the Greeks themselves as a spiritual victory over nature through myths of the gods' war (*der Götterkreig*), where the Olympians defeated the Titans (*PhH*, 244–245, cf. 234–236; *Phen*, 707). Though Greece's wars were initiated (like most) for particular objectives (*PhH*, 223–224, 256, 277), their contributions to spirit's progress were of universal significance. Commenting on the victories over Persia, "it is indisputable that greater battles have been fought, but [these] . . . are world historical victories; they were the salvation of culture and spiritual vigor, and they took away the power of the Asiatic principle" (*PhH*, 257). Even the corruption contributing to the catastrophic Peloponnesian War was uniquely spiritual. "The principle of corruption (*Verderbens*) displayed itself first in the . . . war of the states of Greece with each other, and the struggle (*Kampfe*) of factions within the cities. Greek ethical life (*Sittlichkeit*) had made Hellas incapable of constructing one common state. . . . A general outbreak of enmities (*Feindseligkeiten*) ended finally in the Peloponnesian War" (*PhH*, 265). Therefore, this political collapse was not produced simply by clashes over interest or influence, but by deeper fissures between the Greece's two spiritual pinnacles. "So stand the two states, Athens and Sparta, against one another. The morality of one [demands] a rigid orientation to the state; in the other one finds a similar ethical relation but with a cultivated (*ausgebildetem*) consciousness and boundless activity in bringing forth the beautiful and also the true" (*PhH*, 264; 258).

Consequently, Greece's fall was not simply a wrenching instance of noble ethical life brutally crushed by external forces. It was instead self-inflicted as cultural contradictions called for historical overcoming by spirit's own negative energy.[26] In the *Lectures*, the collapse of Greek *Sittlichkeit* was not decisively marked by Athens' defeat in the Peloponnesian War (by a Sparta that was in many ways inferior—*PhH* 262–264, 265–266, 271) but by the cultural erosion of civic virtue at the hands of an individuality that Athens itself fostered (*PhH*, 226, 242, 246, 250–253, 265). The sophists of the fifth century demanded proof and justification for everything, undermining the influence of habitual obligations; Socrates insisted on grounding right action in the examined life, speaking in the name of "spirit in its depth and truthfulness" (*PhH*, 269; cf. 251, 260). Still, both projects disintegrated "fatherland and ethics (*Vaterland und Sitte*)" (*PhH*, 270, 252–253, 269). Greek *Sittlichkeit* stimulated an energy and reflection (*PhH*, 260–261) that undercut the devotional virtue it cherished (*PhH*, 252, 267).

A parallel examination of Greece's ethical instability is offered in chapter 6, Part A of the *Phenomenology*. The text offers Hegel's well-known interpretation of Sophocles's *Antigone*, tracing how Creon's and Antigone's dispute over burial rites for Polyneices drew the Greek city's (here, Thebes') equally essential human and divine laws into a conflict ending in the destruction of both sides (*Phen*, 471). I will not add anything to these numerous studies here. Instead, I emphasize the dialectical representations of Greece's wars that frame this portion of the *Phenomenology*. In *Phen* 455 (cf. 450–451) war is introduced as the instrument government (*die Regierung*) uses to pry individuals away from familial attachments in the name of community. War "repels the tendency to fall away from ethical life (*aus dem sittlichen*) . . . and preserves and raises conscious self into freedom and its own power. The [seemingly] negative essence shows itself as the real power of the community (*die eigentliche Macht des Gemeinwesens*) and the strength of its preservation."[27] Yet as the narrative plays out, war's dynamics are less controllable and the social categories less clear.

Nearing the end of the *Antigone* interpretation, Paragraph 473 notes that the deaths (of Eteocles, Thebes' ruler, and Polyneices, his exiled brother) creating the tragedy's burial dispute originated not from a stable government's coercive effort to reinforce civic community but from a politically disruptive familial strife with rule over the city as its prize. The "natural accident" of there being two brothers, one older, one younger, challenged community institutions that both demanded unified rule and rejected birth order as a relevant criterion for assigning political authority. Impressions that the confrontation between Creon and Antigone was caused by a political incursion into attachments that were somehow prepolitical are misleading. This family became civically dangerous not because of its cloistered privateness but because of the expansion of a brothers' war into the city.[28] Paragraph 455's separation of government from family, public from private, may represent how these categories are (mistakenly) understood by those in power. They may be singularly and exclusively accepted by Creon and Antigone (*Phen*, 469–471), but they have already been blurred and disrupted by fraternal competition.[29]

At the conclusion of the section, the narrative moves (*Phen*, 475) away from archaic Thebes' political implosion to diagnose the more widespread fracturing of classical Greece. By demanding that its young men leave their families to fight, the city did not simply trigger a conservative familial outrage. Instead it violently unsettled the character of both family and *polis*, eventually constructing a politically aggressive individuality that subverted public service into "a possession and ornament of the family" and laid the groundwork for the historical overcoming of the *polis* itself. Acutely linking the *Phenomenology* with Aeschylus's *Seven Against Thebes*, Markell (2003, 115–117) argues that Hegel blames this civic unravelling on the intrigues of "womankind" set against the universally significant "manhood (*die Mannlichkeit*) of the community" (*Phen*, 475). Yet as Jocelyn Hoy observes (2009, 187), the *Phenomenology* represents *both* masculine and feminine political roles as cultural constructions, polemically driven and dialectically fluid. In attempting to secure its own authority, the community "generates for itself what it suppresses and what is equally essential to it, its internal enemy (*Sein inneren Feind*) that is womankind in general." The woman is not simply resolute defender of the sacred family but aggressive advocate for youthful power. The *Lectures*' signature Greek identity of youthful aggression now seems traceable to influences of the politicized woman. Further instabilities follow within both family and city. Family relations become politically structured. "The power of youth (*die Kraft der Jugend*) is valued over all, the son as lord (*Herrn*) of the mother who bore him, the brother as one in whom the sister has a man as her equal (*als ihresgleichen*), the youth as one through whom the daughter . . . achieves the joy and dignity of wifehood" (comparing with 456–457). And because the Greek city can only act as an individuality when it is "outwardly self-assertive" (475), it must use the aggressive individualities that it has tried to suborn as weapons. Because of his essential role in the wars that "preserve the whole, the brave youth . . . now comes to his day and to his valorization (*das Geltende*)." Yet this valorizing is no cooptation of youthful energy by civic power; it signals civic dependence on the turbulent energies of unreliable saviors (Alcibiades?). Vulnerable to contingencies of strength and luck, Greece eventually collapses when faced with Rome, "a nation out of which emerges a higher spirit" (*höhere Geist-PhH*, 224). The war intended to reinforce the Greek city's cohesion and independence first escapes the community's control and then dissolves and overwhelms it. If the most universal aspirations of Greek *Sittlichkeit* are retained and elevated within modernity, we should expect more rationally stable societies that wage controlled and limited wars, exposing the history of Greece's wars as ephemeral (childish, not youthful) within *Geist*'s self-actualization.[30]

But what if the importance of the Greeks, including their wars, persists in other ways, complicating Hegel's synopticism by underscoring particularities not so easily absorbed into universality? In light of Hegel's insistence that the "rightness of world spirit overcomes all particular claims to right" (*PhH*, 40), this Greek persistence would underscore—if nothing else—how much of Hegel's historical narrative must be forgotten if his philosophical history is to be accepted, prompting questions about the completeness of that synopsis and the dominance of its voice. At least two relevant particularities within Hegel's Greek narrative are notable; the differentiation among the wars of antiquity and the treatment of individuals (not simply individuality) within the representation of classical Athens.

Differences across antiquity's wars reveal cultural textures eventually flattened by the violent, though ultimately progressive, emergence of historical freedom. First, there are the striking differences between Greece and Rome. Despite its allegedly higher spiritual character, Roman politics and culture were dramatically inferior to the Greek *polis* and its *politeia* in virtually every respect. Taking only one example, instead of tragedies and comedies, Roman cultural entertainment saw "the taste for the baiting of beasts and human beings [become] particularly keen" (*PhH*, 94).[31] Seen on their own, Rome's wars did not signal freedom's spiritual advance but spread domination (*Herrschaft* as predatory lordship) ever further, ending in a despotism whose brutality became fully clear only with its overthrow (*PhH*, 251, 279, 281–282). Thus, Hegel's history is no crude map of linear progress and readers may further appreciate why the Greeks were special. Yet he eventually supersedes both ancient cultures within his more elevated theorization of spirit's development, equating them as states where only some were free (*PhH*, 22), thus implying that the most important dimension of spirit's actualization of freedom is a scope mapped universally rather than a content to be interpreted particularly. However, this generalized verdict is less evidence for than outcome of the alleged knowledge of the whole that allows Hegel to write his completed history. Read more locally (through Markell's "diagnostics"), Hegel's cultural interpretations imply that Greece's differences from Rome should matter significantly to a history of spirit, potentially disrupting the synopticism that collapses them. Perhaps the experiences of the Greeks display less the permanence of "the very same course, we can say once and for all, we will always encounter in the life of every world historical people" (*PhH*, 224) than the persistence of continued challenges to historical resolution and (Hegelian) philosophical closure.

War's particularities also complicate Hegel's praise of Greece's two spiritual pillars. Athens follows its liberation of the Greeks from Persia with a war of conquest (*Erberungskriege*) against other *poleis* (*PhH*, 258). The edifying strictness of Spartan morality stands alongside ongoing internal wars against the subjugated helots (*PhH*, 262). Such wars disarrange cultural narratives aiming to inspire, starting with those offered by Thucydides (Hegel's "original historian") as the two paradigmatic Greek self-understandings, that of Athens' Pericles who praises his city as a brilliant achievement whose deeds will live in eternal memory (2.35–46; 2.64) and that of Sparta's Archidamus who reveres his community's enduring culture of deferential obedience (1. 80–85). How might these disruptions affect Hegel's aspiration to see through the conflicts of Athens and Sparta to "show what each would be in itself as a necessary and worthy form (*notwendige wurdige Gestalt*) of the Greek spirit" (*PhH*, 258)? Athenian aggression against fellow Greeks is a darker side to Periclean energy; domestic political violence against the helots is the underworld of Spartan discipline. Hegel's interpretive history reminds us of these disruptions even as his synoptic history insists that we ultimately ignore them.

How war destabilizes cultural narratives is a concern for some of Hegel's most remarkable Athenian individuals. The introduction to his philosophical history claims that its individuals are communities (*PhH*, 16). "The particular is mostly too slight [when compared] against the universal; individuals are sacrificed and abandoned" (*PhH*, 35). Yet the figures emerging within the construction and erosion of Greek culture present a more complicating picture of both individual and cultural variations.

On its own, Greek *Sittlichkeit* interpreted its culture and its citizens' individualities as coconstitutive, functioning within a horizon where "maturing spirit [first] makes itself the content of its willing and its knowledge; but in such a way that state, family, right [law], religion, are likewise objects (*Zwecke*) for individuality, and [yet] this is individuality only through such aims" (*PhH*, 223; 260; *Phen*, 447). Greek individuality was constructed within, not simply secured or enlisted by, culture's spiritual activity. Greek cultural institutions and practices were established through, not organically prior to, individual action.[32] Yet these self-understandings were the self-misunderstandings of a flawed consciousness that interpreted its laws as immediately compelling (*Phen*, 476), recognizing no need or prospect for rational acknowledgment or criticism. In tracing the disintegration of this illusory solidarity (*PhH*, 253, 268–269), the *Lectures* seem to confirm the *Phenomenology*'s representation of Greek individuality as destructive, redeemable only retrospectively within the achievements of modernity (*PhH*, 442–444).

However, Hegel's more granular representation of Athens' individuals is intriguingly richer, making us linger over what he claims to see beyond. In commenting on the uniqueness of the Greeks in the *Lectures'* introduction, he notes that "if we want to arrive at a general representation and thought of what the Greeks had been, we shall find it in Sophocles and Aristophanes, in Thucydides and Plato. In these individuals, the Greek spirit has established itself in representation (*Vorstellung*) and thought (*Gedanke*)" (*PhH*, 79–80; 260–261). Here, the historical trajectory of spirit does not confer significance on individuals; instead, notable individuals etch cultural character. The Greek etching is contested. At one point, Hegel embraces political energy as its most estimable individual expression. It was the statesman and general Pericles, "in whom Athens' highest point of brilliance (*der grosse Glanzpunkt*) [resided]" (*PhH*, 254, 261). Within an expansive paraphrase of Thucydides's rendition (2. 39) of Pericles's funeral oratory—claiming that "we [Athenians] love wisdom without softness (*philosophoumen aneu malakias*)"—Hegel adds parenthetically "for when men dwell on thoughts (*Gedanken*), they distance themselves from practice, from activities [done] for the public, from the common [good]" (*PhH*, 261). In one sense, this endorsement anticipates the eventual valorization of those world historical individuals who are both drivers of change and instruments of reason's craft (*PhH*, 35, 71–72). Yet the Athenians distinguished in representation and thought, rather than in politics or war, offer more critical judgments on Periclean Athens, including its wars. Thucydides's own treatment of Pericles goes beyond his representation of the funeral oration. In two different explanations of why the Peloponnesian war is worthy of being spoken about (*axiologōtaton*), Thucydides points initially (1.1) to its motion and energy, criteria that might be called Periclean (2.41–44, 64). Yet his second statement (in 1.23) reveals unprecedented violence and pain. "For never had there been so many cities captured or left desolate, some by barbarians and others by the Hellenes as the fought each other . . . nor were there so many men exiled or slaughtered, both in the war itself and because of *stasis*." While no ironic deconstruction of Periclean energy, this recognition of the war's misery is as important as any appreciation of Athenian achievement.[33]

The presence of competing expressions of individuality within a surrounding Athenian *Sittlichkeit* complicates narratives of cultural cohesion or corruption. The tragedies of Aeschylus and Sophocles were performed in a seemingly healthy moral environment displaced by the later corruption that infected the works of Euripides (*PhH*, 260). Yet this judgment is surely premature (immediate, suspect). In Hegel's reading, Sophocles's *Antigone* represents Greek ethical life (in archaic Thebes but for a classical Athenian audience—Zeitlin, 2009, 154–155) as already disturbed by the contradictory demands of consciousness' human and divine laws. And Aristophanes's comedies "preserve the entire political seriousness of his people at the time when it was being corrupted . . . with a view to his country's well being" (*PhH*, 261, 271; *Phen*, 744–747). What might superficially seem to be ridicule may have been cultural therapy.[34]

The complications posed to Hegel's narrative by Athens' individuals are sharpest in the activities of its most unusual figure. Allegedly alone among the Athenians, Socrates refused initiation in the Eleusinian mysteries; "he knew well that science and art do not come forth out of mysteries" (*PhH*, 238, 247). This refusal begins another fatal Greek confrontation, between the city's ethos and an alternative vision of the best human life. "It is in Socrates, for whom, at the beginning of the Peloponnesian War, the principle of individuality, the absolute independence of thought, achieved its free expression. He taught that a human being (*Mensch*) had to find and to recognize in himself what the right and the good are, and that the right and the good [hold] universally by nature" (*PhH*, 269; *Phen*, 712). Because Socrates's negative discourses stood "as revolutionary against the

Athenian state" (*PhH*, 270), he was executed as its "greatest enemy" with "the highest degree of justice" that was also inseparable from the "highest degree of tragedy." Socrates was condemned for a corruption rooted in the city itself, contradictions remediable only through the integrating structures and meanings of modernity.

Alternative readings of Socrates's practice have been offered by commentators too numerous to name. Yet even on its own, Hegel's representation is more puzzling than intended. From one perspective, Socrates's challenge to Athenian morality is one expression of a more general cultural disruption. Yet Socrates's challenge is strange,[35] for he does not argue for sovereign individuality in the name of either epistemic subjectivity or pragmatic self-advancement, the overlapping agendas of the sophists and the politicians. He insists that cultural standards be subjected to the critique of thought or *logos*.[36] Such a critical *logos* may be initiated by Thucydides's conflicting assessments of the Peloponnesian war's significance or by the opposing ethical commitments represented in *Antigone*.[37] However, Socrates's unconventional exploration of "the right and the good" is, in provocative ways, often a defense of conventional justice.[38] Socratic practice may not expose the fatal contradictions of Greek culture as much as represent a set of dilemmas always accompanying the actual practice of ethical life.

War's Contradictions in the Rational Society

Hegel's fullest theorization of modern political structures is offered in the *Philosophy of Right* where he continues the phenomenological and historical investigations of how war relates to the maturation of spirit.[39] On first view, war has a limited place within the foreign policy of the rational state and spiritedness is transformed into institutional courage.[40] Yet even here, persisting wars challenge the completeness of Hegel's philosophy.

PhR argues that objective ideas of right and subjective inclinations toward freedom and morality are integrated within modern constitutionalism's rational self-governance. "The state is the world that spirit has made (*hat gemacht*) for itself" (*PhR*, 272). Hegel hints this arrangement in the *Lectures*, anticipating political relations far more advanced than the primordial and unstable lord–bondsman dynamic. A state constitution (*Staatsverfassung*) structures differences between those commanding (*Befehlen*) and those obeying (*Gehorchen*). He imagines the objection that "obedience . . . seems not to be in accordance with freedom, and those commanding appear to do that very thing which opposes the concept of freedom, which is the foundation (*Grundlage*) of states" (*PhH*, 46). Responding, he shifts terms from command and obedience to governing and governance (*Regierenden und Regierten*). Mutuality among citizens is achieved through the mediation of differentiated social and administrative structures that are considered more fully in *PhR*. "The constitution is essentially a system of mediation (*Vermittlung*)" (*PhR*, 302), integrating family, civil society, and state (*PhR*, 258, 261–265).[41]

On first view, this perspective vaguely resembles Aristotle's understanding of the *polis* as a partnership of ruling and being ruled among equals (*Politics*, 3.4).[42] However, Hegel's governance emphasizes administrative performance and civil regulation (the work of estates—*die Stande*—and police—*die Polizei*)[43] rather than the civic activities of ruling and judging.[44] Explicitly political functions belong to a general estate (*der allgemeine Stand*) of civil servants acting within the constitutional order (*PhR*, 297).[45] This framework challenges the adequacy of Lockean or classical liberalism, a "view of the state according to which its sole function is to protect the life, property and capricious will (*der Willkür*)[46] of everyone . . . merely as an arrangement (*Veranstaltung*) with a view to necessity" (*PhR*, 270).[47] And while this state needs citizen loyalty— otherwise, the constitution "has no meaning and no worth" (*PhR*, 274)— affective attachments are embedded within the objective actualization of spirit. Patriotism "is only the result of existing institutions in the state, as [those things in which] rationality is actually present" (*PhR*, 268; cf. 270, 274). This focus thus also separates Hegel's political theory from both an affectively grounded communitarianism[48] and an agonistic politics that embraces fluidity and indeterminacy (*PhR*, 189, 318).

Hegel thus anticipates sociological theories emphasizing civil society and the distinction between state and society, generally.[49] The modern state's network of differentiations advances it well beyond the vibrant but politically underdeveloped Greek *polis* (*PhR*, 273; cf. 150, 261; *PhH*, 50). However, this modern advance is not merely a functional efficiency that rationalizes cooperation. Its social structures originate from human intelligence and are recognized as rationality's establishing itself in the world in a way that is both tangibly concrete and universally significant. "Because [the state] is not a mechanism but the rational life of self conscious freedom and is the system of the ethical world, so the disposition and also the consciousness of the same in [its] principles (*Grundsatzen*) is an essential moment in the realized (*wirklichen*) state" (*PhR*, 270).

This theorization frames Hegel's attention to war. Though states have often displaced one another through violent conflict, the flourishing of a rational state presumes a peace that reflects not simply contingent political stability but conceptual necessity (*PhR*, 326).[50] Yet Hegel does not follow Kant to envisage the eventual disappearance of war. The occurrence of wars and the need for those able to fight them are persistent realities facing modern states (*PhR*, 324, 326, 329, 333). Hegel's response to these realities is both complex and surprising.

In one respect, continued wars reflect political fluidity and contention. States will have disputes; when negotiated settlements fail, wars erupt with peace eventually restored. (*PhR*, 334–340) Allen Wood's judgment that Hegel does not believe that "wars are a good thing, or that we should not do our best to avoid them . . . [indeed] even during war . . .war always has the character of what should cease" (1991, xxvi) sketches what we would expect from a Hegel who situates war within the practices of rational modernity. Lucio Cortella is less satisfied, suggesting that only a revised, globalized Hegelianism can move humanity away from using war as the normal way of settling disputes (2015, 125, 128–129, 145). However, Hegel says something different from both, contending that experiences of war are essential to ethical life. Paradoxically, conflicts provide the clearest insight into the connections between civic membership and universality. Finitudes of particular interests, goals, external goods, and even biological life itself become universally significant once their transience is recognized within demands for sacrifice in the name of a state's ethical identity (*PhR*, 327). The refusal to remain bound to such attachments cannot achieve such significance under pressures of natural urgency (fight or flee?) but only through spirit's willing its own freedom under political duress. When "necessity takes the form of natural power (*Naturgewalt*) . . . everything finite is mortal and transient. However, in the ethical essence, the state, nature loses this power and necessity is raised to a work of freedom, to something ethical (*Sittlichen*)" (*PhR*, 324; cf. 149). Dutiful obedience to the state in times of war, liberates from "a dependence on mere natural drives" and from "that indeterminate subjectivity which . . . remains unactualized" (*PhR*, 149). The "ethical moment of war" (*das sittliche Moment des Krieges*) is revealed in citizens' readiness to sacrifice their lives (*PhR*, 324). Implicitly agreeing with Hobbes's critics, Hegel admits that such a sacrifice cannot be justified if the state is simply a security guard. "For this security cannot be achieved by the sacrifice of what should be secured" (*PhR*, 324).[51] Rather, "[war] has the higher meaning (*die höhere Bedeutung*) [to the degree] that through it . . . the ethical health of peoples is preserved/achieved (*erhalten*) in their indifference toward the consolidation of finite determinations" (*PhR*, 324). Wars are not simply the tools used by anxious governments concerned to strengthen civic bonds (*Phen*, 455). They are historical events to be conceptualized by a philosophy appreciative of spirit's construction of itself within modernity. The *polis'* employment of war for purposes of social actualization has been universalized, not outgrown.

Even the willingness of the primordial lord to die in a life and death struggle over recognition may be redeemed retrospectively once transformed into the courage demanded by the modern state at war. "Courage is for itself a formal virtue because it is the highest abstraction of freedom from all particular ends, possessions, pleasures, and life . . . [but] it is not in itself of a spiritual nature; its inner disposition may [have] this or that ground and its actual result may be only for others and not for itself. . . . [Thus] the courage (*Mut*) of an animal or a robber, bravery (*Tapferkeit*) for the sake of honor, knightly courage, are still not the true forms. The true courage [found within] cultivated nations is the readiness to sacrifice in service to the state, so that the individual matters only as one under many. Not personal courage but integration with the community (*das Allgemeine*) is what matters here" (*PhR*, 327). However, while Kant prefers citizen soldiers to standing armies, Hegel gives a particular civic estate responsibility for fighting. Even though "sacrifice for the individuality of the state is [the] substantial relation of all and thus a universal duty, so it also becomes . . . a particular relation with its own particular estate devoted to it" (*PhR*, 325), not a class of naturally thumistic guardians (*Republic*, 357a–b) but members of an "estate of courage" (*der Stand der Tapferkeit*).[52]

Because modernity's wars should clarify the ethical meanings constitutive of modern political life (*PhR*, 340), we would expect them to escape the contradictions of Greece's struggles. Yet one can argue that the continued presence of war deepens rather than resolves puzzles within Hegel's political theory. Such puzzles arise along several axes.

First, war blurs relations between political and philosophical languages. Initially, the recognition of a civic duty that can motivate the sacrifice of citizens' "property and life, as well as their beliefs and everything of theirs enclosed within the compass of life" (*PhR*, 324) suggests that political appeals to community can overlap with a philosophical comprehension of war's higher spiritual significance. From both perspectives, essentials of ethical life supersede contingent attachments and the philosophical language of actualized self-consciousness reinforces a political language of patriotic duty.[53] Yet this convergence extends only so far. In its distance from the immediacies triggering political conflicts, Hegel's synopticism transcends rather than validates the vocabularies of citizens whose justifications for wars can apparently only be offered as defenses of particular collective interests, rights, or identities under threat from "the passions of rulers or peoples" or rectifications of "injustices or . . . anything else that is not as it should be" (*PhR*, 324). At the same time, Hegel's synopticism may move problematically away from a critical judgment about both war's immediate causes and its justice or injustice, introducing a potentially more dangerous language of a national ethical health that congratulates itself for progressing toward the actualization of universal freedom.[54]

Second, war disrupts the philosophical mapping of modernity's structures. By underscoring the dependent nature of "mere" attachments to life and property, Hegel acknowledges the contingent status of estates managing civil society's ethical life. "In peaceful times, the particular spheres and occupations proceed so as to pursue their particular occupations and purposes . . . in times of [intense] need (*Not*), however, be it external or internal, it is sovereignty, in whose simple concept all of the formerly existing determinations of the organism were joined, and to which the rescue (*Rettung*) of the state is committed, while those previously justified occupations are sacrificed, [this is] where that idealism comes to its distinctive actualization" (*PhR*, 278). What initially appear as necessary determinations of spirit within the texture of a rationalized society become dispensable variations in the harsh light of war.[55]

Third, modern war may diminish rather than elevate the estate of courage. Yes, "the courage of the animal, the courage of the robber [and] courage for the sake of honor" (*PhR*, 327) seem primitive in the face of rationalized combat. Yet when the estate of courage functions more rationally thanks to such technological advances as firearms (328), its presence as an estate of *courage* may be compromised. When "the more purely personal form of courage [is converted] into an abstraction," is spiritedness preserved within modernity's spirit or does the courageous soldier become another of Kojeve's working artisans?

Finally and most importantly, the ongoing possibility of war may unsettle relations between particularity and universality even though this structural clarity is essential to Hegel's philosophy (324). In one sense, particularity and universality should cohere within a consistent Hegelian framework. Though wars originate from particular quarrels, they reinforce the universally significant spiritual dynamic constitutive of modern political and ethical societies (340).[56] Yet war is also intensely particular, fought not for *the* state but for *this* state (329, 337). It is not simply that modern political communities continue to be exposed to contingencies (333, 340).[57] War pointedly underscores the state's objective spiritual existence as a concretely established political community (324, 337, 329). Questions about its political directions and choices must be referred to principles framed by its own vivid particularity (324). No generalized distinctions between defensive and conquering—and perhaps between just and unjust—wars seem possible (326). Yet when particular political communities are engaged in such conflicts they rely on the explanatory and justificatory power of distinctions, just war language if not just war theory, that gesture toward universalizations (*Phen*, 508, 511, 652–653) that may come back to haunt particular appeals. The justification of a particular war as defensive or the accusation against another as aggressive articulate considerations that need to be taken seriously in judging future wars, including one's own. Clarifying the differences between the spiritually universal and the politically particular, the enduringly significant versus the immediately compelling, becomes not a conceptual project for a philosophy functioning beyond politics (Pippin, 2008, 267) but a complex, hazardous task for an embedded practical judgment that can easily go epistemically wrong, either reinforcing overconfidence in reason's ability to control events or undercutting attempts at rational criticism and improvement.

The introduction of war into *PhR* eventually makes the status and coherence of Hegelian political philosophy itself uncertain. Hegel's philosophical wisdom is presented as an intellectual achievement suitable to "a present [that] has cast off its barbarity and unjust willfulness . . . that reveals the state as the image and actuality of reason" (*PhR*, 360). In revealing the state as the actuality of reason, wisdom encounters itself as the *Phenomenology*'s "absolute knowing, spirit that knows itself as spirit" (*Phen*, 808). Within this actualized rationality, war may be coherently conceptualized and limited by international law (*PhR*, 326). Yet Hegel communicates the effect of war on ethical health through a different image. After admitting that war "should not be regarded as an absolute evil," he compares war's effects on "the ethical health of nations" to "the movement of the winds [that] preserves the sea from that stagnation (*Fäulnis*) which a lasting calm would produce—that [condition] for nations which a lasting not to say a perpetual peace (*ein ewiger Friede*)[58] would establish" (324). Now, war is neither the immaturity of a reckless lord fated to disappear nor the remnant of a dangerous nationalism that demands further reform (Cortella, 2015 128–129). As a revivifying disturbance it is neither a confirmation of the tragic character of human life (Williams, 1997, 357, 360)[59] nor a minor coda to spirit's rationally structured political actualization (Franco, 1999, 333).[60] This recognition of war as spiritual renewal could reflect a modern preservation of the Greeks' distinctive ethical life (*Phen*, 455). However, war's turbulence disrupts as much as it reinforces *Sittlichkeiten*.[61] Flows endlessly destabilize and recreate (*Phen*, 730). The ethical world disclosed by this oceanic metaphor seems closer to Machiavelli's, where cultural flourishings and destructions are also imaged as inundations (*Disc*, 2.8), making boundaries between land and water historical in a more unstable sense. Yet can this kind of politics be adequately theorized by Hegelian philosophy? Instead of contemplating its own active presence in the world, philosophy may now find itself alienated from a turbulent other resistant to rationality.[62] In one sense, this frustration might continue the pattern of constructive failures that Hegel traces in the *Phenomenology*. Yet if Hegelian philosophy becomes unstable precisely at its self-understood point of resolution, can there be any resolution on Hegelian terms?

Here, we might reinvolve Hegel's Greeks. Athenian culture's individual expressions of representation and thought challenge Hegel's philosophical history from two directions. The first affirms resilient particularity as a challenge to the synopticism that Hegel continually tries to impose. Because spirit's historical completion displays the whole (*PhH*, 442), Hegel's narrative is privileged as the maturation of the Greek originalists,' engaging spirit's movements directly but more deeply, contemplating its structures, not just reporting its immediacies (*PhH*, 457). Herodotus and Thucydides must have their works rewritten retrospectively by a truly philosophical historian. Hegel's reading of *Antigone* effectively insists that Sophocles cannot grasp the full significance of his tragedy without its translation into Hegelian dialectical categories.[63] Antigone, Creon—indeed, Sophocles himself—become Hegelian characters in the *Phenomenology*'s narrative. Socrates's political statements in the *Republic* are treated literally as Platonic proposals (*PhR*, 46, 185, 206, 262), discounting Socratic irony and the dialogue form in favor of the "substantial ideas" of a Platonic philosophy (*PhR*, 46) itself destined to be transformed within the science of wisdom.

These Greek voices disagree, claiming that human activities and cultural forms must be seen more perspectivally with no single vocabulary in control. As tragedies, comedies, histories, and dialogues, their texts are constructed around particularity and plurality. Though they think within the horizon of the species and offer their insights to indefinite audiences (including classical Athenians, Hegel and us) their thinking is not destroyed (*zerstören—PhH*, 81)—or exposed as naively immediate—by particular determinacies. Instead, it arises within them. The human experience is not raised to universal significance by final narratives of mature institutions, completed struggle, fulfilled recognition, or absolute wisdom. It persists as a problem to be continually revisited.

Yet while such forms of representation and thought accompany or are embedded within pluralized action, they do not simply need to catch up with political fluidity (Markell, 2003, 94; cf. 68–69, 86, 88) and do not involve themselves so completely in particulars as to foreclose all claims to permanent validity. The second Greek challenge to Hegel does not displace political theory with politics, but offers political philosophical challenges (plural) to Hegel. His contention (*PhH*, 55) that all spiritual activity is limited by its time[64] is disputed by the self-understandings of many of his Athenians. For Nussbaum (2001, 67), Hegel's interpretation of *Antigone* is structured by a vision of a conflict-free world whose closure is fundamentally disputed by Sophocles. The Platonic Socrates defends his self-examination within the frame of reference of the species (*der Mensch* or *ho anthrōpos*) as a permanent, not simply a historical possibility, presuming a vantage point that both draws upon and goes beyond Athenian culture (*Apology*, 38a).[65] If we test Hegel's judgment that Thucydides and Herodotus are original historians "not concerned with offering reflections on . . . events, for [they write] within the spirit of the times and cannot as yet go beyond them" (*PhH*, 4) against the Herodotean and Thucydidean texts themselves, we find something different. Though less openly confident that they have seen the whole, their books are hardly unreflective representations of Greek culture. Herodotus imagines a conversation about the best regime as a Persian deliberation and not as a specifically Greek discovery.[66] Thucydides problematizes any permanent separation of Greeks from barbarians and frames his treatment of the war within the horizon of the human. In his "deathless work [that is] the absolute gain that humanity (*Menschheit*) has [derived] from that struggle [between Athenians and Peloponnesians]" (*PhH*, 266), he identifies the problems posed by war as persisting as long as human beings have the same nature (3.82), a possession forever (*ktēma to es aiei*—1.22) very different from a world historical narrative.

Hegelian Legacies?

Modern social and political theories aspiring to use Hegel as a resource face a set of questions not altogether different from those that he elicits. Potentially, his categories can enrich structural analyses of differentiated modern societies and perhaps even (*pace* Williams) of conflictual modern international politics (Cortella). Though Hegel's political theory is not democratic in itself, modern democratic theory can employ his framework in both domestic and international contexts to identify alternatives to the estate bureaucracy that he embraces.[67] Especially because of these positive potentials, an appreciation of Hegel's difficulties can stimulate awareness of parallel problems within more contemporary statements.

Modern deliberative democratic theory replaces Hegel's distinction between the universality of spirit's actualized freedom and the particularity of its political immediacies (*PhH*, 457) with a distinction between the universality of communicative reason and the particularity of cultural lifeworlds and historical circumstances.[68] The premise of deliberative democratic theory is that procedurally responsible political communications validated by discourse ethics can generate moral outcomes within this fluid political world, successfully negotiating the hazards of formal proceduralism and contingent entrapment through the regulation of particular policies and decisions by universally valid moral norms. Prospects for the continuation of violent political conflicts within the world as we know it make the need to act morally in such circumstances a matter of the highest urgency. Under what conditions and for what purposes should wars be fought in historically unstable contexts? The political theories of Rawls and Habermas presume to answer that question by structuring the relationship among nations according to the priorities of deliberative democracy. To this extent, deliberative democratic theory both presumes and develops a politics structured by international law (as in Rawls, 1999, 41), appreciating (like Hegel) its rationality while downplaying (unlike Hegel) its limits and distortions.[69]

Yet if critical readings of Hegel's narratives ultimately problematize the distinction between universality and particularity, they also implicitly question whether discourse ethics can endorse a universal structure for political communication without presuming the influence of contingent historical forces and therefore whether its commitments to fair procedures can simply be justified universally. In its confidence that it has reconciled an ethically privileged proceduralism with a highly specific substantive particularity, does deliberative democratic theory risk repeating Hegel's mistaken claim to have successfully resolved ambiguities between necessity and contingency or essence and semblance? If the cultural influences of Rawls's constitutional democracy or Habermas's international democratic lifeworld are necessary to ground procedural commitments, can a deliberative democratic theory valorizing such procedures exercise critical scrutiny over its own conditions without a circularity blind to its own shortcomings? Can Rawls's theory of justice be an effective critic of the liberal constitutionalism upon which it intellectually depends? If not, the outcome may not be the successful reconciliation of procedure with substance (setting the agenda for an emerging law of peoples) but a contestable allegiance to the circumstances that have tenuously forged Western modernity. Here, historical circumstances and cultural differences may be judged according to a master narrative that is not uncontroversially procedural but problematically substantive, validating the priorities and structures of the powerful and progressive, yet very imperfect West.[70] Failure to see that the challenges of political necessity and historical contingency cannot be met by any resolutive theoretical narrative may have damaging implications for both a suitably critical political theory and an effective political agency. Within the reconstructed democratic Hegelianism of Cortella (2015, 165) or Church (2012, 85), war implicitly disappears as a political problem.[71] At one level, this invites the harsh skepticism of the realists. At another, it prompts a harder rethinking of the kinds of political conditions that would be needed to eliminate wars between nations. Perhaps we need a more aggressively critical political theory that draws both its concerns and its energies from the contingencies and conflicts of politics itself. For many of those embracing this direction, the ally is Nietzsche.

Nietzsche's Polemical Worlds

Nietzsche responds to war's disruptions not by rationalizing its practices but by redirecting its energies, away from conflicts between peoples, toward struggles within the self. However, this revision cannot redirect the self away from politics and the resilience of political conflict within Nietzsche's proposals both enriches and complicates his contributions to political thinking. I will explore how this byplay structures Nietzsche's *Beyond Good and Evil (BGE)*, as it examines the dynamics and meanings of war within a variety of registers.

BGE invites "philosophers of the future" to the new task (*eine neue Aufgabe*) of revaluing values, resisting modernity's mediocrity and nihilism (*BGE*, 224, 263) in the name of higher forms of life (noting *Uses and Disadvantages of History for Life*, 10; *Gay Science*, 343). Though addressed to "philosophers," much of its language is political, assailing democracy and embracing some form of aristocracy (202–203, 224, 239, 257, 268), often through disturbing valorizations of war (200, 209, 262), struggle (208, 262) and tyranny (22, 82, 188, 242).[72] How should such language be interpreted? One set of commentators argues that Nietzsche's severity signals the need to construct and sustain a stern aristocracy able to foster human excellence.[73] A second, broader group contends that such images are metaphors for an intense psychological project characterized, variously, as self-creation, self-transfiguration, exemplary achievement, or the construction of agency.[74] My reading appreciates but adjusts both perspectives. I argue that the language of war plays an essential role in Nietzsche's political philosophy but that it signifies something deeper than a recognition of the harsh demands of aristocratic politics, describing not simply how social and psychological dynamics are understood, but how ontological conditions are represented and how the activity of philosophy is construed. In this respect, Nietzsche's registers of war parallel Machiavelli's. Yet the two authors eventually weave very different, though equally constricting, intellectual webs. While Machiavelli's broadly philosophical concerns always return to the aggressive political paradigm that both informs and distorts them, Nietzsche's efforts to reinscribe conflict within the psyche cannot escape political entanglements. Though we should not take Nietzsche's vocal embrace of warrior aristocracies at face value, his affirmative, if vague, political projections are problematized by the persistence of an aggression that he too often marginalizes. These issues continue within attempts to adapt Nietzsche's perspective to postmodern democratic politics.

Images of struggle persist within Nietzsche's characterizations of both human and nonhuman worlds.[75] In Part One of *BGE* Nietzsche sets his perspective against the theories of nature (teleological or mechanistic— 14; *GS*, 301, 355, 373) that have informed so much of the West's philosophical development. Yet this does not dismiss nature's relevance. Because every appeal to what is allegedly "according to nature" (*gemäss der Natur*) is really the imposition of a morality ("Physics . . . is only a world-interpretation and world-presentation not a world-explanation"— *BGE*, 14; *GS*, 301, 355, 373), Nietzsche can confidently state his own alternative vision. Nature is "wasteful without measure, indifferent without measure, without intentions and considerations, without pity and justice, fertile, desolate and uncertain altogether; think also of this indifference itself as power (*Macht*)—how could one live according to this indifference?" (9). Such a nature undermines any condition of stability, exposing claims to permanence as illusory.[76] Any resistance to this indifference within an affirmation of life (*Uses*, 1, 5; *The Birth of Tragedy, Attempt at a Self-Criticism*, 4; *GS*, 349) might then be valorized for courageously defying nature. Yet if such resistance demands its own distinctive struggles, then living according to life (*gemäss dem Leben leben*) (9, 188, 230; *GM*, 2.12) is natural as well, for "life itself is essentially (*wesentlich*) appropriation, injury, overpowering what is alien [or foreign] (*Fremden*) and weaker" (259; cf. 130). Like Machiavelli, Nietzsche frames his call for value re-creation with a polemical interpretation of nature. [77]

Yet while Machiavelli argues that countering the effects of disorder by channeling its own origins (loves of gain or glory) cannot construct any permanent order, Nietzsche's diagnosis of modernity warns of turbulence's cultural disappearance. Instead of ceaseless ascensions and descents (*Disc*, 2, Pr.), the species faces dehumanization through a mediocrity imposed by the convergence of Christianity, democracy, and mass society (262, 202; *GS* 377; *Schop Ed*, 3.6). Nature's harsh indifference will be replaced with the last human being's comfortable indifference (the well-known image of *Zarathustra—Prologue* 5; *BT*, 9; *GM*, III. 14). The philosophers of the future will not oppose turbulence; they must rescue it (229).

The violent character of this rescue is anticipated in Nietzsche's representation of the revaluation of values as a kind of war. Part Nine of *BGE* describes the future philosopher as "a human being who . . . is perhaps himself a storm pregnant with new lightnings; a fatal human being (*ein verhängnissvoller Mensch*) around whom there is always groaning and humming, gaping opening, uncanny (*umheimlich*) motion" (292; *GM*, 1.16). Philosophy cannot be understood without recognizing its cruel and warlike character. "In every willing to know (*Erkenne-Wollen*) there is a drop of cruelty" (229), though a cruelty eventually sublated to a higher purpose.[78]

In reconceiving philosophy polemically, Nietzsche implicitly acknowledges a conflicted debt to Kant.[79] While Kant advanced philosophy by turning its critical capacities inward (11, 211; *BT*, 18), he did not delve deeply enough into its origins and strivings (23, 54); instead of just explaining how synthetic judgments a priori are epistemologically possible he should also have asked why belief in them is psychologically necessary (11, 187). This inquiry reveals that will to truth originates in what is called will to power (1), also clarified via a metaphor of aggressive discharge, opposing "superficial physiologists and teleologists" (noting the qualification) who mistakenly posit the drive for self-preservation (*Selbsterhaltungstrieb*) as the "cardinal instinct of an organic being." Rather, "before everything, a living thing seeks to discharge (*auslassen*) its strength—life itself is will to power (*Leben selbst ist Wille zur Macht*" (13; *GS*, 349; *GM*, 3.7, 3.27). Power is indexed not by acquisition (Hobbes) or influence (Machiavelli), but by energy.[80]

In spite of these images, Nietzsche does not anticipate Schmitt and valorize political war.[81] Instead, he turns such images inward, sketching a psychological profile of one at war with oneself (158). The modal moralities that *BGE* sets against one another, the master and the slave, "at times . . . occur directly alongside one another—even in the same human being, within a single soul (*innerhalb Einer Seele*)" (260). This is no romantic celebration of turbulence, for the psychically strong organize chaos within themselves (*Uses*, 10), a self-creation always pursued but never completed (*GM*, 3.27). Internal warfare correctly understood is not the pathological disruption of psychic stability but the energetic activity of a strong identity. Still, this self is not isolated. The psyche is socially constructed (*GS*, 354) and psychic activities have social effects (188). Though Nietzsche does not propose definite structures for arranging political or social institutions, he does treat the cultural functions of politics as central to the enhancement or decline of human life.[82] While this focus recalls Hegel's mapping the dialectical influence of *Sittlichkeit* on *Moralität*, it criticizes Hegelian theorizations for underappreciating the full significance of ethical struggle, revising them in ways that make such battles ongoing.

Genealogies of Tyrannies and Rebellion

BGE's concluding Part Nine begins by linking the emergence of higher human beings to a stern and inegalitarian politics. "Every enhancement of the type 'human' (*Mensch*) was so far the work of an aristocratic society (*das Werk einer aristokratischen Gesellschaft*)—and it will be so again and again: as a society that believes in the long ladder of rank and differences in value between man and man and has need for slavery (*Sklaverei*) in some sense. Without the pathos of distance which grows out of the confirmed differences of strata (*Stände*), when the ruling caste (*der herrschende Kaste*) constantly looks afar and looks down upon submissives

(*Unterthänige*) and instruments and just as constantly their practice is obedience (*Gehorchen*) and command (*Befehlen*), keeping down and keeping at a distance, that other more mysterious pathos could not have emerged either, the longing for an ever new widening of distances within the soul itself . . . in brief, simply the enhancement of the type 'human,' the continual 'self overcoming of the human' (*Selbst-Uberwindung des Menschen*) to take a moral (*moralische*) formula in a supermoral (*übermoralische*) sense" (257; cf. 219; *TI, Skirmishes*, 37; *GS*, 377; *Greek State*, 172).

Read politically, this statement parallels but challenges central Hegelian claims. Like Hegel, Nietzsche imagines a society of differentiated and hierarchical *Stände*. Yet the outcome is not integrated rationality but "the pathos of distance." While Hegel's analysis of modern politics substitutes governance and being governed for command and obedience (*PhH*, 46), Nietzsche retains commanding and obeying . And whereas Hegel's mature (Western) political culture is a state where all are free, Nietzsche's imagined aristocracy preserves a need (*nöthig*) for slavery "in some sense."[83]

This vision of an aristocratic society confronts debilitations created by what Nietzsche condemns as the slave rebellion in morals (195). His account of this rebellion seems a politicized reversal of Hegel's lord/bondsman narrative. While retaining the German designation masters (*Herren*), Nietzsche converts bondsmen (*Knechten*) into slaves (*Sklaven*). In both narratives, the oppressed eventually triumph, yet Nietzsche's version of this victory promises not the historical maturation of spirit, but the displacement of a morality valorizing strength by one rooted in weakness (260; *GM*, 1.10). Yet Nietzsche's narrative eventually points not only to the contingent character of political cultural forms (these sequences were not necessary, even read retrospectively) but also to the uncertain but not hopeless possibilities of political change. Replacing (Hegelian) history with genealogies means that there are no historical last words (cf. Geuss, 2008, 68).

By mourning nobility's eclipse Nietzsche seems to regret the lost warrior culture and to remain stubbornly attached to spiritedness. "One should give in to no humanitarian illusions about the origins of an aristocratic society. . . . Let us say to ourselves . . . how every higher culture (*höhere Kultur*) on earth has so far begun. Human beings with a nature still natural, barbarians in the very terrible sense of the word . . . hurled themselves upon weaker, more civilized, more peaceful . . . races" (*BGE*, 257). For all of their violence, however, this noble caste did not establish its "predominance (*Übergewicht*) [through] physical strength but [through] strength of soul (*Kraft . . . in der seelischen*). . . . they were more complete (*ganzeren*) human beings." From this perspective, the new task confronting philosophers of the future might be an attempted reinvention of a premodern political culture within a modern age.[84] Many Nietzschean texts support this reading. Yet his eventual assessment of the sequences of moralities in Europe is more complicated, its histories/genealogies and outcomes more unsettled.

The tracking of slave morality's victory begins in *BGE* Five, "Toward a Natural History of Morals (*zur Naturgeschichte der Moral*)." The project continues in Nine and then in an extended treatment of the same set of questions in *On the Genealogy of Morals*. What does a *Naturgeschichte* reveal? The prior treatment of religion in Part Three fell under the title of *das religiöse Wesen*, the religious essence or religiousness itself. This eventually becomes a mapping of "the whole history (*ganze . . . Geschichte*) of the soul up to this point and its undrunk possibilities" (45). Religiousness itself is its history as experienced genealogically, in a soul formed by its past but constructing indefinite futures (12). A parallel trajectory implies that Five's natural history will also reveal morality itself.

At the beginning of Five, histories of the soul and histories of morals intersect bidirectionally. Souls individuate themselves by their tables of goods or values (194), but values are framed by moral/cultural templates. In the earlier *Uses* Nietzsche interprets cultures through metaphors of nature, atmospheres that "every living thing" needs if it is not to become "withered, hard and barren" (*Uses*, 7; *GS*, 110; *BGE*, 34). While the initial impression is that all cultures support forms of life, *Uses* argues that modern culture suffocates (7–9). In *BGE* Five, atmospheric horizons become forged moralities exerting control though discipline.[85] Opposing liberationist "free thinkers" Nietzsche insists that "every (*Jede*) morality is, as against *laisser aller* [letting go], a bit of tyranny against 'nature'. . . . What is essential and invaluable in every morality is that it is a long compulsion (*langer Zwang*). . . . [And] the wondrous fact is, however, that all there is or has been on earth of freedom, subtlety, boldness, dance, and masterly (*meisterlicher*) confidence . . . even in ethical lives (*Sittlichkeiten*), has been able to develop itself only because of the 'tyranny of such willful laws (*Willkür-Gesetz*)'" (188; cf. 44; *TI, Skirmishes*, 41; *GS*, 352).

Far from rejecting the cultural conditions enabling moral development (as for MacIntyre, 2016, 48, 58), this statement potentially approves every morality. "One must see each (*jede*) morality this way" (188). While the call to move beyond modern morality apparently does not demand overcoming morality simply,[86] it needs to explain why movement away from modernity's moral landscapes is necessary and an account of what the eventual alternative(s) might be. Consequently, comparisons of moralities are expanded to enable the discovery of the different types of obedience demanded and compulsions imposed. A typology of morals ("the task of description—though for it the finest fingers and senses can scarcely be fine enough" [186; cf. *GS*, 112]) must compare the different ways in which moral tyrannies function (cf. 228).

This comparison initially seems straightforward; modern morality's categories of good and evil are excoriated as herd instincts that crush individual distinctiveness. Siding with Hobbes, Nietzsche traces this morality to fear, to "herd timidity" (*der Heerden Furcht-Samkeit*) that cries out: "we want that someday there will be nothing more to fear" (201; cf. 49, 197, 221; *GM*, 3.18).[87] As fear's offspring, slave morality is terrified by the "highest and strongest drives [which] when they break out passionately and drive the individual far above the average and the flats of herd consciousness (*Heerdengewissens*), destroy the self confidence of the community. . . . Hence these drives are branded and slandered most" (201; *GM*, 2.16). Here, Nietzsche's concerns seem to parallel John Stuart Mill's in *On Liberty*. Both recoil at mass society's impacts on individual excellence. However, while Mill tries reconciliation by insisting that the achievements of the gifted benefit society (*On Liberty*, 3), Nietzsche emphasizes distances between higher and lower humans. In *BGE* Two, "what gives the higher type of human beings nourishment or refreshment must almost be poison for a very different and inferior type" (30; cf. *GM*, 1.17; *GS*, 3, 4, 76) [88]. Yet modernity's deficiencies go beyond its hostility toward higher lives (Church, 2015, 151). The seemingly victorious slave morality is internally unstable. Common utility undermines the Christian commitment to "neighbor love" (201; cf. 60; *GS*, 21); appeals to popular sovereignty and political equality mask a willingness to submit to "one who commands unconditionally" (Nietzsche's example is Napoleon) (199; *GM*, 1.16).

Yet as the investigation expands, its conclusions are less certain and its moral categories less stable (cf. 2, 24, 31, 34). Eventually, when Nietzsche confronts (in Eight) the German anti-Semitism that he clearly holds in contempt (cf. *GM*, 3.26),[89] he introduces the deeper question of what Europe owes to the Jews. The provocative answer is "many things, good and bad, and one thing above all that is equally best and worst; the grand style in morality, the terribleness and majesty of infinite demands, infinite meanings (*unendlicher Forderungen, unendlicher Bedeutungen*)" (250; cf. 248).[90] This should prompt re-examination of the earlier claim in Five, "the significance of the Jewish people [is that] with them begins the slave rebellion in morals" (195; *GM*, 1.7). To the extent that this moral upheaval was a terribleness and majesty of infinite demands, its responsibility for the "overall degeneration of man" diagnosed at the end of Five is puzzling. Is modern morality a departure from the rebellion's initial character, reflecting the indeterminacies of any *Naturgeschichte*? Or was there something particularly dangerous about *this* revaluation of values?[91] Puzzles deepen as Nietzsche implicitly challenges both the ancient Roman dismissal of the Jews as "a people born for slavery' " and the scriptural understanding of the Hebrews as the chosen people (195). By 251, far from being born slaves, the Jews are "the strongest, most tenacious and purest race now living in Europe; they understand how to establish themselves throughout (*sich durchzusetzen*) even under the worst conditions . . . by means of virtues that today one would like to stamp as vices." Their strength has arisen through their own activities in confronting these worst conditions, perhaps confirming that "a species (*Art*) comes into being, a type fixed and strong, through a long fight with essentially constant unfavorable conditions" (262; cf. *GS*, 136, 361). The Jews now seem self-chosen because they were strong, not strong because they were divinely chosen. The power of the slave rebellion in morals is therefore ambiguous. How can a morality that dominates through a terrible majesty resisting the worst conditions be slavish? How have the virtues of a morality that has so dominated (*GM*, 1.7, 10) become vices?

Consequently, the eventual examination of the noble in Part Nine will be posed as a question (*was ist vornehm?*—287). Just after claiming (257) that an aristocratic society is needed for human enhancement, Nietzsche distances himself from any historically recent, indeed from any modern, aristocracy. By the time of the Revolution, French aristocrats were useless functionaries. By contrast, "the essential characteristic (*das Wesentliche*) of a good and healthy aristocracy . . . is that it experiences itself not as a function (whether of a monarchy or a commonwealth) but as their meaning (*Sinn*) and highest justification . . . it therefore accepts with a good conscience the sacrifice of a host of human beings who must for its sake be reduced and dragged down to incomplete human beings, to slaves, to instruments" (258). This previews what seems a valorization of domination according to the imperatives of life, which essentially means "appropriation, injury . . . and at least, at its mildest, exploitation" (259). Affirming this principle of exploitation rejects theories of mutual accommodation (the social contract) "as [establishing] the fundamental principle of society (*als Grundprinzip der Gesellschaft*)" (cf. *GM*, 2.17). Such cooperation is in reality "a will to the denial of life, a principle of dissolution and decline." By contrast, "exploitation does not belong to a corrupt or incomplete and primitive society; it belongs to the essence of what lives as a basic organic function; it is a consequence of a will to power (*Willens zur Macht*), which is after all, the will of life (*der Wille des Lebens*)" (259; *GM*, 2.12).

Nietzsche follows this severity with a return (beginning in 260) to the typology of morals initiated in Five. Though he initially encourages "wandering through the many more refined and cruder moralities which have so far ruled (*geherrscht*) on the earth, or are still ruling (*herrschen*)," he arrives at a divide. "There are master morality (*Herren-Moral*) and slave morality (*Skalven-Moral*)." Yet essentializing these would be mistaken. The basic difference between them is blurred in "all the higher and more mixed cultures" where there are "attempts at negotiation between these two moralities and yet more often the confusion and mutual misunderstanding of both" (260; cf. 215). Any inclination to separate these moral forms decisively is confounded by the observation that "at times [the two] come to light in their severity directly alongside each other—even within the same human being, within a single soul." From this perspective, the genealogical account that Nietzsche offers both in *BGE* and in the First Essay of *GM* may be a critical dissection of both moral types, informing a deeper understanding of modern morality and the possibilities beyond.[92]

The difference between master and slave moralities is expressed both in their differing value categories (good and bad, *Gut und Schlecht*, rather than good and evil, *Gut und Böse*) and in the distinctive political cultural sequences that established them. Master morality begins with affirmation, where "the exalted, proud states of the soul . . . [confer] distinction and [determine] the order of rank." The "noble human being (*der Vornehme Mensch*) separates his essence from those in whom the opposite of such exalted, proud states finds expression . . . in this first type of morality the opposition of 'good' and 'bad' means largely the same as 'noble and 'contemptible' " (260). While such higher cultures began in violence (257; *GM*, 2.6), their moralities were sustained through the construction of networks of meaning and evaluative vocabularies. "The common human being (*der gemeine Mensch*) was such as he was valued (*galt*) . . . he attached no other worth (*Werthe*) to himself than his masters attached to him (it is a distinctive right of masters to create worth—*zu schaffen Werthe*)" (261). This theme is developed more fully in *GM* when Nietzsche defends the proposition that "the lordly right of giving names (*Herrenrecht, Namen zu geben*) extends so far that one should allow oneself to apprehend the beginning of language itself as an expression of power (*Machtäussenrung*) by the rulers" (*GM*, 1.2; cf. 1. 4–5; *Tragic Age*, 3).[93]

This noble morality individuated its members through linguistic categories and cultural practices separating human types, applying to actions only derivatively. Actions were praised or blamed according to the agent's character. Judging actions apart from agentic character reflects the flattening agendas of democratic utility and moral consequentialism (260, 268; cf. *GM*, 1.3; *GS*, 13). Noble compassion was not pity but largesse, prompted "more by an urge produced by an excess of power" (260; cf. 171). Insofar as the noble morality imposed duties they were "duties only to one's equals . . . against beings of a lower rank, against everything other (*Fremde*), one is permitted to act at discretion or 'as the heart wills'" (260). Noble morality thus seems to originate in a self-affirmation that does not require demonizing some other. This supposedly stands in contrast to a slave morality borne of resentment. "The slave's eye is resentful of the virtues of the powerful" (260).[94]

Yet these contrasts may represent only how such moralities looked from the inside. "The noble type experiences itself (*fühlt sich*) as value-determining" (260). Seen more critically, the self-understandings of noble cultures may be as partial and misleading as those of their alleged inferiors (262). Though noble morality prided itself on self-affirmation, much of what Nietzsche writes about its emergence implies reactivity. Practices within a society that was violated (*Vergewältigten*), suppressed (*Gedrücten*), and unfree (*Unfreien*) created an oppressed other whose "contemptibility" led the masters to designate themselves as noble (*GM*, 1.11). Much of *BGE* 262 thus traces the construction of fixed and strong types to prior conditions of warlike hostility and abuse. Though noble societies saw themselves as freely self-affirming, they also created themselves in response to necessities, "a constant battle with [their] neighbors or with the oppressed who are rebellious or who threaten rebellion," a process perhaps not altogether different from the genealogy of a herd morality where "here again (*wieder*) [that is, not uniquely] is fear the mother of morals" (201). Given these continuities in the instinctual bases of ethical communities, it becomes be less clear that the morality of timidity (197) was established through timidity alone (*GM*, 2. 16–17).

To the extent that moralities of good and bad valorize their own categories of nobility and baseness, they may conceal or ignore the extent to which such terms are rooted in raw power and domination (*GM*, 1.11). In both *BGE* (260) and *GM* (1. 5), Nietzsche comments on the noble Greeks' reputations as the truthful (*die Wahrhaftigen*). In *GM* he adds that such terms of worthiness were grounded in power imbalances. The noble Greeks "call themselves" (*heissen sich*) truthful. In *BGE*, the various forms of hardness demanded by necessity are what masters name (*nemmt*) the virtues (262). Contempt for softness is "itself reckoned under the virtues, under the name of justice." In commenting on the achievements of Periclean Athens in *GM* Nietzsche considers Thucydides's representation of the funeral oration but offers a different assessment from that voiced by Pericles (or Hegel). In the oration, Pericles praises Athens as the regime representing an "education to Hellas," but Nietzsche begins his commentary by noting that "the noble races . . . have left as their mark the concept 'barbarian' wherever they have gone; even their highest culture gives away its consciousness of it and indeed a pride in it (for example when Pericles says to his Athenians in his famous funeral oration 'our boldness has opened [broken] the way to every land and sea, everywhere raising up everlasting memorials of goodness and badness'" (*GM*, 1.11). While the Athenians elevate their cultural identity by distinguishing themselves as the pre-eminent Hellenes standing in opposition to the barbarians, Nietzsche represents their achievements as being themselves somehow barbaric.[95] If nothing else, it is now clearer what the so-called slaves were rebelling against.

Moreover, though every morality presumes some psychological depth (32), these noble masters lived too much on the surface, in "war, adventure, hunting, dancing, war games and in general all that involves strong, free, joyful activity" (*GM*, 1. 7; 1. 5). Did this morality's privileging of character as the definitive basis for praise mistake appearance for depth? Absent depth, there is little space for self-knowledge. In despising the common, the "noble ones, . . . [the] good, beautiful, happy ones" have also deprived themselves not only of a knowledge of the common (*GM*, 1.10), but also of any prospect for knowledge generally.[96] Someone not pushed toward the crowd by the stronger instinct that overcomes distaste "was not made . . . was not preordained for knowledge" (26), reinforcing the sense that knowledge must somehow be knowledge of the other. Their brilliant but shallow energies may have blinded noble masters to other human possibilities.[97] The psychic deepening that allows self-interrogation only emerged through the slave revolt. "While the noble man lives in trust and openness with himself. . . . the man of resentment . . . loves hiding places, secret paths and back doors" (*GM*, 1.10; cf. 1.6).[98] Challenging the outcomes of this now ambiguous moral rebellion may depend on resources that the rebellion itself created. Nietzsche eventually adjusts the pessimism of *BGE* Three that despaired (62) of religiously bred sickness and mediocrity.[99] By Five, "the long unfreedom of the spirit, the mistrustful constraint in the communicability of thoughts, the discipline that thinkers imposed on themselves to think under the direction of a church or court, or under Aristotelian propositions, the long spiritual will to interpret all events under a Christian scheme . . . all this, however, forced, willful, hard, gruesome, and anti-rational, has shown itself to be the means through which the European spirit has been trained (*angezüchtet*) in its strength, ruthless curiosity, exquisite mobility, though admittedly in the process an irreplaceable amount of strength and spirit had to be crushed, stifled and ruined" (188; cf. 219). The philosophers of the future must treat the consequences of modernity not simply as descents into nihilism but as resources for change.[100]

Philosophical Contests

In one respect, the principal task for philosophers of the future resembles what Pippin (elsewhere) characterizes as the establishment of normative authority within an unsteady moral context.[101] Yet this project is inevitably confrontational, frustrating Pippin's more stabilizing (more Hegelian) normative projections. The new philosophers' task extends along vertical and horizontal axes that are contentious both in themselves and with one another. We might (imperfectly) call these axes psychological and political/cultural.

After offering his preliminary analysis of morality's cultural dynamics in *BGE* 188, Nietzsche turns (190–192) to its psychological infrastructure, now insisting on the significance of instinctual commitments and challenging those seeking to establish morality on exclusively rational grounds. A surprising ally is Socrates.[102] The Socratic dictum that knowledge makes one good "smells of the rabble," for it makes the "good" identical with utility (190; cf. *GS*, 354).[103] If this proposition became at all "refined and noble" it was due to Plato's artistry. Yet whether it was the historical or the Platonic Socrates, "the superior dialectician [who] had stood first on the side of reason . . . in the end, however, privately and secretly . . . laughed at himself too . . . [for] he had seen through the irrationality in moral judgments" (191; *GS*, 340; *TI, Problem of Socrates*, 4). Plato's attempted dialectical overcoming of this dilemma employed "the greatest strength (*der grössten Kraft*) any philosopher so far has had at his disposal—to prove to himself that reason and instinct (*Vernunft und Instinkt*) of themselves tend toward one goal, toward the good, toward 'God' " (191). While these strengths were eventually corrupted by democracy, Christianity, and utility, Platonic philosophy still challenges modern rationalism by recognizing the significance of instinct. "Descartes . . . conceded authority only to reason, however reason is only an instrument (*Werkzeug*) and Descartes was superficial" (191). Notably, this apparent rejection of reason challenges only Cartesian rationality and Nietzsche does not simply ground moral authority in liberated instinct. This is suggested when he claims to offer a certain kind of truth, not "the truth" or "my truths" but "our truths" (*unsere Warheiten*) (202; cf. *BT*, 8; *GM*, 1.1, 2.4).

Redeeming instinct's moral role begins by critically revisiting the ironic and self-deceiving Socratic compromise that "one must follow the instincts, but persuade reason to help them" (191). Initially, this formulation elevates the instincts; in demanding followers they reinforce reason's subservience. Yet in soliciting help (*nachzuhelfen*) and in relying on persuasion (*überreden*), instincts also acknowledge their neediness for reason. The relation between instinct and moral rationality now emerges as a problem or a puzzle. Further, whatever bonds might come to connect them cannot be constructed through peaceful collaboration. Not every instinct is redeemable. The fearful need for safety and the seemingly humane inclination toward pity have spread spiritual degeneration (191). Within modernity, reason has helped these instincts by constructing utilitarian morality (so Descartes is not just superficial but an outlier). The antidote would seem to demand that a harsher form of reason judge the instincts mercilessly, disintegrating the foundations of utility. However, a vaguely Kantian reason disconnected from the emotions, unaware of "what in us really wants truth" (186) cannot exercise or implement this kind of judgment. [104] Instead, Nietzsche reconstructs the discoveries and applications of truth claims according to the imperatives of a vigorous emotional life which is always an aggressive and risky work in progress. Those with higher instincts are always waging war with themselves (200; cf. 76; *GM*, 2.16). Reason's collaboration with instinct requires a confrontation that is mutually enhancing (not simply instrumental, one way or the other) yet also mutually winnowing (not simply persuasive).

If his concern is with "our truths," Nietzsche must also reject monologic normative authority. His use of the first person plural signals neither Kant's universal imperatives nor Habermas's forceless force of the stronger argument. For Nietzsche, an argument is true (or forceful) only for self-selecting readers whose sign language is affectively healthy (187). True statements have normative authority only for exemplary human types (257). Nietzsche's interpretation of morality's possibilities must be accepted as "our truths" by others whose qualifications are both shown and developed in their pragmatic responses to his texts.[105]

Consequently, renovating morality's infrastructure is not simply an epistemological correction. Explorations of the psychological infrastructures of morality must recognize both reason and instinct as socially constructed, requiring challenges to the cultural distortions of modern education (194). Nietzsche's creative Socratic attempt to reclaim the instincts contests the hollow (counter-Socratic) confidence of modern morality, which claims that "one clearly knows in Europe what Socrates thought he did not know and what that famous old serpent once promised to teach—today one 'knows' what is good and evil" (202). But this challenge occurs within a more politicized attack on moral timidity launched by strong and dangerous drives (*starke und gefährliche Triebe*; 201). This means that no agreed upon truth or normative authority can escape the contingencies and conflicts of politics; indeed, "our" moral truths would seem to become true only if acted upon.[106] "Where then must we reach with our hopes? Toward new philosophers . . . spirits strong and original enough to give the impetus for opposite valuations and to revalue and reverse 'eternal values'" (203). Such truth claims may parallel the *verita effetuale* of *Prince* 15 and we can understand why Nietzsche reads Machiavelli (*TI, Ancients*, 2) as an antidote to rationalist moralities striving to dominate contingency.

Future philosophers' horizontal and vertical explorations continue to be tracked in *BGE*'s transition from Five to Eight and Nine. Both are aggressive, though in markedly different ways. Consistent with the byplay initiated in Five, the horizontal direction critically engages the political and cultural templates of modernity while the vertical exploration challenges the psyche to undertake exhilarating yet painful self-overcoming. Ultimately, self-engagement becomes primary, but its inner explorations cannot avoid politics and its conflicts.

At the end of Five, Nietzsche reiterates the linkage between morals and physiological instincts within a seeming condemnation of the consequences of modern Europe's demographics. Within "an age of dissolution that mixes races with one another, with such an inheritance, [they] have in their bodies varied origins, that is, opposite, and often not merely opposite, drives and value standards that fight (*kämpfen*) each other and rarely give each other any rest" (200; cf. 224; *GM*, 3.14). Such mixtures foster anxiety among the members of "late cultures and refracted lights" whose "most fundamental desire is that the war who they are [or it is] (*der Krieg, der er ist*) should come to an end." Did limited pacification among earlier societies suggest that the permanent elimination of fear is possible, and that the cultural condition of modern happiness or quietude (200) is altogether better than being afraid (44)? However, the continuation of anxiety exposes the failure of modernity's empowered fear as another of its internal contradictions. Nietzsche responds not with a call to reestablish prideful homogeneity, but with an appreciation of how anxious and unsettled differences can be resources for confronting a modernity whose chief flaw now seems to be its arrogance. Herd morality is "merely one type of human morality beside which, before which, and after which many other types, above all higher moralities are, or ought to be possible. Against such a such a 'possibility,' such an 'ought,' this [herd] morality fights with all its strength (*Kräften*); it says stubbornly and relentlessly, 'I am morality itself and nothing else is moral'" (202). In contrast, those with higher instincts may emerge when their anxieties intensify and "the opposition (*Gegensatz*) and war (*Krieg*) in such a nature effect one more charm and stimulus of life" (200). [107] Yet because "it has now come that we find in political and social arrangements an even more visible expression of this morality" (202), such wars cannot be exclusively internal.

The title of Eight, *Peoples and Fatherlands*, implies political engagement, yet much of the text concerns German music (240, 252, 254–255), continuing and anticipating more explicit critiques of relations between culture and politics.[108] While we might worry that this narrative will embrace music's contributions to cultural myths (as in *BT*, 23), *BGE* eventually takes more critical directions. Paralleling section 200 of Five, Eight's last section (256) reflects on exemplary political figures and artists. In both sections these figures fight psychological and cultural wars. In 200, whose figures wage war against themselves and stand against modern complacency, one artist (Leonardo) crashes a circle of politicians (Alcibiades, Caesar, Frederick II). In 256, whose focus is on "the more profound and comprehensive men of this century," one political leader (Napoleon) is placed among the artists. These profound and comprehensive men stay away from nationalist politics: "they were merely taking a rest from themselves when they became patriots." Yet the eventual implication goes beyond counseling political distance. Just as Leonardo's place in 200 recalls politics' cultural functions, Napoleon's presence politicizes culture, suggesting that we should read Eight's cultural diagnoses as political, not simply aesthetic, judgments.[109] As Eight begins, Nietzsche moves from reflections on Wagner (240) to political criticism (241). In 247, reading aloud is a public act. Are withdrawal and patriotism the only political alternatives?

In 242 Nietzsche detects politically critical potentials within the features of modern society that earlier were blamed for causing homogeneity and compliance. While the "Europeans are becoming more similar to each other," "the same new conditions under which on the average will foster the leveling and mediocritization of humans . . . are likely in the highest degree to give birth to exceptional human beings of the most dangerous and attractive quality." Now sounding like Tocqueville, Nietzsche warns that despotism threatens this radically egalitarian society. "Future Europeans [may be] as much in need of a master and commander as of their daily bread." One counter may be the exceptional human beings whom democratization fosters. "But while the democratization of Europe leads to the generation of a type that is prepared for slavery in the subtlest sense, in single, exceptional cases the strong human being must turn out stronger and richer than perhaps ever before . . . the democratization of Europe is at the same time an involuntary arrangement for the cultivation of tyrants, understanding the word in every sense including the most spiritual (*geistigsten*)." The most spiritual tyrants may both cohabitate with and confront the most despotic, perhaps by challenging the society in which despotism is likely to grow.

Though Part Eight devotes less attention to narrowly political questions than to broadly cultural ones, its cultural reflections reverberate on politics in scathingly critical ways, first targeting power politics, where "a monster of empire and power" is mistaken as greatness (241; cf. 254) and then German nationalism (251), an example of "nationality-insanity (*Nationalitäts-Wahnsinn*)" (256; cf. 156, 241, 245). Such critiques do not simply resist power's oppressiveness and nationalism's insanity in the name of individuality (Shaw, 2007, 29, 61). They challenge the public culture that empire and nationalism foster. One reason why nationality is insane is that it induces the "pathological estrangement" of a separatist politics denying the truth "that Europe wants to become one" (256; *GS*, 377). This Europeanism might be read simply as an expanded form of localism, especially in light of Europe's dominance over other lands (202, 255). Yet the boundary crossings and population mixtures that Nietzsche at times decries also stand as potential antidotes to the reduction of Europe to something analogically nationalist (*BGE*, Pr). More generally (whether this is Nietzsche's express intent or not), the critical political stance that Nietzsche adopts warns against the dangerous possibility that attachments to Europe will become yet another political insanity (210). These critical potentials are, of course, just that. However, as potentials they are both generous and demanding, revealing both the insights and the inadequacies of Nietzsche's political thought more fully.

However, critical politics becomes secondary as *BGE* concludes with struggles that are more deeply introspective (sections 263 through 296). Nearing the end of 262, Nietzsche intensifies the earlier claim that master and slave moralities may coexist within the same soul. "The dangerous and uncanny (*unheimliche*) point has been reached where the greater, more manifold, more comprehensive life overcomes and lives beyond the old morality; the 'individual' stands there, obliged to his own laws, his own arts and cunning for self preservation, self elevation, self-redemption (*Selbst-Erlösung*)." The harsh environment that demanded nobility has disappeared and slave morality cannot protect against nihilism. Yet the restoration of the old master morality is neither possible nor desirable. Countering the frightening consequences of slave morality must occur within the deepened modern soul that now displaces morality or culture as the primary unit of analysis ("the values of a human being give away something of the structure of his soul"—*Aufbau seiner Seele*—268). Nietzsche's goals are to call, test, and strengthen individuals, inviting members of his readership to discover resources for higher achievements within themselves, both encouraging and warning those who might (263; 41). Read cumulatively, *Beyond Good and Evil* may offer a performative example for those "most spiritual" tyrants seeking to re-create themselves within modern democratic chaos.[110]

This project requires that the noble separate themselves from any community (270, 271; 40–41, 212), for "every community (*Geimeinschaft*) makes somehow, somewhere, sometime, the common" (284).[111] What enables noble separation is not Stoic withdrawal from life's vulnerabilities (9; *GS*, 326) but experiences of deep suffering (*das tiefe Leiden*), another instinct linked to a certain kind of knowledge. "Through his suffering (*seines Leidens*) [the noble human being] is capable of knowing more than the cleverest and the wisest could know" (270), perhaps by empathizing with varied forms of suffering from the inside (Clark and Dudrick, in Clark, 2015, 122–123). This wider scope does not, however, bespeak egalitarian cosmopolitanism. Such experiences reinforce the critical recognition of hierarchy among sufferings and sufferers, the intellectual advance which is "the pride of the elect of knowledge" (cf. 39).

Within the reflections on the virtues in 284, mastership turns inward. One mark of nobility is being able "to remain master (*bleiben Herr*) of one's four virtues, courage (*Muthes*), insight (*Einsicht*), sympathy (*Mitgefühls*) and solitude (*Einsamkeit*)." In naming four virtues Nietzsche may reimagine scholasticism's (*ST*, II–II. 58.3) cardinal virtues, prudence, courage, moderation, and justice, though there is no parallel (here) to the theological virtues. While the scholastic framework adapted the classical Aristotelian tradition since rejected by modernity, Nietzsche avoids simple affiliation with ancients or moderns.[112] By beginning with courage he gestures toward a Homeric legacy but the three succeeding virtues affirm non-Homeric strengths.[113] Because all community makes humans common , the highest virtues must be self-creations, with the noblest mastery more authentically agentic and innovative than the surface displays of the ancient heroes. Insight might imply the continuous recognition of "our truths," the nobly instinctive, non-Cartesian rationality that demands actualization. The greatest thoughts (*grössten Gedanken*) are the greatest events (*grössten Ereignisse*) (285). While sympathy superficially recalls Aquinas's charity, it is extended only to those meriting it. The capable who are prevented from reaching heights of achievement that are otherwise within their grasp (those for whom "the call that awakens . . . comes too late"—274) elicit a kind of pity (203), while the sufferings of the mediocre should be dismissed (171, 225; *GS*, 338). Yet this assemblage of virtues is also discordant if not conflictual. How are sympathy and solitude reconciled (44)? Aristotle's schema in *NE* envisages the integration of potentially incompatible virtues within a moral personality (*hexis*) guided by practical wisdom (6.13). Nietzsche's cohesion is, on the other hand, forged by a willful mastery that controls insight (283; 117, 212), perhaps explaining why courage remains as first virtue (the only kind of admirable moderation?).[114] And when the "noble soul . . . accepts this standing fact of its egoism without any question mark . . . if it sought a name for such a thing it would say 'it is justice itself'" (265; *GM*, 1. 11).[115]

The imperative of agentic control reconstructs philosophy along radically self-referential lines. "A philosopher—is a human being who constantly experiences extraordinary things, sees, hears, suspects, hopes and dreams; who is struck by his own thoughts as from outside, as from over and under, as by his type of experiences and lightning bolts. . . . A philosopher . . . always [comes] back to himself" (292; 175). This contrasts strikingly with the Socratic definition of the philosopher in *Republic* Five as someone open to all kinds of learning (475d). Unlike the cave image in *Republic* Seven which represents "our nature" as it grows within yet aspires beyond its cultural shadows, Nietzsche's caves (plural) are personal depths that can always be plumbed further (289; 214), asking "whether behind every one of [these] caves there does not lie, must not lie some deeper cave."[116] This deeper excavation is presented in metaphors of violence. While Plato's violent images are political (*Rep*, 517 a), Nietzsche's seem naturalistically physical (292). And while Plato envisages some cessation of psychological, though not political, turbulence in reaching the light (*Rep*, 516 b–c; 517 a), Nietzsche emphasizes the continued wars that the best wage against themselves (cf. 200; 76).

The philosopher's turbulent self-referentiality is both challenged and refined by a figure Nietzsche calls the tempter god (*der Versucher-Gott*), eventually identified as Dionysus (295).[117] Touching even the deepest psyche, this god knows (*wissen*) how to access the cave of every soul (*jeder Seele*). Its temptations are potentially democratic, though responses to them are not (42).[118] Those responding appropriately become disciples, pressing "ever nearer to him in order to follow him ever more inwardly and thoroughly." Yet discipleship is not rote following (43, 194), and philosophers of the future will not repeat Nietzschean dogma (Satkunanandan 2015, 38). Implicitly countering images of Dionysian frenzy, the god's influence is represented as calming, "making silent all that is loud and full of itself." Avoiding images of war and churning seas, the god "smooths rough souls and lets them . . . lie still as a mirror, that the deep sky may mirror itself in them." Perhaps like the education imaged in Socrates's cave narrative, the tempter god may turn "the soul around . . . until it is able to endure looking at that which is" (*Rep*, 518c). The tempter god pacifies with visions of the sky (yet noting 71).

However, less pacific implications are hinted as Nietzsche imagines the gods (plural) philosophizing. "Even that Dionysus is a philosopher and that the gods too thus philosophize seems to me to be a novelty that is not without danger and might arouse mistrust precisely among philosophers." This statement provocatively recalls Aristotle's claim in the *Nicomachean Ethics* (10.8) that *theōria* is the only activity suitable for gods. However, the differences between these two projects underscore the radically aggressive character of Nietzsche's version. Like Nietzsche, Aristotle appeals to divine activity to revise conceptions of the best human life (*NE*, 10.7). Human beings should not confine themselves to thinking "only about mortal things because one is mortal but rather to make oneself immortal insofar as that is possible." Yet such a life would also "exceed what is human." Aristotle thus clarifies the borders of the human by showing its limits, encouraging his readers to reach toward a divine that is beyond mortal thoughts, yet still somehow human (*Metaphysics*, lambda, 7). By contrast, Nietzsche vision of the gods' philosophizing intensifies the aggressively human by suggesting that nothing permanently limits the value creations of the overman. Every soul touched by Dionysus "goes forward richer, not graced and startled, not as blessed and oppressed by alien goods, but richer in himself (*reicher an sich selber*), newer in himself (*sich neuer*) than before . . . full of new wills and streams, new unwillingnesses and countercurrents."

The unsettled relations between humans and gods are explored further as Nietzsche speculates on the tempter god's "pomp and virtue names" (*Prunk- und Tugendnamen*).[119] These are not discovered by grasping some divine nature but by deploying human interpretations of divinity. None of these pomp and virtue names reflects the dominance of slave morality. As named/praised by Nietzsche the virtues of the god are also four: "his explorer and discoverer courage, his daring honesty, his truthfulness, his love of wisdom." This quartet intersects provocatively with the virtues of noble humans. The god's courage parallels the first human virtue; daring honesty occupies the place of insight (227) and truthfulness replaces sympathy, though "under some circumstances (*unter Umständen*) [the god] love[s] (*liebe*) what is human," and we recall that in some cases sympathy may be a condition for (our) truthfulness (*BGE*, 26). Love of wisdom (*Liebe zur Weisheit*) takes the place of solitude, perhaps underscoring that "every philosopher was first of all a hermit" (289; 25, 204).[120] Love of wisdom may divinize solitude and delving into one's own deepest caves may humanize the love of wisdom. Yet it remains questionable how the god's virtues, even as interpreted by the most ambitious, can serve as stable models for human nobility. This is not simply due to human limitations, for errors and imperfections afflict both sides. Humans name the god's virtues under the (distorting?) influence of pompous solemnity. Yet what the god thinks it knows about humans may also be wrong and there are things that gods may learn from humans. Being more humane (*menschlicher*), humans have characteristics (a sense of shame, not one of the virtues) that gods may lack.[121] The re-creative power of the overman is paralleled by the imperfections of the gods. Does this mutual mismatch temper or further incite the ambitions of the overman? Dionysius says that the human—*der Mensch*—has no equals on earth.

So far, this schematic reading of *BGE*'s trajectory toward greater self-excavation seems broadly consistent with Nehamas's (1985) focus on Nietzsche's self-creative philosophy of life as literature, making war, indeed politics generally, into a history visited only recreationally (256). Yet by representing his future philosophers' new task as the revaluation of values, Nietzsche returns not just to a recognition of the persistence of cultural forms but to an affirmation of energetic politics (21, 205), genealogy as historical activity.[122] The philosopher's new lightnings (292) recall the lightning flashes of wars between states (*Greek State*, 170). The tempter god's pacifications may only be rest stops where energy is marshaled for further overcomings (273; 189). When this god is given its own voice, it "often reflect[s] how I might yet bring [a human being] forward, make him stronger, more evil (*böser*) and deeper than he is" (cf. *GM*, Vor. 6). Making strong human beings more evil may undo some of the outcomes of the slave rebellion in morals but it may also reignite the resentful suspicions that triggered that rebellion, drawing on fears of domination not entirely misplaced.[123] That prospect parallels the *Republic*'s cave dwellers' hostility toward the philosopher returning from above (517a), a reminder that there are horizontal as well as vertical caves, the love of one's own country or culture that refuses to look too critically within and violently punishes those who do. Perhaps another way in which Nietzsche cannot separate himself from Socrates (Nehamas, 1985, 30) is that neither can avoid politics and its contentions.

Nietzschean Resonances?

While this inward philosophical turn cannot disconnect itself from politics, the trajectory of *BGE* still leaves politics, especially the severely polemical form that Nietzsche's language continually images, undertheorized. Commentators trying to decipher his political theory offer controversial reconstructions that inevitably encounter anomalies.

One set reads 257's aristocratic society—structured by a pathos of distance and embracing slavery "of some sort"—programmatically, seeing some forms of internal and external domination as essential to Nietzsche's cultural regeneration.[124] It is, however, hard to see either the critical or the self-reflexive philosophies represented in *BGE* taking this stand without posing their own challenges to that project. If Nietzsche persists in pressing for this political aristocracy, he invites the Hegelian rebuke that he is regressively ennobling the primitive consciousness and aggression of premodernity, supplanting spirit with spiritedness. Yet Nietzsche might reply that this critique overlooks how the emotive politics of war contributes to Hegel's own vision of ethical health (*PhR*, 324), leaving the status this most intense politics unsettled.[125]

Perhaps Nietzsche envisages an aristocratic society constituted not by a pathos of social distance but by networks of noble individuals. This proposal is consistent with Nietzsche's recognition of the importance of cultural contexts for individual achievement and his insistence that creating a nobler human culture is one of future philosophy's new tasks (61, 203, 211).[126] Yet the political dimensions of this higher culture of excellence are unclear. To the extent that such readings reconceive politics as personal self-overcoming, what Leslie Thiele calls a "politics of the soul," they retain a language of politics while eliminating much of its focus.[127] And this higher culture may not lead its members to what Tamsin Shaw interprets as engaged political skepticism (2007, 2, 33) but to a severely judgmental moral aloofness disconnected from any politics once rational legitimacy is seen as impossible.

Nietzschean polemics are dramatically resituated within the sympathetic but critical perspective of Richard Rorty who recommends privatizing Nietzsche's call for self-overcoming. Exploitation and domination should be reinterpreted as metaphors for the severity toward one's own commitments needed by strong poets.[128] The last word of public philosophy must, on the other hand, recommit to Mill's two liberal cornerstones, reducing pain and leaving people's private lives alone (Rorty, 1989, 45). Nietzsche becomes politically benign once politically marginalized. Yet this attempted reconstruction encounters challenges from Nietzsche's own genealogies of the social dynamics that create the self. For both Nietzsche and Rorty the public/private separation is not a permanent ontological condition, but a revisable outcome of political discourses creating pragmatic categories and responding to historical needs. Nietzsche's tracing the influence of culture on the self clarifies the framework upon which Rorty relies, but it also exposes any claims to political last words as arbitrary.[129]

For postmodern democratic theory, on the other hand, Nietzsche's political importance lies precisely in his genealogies as he challenges theorizations (Hobbes's, Kant's, Hegel's) that overlook politics' continued risks and disruptions. In place of closure Nietzsche reinforces the need to contest oppressive social forms, reconnecting the philosophers' vertical and horizontal struggles and forging a connection with Foucault and postmodern theories of agonistic democracy.[130]

Yet questions persist. Tracy Strong's and Lawrence Hatab's illuminating books offer good examples. Though both insist that readers must recognize Nietzsche's hard edges, their interpretations eventually replace references to war with images of games, laughter, play, music, and dance.[131] These moves may be faithful to Nietzschean philosophers who are joyfully self-creative (*BT, Attempt*, 7; *GS*, 382), but may also sidestep the darker sides of politics, failing to treat political violence with the seriousness it merits. Is Nietzsche's transfiguration of politics politically distorting? When contestative agonism persists it does so within

Connolly's "gentle wars" tempered by a broadly civilized context or within Hatab's replacement of war with tragedy (1995, 222), effectively placing the most violent politics outside of the epistemic and pragmatic horizons of democratic political action.[132] How will such events be made sense of? What responses to their prospects and occurrences are appropriate? What limits exist and how can they be identified? Is war simply the other of egalitarian democracy?[133]

Possibly, though, Nietzsche's most important political contribution is indirect, a critical diagnostic of modernity's contradictions (Geuss, 2008, 69; Sluga, 2014) that could engage questions of just and unjust wars. The power of this critical perspective is, however, limited by Nietzsche's representation of philosophy as self-exploration driven by commitments to overcome restrictive normative attachments and constraining social hierarchies. While this reframing may correct inflated beliefs that the right philosophy can prove moral theorems,[134] it may also (and paradoxically) limit philosophy's critical potential. Here too, Strong and Hatab are provocative. For Strong, one of Nietzsche's contributions is his representation of philosophy as a practice distinctively concerned with intelligibility (2000, 305, 309). While claims to intelligibility are presumed in other practices, economic, artistic, rhetorical, or polemical, philosophy may stand out as the practice that subjects all claims to intelligibility, including its own, to radical questioning. Yet does such questioning originate in anything beyond philosophy's own willful demands? Hatab's focus on Nietzschean agonism, perspectivalism,[135] and suspicion (1995, 61) raises doubts, essentially redefining philosophy as an agonism (154, 158, 182, 184) that courageously opens itself to agonistic challenge. These readings may well be consistent with Nietzsche's express prioritization of will to power over knowledge, but they also seem to valorize the practice of philosophy as a distinctive form of warlike willfulness.

Yet mustn't philosophy's distinctively aggressive critical thinking go beyond critical self-assertion? Arguably, the relationship of willfulness to truthfulness remains more ambiguous for Nietzsche (*BGE*, 202)[136] than it does for those democratic descendants who award a more pronounced role to contestation.[137] However, by emphasizing contestation itself rather than the grounds and purposes that contestation serves does Nietzsche's (or Nietzschean) agonism ignore other important political realities, particularly the reflective assessments of public purposes that are essential to political choice, the considerations that deserve not simply to be energetically asserted but to be taken seriously?

Unsettled Histories

For all of their differences, neither Nietzsche nor Hegel really succeeds in making political war history. Their own texts acknowledge that such wars cannot be overcome within a historical dialectic or resituated within a psychology of self-creation. Though Hegel emphasizes the ordered rationality of modernity's objective spirit, his healthy politics still needs the vigorous contributions of war to oppose the stagnation of perpetual peace. Nietzsche's inward philosophical turn remains embedded in surrounding, often aggressive, attachments to political power and cultural identity.

These complications do not simply leave war undertheorized, they may also leave philosophy diminished, for one of political philosophy's strengths must be its capacity to contribute to public discussion about this most wrenching political phenomenon. Each author's metaphor of color is illuminating. Hegel's philosophy paints its grey in grey, coming to the world too late to change it, Nietzsche's prizes colors marked by variety and brilliance (*BGE*, 296).[138] Yet neither a philosophy shrouded by dusky rest nor one inflamed by glimmering motion seems capable of engaging war's harshness in a way adequate for thoughtful practice. In spite of their grounding in epistemologies of historicism, neither perspective seems fully able to assist serious efforts to deal with violent historical change. Appreciating this problem, we might reconsider two classical authors whose presence continues to influence modern and postmodern political discourses, Thucydides and Plato.

5 | Political Philosophy Between Peace and War

THUCYDIDES, *Peloponnesian War*
PLATO, *Republic*

Different Texts, Different Worlds?

The interpretations offered so far have used the ideas of war and peace as apertures into the intellectual structures and the rhetorical practices of a series of seminal texts. War and peace have been understood not simply as alternative political conditions to be engaged but as fundamentally different characterizations of the practical world, the moral choices facing those within it, the epistemologies that access it, and the language in which it is represented. Though resisting oversimplification, these readings have also argued that the texts considered thus far have been guided by one or the other of these perspectives. In some ways, each of these networks might seem to engage different worlds. While this divide is most pronounced in the colliding perspectives of Schmitt and Derrida, the tendency to elevate one or the other of these conditions to pre-eminence continues across this archive. Aquinas's hierarchy of human and divine laws not only structures a created normative order that unjust wars threaten and just wars restore but also reveals that membership in the community of the saved, held together by charity, is the highest, most fulfilling human aspiration. Hobbes's thought experiment of the state of war and Kant's acknowledgment of the persistence of historical wars are both transformed into programmatic outlines for perpetual peace. Hegel's narrative of the historical self-actualization of spirit subsumes warlike spiritedness within stable rationality. Countering such perspectives in numerous ways, Machiavelli's political agency and Nietzsche's psychological overcomings affirm the permanent place of confrontation within human life and its world.

While their intellectual structures and narrative styles differ markedly, each of these authors/texts also intends to settle the most important political philosophical questions. The destabilizing Nietzsche remains committed to "our truths." The Derrida who cherishes openness to the other paradoxically rejects most competing voices within the Western philosophical tradition as androcentric dominations whose instructiveness depends on their deconstruction. I have tried to argue, however, that all of these conceptual frameworks are unsettled internally by lingering complications or roads not taken, the politics beyond enmity implicit in Schmitt's valorization of meaning, the persistent anxieties of sublunar politics for Aquinas, the political disruptions to Hobbes's prudential and Kant's moral sciences, the persistence of the spiritedness that allegedly gives way to Hegel's spirit. These observations are not intended to assail unsuccessful efforts at intellectual resolution, but rather to note disconnects between ambitions for such closures and inevitably frustrating political complications. One response to this apparent dead-end is offered by philosophers pulling back from philosophy itself. Raymond Geuss and Bernard Williams argue that abstract or hypermoralizing political theories need to be replaced by a political thinking more embedded in the uncertainties and tragedies of politics itself. Among the authors considered thus far, Machiavelli seems most committed to this kind of project. However, I have argued that his apparently anti-philosophical turn toward politics itself presumes philosophical claims, retaining the need for philosophy (committed to *verita effetuale*) within even the most aggressive turn toward politics. The unintended consequence of this collision has been to limit the contributions of political philosophy even as they are performatively represented as necessary. In place of a philosophical structure that oversimplifies politics or a political thinking suspicious of philosophy, we may need a philosophy that takes politics seriously and a narrative of politics that is open to philosophy. This chapter argues that we can find that mutuality in Thucydides and Plato.

But why read these two together? Scholarly commentaries have, as rule rather than exception, offered deeply illuminating readings of one without paying significant attention to the other. Why stray? The most immediately contrarian reason is that we are frequently told that we need and should not, precisely because the two inhabit such different intellectual worlds. Plato's true philosophers allegedly occupy an unchanging world of intellectual forms (ideas) existing, in the language of the *Republic*'s cave story, above and in the light, far removed from darker politics going on "down here" (*Rep*, 521a). In contrast, Thucydides's world is passionate and disorderly, diagnosed with frightening intensity by the character Diodotus in Book Three's debate on Mytilene. "Hope and *erōs* [which] are everywhere . . . extend human nature relentlessly toward [some] action (*tēs anthrōpeias phuseōs hormōmenēs prothumōs ti praxai*)" (3.45).[1] Nietzsche reinforces this separation in *Twilight of the Idols*, "What I Owe to the Ancients." "It is courage before reality that at last distinguishes natures like Thucydides and Plato. Plato is a coward before reality, consequently he flees into the ideal; Thucydides has himself in control, consequently he also keeps control of things." Though offered for its own controversial purposes, Nietzsche's judgment is seconded by many current scholars. Jacqueline de Romilly (1963, 362, 365) and Gregory Crane (1998, 324–325) contrast abstract Platonic idealism with gritty Thucydidean realism. Placing Thucydides among those skeptical of any strictly philosophical approach to politics, Geuss asks "who is a better guide to human life, Plato or Thucydides?" and answers the latter, precisely because of his recognition of what Geuss sees as the real world (2005, 219–233).

According to these assessments, we find these two (Greek) authors speaking such different intellectual languages that prospects for dialogue seem impossible. In spite of the discursive and narrative approaches of both, some readers find their texts frustratingly rigid. Though Plato represents the human world through dialogues, many interpret their conversations as opportunities for a theorizing Plato to demonstrate philosophically grounded imperatives (Nussbaum, 2001, 69, 139; Reeve, 1988, 234). Thucydides's narrations of the speeches and practices of political agents allegedly confirm coldly lawlike explanations of political disorder. Thus, the so-called Melian dialogue in Book Five becomes a parody of dialogue, limited by compulsions of power (Athenian military superiority—5.86) and distorted by attachments to political imaginaries (Melian visions of an ordered world ruled by the divine—5.104—and Athenian acceptance of the imperatives of empire—5.95, 97, 105). Even the parody unravels as the substitutes for dialogue—Melian appeals to piety and just gods and Athenian affirmation of a natural law subordinating the weaker to the stronger—collapse into disasters in the narratives that follows (Mara, 2008, 53–54).

The contrarian impulse is refined by more serious considerations. Eventually, such striking disjunctures between Platonic and Thucydidean worlds discourage us from seeking a resource for critical political philosophy in either author. For many commentators, both skeptics and defenders, Plato's transparently monologic dialogues (Bercovitch, 1998,

75) at best approximate the decisive clarity of a philosophy conducted in an enduring but distant space where ordinary politics are irrelevant or forgotten. Instructed by Thucydides, we speak and act within a turbulence whose dynamics may be explained by science but not placed under the scrutiny of thoughtfulness and care of agency. Thus read, each author imposes a conclusive frame of reference that dismisses alternative views of the world and discourages attempts at practical change, previewing rather than avoiding their successors' difficulties.

I challenge that conclusion by interpreting Thucydides and Plato dialogically, expanding insights about each by reading both.[2] Interpretations sensitive to mutuality may disclose possibilities missed by more sequestered readings, especially questions of war and peace posed by the experience and memory of the Peloponnesian War. As texts, both Plato's dialogues and Thucydides's book revolve around interactions and conversations that arise within intensely particular circumstances but that also engage problems of permanent significance, moving from the immediacies of war to what might be known about human beings and the world. Implicitly, each author invites the conversational contributions of the other. It is not immodest to ask that the value of this approach be judged by the interpretations that it makes possible.

Substantively, I argue that this interactive reading avoids the binary frames of reference of abstract and illusory peace or ongoing and inescapable war, drawing attention to experiences in need of continued intellectual negotiation and opening spaces for practical improvement. Beyond revising our understanding of these authors, such mutual readings help us to appreciate the possibilities of a dialogic or conversational political theory that challenges both the possibility and the desirability of the attempted closures that I have attributed to the positions considered previously. Plato and Thucydides are read as participants in a conversation that should be expanded to welcome and interrogate the contributions of this book's range of texts.

Texts and Contexts

For both authors, relations between texts and contexts are bidirectional. Plato's philosophical dialogues do not simply respond to political events in Athens' fifth century; they inscribe those events, particularly those of the Peloponnesian War, within their dramatic structures. While Thucydides's narratives (never called a history) are not explicitly philosophical, they gesture toward philosophical concerns and invite philosophical reflection.

Socrates's practices within the dialogues largely parallel the war (431–404, bc).[3] He makes his first public impression in the *Protagoras*, historically set in 432, just before its outbreak (Nussbaum, 2001, 91). Seth Benardete (1991, 7) and Arlene Saxonhouse (1983, 139–169) note that textual references in the *Gorgias* extend virtually through the war's entire course.[4] In the *Meno* (set circa 401), the angry encounter with Anytus, Socrates's principal accuser in his capital trial (399), recalls Athens' internal political disturbance after its defeat by Sparta (404), where the short lived oligarchy of the thirty (404–403) was overthrown by a returning democracy involving Anytus. Even dialogues more overtly philosophical are politically situated. The mathematical cosmology offered by the Locrian Timaeus is the first of a series of responses to Socrates's request to see a regime resembling the *Republic*'s city in speech in motion or at war (*Tim*, 19 b–c). A projected sequence and structuring of speeches is organized by a character named Critias, likely, though not certainly, the eventual leader of the thirty, and is designed to culminate in the revelation that such a city existed historically as ancient Athens (*Timaeus*, 26 c–d).[5]

In the *Republic*, we find reminders and images of the war that implicitly engage portions of Thucydides's narrative (Bloom, 1968; Nails, 2002). The dialogue's interlocutors, some of whom will be among the thirty's victims, anticipate the oligarchy's violence (Frank, 2018, 13). The conversation's physical location connects to the democratic victory over the thirty won in a battle fought near the temple of Bendis, the Thracian goddess whose festival prompts Socrates's and his companion Glaucon's visit, "down to the Piraeus" (327 a).[6] Socrates's eventual representation of a philosophy "making no use of anything sensed in any way, but [only] ideas themselves, through ideas to ideas, . . . ending in ideas" (511 b–c) is no simple metaphysical projection. It reveals "a life better than ruling" (520e–521a) to Glaucon, who is addressed, in the language of oligarchic political clubs, as a *hetairos* and thus as someone potentially attracted to the thirty. Just as his relation Critias proclaims the historical existence of a Socratic city in speech, Glaucon eventually demands to be shown how the *Republic*'s city can be realized (471d–e). Identifying a life better than ruling is a speech act within a conversation that shows how forms of tyrannical and democratic *kratein* are connected (562b–c) and presents a different kind of ruling and being ruled (427c–e) as an alternative.

Reversing direction, Thucydides moves from the anxieties and agendas of particular individuals and regimes to broader ways of understanding and engaging the world. Here, we might reconsider Donald Kagan's judgments about the place of the characters' speeches in the narrative. For Kagan (2009, 17), Thucydides either reports these speeches as accurately as possible or violates objective history. In his own methodological sketch (1.22), Thucydides notes that he aims to be as accurate as possible about the war's deeds (*erga*) and, as to the speeches (*logoi*), because "recalling precisely what was said was difficult" he has offered what "seemed . . . each would have said [as] especially required (*ta deonta malist' eipein*) on the occasion, [while] maintaining as much closeness as possible to the general sense (*gnōmēs*) of what was truly said." This might mean reporting the *logoi* with as much factual accuracy as possible. However, another possibility is that the book represents the most appropriate speeches to be given on *these* occasions, by *these* speakers, before *these* audiences. This does not mean that Thucydides simply fabricates (Nichols, 2015, 16), but it does acknowledge an authorial discretion in crafting *logoi* that most clearly reveal the priorities or identities of the speaker or regime in question. Differing from straightforwardly factual reports, such representations invite the critical scrutiny that Thucydides applies through a range of narrative strategies. The speeches are also speech acts with their own pragmatic intentions (achieved or not) and consequences (foreseen or not). Each *logos* is itself an *ergon* connected to other narrated *erga*. Pericles's funeral oration (2.34–46) valorizing a distinctive civic identity reads differently after we encounter Thucydides's subsequent plague narrative (2.47–2.54) diagnosing civic disintegration. Likewise, his last speech proclaiming (2.64) that the daring exhibited by Athens' multiple wars will forge a name persisting in eternal memory (*aieimnēstos*) must be critically reassessed in light of the severe distress caused by the city's fighting two wars at once (7.28).[7]

Though politically situated, Thucydides's speeches show the limits of those situations by gesturing beyond them, as in the Athenian statements on Melos about the significance of nature and the gods as justifications for their political adventurism (5.105). In pointing beyond immediate political horizons such appeals acknowledge that cultural meanings are insufficient justifications for controversial practices. Yet the practical character of these appeals implies that visions of nature, the gods, and the human things (*ta anthrōpeia*) generally, are neither deduced from scientific or moral first principles nor disclosed by divine revelation. They emerge within pragmatic contexts continually subjected to challenge and revision. When Athenian (1.76; 5.105) and Syracusan (4.61) speakers say that nature mandates the domination of the weak by the strong, they speak within powerful regimes that construe imperatives of nature as validations.

Interpreting the speeches as more than factual reports means reading them as representations of political, ethical, and epistemic alternatives that are scrutinized within a broader narrative. Critically examining *logoi* of all sorts may be Thucydides's core intellectual project. The war's *erga* are accessed through investigations of others' accounts and the *logoi* offer distinctive and controversial possibilities for politics. Read this way, the book is multivocal and Thucydides's own *logos* takes other *logoi* seriously, while nonetheless subjecting them to critical examination.[8] This multivocality allows dialogic intersections with the *Republic* that are both illuminating and critical.

In what follows, I test this grounding claim by considering two questions. The first is epistemically foundational, asking whether extremity clarifies or distorts our understanding of human affairs. The second is politically charged, examining allegations of the necessity of war. In both cases, Thucydides's frame of reference seems to exclude serious engagement with Platonic political philosophy, while Plato's philosophical allegiances draw us away from Thucydides's violent political world. I will try to smooth some of these edges by uncovering interactions that are more mutual, inviting and examining the contributions of a variety of voices.

Politics and Extremes

Speaking in what may be his darkest tone, Thucydides implies that the human things—*ta anthrōpeia*—are clearest during times of what Jeremy Mynott (2013, 3) calls upheaval.[9] Concerning the *stasis* in Corcyra, Thucydides writes: "And so many hardships fell upon the cities on account of *stasis*, things that happen and will always happen as long as human beings have the same nature (*hē autē phusis anthrōpōn*) . . . In peace and good circumstances (*eirēnē kai agathois pragmasin*), cities and individuals hold better thoughts (*ameinous tas gnōmas*) because they do not have to confront involuntary necessities, but war (*polemos*), generally depriving [human beings] of daily resources is a violent teacher (*biaios didaskalos*), making the dispositions of both [cities and individuals] like that [harsh] condition" (3.82).

In interesting ways, this statement intersects with the controversial judgments of Schmitt, Machiavelli and Hobbes. At first blush Thucydides seems to anticipate Schmitt's understanding of politics as "the most

intense and extreme antagonism . . . [becoming] that much more political the closer it approaches the most extreme point, that of the friend
enemy grouping" (*CP*, 27). Yet differences eventually overwhelm
similarities. While Schmitt's extreme defines politics, Thucydides's
destroys it. As I have suggested in chapter 1, Thucydides's Corcyrean narrative underscores processes that destabilize Schmitt's focus on violent
conflict as the conceptual essence of politics. Thucydides does not stop
at Derrida's hyperpoliticization; he traces the unravelling of politics itself.[10] For similar reasons, Machiavelli's reading of the Corcyrean episode
(*Disc*, 2.2) as a forceful reminder of the vengeful republican love of liberty
(*Prince*, 5) is challenged . For Thucydides, what may look (to Machiavelli)
like energy within a polemically intensified vision of politics is really social suicide. If such a violent extremity reflects the underlying nature of
ta anthrōpeia, the establishment and exercise of political power are not,
as some of Thucydides's characters allege, natural, but counternatural.[11]
Schmitt's interesting dangerousness and Machiavelli's energetic vengeful-
ness dissolve politics all the way down.

Seeing politics as a bulwark against natural chaos seems more
Hobbesian; indeed, the Corcyrean narrative may be one source for
Hobbes's disordered state of nature.[12] Yet this parallel, too, is limited. The
inhabitants of Hobbes's "natural condition" do not, as in Diodotus's diagnosis, extend themselves relentlessly toward action. Their anxieties block
any effective action and they long for a security that will assure commodious living (*Leviathan*, 13.9). Moreover, while Hobbes offers *Leviathan*'s
institutional designs as stable remediations (29.1), Thucydides sees such
attempts as, too often, self-undermining. The very drives for gain and
honor that converged to create stability in the archaic period prior to the
Trojan war (1.8) are the roots of political disintegration during the present
period of the Peloponnesian war (3.83). Though the hegemonies established by Athens and Sparta after the Persian wars ordered Hellenic political life (1.18–19), their competition now threatens to destroy it. The civic
disruption in Corcyra previews a condition that progressively threatens all
of the Greek cities.[13]

Such a narrative could not be further from a *Republic* structured by a
two world ontology dominated by a metaphysics of ideas. We can understand why Romilly concludes that Plato's purposes "could not in fact have
had either meaning or relevance within history" (2012, 141). Yet this judgment overlooks the ways that political turbulence frames discourses within
this most philosophical dialogue. This influence is observable not only in
the regime-driven narratives of Books Eight and Nine (which draw heavily

on the disruptions of 404/403) but also in portions of the work that seem on first reading more philosophically analytic. For example, in his characterization of the appetitive part of the soul in Book Four, Socrates insists that the desires (*epithumiai*) aim only at their appropriate satisfactions, disregarding concerns for quality. "Let no one make an uproar if [we are] inattentive . . . that no one desires drink but good drink (*chrēstou potou*), not food but good food (*chrēstou sitou*), for all, of course, desire good things (*tōn agathōn*) . . . [A] particular kind of thirst is for a particular kind of drink, but thirst itself is neither for much nor little, good or bad, nor, in a word, for any particular kind, but thirst by itself is naturally only for drink" (438a; 439a).

Some commentators (Reeve, 1988, 138) read this as a logical analysis of the character of desire as such. Yet even this "analytic" is part of a dramatic trajectory, as Socrates attempts to identify psychic justice and injustice by constructing images of their civic parallels (368d–369a). If desire is blind to satisfaction's quality, calculative rationality (439c–d) must govern the soul (Weiss, 2006, 175) as a separable, regulating faculty. This psychic order parallels the just city's stratified political structure, reinforcing the interlocutors' agreement that cities should be ruled (*kratoumenas*) by the *epieikesteroi*, translated by Bloom as "the more intelligent" (431c–d). Yet though presented as analogy, the civic/psychic parallel eventually diverges. A sharply stratified psychic structure implies the disconnection of desire *qua* desire from any concern for the good, splitting emotional and rational psyches. This chasm is challenged by Socrates's own choices of words. In its yearning (*orexis*) and urge (*hormē*) for satisfying drink, the thirsting soul also takes counsel (*bouletai*) (439a–b), implying deliberation. The *epieikesteroi* are identified by both their desires (*epithumiōn*) and their prudence (*phronēseōs*). Eventually, the framing analogy of soul/city itself becomes provisional and controversial (434c–435a), introducing puzzles, not demonstrating solutions. In the revised account of Book Nine, each of the soul's parts is distinctively appetitive, characterized by its particular desire, now intensified into love (580d ff).

If Book Four's analytic of desire is misleading, are there alternative readings ? Taking the dialogue's politically turbulent backstories seriously, may we interpret desire's unconcern with quality as a representation of desires experienced under extreme circumstances, where demands for preservation render judgments about quality otiose? Survival becomes the strongest imperative for those afflicted by war and *stasis*. Looking to Thucydides helps us to grasp this point. Both the plague narrative of Book Two and the account of the slaughter of Nicias's army in Book Seven offer images of intense thirst absent any concern for the quality of what is drunk. As Nicias's horrific retreat from Syracuse ends, "the Athenians pushed on to the Assinarus river . . . partly because of their weariness and desire to drink (*piein epithumia*) . . . The Syracusans hurled missiles down upon the Athenians most of whom were drinking greedily . . . The Peloponnesians went down to the water's edge and butchered them, most of all those in the river. The water at once became foul but was drunk all the same, though muddy and full of blood, it was fought over by many" (7.84). We can extend this parallel to extreme hunger. During the siege of Potideia, the inhabitants had "sometimes eaten one another" (2.70). In anticipating the control of the thirty, the *Republic* presumes Athens' defeat through siege. When Xenophon extends Thucydides's time horizon through the defeat in *Hellenica* 2.2, he repeatedly references starvation and famine. Read in these contexts, the divide between desire and rationality is far from abstract and the psychic scenario wherein calculation masters desire becomes a disturbing commentary on how political extremes distort or disintegrate practical judgment just when it is most needed. Subsequently, Socrates imagines warring (*polemein*) and faction (*stasiazontoin*) between calculation and appetite (that by which the soul loves—*era*, the *hetairos* of satisfactions and pleasures) in his story of Leontius (439e–440b). In its collision with desire, calculation loses, leaving anger (*orgē*) in its wake. Here, at least, Plato does not run away from reality "to prove to himself that reason and instinct (*Vernunft und Instinkt*) of themselves tend toward one goal" (*BGE*, 191).

According to this reading, Socrates's representation of desire in Book Four recognizes political influences on even the most basic psychological functions. The significance of warlike politics is anticipated earlier in the same book when Socrates's explains how the city constructed thus far (since 368e) will fight (422a). Pressed by Glaucon's brother Adeimantus, he proposes that it exploit cleavages within its competitors, each of which sounds like a potential Corcyra, "two [cities] warring with each other, one of the poor, the other of the rich." Intensifying *stasis* is the key to victory (422e–423b). For someone committed to defending justice (354b–c), Socrates is remarkably clinical about the consequences of this strategy for Greek political life.[14] Yet the destructive influence of cultural forces, one exploiting, the other vulnerable to, *stasis*, highlights the politically created character of extremity and the possibility, though hardly the guarantee, that things could be otherwise.

Socrates gradually softens this extreme polemicism in a different war narrative, offered in Book Five (Kochin, 1999; Frank, 2007). For Glaucon, this discussion is a tangent that postpones hearing how their city in speech could be realized (471e). While the eventual outcome may confirm that this achievement is impossible (Roochnik, 2009), a more pragmatic implication is that the violent wars waged both among Greeks and between Greeks and barbarians can be moderated. In a passage that draws considerable attention from both Schmitt and Derrida, Socrates distinguishes Greek wars (*polemoi*) with barbarians from internal conflicts (*staseis*) among Greek cities. Unlike Pericles (of 1.144; 2.64), he does not see Greek wars as venues for achieving timeless renown. Abandoning Book Four's cynicism, he envisages how wars among Greeks would be less devastating. Both linking and revising Thucydides's plague and Corcyrean narratives, *stasis* is curable disease, not inevitable collapse (470c–d). Socrates next imagines that Greeks might fight barbarians the way that they now fight each other (471b), opening the possibility of further moderating wars with barbarians as well. Is the divide between Greeks and barbarians itself capable of being bridged? By problematizing both the relationship between *polemos* and *stasis* and the permanence of the hostility that these polemics reflect, Socrates disputes Schmitt's concept of the political as that which telescopes the most deadly enmity and moderates Derrida's vision of a future that may come, offering daunting but workable prospects for more modest political change.

Such practical moderation presumes a distinctively non-Periclean regime. In honoring "those who have been judged exceptionally good in life when dying of old age or in some other way" in the same fashion as it memorializes those killed in battle (469b), this regime does not base its reputation on the scope of its wars; its funeral orations would revise conceptions of conspicuous men (Thuc 2.43–6). Eventually, the principal condition of this city's emergence is the coincidence (473c) of philosophy and political power, an association that, while neither natural nor necessary, is not impossible (497a). If nature does not simply order things for the best—one implication of Timaeus's ambitious cosmology[15]—neither is it the nightmarish chaos of Corcyra. Human nature might instead be understood as indeterminate, offering possibilities as well as hazards. In recognizing extremes without surrendering to them, the *Republic* encourages deeper inquiry.

Can this interpretation of the *Republic* reflexively enrich readings of Thucydides? Speculatively, a byplay between the sharpness and distortions of extreme statements may help to identify the controversial place of chapter 84 in Book Three. There, *stasis* is said to reveal "human nature (*hē anthrōpeia phusis*) dominating (*kratēsa*) the laws and inclined even against the laws to do injustice, well pleased to show its passion (*orgēs*) as uncontrollable, stronger than justice, enemy to distinction." Because "the language has a more rhetorical character [and] the criticism of human nature . . . [is] less nuanced than in 3.82" (Lattimore, 1998, 171), some commentators have read the chapter as spurious. Alternatively, while acknowledging Thucydidean authorship, others marginalize the chapter as part of an earlier draft (Connor, 1984, 102; Mynott, 2013, 219; Orwin, 1994, 176). However, the chapter's own extreme stance could be read as a textual acknowledgment of both the distorting consequences and stark clarity of seeing "human things" extremely. Perhaps Thucydides's treatment of human nature shares some of Plato's ambiguities. Three Thucydidean references to women may illuminate. Within the funeral oration, Pericles advises women hearing his encomium to conspicuous males (2.43) to respect nature's standard (*huparchousēs phuseōs*) by avoiding manly *kleos* (2.45). Yet by speaking in nature's (authoritative) name to reinforce a controversial view of the human good, Pericles's rhetoric acknowledges that there may be counterpossibilities framed by alternative views of nature. Concerning Corcyra, Thucydides comments (3.74) that *stasis* drove the city's women to a boldness and endurance (the political behaviors of Athens and Sparta) counter to nature (*para phusin*). Nature may include a gentleness violated by political extremities that may themselves be moderated. Is it accidental that a sequel narrates the peaceful festivals of the old Ionians, with a focus on the women's chorus (3.104)? Those told to avoid *kleos* (2.45) by a statesman dismissing Homer (2.41) receive Homeric praise.

In backing away from his revised Corcyrean narrative with a revised Periclean narrative in *Republic* Five, Socrates encourages reconsideration of Thucydides's authorial narrative in ways that reinforce skepticism about Hegel's verdict that Thucydides writes "within the spirit of the times and cannot as yet go beyond them" (*PhH*, 4). Recalling the critique of Hegel in chapter 4, in writing why the war is most worthy of being spoken about (*axiologōtaton*) in 1.1, Thucydides underscores the scope and intensity of its motion, drawing on Periclean criteria of daring and energy, considerations intended to go beyond the spirit of the times. "For this was the greatest motion (*kinēsis . . . megistē*) that had come to be among Greeks and even [among] portions of the barbarians, indeed one may speak of [the involvement of] most of humanity" (*pleiston anthrōpōn*) (1.1; cf. 2.64). Further complications arise in 1.23 where the war's greatness (*megiston*) shows another side, "such sufferings as came to afflict Hellas unlike those [experienced] in any [length of] time; for never had there been so many cities seized and abandoned . . . nor were there so many human beings dislocated or slaughtered, both on account of the war itself and because of factional fighting (*stasiazein*)." Widespread human misery accompanies Athenian greatness and their byplay provides a lesson that will be relevant as long as human beings have the same nature. Both explanations of the war's significance offer visions of extremes (*erga megista*) that challenge the better thoughts of peace and good circumstances. The appropriate response may not be retreat to those better thoughts within a more conventional but therefore more tenuous political moderation, but critical judgment applied to extreme prospects, including extremes of enmity and friendship, realism and idealism. By following *kinēsis* with *stasiazein* across his explanations of the war's importance, Thucydides implies that the extremism of the Corcyrean narrative should become part of a critical examination of Pericles's Athenian narrative. We can begin that critique by considering claims about the origin of war.

The Necessity of War and the Possibility of Logos

The proposal to moderate wars in *Republic* Book Five presumes regime functions beyond both defense and aggrandizement. In addition to exercising power, political cultures may enable or frustrate discursive practices that can inform critical judgment. Judgment and *logos* are linked by Socrates in Book Nine when he asks "by what must things that are going to be finely judged (*kalōs krithēsesthai*) be judged? Isn't it by experience, prudence, and *logos*?" (582a). The question is prompted by the need to delve deeply into the tyrant's *psychē*, but the bidirectional connections between soul and city, reflected in the byplay between the tyrant's soul and the character of democracy (*Rep*, 565c–d), imply the need for a *political* judgment.

The political judgment central to the *Republic* chooses between the just and the unjust life (347e; 618b–619a) and the dialogue as a whole proceeds by examining a series of *logoi* about justice and its opposites. What *logos* means within the Platonic dialogues is not obvious of course (*Gorgias*, 523a), yet prospects for its exerting the positive influence envisaged by Socrates seem on first view discounted by Thucydides. The actions and deeds represented in his book appear to reinforce the subordination of *logos* to passion (*orgē*) or power (*dunamis*). When Thucydides's own rationality is brought to bear, it seems only to offer a disheartening, analysis that discloses the inexorability of overreaching.[16] Yet this impression misleads. The importance and fragility of *logos* within political judgment emerges thematically within Thucydides's complex treatment of the necessity of war.

In his last speech, Pericles considers whether the war against the Peloponnesians was chosen or necessary, answering the latter. "For those in good fortune and [able to make] a choice (*airesis*), waging war is altogether thoughtless (*pollē anoia*), but when from necessity (*anankaion*) they must [either] submit by giving way to their neighbors or prevail by running risks (*kinduneusantas*), those who flee from dangers are more blameworthy than those who stand up to them" (2.61). Thucydides apparently agrees with this judgment when he comments, twice (1.23; 5.25), that the Athenians and Spartans were compelled (*anankasai*) to fight. However, both the Periclean and the Thucydidean statements provoke questions. For Pericles, war is necessary when cities confront the alternatives of subjection or prevailing; running risks is necessitated by the starkness of that alternative, thoughtfulness being overwhelmed by immediacy. Yet in his first speech, running risks is valorized and choiceworthy as the source of "the greatest honors (*megistai timai*) for both cities and individuals" (1.144).[17] Submitting to Lacedaemonian demands is dishonorable slavery for a regime of Athens' stature (1.141).[18] Within Thucydides's narrative, the meaning of compulsion (*anankē*) itself is a problem requiring critical thoughtfulness and his own judgment about the war's necessity is not settled.

The Athenians' speech at Sparta in Book One (1.73–78) traces the creation of Athens' empire to necessity, the three compelling (*katēnankasthēmen*) or conquering (*nikēthentes*) forces of fear, honor, and interest. Thucydides's various representations of this claim, both within the speech and across the narratives that follow, raise questions about its meaning. The speech is intended (1.72) to show Athens' power (*dunamis*) and thus to deter hasty Spartan reactions to their allies' warnings about Athens' growing aggressiveness. Yet the Athenians' confidence that recognizing their power will restrain may ignore its propensity to distress, making war more, not less, likely. Athenian greatness and Spartan fear are identified (1.23) as the truest *prophaseis* of the war.[19] By explicitly referencing these regimes and inviting the reader to consider how greatness and fear intersect within them (Mara, 2008, 150–151), Thucydides suggests that *anankē* can be interpreted not as a causal sequence dictated by historical laws (Romilly, 1963) but as a controversial thesis (Orwin, 1994, 64) made within and across political cultures. These allegedly conquering forces are variably ordered within the Athenian speech (1.75–76). There is no necessary sequence. A second statement gives primacy to honor, not fear, implying different perceptions of necessity and shifting priorities for practice. If fear dominates, reputation is valued principally as deterrent. If honor prevails, the greatest fear may be loss of reputation.

Yet the Athenians also claim they deserve their empire because of their decisive role in defeating Persian aggression (1.75). Moving from the origins of its empire to its manner of rule, Athens especially merits praise (*epaineisthai te axioi*) because it treats its subject cities more justly (*dikaioteroi*)—because with more equality (*apo tou isou*)—than its superior military power dictates (1.76–77). This justice is not Thrasymachus's advantage of the stronger (*Republic*, 337c), but works to the advantage of the weaker. Yet complications persist. How do claims to distinctive worth fit with necessity's overpowering influences? By representing their regard for equality as discretionary, the Athenians give the generosity of the powerful literal *pride* of place. Yet the speech also implies a countervailing dynamic between power and justice. While Athens' justice is enabled by its power, this same justice can criticize applications of power in the name of an equality different from the equal balancing of material forces. The outcomes of such criticism cannot be presumed, for influences of fear, honor, and interest persist. Yet the possibility of judgment attentive to a justice not dictated by power acknowledges the potential integrity of *logos*. For such a *logos*, "realism," including the later (5.89) Athenian claim that justice holds only when material powers offset, is not a science to be demonstrated but a discourse to be interrogated.[20]

Logos is thematized politically in Book Three by the character Diodotus, as he argues for a prudently humane treatment of the city of Mytilene, which attempted to defect from the Athenian empire in the fourth year of the war. The revolt was suppressed by an Athenian force cooperating with Mytilene's *dēmos* (3.27; the rebellion was apparently initiated by the oligarchs) and the thousand men held responsible are sent to Athens for trial. In Athens, the incensed assembly initially votes to kill all of the adult males (regardless of their roles in the revolt) and to sell the women and children as slaves. The next day, there are widespread second thoughts and a reconsideration begins. The debate that follows involves numerous voices but we hear (or read) only two, that of the demagogue Cleon, who reaffirms the initial decision, of which he was the principal architect, and that of an otherwise unknown citizen named Diodotus who opposes it.

While Cleon dismisses *logos* as a nonserious and dangerous distraction (3.37–38), Diodotus defends it, arguing that a good citizen (*agathon politēn*—3.42) speaks to his colleagues on equal terms (*apo tou isou*), attempting to persuade them toward the better course.[21] Unfortunately, deficiencies in the assembly's practices, largely spawned by the demagoguery of speakers like Cleon, make this kind of persuasive speech impossible. Consequently, even those proposing good policies (as well as those who push for terrible things) must lie to be believed (3.43). Diodotus then makes a case for moderation based exclusively on advantage, discounting justice altogether (3.44). Yet because this argument follows his admission that he is probably lying, we are cautioned against taking his claim that moderation is only a matter of expedience as his last word. Perhaps he is dismissing only *Cleon's* justice, arguing for moderation on the basis of another, better way.[22] However this may be, the crucial point is that Diodotus identifies the persuasive work, the *logos*, of the good citizen as the standard by which Athenian political practices should be judged.

However, the outcomes are disappointingly mixed. While a large number of Athenians recoiled at the original decision (3.36), the moderate position eventually loses votes with Diodotus's proposal (explicitly so designated), prevailing only narrowly (3.49). And while Diodotus proposed that the thousand interned oligarchs be judged calmly (*hēsuchian*—3.49), they end up being executed summarily (3.50). Yet while this Athenian debate is highly flawed in both process and outcome, its *logoi* still matter. It contrasts sharply with the longer antilogy before Spartan judges deciding the fate of the defeated Athenian ally Plataea, a narrative that follows closely in Book Three (3.52–68). Though both the desperate Plataeans and their aggressive Theban adversaries speak at great length, each addressing the Spartan commitment to avoiding injustice, Thucydides's final comment is that the outcome, fatal to Plataea, was settled in advance. "It was almost entirely because of the Thebans that the Lacedaemonians came to turn against the Plataeans, thinking that the Thebans were useful to them in the war that was now beginning" (3.68; Mara, 2009, 121; Nichols, 2015, 73–74; Thomas, 2017, 581–582). To the extent that Athens supports a serious, though always fragile, attention to *logos*, it is closer than Sparta to a community that Diodotus—and Socrates—might identify as political.[23]

The place of *logos* is critical but ambiguous within Thucydides's comments on Pericles's leadership (2.65). "Whenever he perceived that [the Athenians] were arrogantly confident in any way . . . he shocked them into a state of fear by his speaking (*legōn*), and again, when they were unreasonably (*alogōs*) afraid, he restored them to confidence." The notable funeral oration prizes Athenian *logos*, as instructing, not impeding, action (2.40). This may distinguish Pericles's Athens from Archidamus's (1.80–85) Sparta, where the shame (*aischynē*) and deference (*aidōs*) fostered by harsh education ensure subordination to the laws (1.84; Balot, 2014, 207–209). Eventually, however, Pericles's rhetoric also subordinates *logos*, not to deferential *aidōs*, but to energetic *ergon*, daring and risky action undertaken for the sake of honor (1.144). Athens needs no Homer because the city's actions, leaving remembrances of harm and good everywhere (2.41), speak for themselves. Athens' standing as an "education to Greece" (*paideusin tēs Hellados*) is "not boastful speaking (*logon*) for the occasion but the factual truth (*ergōn alētheia*) [as] shown by the power (*dunamis*) of the city." To this extent, Pericles's rhetoric is consistent with Hegel's assessment that the Athenian branch of the Greek world valorized *erga* over *logoi* (*PhH*, 261). It is less clear that Thucydides accepts either. As represented in the text, the oration's appeal to factual dynamism needs its own controversial and therefore questionable rhetoric to succeed. Pericles may imply that Athenian power has replaced Homeric poetry as Greece's educator, but the city's complicated legacy may persist through the enduring and critical *logos* of Thucydides.

Within Thucydides's *logos*, Pericles's political speaking and leadership depart from the discursive practices of Diodotus's good citizen. In all of his direct speeches, Pericles attempts to silence views of the human good different from his own. Those offering alternatives are dismissed as do nothings (2.64) who, when thought of at all, are considered useless (2.40). Though explicitly complimenting Athens' *logos*, Pericles's *logos* is performatively nondiscursive; Thucydides does not pair his speeches with any others. Under Pericles's influence, what was in name a democracy was "in fact the rule by the first man (*archē tou prōtou andros*)" (2.65).[24] His success in taming and encouraging the city is troublingly followed by political failure caused by the machinations of vying successors, who "stove each to become first (*oregomenoi tou prōtos hekastos gignesthai*) [and] resorted to handing over the city's affairs to the pleasure of the *dēmos*." Though this behavior is generally consistent with Athens' competitive political culture, the standing of Pericles and the destructive ambition of those following are expressly connected by the adjacent references to first positioning, contrasting dramatically with the political *logos* endorsed by Diodotus.

Even at its best, however, *logos* is vulnerable. In 4.108, as the war drags on, Thucydides notes how rationality can be suborned by passionate ambition when he narrates how revolts against Athens spread across the Chalkidikean cities. Inspired by the Spartan Brasidas's successes in the region, they "secretly sent proposals to [Brasidas] . . . each wanting to start the first revolt. It seemed to them they could do so with impunity, a mistake about Athenian power as great as the obviousness of that power later on, but their judgments were based on vague wishes not on clear foresight, according to the human habit of giving desire over to thoughtless hope, while using [in Crawley's translation] sovereign reason (*logismōi autokratoi*) to dismiss anything unattractive" (4.108). Here, the sovereignty of *logos* can only be ironic, for it is not a resource for critical judgment, but a ruling power sweeping judgment aside.

Finally, political *logos* cannot firmly control its benefits and harms. Commentators (Johnson, 1993, 107–110; White, 1984, 75) observe that Diodotus's advising Athens to consider only advantage when deciding about Mytilene returns as a harsh ultimatum delivered by its envoys some dozen years later to Melos (5.87, 113). Absent a narrative of the assembly's debate, we cannot directly connect its brutal treatment of Melos (which suffers as a population the fate deflected from Mytilene's democrats) to these demands (Zumbrunnen, 2008, 104–105). Still, this disquieting linkage points to politics' inherent unpredictability. What rescues in one context destroys in another. If Diodotus is indeed one of Thucydides's heroes,[25] his heroism is not that of Kant's moral politician, offering "a sight worthy of a deity" (*TP*, 86). Though named as a "gift of Zeus," Diodotus is an imperfect human being needing to make do within circumstances that he cannot altogether control or predict. The pragmatic character of Thucydides's book may lie in its aspiration to instruct under conditions of uncertainty, with *logos* remaining the best, though still flawed, resource for the citizen confronting political contingencies.

Building on this reading of Thucydides, we can revisit the Socratic narrative of war's origin (*genesis*) in *Republic* Book Two and the elusive place of *logos* within it. The first city in speech is of "the most extreme necessity" (*anankaiotatē*—369 d), meeting only basic needs. At Glaucon's insistence, Socrates adds luxurious (*truphōsan*) adornments. Because its territory is now inadequate, "we must cut off a piece of our neighbor's land, if we are going to have enough for grazing and growing, and they in turn from ours, if they give in to the acquisition of money, overstepping the boundary of the necessary" (373d). Given the dialogue's focus it is surprising that questions about such wars' justice are not raised. Perhaps necessity knows no law and greed is there for all to see. Yet it turns out that both the appeal to need and the accusation of aggression are suspect. As noted earlier (in chapter 2), while different motives allegedly drive the needy city and its avaricious neighbor, the assessments themselves are articulated within a political culture that treats its luxuries as necessities and demonizes its neighbors' needs as aggression.[26] Given the pragmatic context of the dialogue, this diagnosis of war's origins is also notably incomplete. There is no acknowledgment of a distinctively Athenian or Periclean ambition for fame and any of *its* accompanying necessities. In contrastive parallel to Pericles's first valorization of the love of honor (1.144), Socrates comments: "Let's not yet say whether war works evil or good . . . but only this much, that we have in turn found the origin of war— in those things whose presence in cities most of all produces evils both private and public (*idea kai dēmousia kaka gignetai*)" (373e). Because necessities are multiple and appeals to their power are always controversial, Machiavelli's reduction of just wars to necessary ones (*Pr*, 26; *Disc*, 3.12) cannot settle things. Justice remains an unasked but significant question. Within the *Republic*, this question emerges not from an inclination to obey intuited natural laws nor from a rational recognition of morality's imperatives but from disputes within politics itself. When does neediness become aggression? Is love of honor an extenuating need? Such disputes point toward a kind of *logos* whose structure is not conclusive and systematic but disputable and pragmatic.

Yet the possibility for political *logos* seems to go in a more transformative direction when the story of war's origin is followed by the introduction of philosophy. Far from being an example of Geuss's abstract hypermoralizing, this philosophy is politically implicated. If wars must be fought, the regime requires a class of specialized warriors (or guardians) qualified by both strength and spiritedness (*thumos*). The recognition of *thumos* introduces the psychic home for an ambiguous love of honor (cf. 581a). More seriously, the seemingly indispensable guardians threaten to become ticking time bombs. "With such natures how will [the warriors] not be savage to one another and the other citizens?" (375b). To ensure they target only outsiders, Socrates proposes that they be made philosophical, led to "define one's own and the other by intelligence (*sunesei*) and ignorance (*agnoia*)" (376b). Thus characterized, however, this orientation is virtually unrecognizable as philosophy. Embedded in familiarity, it cannot turn a critical eye within; its presumptive definition of justice is the already discredited "helping friends and harming enemies" (334c–335a). Yet by calling this grounding *philosophia*, the love of wisdom, not the love of the city, Socrates points to other possibilities. Yes, intelligence may be enlisted for the advancement and justification of one's own (as for Machiavelli), but it also may be self-critical and open to the other, resisting the darknesses of politicized caves.

A more critical possibility arises within the recast philosophy of Book Five whose philosophers love learning of all sorts. "One who is willing to taste every sort of learning . . . and is insatiable we shall justly (*en dikē*) say is a philosopher" (475c). Since this philosophy is present in the city by coincidence, political contingencies remain. While this regime might fight more moderately, wars persist. In response to this persisting necessity, this philosophical city must employ resources that its premise mistrusts, appealing to a thumistic drive toward honor tied to *erōs*. Here at least, spirit's estate of courage cannot be sustained without spiritedness. Erotic rewards are promised to "the man who has been best and earned good repute" so that he will "be more eager (*prothumoteros*) to win the rewards of valor" (468b–c). The love of honor is motivational tool not consummate goal.[27] Yet as the narrative progresses, the drive toward honor refuses to stay auxiliary.[28] Socrates's heroic and tragic point of reference is Ajax (468d), driven insane by a destructive need for recognition that violently escapes control. Consequently, this regime's philosophy carries no assurances against abuse or pathology as long as wars, however just or necessary, are engaged. As Jill Frank notes (2007, 454; though see Pritchard 2010, 20), Socrates's attempts to soften the waging of wars in Book Five recall traditional restraints that were, even at the time of the dialogue's performance, already being shattered by the Peloponnesian War. The inability of philosophy to control *erōs* is eventually confirmed by the emergence of a faction that disintegrates the supposedly perfect polis (546a ff).[29]

One reason for this failure is that the philosophy introduced in Book Five is, while corrective of Book Two's caricature, also deeply flawed. As others have noted, its pretenses to closure are exposed as hopeless and dangerous, especially when compared with the aporetic philosophy of Socrates.[30] The dangers intensify as the training of philosophers becomes the overarching purpose of this city. Yet the drama of the *Republic* suggests that no coincidence of political power with philosophy, however just, can eliminate the persistence of war and its threatening implications.[31]

Philosophy's vulnerability to violence is reinforced by reminders of Athens' turbulent politics in Books Eight and Nine, returning to Thucydidean themes, if not immediately to the Thucydidean narrative. The futures of the interlocutors signal the violent domination that follows the defeat (Frank, 2018, 13; Ferrari, 2003, 11). Though Thucydides's book ends prior to these events, we might detect, with Simon Hornblower (2008, 850), the "seed" of a judgment on the thirty sown in Thucydides's account of the violence of the four hundred (in 411) and his comments on the destructive character of oligarchy generally (8.66, 68, 89). Plato may go further historically and anticipate the democratic removal of the thirty in Book Eight's account of democracy's victory over oligarchy (556d–557a). Within the continuing narrative, however, this victory is unstable. The disorder of the democratic man parallels the deterioration of a city under conditions of *stasis* where *logos* or language is perverted by *pleonexia*.[32] Tyranny re-emerges from democracy's "extreme freedom" (*akrotatēs eleutherias*—564a). The hypothetical tyrant's political success story parallels events in the early career of the historical Athenian tyrant Peisistratus.[33] In hinting these connections, Socrates not only challenges democratic triumphalism but also rejects any political community's confidence that it stands permanently on the right side of history. Political time horizons now seem fluid and contestable, paralleling Thucydides's complex narrative arcs.[34] In this respect, Plato may challenge the transformative historical narratives of Kant and Hegel not by moving even further above the particularities of heteronomy and original history but by taking the contingencies signaled within the dialogues more seriously. By acknowledging a lingering Peisistratid or tyrannical possibility in Athens, Socrates might seem to manipulate the democratic fear sketched in Thucydides's Book Six (6.15, 27–28). Yet this would do nothing but polemicize politics even further. Instead, he advises Glaucon to construct a regime within himself (592b), refocusing on soul, not city and seemingly rejecting both Hegelian and Thucydidean historical narratives in favor of a politics of the soul. However, the goal of this inner politics is not relentless Nietzschean excavation but serene stability, "always . . . adjusting the body's harmony for the sake of the accord in the soul" (591d).

Yet Socrates is no more successful than Nietzsche in keeping clear of politics. The dialogue's concluding myth represents "the whole risk for a human being (*ho pas kindunos anthrōpō*)" (618b) as an inescapable need for pragmatic choice amidst a welter of contingencies (618b–619b). Risk is not opportunity to achieve a name that will persist eternally, but anxiety surrounding the ongoing need to examine one's life, not escaping time, but always recurring in times, not decisive, once and for all, but uncertain, again and again (Mara, 1997, 74–80). The indeterminacy of such choices is reinforced in Socrates's final, ironic exhortation to his conversation partners. "If we are persuaded by me . . . we shall practice justice with prudence . . . And here and in the thousand year journey that we have described we shall do well (*eu prattōmen*)" (621c–d). However, the immediate interlocutors and witnesses will not unambiguously "do well." Polemarchus and Niceratus will be two of the thirty's victims; Glaucon's and Adeimantus's relatives will kill their friends; Socrates will be executed. That the *Republic* occurs in the midst of a war destined to be lost, to be followed by a tyranny with murders close to home and then by a democratic restoration that prosecutes philosophy (*Apology*, 29c–d) is a dramatic reminder of frightening risks continuing across times and spaces. The ending of the dialogue may be as inconclusive—or as textually arbitrary—as that of Thucydides's book, prompting us to reconsider whether the Thucydidean ending is circumstantially accidental or authorially chosen.

The Greeks and Beyond: Different Texts in a Shared World

Beyond existing in a common historical space (Ober, 1998), Thucydides's and Plato's texts share an intellectual space where they can interrogate and instruct both one another and their readers, making the two authors open to a mutuality that other texts examined in this book too often resist. Guided by Hunter Rawlings and Jeffrey Rusten (Romilly, 2012, intro, ix), we can interpret Thucydides's claim to have written a possession forever, *ktēma te es aiei*, not as offering a conclusive last word, but as providing a resource to be listened to again and again. Though the complicated structure of the written text (Lattimore, 1998, xx; Geuss, 2005, 228–229) may frustrate efforts to listen straightforwardly to its oral presentation, we can become more attentive by speaking about it with others, offering our own interpretations, commentaries, and critiques, and listening to theirs. Thucydides's writing about (*synegrapsein*) the war intends to uncover those things most worthy of being spoken about (*axiologōtaton*), explicitly linking his particular written text with the speeches of indefinite audiences. As we read his representations of his characters' speeches, we are encouraged to hear them both in the ways of their immediate audiences and as they might be heard critically by us, requiring continued returns to a written text that offers a *logos* about *logoi* and *erga*, and giving that text a voice structured by, but not limited to, Thucydides's own. By recalling and reconstructing Thucydidean themes, the *Republic* dramatizes the kind of conversation able to read, listen to and speak about Thucydides's book in serious, critical ways. Socrates's revisions of the Corcyrean and Periclean narratives are provisional and incomplete, not only because of challenges and revisions within the dialogue but also because they invite Thucydides's involvement as interlocutor, pointing not toward a fuller theoretical completion but to continuing exchanges that will always revisit the most intractable problems of politics.

By representing the *logoi* and *erga* of the war so that they may be read, listened to and spoken about reflectively, both authors point to the educational possibilities of a certain kind of peace or stability even as they write about—and within—turbulent frames of war.[35] Their projected readers occupy what might be called a space of anxious leisure, with neither war nor peace dominating as a single frame of reference. Without anxiety there would be no good reason to turn our attention (one way of describing *theōria*?) toward the deeply disturbing Thucydidean images of Corcyra, Melos, Sicily, and Mycalessus. Absent a leisure capable of resisting both charm (the *Republic*'s promised torch race on horseback, 328 a) and terror (Athens' devastating war and violent oligarchy), we may be driven to follow the realists and dismiss attempts at *theōria* as distractions or denials. Because it is always situated between war and peace, this anxiety is not a Hobbesian concern for future time removable by political science but an ongoing practical uncertainty with no foreseeable intellectual or historical termination. And this leisure is not a sequestered space for either objective theorizing or ironic play—though both theorizing and playfulness are part of what goes on—but a contested space where the problems that make its practices necessary always threaten to disrupt their possibility.

If Thucydides and Plato do indeed practice a kind of political philosophy that is not limited by either abstract (and illusory) serenity or immediate (and overwhelming) disruption, we can correct Nietzsche's judgments about both authors. In exhorting his listeners to "practice justice with prudence in every way" Socrates does not preach Geuss's (2005, 230) hypermoralisms but pragmatically responds to "the whole risk for a human being." And in attempting to provide a text to be heard and spoken about repeatedly, Thucydides does not face harshness resolutely but impotently. Diodotus's image of the seemingly inevitable destructiveness of *prothumia* (3.45) is articulated as a part of his *euboulia*, his political good counsel.

This interchange between these classical Greeks might also enrich our current approach to political theory, though in ways that can only be sketched here. We can start by reconsidering Geuss's (2008) critique of modern political philosophy in the name of a political thinking that takes real politics more seriously. This proposal is valuable, but it needs nuances that the approach taken here may help to provide.

First, a dialogic political theory sees Geuss's categories as too binary. There is more variety to Western philosophy's approaches to political problems than Geuss's critique of Kantianism and its descendants (2008, 8, 98–99) acknowledges. Interpretive attention to the different texts within the history of Western political philosophy reinforces this richness. Reading these texts simply as systematic statements to be proven or refuted concedes too much to modern Philosophy departments working exclusively within an Anglo-American analytic paradigm. Read less restrictively, the texts considered here not only follow different philosophical paths but also acknowledge multiple and plural political realities. Sometimes these realities are inscribed within the texts, at others their presence is elicited by the flow or the frustration of an argument. Whether intended or not, however, they draw political philosophy toward a politics that no philosophical framework can simply control. Concerns about the competence of authority, the justice of causes and the rightness of intentions are not conclusively resolved by appeals to Aquinas's hierarchical laws. Machiavelli acknowledges political functions different from and challenging to the organization of struggles for riches and dominion. Hobbes's proof of the logic of obedience collides with urges to resist oppression and recognizes the importance of social goods beyond commodious living. Hegel's messy local knowledges challenge the completeness of his synoptic history. Such multiple political realities are misrepresented and distorted by both abstract philosophizing and reductive versions of "realism."

Within these texts, philosophy and real politics do not inhabit different worlds but are mutually constitutive and corrective cohabitants. The political importance of a security beyond bare preservation prompts a reconsideration of Hobbesian rationality that discovers a mutual engagement not reducible to the bargaining of fearful egoists. Political problems that Kant must eventually acknowledge force us to rethink the philosophical assistance needed by the moral politician. Political demands for (Glaucon, Adeimantus) and controversies over (Thrasymachus, Polemarchus, and Cleitophon) justice continually reshape Socrates's narrated dialogue about what justice is and why it is a human good. A sympathetic reconstruction of Geuss's project executed according to the perspective offered here might be alternatively titled *Philosophies and Political Realities*.

Second, Geuss's suspicion (2008, 38) of ahistorical philosophical programs overcompensates by giving too much away to contingency. Historical readings of these texts are inadequately historical if they ignore authorial claims to permanent significance. Designations—such as "metaphysical," "epistemological," "hypermoralizing" or "premodern"—that exclude all such claims before the fact should be suspected as peremptory. The verdict that there are no interesting eternal questions in political philosophy (Geuss, 2008, 13) may only be true for an eternity conceived in opposition to Thucydides's *ta anthrōpeia*. If we replace "eternal' with "recurring" or "unavoidable," we find a number of foundational political questions. Some good candidates are: How is political power distributed and exercised? What are power's contributions and dangers to social life? How can the deployment of power as violence be justified? How does power exercised within a political community differ from power leveled against outsiders? What grounds differences between insiders and outsiders, friends and enemies? What considerations (if any) justify their differential treatment? What ways of life does a political regime foster or suppress? How do ways of life impact exercises of power and projects of justification? Can any successfully constructed political justice avoid creating its own forms of injustice? The recognition of such questions does not separate political philosophy from real politics. Kant's timeless moral rationality and Nietzsche's contingent genealogies are not the only alternatives.

Third, granting that political theory should be connected to political interventions (Geuss, 2008, 95), we should consider what "connected" means. The view challenged by Geuss insists that political actions and choices be subjected to tests imposed by philosophical ethicists and be corrected or held accountable when they fail (noting Rawls, 1999, 89–90). Another approach, drawing more of Geuss's sympathy, treats political philosophy as a form of politics, as it theorizes connections between policies and outcomes or as it criticizes—or reproduces—ideological bonds. This book proposes a third alternative, reading political philosophical texts as contributions to an education that informs, rather than lectures or regulates, the practices of political agents, while still retaining critical distance from political events.

Discoveries about what is politically *axiologōtaton* do not, therefore, establish some new theoretical structure that is somehow superior to competing or preceding perspectives. Any persuasiveness that emerges depends on insights arising from the intersecting, questioned interpretations that this space enables. Outcomes are perspectival, not taking the form of "you must agree" or "that is wrong" but rather of "yes, but . . ." or "perhaps, but only if . . ." or "have you thought of . . . ?" Such conversations draw philosophical theorizations into the kinds interactions connecting Plato's dramatic characters or Thucydides's statesmen and citizens. We might interpret the authors considered here as participants. So, while Kant and his successors (Rawls, 1999, 19, 28, 46) anticipate a time when political influences of fear, honor, and interest are significantly diminished by international institutions supporting universal human rights, Thucydides disagrees. Fear, honor, and interest (in varying orders) are more resilient. However, the same conversation takes Kantian contributions seriously though avoiding Kantian resolution. Even if the rationally conceived moral politician of *Toward Perpetual Peace* is problematically separated from politics, Kant's construction of such a figure reminds us of the hazards of becoming too politically embedded. On the other side, though Thucydides does not talk about rights, he does (1.23) recognize suffering, bloodshed, and dislocation, forms of loss that may come closer than abridgements of rights (Geuss, 2008, 65) to universal loss. Though not (like Butler) making precarity his theme, Thucydides reminds his readers of sufferings that occur as long as human beings fight one another. Does confronting political abuses from more abstract vantage points—not just power and interest but also rational morality and legality—threaten to diminish anxiety by obscuring the sufferings involved?

Clearly, there are parallels between the activities of textual interpretation and critical citizenship. Both require the byplay of openness (listening to other voices) and skepticism (detecting both insights and errors), and they can each be strengthened by mutuality. Interpretive reading can provide resources for critical citizenship, just as experienced citizenship can deepen resources for interpretation. Geoffrey Harpham (2017) captures this nicely. "Interpretation—by which I mean the effort to divine the author's meaning through a close study of the text and disciplined and informed speculation about context—represents the highest calling and most refined form of the everyday citizen's activity of opinion formation." Both activities also establish their own forms of contestable power, requiring their own virtues and running their own risks. When Thucydides is exiled from Athens, he responds by writing about the most important political things, not by attempting to reestablish his political presence, sharply contrasting with the activities he attributes to Alcibiades (8.47). This activity of writing is more an alternative politics than an alternative to politics, for it performatively challenges claims that honor, fear, or interest are the only political influences worth noting. Socrates is executed for the political consequences of the leisure that he tries resolutely to create. Finally, since the creation of conversational space is a political act, there can be no uniformity of outcome. According to the *Letter to Vettori* (Machiavelli, 1998, 107–111), Machiavelli, like Thucydides, has his leisure imposed on him but (seemingly) unlike Thucydides, aspires to use the product of his leisure (the *Prince*) to return to political influence. Like Socrates, Machiavelli sees his work as constructed through interactions, though his are with "the ancient courts of ancient men" not with contemporaries in a condition of dialogic equality. While Machiavelli says he delivers himself entirely to these ancient men, his books end by trying to control their voices as he aspires to put himself "at the head of introducing new orders." Machiavelli's activities are monologic, feeding "on the food that alone is mine." Socrates tells his interlocutors at the end of the *Republic* that "*we* shall do well." Political leisure and the philosophy that it enables give us both the *Republic* and *The Prince*, both the *History* and the *Discourses on Livy*. These parallels between reading and acting points to differences between Richard Rorty's and Michael Oakeshott's overlapping images of philosophy as a series of continuing conversations (Rorty, 1979, 317–318, 389–392; Oakeshott, 1989, 97–98, 151, 154) and the project sketched here. Dialogic political philosophy does not avoid the agora to stay in the academy, rejecting Rorty's pragmatic divide between private and public.

Yet dialogic political theory also recognizes the distances between interpretive and civic activities. Interpretations invite reinterpretations; ongoing do-overs are both possible and appropriate. By contrast, political activities and the decisions to which they contribute are often painfully final. Their substance might be reconsidered, even reversed, but their material consequences cannot simply be remediated, let alone erased. We see this finality illustrated by the different kinds of political risks undertaken by Plato's Socrates and Thucydides's Diodotus. The dramatic setting of the *Republic* is a sobering reminder that most of Socrates's conversations end in failure. In response to such frustrations, Socrates usually proposes more of the same, conversations guided only by what his interlocutors have failed to refute and looking toward better deliberations (*Gorgias*, 527d). Prospects for improving particular conversation partners such as Alcibiades and Critias may not be encouraging,[36] but the possibilities opened to the indefinite readers of the dialogue may be more promising.[37] Diodotus's situation is different. Concerning Mytilene, he only gets one chance. There will be no do-overs for its democrats should he fail and there end up being no do-overs for its oligarchs, period. So, when Socrates's anticipates his trial and eventual execution (*Republic*, 419a, 496d–497a; *Gorgias*, 521b–c) he speaks in a tone that is both aggressively defiant and serenely confident, assuming a rectitude that parallels Kant's praise of the moral politician. He may suffer injustice but he will never inflict it. By contrast, the political consequences of Diodotus's speech on Mytilene escape control as they play out with unpredictable severity on the Melians. While Socrates's immediate rhetorical failures are rescued by the hopeful nature of dialogues, Diodotus's immediate political and even moral success eventually enmeshes him in a political and moral liability that, however unfairly, he cannot escape. His activity becomes critically distant only in a Thucydidean narrative that we are invited to consider again and again. We can only imagine a conversation between Plato's Socrates and Thucydides's Diodotus. The best we can do is to interpret the texts that give them presence within continuing and expanding political and philosophical conversations about politics.

This dialogic approach to political theory neither transcends nor surrenders to "realism" and it does not take frames of either peace or war as decisive. Instead, it engages a perplexing and disturbing variety of political realities, from Thucydides's and Plato's through Hanson's and Butler's, depending on a continued awareness of politics that stimulates rather than disables philosophy.

NOTES

Chapter 1

1. Bendersky (1983, chapter 11); Seitzer and Thornhill (2008, 1–2, 25–26); Slomp (2009, 34).

2. Habermas (1998, 188). For a more extended discussion see Müller (2003, 78, 174, 195).

3. "The concern here is neither with abstractions nor with normative ideals but with inherent reality" (*CP*, 28). That Schmitt is a "realist" in any simple political sense is challenged by Müller (2003, 9); Slomp (2009, 125); and, of course, Derrida (1997, 115).

4. Cf. *The Age of Neutralizations and Depoliticizations* (*AND*) in *CP*, 89–76; see also Schmitt (2005, 65; 1996, chapter VI).

5. Translations largely follow Schwab's (2007), though I have made some adjustments. I thank Friederike Eigler for her guidance and assistance. Schmitt's text is the 1932 edition (München: Duncker, and Humblot, 1932).

6. Differing from Slomp (2009, 49, 65–66).

7. For Slomp (2009, 17) Schmitt's truly political bonds are total and his healthy domestic society is a homogeneous one.

8. Schmitt's recognition of the political importance of friendship (Slomp, 2009, 24, 113), presumes the conceptual priority of enmity.

9. Slomp (2009, 11, 30) sees opposition to total war as one of the cornerstones of Schmitt's work.

10. Meier (1998, 39; 1995, 62–64) argues that by validating the establishment of peace as a legitimate political goal, Schmitt counters arguments that his politics are essentially agonistic. Schmitt emphasizes that "the political does not reside in the battle itself" (*CP*, 37). Yet a liberal politics dedicated exclusively to providing peace and security is anathema to Schmitt's project (*CP*, 45, 70–71). Locating politics not in "the battle itself" but "in the mode of behavior determined by this possibility" seems to separate politics from a narrow agonism while inscribing a broader agonism within politics.

11. Differing from Rawls's (1999, 37, 42, 44) projections.

12. Differing from Kennedy (1998, 100).

13. What Habermas calls a "weird vitalistic aura" (2006; cf. 1998, 197). See also Richard Wolin (1992, 430–435).

14. Schmitt's reliance on nationalist mythologies is noted by McCormick (1997, 193, 232). Meier (1998, 144) disagrees: "it would not have occurred to anyone whose political thought revolves around the nation to develop the conception of the political that Schmitt develops." Yet since Schmitt insists on the contingency of political groupings (*CP*, 26), theoretical and practical connections with radical forms of nationalism seem hard to dispute.

15. Within what Meier calls (1995, 6–7, 30–36, 50, 58–59; 1998, 69) the "hidden dialogue" between Schmitt and Strauss. "Dialogue" is not agreement and "hidden" does not mean conspiratorial.

16. See Robert Alter's (2004, 542) alternative assessment of biblical theology ("ontological division or chasm between the Creator and the created world . . . sets off biblical monotheism from the worldview of antecedent polytheisms") and Murad Idris's (2014) alternative assessment of Erasmus's Christian political theology ("Peace is a theologized concept, referring back to God and Christian community").

17. Strauss (1997, 30), citing *Deuteronomy* 4.6. This comment is made in Strauss's introduction to the English translation of *Spinoza's Critique of Religion*, which originally (1965) included the review of *CP* as an appendix.

18. Noting Smith (2016, 265) and agreeing with Müller (2003, 11, 225) about a need to focus on Schmitt's philosophical anthropology but wondering whether calling this perspective "conservative" settles things. Meier argues that because "Schmitt does not make his conception of the political dependent on a primary tendency of human nature to form exclusive groups" (1995, 69; differing from Slomp, 2009, 49) his political theory is not simply grounded in anthropology. Yet dispensing with human nature's instincts may prompt revision rather than rejection of anthropological claims.

19. Strong (2007, xviii). See also Müller (2003, 249); Slomp (2009, 35, 119).

20. For Meier (1995, 50–54; 1998, 56–58), Schmitt eventually moves from a focus on human problematics to a darker statement about human evil. Yet the focus on evil may emerge not only from scriptural images of fallenness (Meier, 1995, 53, 57; 1998, 81) but also within a political rejection of assumptions about the innocence of human motives that Schmitt sees as common to liberalism, socialism, and anarchism (*CP*, 60).

21. Strauss (2007, 120). For Meier (1995, 62–69) this provisionality pushes Schmitt to make the foundations of his position explicit.

22. Slomp (2009, 136–137) images Schmitt's politics as a dynamic "rigid and shapeless like water" that nonetheless follows "the contours and character of the terrain."

23. Perhaps one way of interpreting Derrida's (1997, 116) "impure purity of [Schmitt's] political as such."

24. Originally the statement of Theodor Daubler. Meier (1998, 44).

25. On the differences between technology and technicity in Schmitt see McCormick (1997, 5, 44).

26. McCormick (1997, 38–42). See Weber (1949, 17–18) and Strauss's (1953, 35–80) controversial critical assessment.

27. McCormick offers a good example. "Just as social democratic theory . . . has absorbed much of liberal institutional, legal and ethical theory . . . liberals must take seriously arguments regarding transforming social practices advocated by progressive scholars to

their left" (1997, 306; 9–10). The resources needed for confronting the problems of modernity are provided by the progressive best of modernity and postmodernity. See also Seitzer and Thornhill (2008, 45–50). There is neither room nor need for critiques that might show modern and postmodern thought's lapses or omissions. Müller (2003, 250) is uncomfortable with the "high liberalism" of Rawlsian moral philosophy, counseling an alternative to Schmitt that is historical and contingent but still somehow philosophical.

28. Where a discourse creates the reality it allegedly describes, explains or interprets (*PF*, 93). Edward Said implies that all texts or representations are discourses because they "are embedded first in the language and then in the culture, institutions and political ambience of the representer" (1979, 94, 272).

29. Noting the parallel with Rawls (1999, 101).

30. Concerning another of Schmitt's books, McCormick comments that "it is almost impossible to recognize when he is talking about normal constitutional operations and when he is talking about emergency ones; all of the former have been subsumed in the latter" (1997, 146).

31. Partially disagreeing with Slomp (2009, 58), who takes Schmitt more at his word.

32. See Ulmen's comment at *TP* 85, n89, quoting Schmitt's *Glossarium*. Meier (1998, 46) notes that the same passage also comments that "Adam and Eve had two sons, Cain and Abel."

33. Butler seems more politically optimistic than Derrida in claiming that senses of future possibilities can inform pragmatics in "the time, 'the now,' in which we live" (2010, 110, 134). Beyond allusions to the need to contest the state (110, 147, 149), she declines to engage Derrida's question of how those activities can be recognizably political.

34. In a different context, Honig (2013, 183) comments, "the move to sorority may . . . turn out only to restage rather than interrupt the fraternity or phallocracy we seek to contest."

35. As in Thucydides (1. 23; 3.83; 7.29, 87); Machiavelli, (*Pr*, 8, 9; *Disc*, 3.49).

36. On the significance of Corcyra's depoliticization for Thucydides see Mara (2008, 156–157); Orwin (1994, 179–180); and Price (2001, 27).

37. Agreeing with Slomp (2009, 20) that Derrida sees "the Schmittian individual as singularly male." Derrida sees a paradigm of masculinity informing a much broader range of thinkers.

Chapter 2

1. Just war theory as developed by Catholic theology originates with Augustine (O'Brien, 1981, 4–5; Johnson, 1986, 1–5; Elshtain, 2003, 50). The Thomistic statements are more analytically precise and more expressly appreciative of the potentials of natural reason (Sigmund, 1993, 217, 228), both inviting and requiring scrutiny from a more self-consciously secular philosophy.

2. References to *ST* are organized by Part (I, I–II, II–II), followed by Question and Article. Citations are to I–II unless noted.

3. Appropriately for Rawls (1999, 34, 55), problematically for MacIntyre (2016, 55–56).

4. The text of *ST* is the multivolume bilingual edition (Blackfriars and McGraw Hill, 1964–). Translations begin with these volumes, though I have made occasional changes.

5. Reinforcement acknowledged, for example, by Rawls (1999, 77, 103).

6. Seagrave (2009, 491–523).

7. Seagrave (2009, 521) comments that *ST*'s opinions and arguments become more disconnected from those of particular human beings as they come closer to the truth.

8. Differing from Seagrave (2009, 512). For appreciations of Aquinas that emphasize differences with Aristotle see Jaffa (1979, 186–188) and Fortin (1987, 248–275). Similar questions arise over the treatment of Cicero in *ST*. Compare Seagrave (2009, 509) with Strauss (1953, 155).

9. Langan (1977, 192) interprets Aquinas's moral theory as a deontological intuitionism wherein thoughtful human beings grasp self-evident moral principles. Though this interpretation is offered as an alternative to teleology (186), the humans who intuit such principles are creatures flourishing in a certain way.

10. Differing from MacIntyre's grouping of Thomists and Aristotelians into one ethical perspective (2016, 118, 168, 206).

11. Complicating Langan's (1977, 194) judgment that Aquinas posits a significant similarity between imperfect and perfect happiness. Jordan (1993, 237–241) offers a different view.

12. For MacIntyre (1988, 186–187), the Thomistic view accommodates a psychological but not an intellectual narrative of tragic choices. Intellectually, "such dilemmas will always rest upon a mistake."

13. 91.4; *DR*, I.11. Moreover, since violence predictably begets violence, successes in unjust wars become self-undermining (*DR*, I.10).

14. Implied by Jaffa (1979, 192–193).

15. Finnis (1998a, 245–252) sees Aquinas as less of an opponent to liberalism than does MacIntyre (1981, 133; 1988, 201–203; 2016, 124–129).

16. Reinforced by the possibility that tyranny punishes the sins of a community (*DR*, I.6).

17. Boyle (1998, 51–52) rejects this direction within Catholic just war theory, though largely in defense of refusals to participate in unjust wars.

18. Recognizing the historical reasons for attending to these controversies. See Heath (1972, 194).

19. On the sources from Augustine see Heath (1972, 81–91). English translations are offered in Fortin and Kries (1994).

20. Bloom's (1968) translation, slightly modified.

21. Drury (2008, 66–68) argues that this prospect compromises Aquinas's general perspective on just wars.

22. Johnson (1986, 34).

23. A range of causes set the (various) allies against the Nazis. Still, the character of that regime influenced the allies' treatment of the defeated nation (Jaspers, 1961, 53–60) and set the agenda for the Nuremberg trials (Rawls, 1999, 98–99). Sometimes, failure to attend to regime character may lead to significant political and moral error. Walzer (1977, 265–256) criticizes the Truman administration for failing to distinguish an imperial Japan, "engaged in a more ordinary sort of military expansion" from the Nazi regime. Insisting that both surrender unconditionally contributed to decision sequence leading to the atomic bombing of Hiroshima and Nagasaki.

24. Compare Walzer (1977, 21) with Johnson (1986, 32). Finnis (1998b, 25) is skeptical about the distinction.

25. See MacIntyre's (2016) extended critique. More appreciative assessments of the evolving use of rational choice in political science are offered by Hardin (1995, 46); and Chong (2000, 14).

26. *Deuteronomy* 20:11–20; 28:52–58; *2 Kings*, 25:1–4, as well as Thucydides on the siege of Potidaea (2. 69) and Xenophon of the siege of Athens (*Hellenica*, 2.2).

27. O' Brien (1981, chapter 1); Elshtain (2003, chapter 3).

28. Anscombe (1961, 53); Walzer (1977, 19–20); Johnson (1986, 31–32); Elshtain (2003, chapter 3).

29. Walzer (1977, 157–159).

30. Elshtain (2003, 56–57); Finnis (1998b, 33–34); O' Brien (1981, 44–47).

31. Anscombe (1961, 57–59). Walzer's treatment (1977, 151–159, 278–283) is also skeptical but more nuanced in its treatment of practical cases. See also Rawls (1999, 95, 99–100).

32. Suggested by (among others) Ignatieff (2004, 15, 33, 34, 110) and O'Driscoll (2015, 375). Butler (2010, 43) is unconvinced.

33. Consistent with Satkunandanan's critique of calculative morality (2015, 83) but suggesting a somewhat different alternative.

34. Noting Boyle (1998, 42) and Finnis (1998b, 18), implicitly criticized in a different context by Satkunanandan (2015).

35. Ignatieff's (2004) recognition of lesser evils acknowledges this ambiguity, though he may underplay the need to confront "dirty hands" (Stocker, 1986).

36. Noted by Jordan (1998, 96).

37. Paralleling Ignatieff (2004, 167).

38. Discussed in Mara (1986, 49–78).

39. Aertsen (1993, 21) notes that references to Aristotle as "the Philosopher" were common within medieval commentary. Yet the term also condenses Aquinas's positioning of philosophy within human practice generally.

40. See MacIntyre (2016, 57); McInerney (1993, 208–209); and Seagrave (2009, 509). All accept the premise but MacIntyre and Seagrave resist the conclusion.

41. Fortin (1987, 271) comments: "contrary to what has often been said, Aquinas did not baptize Aristotle. If anything he declared invalid the baptism conferred upon him by his early commentators and . . . made him a slave or servant in that City." See also Jaffa (1979, 186–188); Jordan (1998, 87–89); Salkever (1990, 174, 206).

42. Mara (1995, 1998); Frank (2005); Salkever (1990, 2009); Tessitore (1996).

43. Nonetheless interpreted by Fortin (1982, 590–612) as departing from Aquinas in substantial ways.

44. For example, Shapiro (2003, 3–4).

45. Discussed in Mara (2008, 143–148).

46. Habermas (1992, 34–39); Rawls (1999, 34, 55; 2005, 134–135).

47. For arguments that neither Rawls nor Habermas avoids this difficulty see Mara (1985, 1989, 2008); Nussbaum (1998); Salkever (2002).

48. Compare Habermas (1996, 309) with Rawls (2005, 145).

49. *Prince* (20); *Discourses* (1.57, 58; 3.30).

50. Differing from De Grazia (1989, 190–191) and Viroli (2010, 68, 190, 199). Agreeing with Mansfield (1979, 250), Orwin (1978, 1225) and Zuckert (2017, 78).

51. Sullivan (2004, 68) notes *Discourses* 1.29, where Machiavelli claims that "a city that lives free has two ends—one to acquire, the other to maintain itself free." See

Hornqvist (2004, 50, 187), but also Coby (1999, 266), Hulliung (1983, 220), and Strauss (1969, 11).

52. Coby (1999, 28); Sullivan (2004, 58–59).

53. For McCormick (2011, 57) "discord seems to be good both in itself . . . and as a means to better policy and military success." He replaces discord with civic participation (2011, 167) perhaps too easily. See Lefort (2000, 130, 133, 136–138); Zuckert (2017, 125).

54. Differing from De Grazia (1989, 172), Skinner (1991, 131), and Viroli (1991, 159, 168; 2010, 189–190). While noting *Prince* 26's contention that a war liberating Italy from the barbarians would be just, Hornqvist (2004, 254–257) argues that Machiavelli's rhetoric, including his use of Livy (9.1), problematizes the justice to which he appeals (cf. *Disc*, 3.12; *FH*, 5.8).

55. Translations of passages in the *Prince* generally are those of Mansfield (1998) and, in the *Discourses*, those of Mansfield and Tarcov (1996), though I have made occasional small changes. The Italian texts are those in Bertelli's (1960) edition. Referenced editions of the *Florentine Histories* (*FH*) and *The Art of War* (*AW*) are the translations of Banfield and Mansfield (*FH*, 1988) and Lynch (*AW*, 2003).

56. A point made variously by Orwin (1978, 1227); Strauss (1969, 281); Mansfield (1979, 140–141); Hornqvist (2004, 187); Fischer (2006, xxxvii) and Zuckert (2017, 467). A more communitarian understanding of the common good is attributed to Machiavelli by De Grazia (1989, 175–176, 186, 190, 270–271); McCormick (2011, 24, 78, 80–81, 84, 90); Pitkin (1999, 48, 81); Pocock (2003, 184, 200–201, 209); Skinner (1990, 138); Viroli (1990, 152–153); and Wolin (1960).

57. Parel (1992, 111), Pitkin (1999, 850), and Hulliung (1983, 136) see the identities of the great and the people as more stable. My reading is closer to Coby's (1999, 94), though he suggests that the people constructs itself only when threatened (1999, 98; see also McCormick, 2011, 24; Lefort 2000, 130).

58. Implied by Masters (1996, 226) and Mansfield/Tarcov (Machiavelli, 1996, xli–xlii) and questioned, differently, by Coby (1999, 282), Pocock (2003, 163, 218), and Strauss (1969, 253).

59. Agreeing with Strauss (1969, 1969, 116–118), Sullivan (2004, 62–66), Mansfield (1979, 250), Mansfield/Tarcov (Machiavelli, 1996, xli) Zuckert (2017, 235) and departing from Coby (1999, 11), Hornqvist (2004, 266), Hulliung (1983, 37–41), McCormick (2010, 31–35), and Skinner (1990).

60. *Disc* (1.6, 20, 33, 34); 2.2. cf. Strauss (1969, 118), Mansfield (1979, 201), and Sullivan (2013, 521; 2004, 58–66). The point qualifies judgments (Coby, 1999, 254–261; Hornqvist, 2004, 50, 187, 290; Hulliung, 1983, 220; and Pocock, 2003, 213) that Machiavelli sees liberty and greatness as mutually supportive.

61. Differing from Viroli (2010, 175, 199).

62. Interpreting Machiavelli as less traditionally republican than Skinner does (1990, 141) and agreeing generally with ascriptions of innovation offered by De Grazia (1989, 233), Mansfield/Tarcov (Machiavelli, 1996, xix–xx), Pocock (2003, 167, 564), Strauss (1969, 59) and Zuckert (2017, 114–115). Differences over what these innovations mean are considerable.

63. Orwin's analysis of *Prince* 15–17 (1978, 1217–1228), arguing that Machiavelli sees old warlikeness as obsolete (1226), should be preceded by appreciating *Prince* 14.

64. Agreeing with Lefort, 2000, 114 and going beyond McCormick (2011, 36–41). Hornqvist argues that the *Prince*, particularly, should be interpreted in light of the political controversies surrounding Machiavelli. Yet while the immediate addressees of both the *Prince* and the *Discourses* are explicit, the extended or potential audiences are indefinite. Who are the princes? This reading draws no fundamental divide between the goals and the content of the two works, though each is—and both together are—rhetorically complex. Cf. Strauss (1969, 21–24); Mansfield (1979, 23; 1998, ix–x); Masters (1996, 44); Zuckert (2017, 6).

65. Differing from Masters (1996, 223).

66. Though religion is not mentioned in the chapter title and is interpreted in light of its political importance, an emphasis continuing across succeeding chapters. Pocock (2003, 192, 214), Strauss (1969, 230), Sullivan (1996, 108), and Coby (1999, 72–75) argue that Machiavelli eventually treats the Romans' religion as less vital for their virtues than his initial statements suggest. Viroli (1990, 156–157; 2010, 1–2) differs.

67. Hulliung (1983, 23, 255–256) notes parallel appeals to violence in Machiavelli's themes and rhetoric.

68. Perhaps paralleling *Prince* 26 where the liberation of Italy is represented as easily achievable. Hornqvist (2004, 261) and Zuckert (2017, 101–105) show why this is false.

69. So, one of *The Prince*'s tasks (chapters 8, 15, 17, 18) is revising beliefs about the qualities that should bring princes praise or blame. The treatment of Agathocles the Sicilian in 8 represents the challenges involved. See especially Weiner (2016).

70. For example, those of Brown (2010, 157); Hornqvist (2004); Pocock (2003, 552); Sullivan (1996, 11); Viroli (2010, xvii); Wolin (1960, 211).

71. Wolin (1960, 211).

72. Appreciating but complicating Mansfield's comment (2013, 651) that Machiavelli's knowledge of worldly things is a polemic against those who argue on the basis of nonworldly things.

73. De Grazia (1989, 31, 74, 77, 219, 267). Seen by Pocock (2003, 167) as a politicized version of original sin.

74. De Grazia (1989, 87); Viroli (2010, 1–2 and throughout).

75. Possibly revisionist history given the mendicant friars' apparent roles in the twelfth-century inquisition. See research summarized (aggressively) by Drury (2008, 4–5).

76. Error perhaps Christianity's language, evil, Machiavelli's.

77. Spinoza appears to make an analogous criticism of the Judaic tradition in *Theologico-Political Treatise*, chapter 3, though he does not claim that political debilitations (also imaged by effeminacy) are caused by false religious interpretations.

78. Strauss (1969, 201–203) and Mansfield (1979, 202–203) emphasize Machiavelli's rhetorical strategy of subtly endorsing this "philosophical" claim by undercutting the objection to it. Yet Machiavelli's response is hardly decisive. The stated objection (absence of recorded memory) is not the only argument against the claims of the ancient philosophers (see Aquinas, *ST*, I. 103.1). The reference to "those philosophers" is both vague and selective. Kahn (1979, 136) comments that "the instinct to explain things by telling how they began . . . dominates all [ancient] scientific or philosophic speculation down to and including Plato's *Timaeus*." For Strauss, the philosophers arguing for eternity are Averroes and his disciples; for Mansfield, they are the Averroeists and Aristotle.

If so, Machiavelli's apparent defense of "those philosophers" is not an endorsement of their philosophy.

79. Mansfield (1979, 203) notes that the Romans failed to obliterate traces of the religion of the Tuscans, though this may have been intended as destruction by absorption.

80. For Bertelli and Mansfield/Tarcov the scriptural source is *Exodus* 32: 25–30, death by the sword as punishment for the golden calf idolatry. The conflated (Alter, 2004, 762) rebellions in *Numbers* 16–17 challenge Moses and Aaron but are punished by divine cataclysms.

81. Blurring old and new testaments, male and female voices, kings and tyrants, human beings and God. On the revision of Luke see Strauss (1969, 48–52); Mansfield (1979, 99–100, 304); Mansfield/Tarcov (Machiavelli, 1996, xxxv); Smith (2006, 39); Zuckert (2017, 153). By contrast, in *DR* (1.1, 8) Aquinas presents David as shepherd of his people and servant of God. Machiavelli's striking image in 1.26 also ignores the deterioration of the Davidic dynasty after Solomon (*Disc*, 1.19).

82. Parel (1992, 153–158; 2013, 587); Strauss (1969, 173).

83. Emphasized also by Rahe (2007, 47).

84. These commentators do not always agree, particularly on the role of some kind of tyranny in Machiavelli's perpetual republic. See Mansfield/Tarcov (Machiavelli, 1996, xxxii–xxxiii); Masters (1996, 223–225); Zuckert (2017, 274).

85. Agreeing partially with Pocock (2003, 167).

86. For Parel (1992, 68–69; 2013, 592–595) the references are astrological, but they could also refigure the philosophical categories of Aristotelianism and Thomism. On the ways in which editors have arranged the treatments of *in universali* and *al particulare* in various Italian editions see Parel (1992, 69–70).

87. Masters (1996, 189).

88. Saxonhouse (1985, 157).

89. Noted within a different political reading by Lefort (2000, 125). Zuckert (2017, 100) doubts that Machiavelli's valorization of impetuosity is serious.

90. De Grazia (1989, 375–376) suggests that "many who have written on this" was a common reference to Plato.

91. For different views see De Grazia (1989, 68); Strauss (1969, 220–223); Saxonhouse (1985, 155); and Viroli (2010, 31, 33).

92. Noting that the five chapters preceding 2.29 emphasize human mistakes.

93. Parel (2013, 591) reads Machiavelli's use of *governare* as astrologically informed, "the control of sublunar bodies by planetary motions," not involving "mental or moral activity." However, *Pr* 25s explicit concern is the extent to which we might govern ourselves.

94. Differing somewhat from De Grazia (1989, 267–269).

95. That Machiavelli sees first personal psychological reform as impossible is argued by Parel (2013, 596) and Pocock (2003, 165, 180). Mansfield/Tarcov (Machiavelli, 1996, xl) and Danford (2006, 106–107) disagree.

96. Noted by Hornqvist (2004, 249–253), Pocock (2003, 157, 183), and Sullivan (2004, 73, 75).

97. Differences between Machiavelli and Polybius are noted by Sullivan (1996, 94) and Zuckert (2017, 124–125) but downplayed by Pocock (2003, 189, 205) and Viroli (2010, 29).

98. See the (different) readings of Hulliung (1983, 155) and De Grazia (1989, 78) versus those of Strauss (1969, 290–291) and Mansfield (1979, 35–37).

99. With *fortuna* seen not as agent but as effect of natural causes.

100. Agreeing with McCormick (2011, 41–43) but with conclusions paralleling Sullivan's (2004, 47–48). Note also Zuckert (2017, 188)

101. Acknowledging Parel's warning against confusing awareness with agreement (2013, 600), Machiavelli's close acquaintance with the text of *De Rerum Natura* seems clear (see Sullivan, 1996, 193, n15; De Grazia, 1989, 217; Black, 1990, 77).

102. *De Rerum Natura* 2.167–181; 3.463–464, 554–557, 612–614, 670–674, 691–693; 4.832–242. Strauss observes (1969, 200, 333 n59) that there are no references to the soul (*anima*) in either *Prince* or *Discourses* but frequent references to spirit (*animo*). Still, as Brown (2010) notes, Machiavelli's focus on religion's political value differs significantly from Lucretius's intent to liberate human beings from superstition (*DRN*, 1.63–72; 5.198–199, 1161–1203; 6.52–55). Yet Machiavelli's political embrace of religion may not be as complete as on first view. And for James Nichols (1976, 18, 84) the atheist Lucretius is eventually more understanding of religious needs than he first appears.

103. Rahe (2007, 45) and Brown (2010) answer the latter question differently. For Lucretius, earth and heaven will pass away (*DRN*, 5.64–67, 93–99, 243–246; 318–331—the last passage making the same objections to the world's eternity as those countered in *Disc* 2.5), but the atoms and the void will not (*DRN*, 1.244–245, 418–421, 518–519; 6.936–941).

104. Though in a narrative that is paradoxically poetic. Lucretius explains in *DRN* 5.1–25. James Nichols interprets in 1976, chapter 2.

105. Mansfield's (1979, 204) comment that Machiavelli's inundation reveals "a reasonable and benevolent purpose in nature" may go too far.

106. Compared with *DRN* 2.1090–1104.

107. Note *FH* 6.34 as Machiavelli narrates a devastating windstorm sweeping Italy. "When arms had been put away by men, it appeared that God wished to take them up himself . . . . the whirlwind, driven by superior forces, whether they were natural or supernatural, broke on itself and fought within itself . . . [so] that the earth, water, and the rest of the sky and the world would return mixed together to its ancient chaos."

108. *DRN* 3.320–322; 5.7–12, 110–114, 1117–1119; 6.35–41. This is compared with the foolishness of ambition, 3.1034–1035; 5.1120–1132.

109. Comparing the tower of Babel narrative in *Genesis* 11.4. This project, too, is undertaken for human beings to "make us a name, lest we be scattered over all the earth" (Alter translation). The result is intended to stand as a permanent image of the human presence and it relies on display not deception. This is punished by a God who sees a common human language as a resource for (a threatening?) ambition, "if this is what they have begun to do, now nothing that they plot to do will elude them" (*Gen*, 11.6). Machiavelli treats the punitive scattering of humans among different languages and cultures (*Gen*, 11.7–9) as a consequence of human activity and a condition for persisting ambition. Smith's essay (2006, 36–57 at 39) stimulated this comparison, though I engage a different section of the *Discourses* and draw somewhat different conclusions.

110. Differing from Strauss (1969, 241, 269) and Mansfield (1979, 435).

111. For Coby (1999, 190, 280) and Hulliung (1983, 227) privileging glory reflects Machiavelli's agreement with Roman or Spartan valorizations. I note a philosophical psychology.

112. For Brown (2010) Machiavelli accepts the Lucretian claim (*DRN*, 2.255–260) that free will is common to human beings and animals, but the love of glory seems different.

113. Agreeing with De Grazia (1989, 280) that *Prince* 15's concern for the "generically true" is constituted by effectuality. Mansfield (2013, 652) notes that this is the only use of *verita effetuale* in Machiavelli's works.

114. Mansfield/Tarcov (Machiavelli, 1996, 114) suggest that the philosopher could be Cicero or Machiavelli's contemporary Pietro Pomponazzi. Viroli (2010, 30) may accept the belief in occult presences as Machiavelli's own too easily.

115. Agreeing with Lefort, (2000, 133) that *Prince* 15 does not erase what ought to be.

116. De Grazia (1989, 98), Lefort (2000, 130), Pocock (2003, 156, 180), Skinner (1990, 123, 137–139), and Viroli (1990, 152, 164; 2010, xiv, 160) see these categories as relatively stable. Mansfield/Tarcov (Machiavelli, 1996, xlii) and Zuckert (2017, 47) differ.

117. Pitkin (1999, 324–325). See also Lefort (2000, 137).

118. *Disc* 1.9. See McCormick (2011, 80–81, 84, 90); Pitkin (1999, 85–86, 96); Pocock (2003, 184, 201); Skinner (1990, 138); Viroli (1991, 153; 2010, 170).

119. Pitkin (1999, 8, 286, though note comments at 1999, 286 n1). Strauss (1969, 221–223), Orwin (1978, 1220–1112), Hornqvist (2004, 168–172) and Zuckert (2017, 463–465) see the differences between Machiavelli and Aristotle as more important. For McCormick (2011, 6.25) Machiavelli opposes Aristotle's elitism in the name of popular government.

120. Coby (1999, 254ff.); Fischer (2006, lvi–lvix); Hornqvist (2004, 50, 187); Hulliung (1983, 5–6); McCormick (2011, 51–52, 58); Sullivan (2004, 10–11, 32–34, 38, 49). This connection is softened (not entirely persuasively) by Pocock (2003, 213) and Viroli (1991, 159).

121. As Coby (1999, 65), Strauss (1969, 149–150), Mansfield (1979, 389) and Zuckert (2017, 237) note Cincinnatus lived his later life in poverty because of financial penalties incurred by his son's flight from criminal prosecution. See Livy, 3.11–14.

122. Moving from judgments (3.22) about Manlius' nature as strong, pious and reverent. De Grazia (1989, 141–142) and Viroli (2010, 75) may take Machiavelli's treatment of Manlius the citizen too much at face value, as may Spinoza, *Theologico-Political Treatise*, chapter 19. For Zuckert (2017, 249) *Disc* 3.34 is mainly commentary on how popular approbation can go wrong.

123. For Livy (7.4), the inhuman treatment of the young T. Manlius at the hands of his father is the relevant backstory. Here, merciless civic discipline may originate in psychopathologies caused by child abuse.

124. Aquinas (*D R*, 1.7, quoting Augustine, *City of God*, 5.18) uses the story of Manlius's execution of his son to reinforce the son's fatal obsession with glory.

125. Sullivan (1996, 82).

126. Departing from Viroli (2010, 68). Machiavelli goes beyond Livy's Lucius Lentulus (9.4) who mentions only nobility and ignominy.

127. See *Disc* 1.49, 58.

128. Coby (1999, 147) calls this appeal to civic virtue Machiavelli's "noble lie," (note also Zuckert, 2017, 262–263) while Sullivan interprets (2004, 79) the focus on the common good as instrumental to the pursuit of honor. Machiavelli's own position may be ambiguous. In *Prince* 26, he represents Italy's disorder as giving "opportunity to someone prudent and virtuous to introduce a new form that would being honor to him and good to the community of human beings," expanding rather than dissecting the common good.

129. Wolin (1960, 224–226). See also De Grazia (1989, 164) and Pocock (2003, 558). Rahe (2007, 38) sees no Machiavellian attention to character due to the rejection of classical teleology.

130. Cf. Strauss (1969, 298–299); Danford (2006, 99). McCormick (2011) elides the borders between citizens and soldiers (11, 26, 33, 61, 93, 101) and interprets the need for broad, harsh punishments as warnings to dangerous elites (76, 126, 128, 136). For Sullivan (2004, 62–64), Pocock (2003, 196–197, 209–211) and Zuckert (2017, 152), Machiavelli's citizens are primarily soldiers, not the other way around.

131. Differing from Viroli (2010, 2, 190) and agreeing with Orwin (1978, 1224).

132. Shown in the reactions of the tribune prosecuting Manlius's abusive father and of the soldiers who witness Torquatus's son's execution, both narrated by Livy (7. 4; 8.7, 12). By contrast, Machiavelli's story of Madonna Caterina Sforza in *Disc* 3.6 dramatically subordinates the love of children (graphically imaged through the self-exposure of the mother's genitals) to political independence. Cf. *AW*, 6.27–33; *FH* 8.34. For various interpretations of the Caterina Sforza story see Pitkin (1999, 249–250), Saxonhouse (1985, 164), Viroli (2010, 110) and Zuckert (2017, 267).

133. Reading potentials in the text differently from Strauss (1969, 295).

134. As in critiques of Sparta offered by Plato (*Republic*, 548a–b) and Aristotle (*Politics*, 2.9). Agreeing with Coby's (1999, 283–284) emphasis on the importance of such critiques, I wonder if Machiavelli's vulnerability to these objections stems simply from his embracing a timocratic ethic.

135. Pitkin (1999, 307–308). Also, Lefort (2000, 137).

136. Pitkin (1999, 110, 136, 165, 182, 230–231, 248, 268, 273–276, 282, 299, 304, 316, 326–327). She acknowledges (19) that "Machiavelli never addressed the topic of autonomy; the term does not figure significantly in any of his writings."

137. Pitkin (1999, 300–301). Reflecting some agreement here with Viroli (2010, 199).

138. Likewise complicating Zuckert's reading (2017, 153) of *Disc* 1.26 as a cautionary warning against radical political change. Does the chapter reveal the stark choices facing those aspiring to be political liberators or redeemers (comparing with *Pr* 26)?

139. McCormick (2011, 45, 65, 115, 128, 136, 161) focuses on the importance of popular judgment in Machiavelli, emphasizing its punitive character, though perhaps not fully engaging the implications. On Machiavelli's treatment of middle ways as they relate to more immediate political challenges facing Florence, see Hornqvist (2004, 98). Coby (1999, 129) notes that Machiavelli's advice to avoid middle ways in *Disc* 2.23 is offered within an example wherein the Romans did pursue a middle course, neither completely liberating nor completely destroying the rebellious cities in Latium. Nonetheless, individual cities were liberated or destroyed as prudence dictated. A general middle way was comprised of particular extremes. On the dispository or punitive character of the judgment imaged in the *Discourses* see Mansfield (1979, 261–262).

140. Both possibilities are implied, generously, by Pitkin (1999, 7, 81, 287, 301).

141. Underscored in Honig (1991, 109).

142. Arendt (1958, 220–230); Honig (1993, 2–3, 74–75). Pocock (2003, 573) notes the connection of his historical reading of Machiavelli's texts to Arendt's political theory.

143. McCormick (2011, 141, 169) suspects philosophy as the weapon of elites or the tool of experts. Pocock (2003, 212) and Lefort (2000, 133) diagnose and endorse the opposition of Machiavellian politics to a hegemonic philosophy. Yet there is no reason to believe that increasing the scope of political participation is threatened by or eliminates the need for a philosophical practice understood in more democratically conversational ways.

Chapter 3

1. Curley (1994, xxvi–xxviii); Gauthier (1969, 76–89); Hardin (1999, 22); Kavka (1986, 111–113); Hoekstra (2007, 117); Slomp (2000, 123ff.).

2. Rawls (1999, 10); Habermas (1997, 124–126); Korsgaard (1996, 33); Nussbaum (1997, 48).

3. As in Williams (2003).

4. Noted by, for example, Tuck (1999, 207–225, 230–231).

5. Ahrensdorf (2000, 581); Cantalupo (1991, 94); Slomp (2000, 55–56). Strauss (1997, 130) disagrees.

6. For Gauthier (1969, 65) and Johnston (1986, 37), Hobbes's natural rights impose no correlative duties. For different reasons, Kavka (1986, 315) and Flathman (2002, 102) disagree.

7. Gauthier (1969, 53); Evrigenis (2014, 71); Sullivan (2004, 83).

8. For different treatments see Evrigenis (2014, 166); Garsten (2006, 25–26, 45); Martel (2007, 38); Skinner (1996, 431–435).

9. Spragens (1973, 173). See also Flathman (2002, 14); Garsten (2006, 49); Johnston (1986, 182); Slomp (2000, 11–12).

10. Evrigenis (2014, 9); Garsten (2006, 46); Johnston (1986, 120–121); Martel (2007, 52, 56–57).

11. The suggestion of Evrigenis (2014, 163, n18) and Johnston (1986, 119–120). Martel (2007, 33, 107) interprets Parts 3 and 4 as reversing the authoritarian elements of 1 and 2 to create more democratic possibilities.

12. Gauthier (1969, 3), Flathman (2002, 55), and Kavka (1986, 7) see Hobbes's scientific and introspective approaches as independent.

13. Why science is treated as an effective trope is not immediately obvious. Kavka's (1986, 5) observation that the conclusions of science are demonstrably certain presumes an audience receptive to such certainty, an expectation that Hobbes does not share. Garsten (2006, 49), Johnston (1986, 91), and Skinner (1996, 4–5, 334, 370, 376, 426) read *Leviathan* as a rhetoric serving science. Evrigenis (2014, 14, 91, 134, 242) argues that a scientific demonstration enlists the reader's participation in drawing conclusions but always under the direction of Hobbes.

14. Evrigenis (2014, 21, 71); Gauthier (1969, 27ff.); Johnston (1986, 11–12); Spragens (1973, 106, 170).

15. Differing from Slomp's (2000, 167) judgment that Hobbes's state of nature represents humans as undifferentiated animals and from Gauthier's (1969, 19–20) that Hobbes's natural men are wild animals who can be tamed.

16. Strauss (1963, 16–17); cf. Gauthier (1969, 17); Johnston (1986, 98); Spragens (1973, 131). Martel's contrarian reading (2007, 12) indicts the sovereign as the source of chaos.

17. Sullivan (2004, 12).

18. For Kavka (1986, 104), the presence of "dominators" within the state of nature makes pre-emptive aggression rational.

19. See Gauthier (1969, 27–28, 40–41, 97); Flathman (2002, 71). Kavka's revision of Hobbes's narrated natural condition into Hobbesian contract theory (1986, 23, 65–67) introduces a normative dimension not found (as yet) in Hobbes. Kavka's Hobbesian contractors inhabit something closer to Rawls's original position.

20. Gauthier (1969, 49) emphasizes the importance of normality.

21. Differing from Slomp (2000, 90; 2007, 185–186), who reads Hobbes as eventually replacing diagnoses of motives with observations of behavior.

22. Going beyond Spragens's (1973, 193) judgment that the task of Hobbesian politics is containment.

23. For Gauthier's (1969, 70) Hobbes's natural law language shows incomplete emancipation from the Medieval tradition. However, perhaps he is appropriating and subverting a traditional vocabulary for innovative purposes. Thus agreeing with Martel (2007, 38, 65) but seeing Hobbes's innovative purposes differently.

24. Differing from Sullivan (2004, 96).

25. Flathman (2002, 96) posits an incipient normative equality in the leeway given to individual motions in the state of nature. Every attempt to interfere with another's pursuit of what she sees as necessary for her preservation requires justification (2002, 102). Yet this condition cannot add normative weight since all such justifications are simply sincerely held first personal beliefs. While my behavior in that condition may affect others, there is no relevant other to whom a second personal justification need be offered and no third personal considerations that would allow first personal judgments to be critically assessed (Hoekstra, 2007, 121). Kavka's (1986, 315, 338) correction of natural right into a status grounding normative postulates belongs more to Kavka's Hobbesian theory than to Hobbes.

26. For Martel (2007, 130) the difficulties are severe enough to undercut Hobbes's endorsement of sovereign power altogether.

27. Hobbes's account of the "Causes, Generation and Definition of a Commonwealth" (*Lev*, 16) notwithstanding, the most significant problem may concern not how political order originates but how it can be maintained, not undermined. Evrigenis (2014, 112, 115).

28. Flathman (2002, 144, 146); Gauthier (1969, 145, 162–163, 169); Herzog (1989, 95–99); Johnston (1986, 206–207); Kavka (1986, 23); Martel (2007, 12, 76).

29. Kavka (1986, 91–92, 223).

30. Implied within Gauthier's (1969, 128, 150) focus on the hypothetical act of authorization.

31. Kavka's Hobbesian theory first (1986, 199) adjusts the terms of agreement needed for the creation of the sovereign from unanimity to near-unanimity and then (237) stipulates the problem of first compliance away.

32. For Slomp (2000, 6), no game theoretic interpretation offers rational actors escape from the state of nature. In different ways, Flathman (2002, 63, 69, 167) and Kavka

(1986, 449) suggest revisions seen as compatible with Hobbesian principles. Martel (2007, 76, 194) goes further to identify grounds for a democratic mutuality in Hobbes, seen as absent by Garsten (2006, 37).

33. Hobbes may identify emotional barriers to the acceptance of authority beyond Johnston's (1986, 158) magical thinking. Confidence in scientifically directed rhetoric (Evrigenis, 2014, 178, 241, 251–252) may be as tenuous as confidence in science itself. The extended reflections on natural punishments imply that Hobbes's pessimism is not confined to the "collective insanity" of the English Civil War (Skinner, 1996, 435–436).

34. That Hobbes's audience is comprised principally of subjects is argued by Evrigenis (2014, 21, 132, 140, 234); Johnston (1986, 88–89, 119, 210); Martel (2007, 1, 19, 41–43); Skinner (1996, 428); Watkins (1973, 75–81); Warrender (1957, 326). For exceptions see Flathman (2002, 86, 94, 107); Mara (1988, 390–411).

35. Taking this statement more literally than Cantalupo (1991, 140) or Martel (2007, 224).

36. Hobbes rhetorically assails the authority of books (cf. Garsten, 2006, 27; Martel, 2007, 44; Skinner, 1996, 334), so as to privilege his book.

37. Skinner (1996, 70) offers a general discussion of counsel within Tudor theories of rhetoric.

38. Kavka (1986, 228) is rightly suspicious of the claim as written but he may downplay its pedagogical role. Martel's alternatives of submission versus subversion (2007, 36) may be too binary.

39. I owe this observation to Roslyn Weiss.

40. Agreeing with but going somewhat beyond Garsten (2006, 40).

41. Such prohibitions extend even to challenges to secular authority on the basis of the love of wisdom, "for disobedience may lawfully punished in them that against the laws teach even true philosophy" (46. 42). Such punishment does not render that philosophy false.

42. Differing from Hood (1964, 10, 12); Warrender (1957, 155).

43. Complicating Hobbes's endorsement of a command theory of law, as in Herzog (1989, 136–137).

44. Hüning (2007) offers an extensive treatment of Hobbes's theory of punishment.

45. Slomp (2000, 68) is skeptical about labeling Hobbes's social theory "bourgeois" because it does not recognize property rights against the state. Gauthier (1969, 90) is comfortable with the designation because Hobbes grounds his moral theory in the need for individual self-preservation. Applied generally, the term probably oversimplifies.

46. Paralleled by Hobbes's representation of Caesar's assassin Brutus, the civic republican hero, as a "mock heroic figure" (Cantalupo, 1991, 46–47).

47. Agreeing with Evrigenis (2014, 234) and Slomp (2000, 62; 2007, 191). Kavka (1986, 225) may be too quick to dismiss Hobbes's insistence that the sovereign be the exclusive source of honor as antiquated.

48. Flathman's (2002, 144) judgment that Hobbes's civic education is intrusive and repressive may oversimplify, though Hobbes does not see this education (*pace* Martel, 2007, 54, 80) stimulating political criticism.

49. Boyd (2001, 395–396, 408) interprets such transformation as correcting the violent impulses of aggressive associations. See also Flathman (2002, 162). Kavka (1986,

210–211) detects a more positive anticipation of welfare state liberalism, disputed by Martel (2007, 76).

50. Mitchell (1993, 59–60) characterizes Hobbesian society as the "equality of all under the one."

51. On Hobbes's iconography see Bredekamp (2007, 29–60). Evrigenis (2014, 125, 131) notes persistent images of war, suggesting that security requires readiness for war. Martel (2007, 124) dissents and interprets the frontispiece as representing the sovereign as a dangerous idol.

52. Hobbes's account of authorization is central to Gauthier (1969, 127–129) but unnecessary for Kavka (1986, 389). Kavka's correction may be an overcorrection that downplays the importance of chapter 16 within Hobbes's developing argument. For Gauthier (1969, 132, 169–171), the logic of authorization can make the Hobbesian polity more representative and less absolute, arguing that Hobbes's obsessions with political destabilization are responses to the "disorders of the present time."

53. Curley (2007, 318); Gauthier (1969, 206); Johnston (1986, 172–173, 182); Skinner (1996, 384); Strauss (1963, 74–76). Kavka (1986, 21) prematurely concludes that religion "plays little role in Hobbes's political and moral system."

54. Hood (1964, 13, 22–23, 31, 38, 40); Martinich (2007, 375–376); Mitchell (1993, 46, 56); Warrender (1957, 278–279, 289, 295–296). Martel (2007, 7–8, 33, 101) sees Parts 3 and 4 as making the problematics of reading any text explicit.

55. Underscored by Cantalupo (1991, 141) and Smith (2016, 68).

56. Hobbes places chapter 12 ("Of Religion") between chapter 11's treatment, "Of the Differences of Manners" ("those qualities of mankind that concern their living together in peace and harmony") and chapter 13's narrative of the terrifying natural condition. Johnston (1986, 191) reads 12 as arguing that religion is equivalent to superstition. Smith (2016, 72) argues that it identifies curiosity about causes as the human seed of religion.

57. Noted also by Gauthier (1969, 178, 200).

58. Yet as Curley notes (1994, xl) in *Leviathan*'s Dedicatory Letter, Hobbes anticipates that his scriptural interpretations are likely to cause the most offense.

59. Seeing darkness as an avoidable danger rather than an inevitable collapse as in Cantalupo (1991, 190, 194, 235, 237).

60. Mitchell's (1993, 46–47) Hobbes empowers the sovereign to interpret scripture because authoritative scriptural guidance is needed to address anxieties about salvation in a world where Christ is temporarily absent. Interpretive authorization is spiritually necessary. My reading is that Hobbes sees it as politically necessary, "to avoid the calamities of confusion and civil war" (38. 1).

61. For a fine discussion of Hobbes's treatment of images of hell, see McClure (2011). Also Curley (2007, 317); Martinich (2007, 383).

62. Martinich (2007, 376, 379, 383) notes that many of Hobbes's controversial theological claims parallel positions taken by Protestant reformers. Hobbes may exploit such parallels to construct scriptural readings reinforcing interpretive agreement and therefore social stability. See Lessay (2007, 243); Farneti (2007, 291).

63. For all of its interesting provocations, Martel's subversive reading (2007, 33) may downplay Hobbes's rhetorical concern for civil and religious peace. Evrigenis (2014, 160–161) notes that Hobbes's varying accounts of the state of nature avoid explicit

linkages to *Genesis* until a paragraph on Cain's killing of Abel is added to the 1688 Latin edition. Nonetheless, the state of nature narrative is infused with the vocabulary of *Genesis* (2014, 176–177). Does this performatively acknowledge the absorption of scriptural interpretation into rational argument?

64. Departing somewhat from Mitchell (1993, 70), more in agreement with Curley (2007, 325–326) and Smith (2016, 86).

65. Curley (2007, 322); Johnston (1986, 172–173, 182); Schwartz (1985, 8, 21–22).

66. Johnston's (1986, 167) and Smith's (2016, 81) views that Hobbes reads the New Testament in light of the Old may underplay bidirectionalities. See Schwartz (1985).

67. Johnston (1986, 192); Lessay (2007, 251, 262–264); Martel (2007, 71, 75); Mitchell (1993, 70); Schwartz (1985, 19).

68. Emphasizing *Numbers* 16 and conflating two rebellions into one Alter (2004, 762).

69. Compare with Aquinas, *ST* I.103. 7.

70. Hood's (1964, 14) assessment.

71. Supporting Curley's (2007, 314–315, 326) and Johnston's (1986, 212) judgments that Hobbes may embrace radical enlightenment. See also Ahrensdorf (2000, 583). This reading may be altogether differ from Martel's (2007, 173, 195) suggestion that Hobbes represents the image of the Holy Spirit as a blank space to be filled by human practices. These are not the only alternatives, however. For Spinoza (*Ethics* II, P. 10. Cor. Dem. Schol; *Theol Pol Tr*, chapter 6), the theological creationists err by separating God from nature (as in *ST* I. 103.2; 105.6), the scientific atheists, by separating natural explanations from any conception of God.

72. Flathman (2002, 13, 30) argues that Hobbes identifies disorder as an ontological condition that can only be stabilized by the science that security allows. Note Evrigenis (2014, 69). Slomp (2000, 15, 17, 20) and Garsten (2006, 52) contend that Hobbes sees political chaos as enemy to continuous identities.

73. Consequently, the advantages of Slomp's (2000, 7) detached perspective are accompanied by liabilities. Spragens (1973, 174–175) reads Hobbes's paradigm of motion as one that both discloses and obscures, though with a different focus.

74. Gauthier (1969, 107–108); Kavka (1986, 424–433).

75. Cantalupo (1991, 26–27, 247–248); Martel (2007, 228).

76. Adapting Bermeo (2003) and differing from Garsten (2006, 177). Flathman comments (2002, 87–88) that nobility of character may be the only reliable support for authority. Need such characters be rare?

77. Slomp's (2000, 184) characterization of the desire for fame after death as an innocent alternative to the dangerous quest for pre-eminence may understate its political importance. Kidder (1983, 140) comments that sovereignty may be "the ultimate prize for glory seekers."

78. Alternatives offered by Evrigenis (2014, 241) and Johnston (1986, 61, 127, 158), though Evrigenis (230–231) is less convinced of Hobbes's utopian intentions.

79. Paralleling but differing from Flathman (2002, 167), who begins with a reading of Hobbes's skeptical philosophy and ends with a more active, though still chastened, democratic politics. Martel equates philosophy with an essentializing metaphysics that creates idols (2007, 104). I suggest a (different) form of philosophy that Hobbes requires but does not recognize (a la Garsten, 2006, 26), one that moves toward a less definite chastening of political activism.

80. For Flathman (2002, 1–2), the state of nature is "making gone wrong" (27).

81. Spragens's judgment (1973, 18) that Hobbes's political theory is informed by a "disillusionment with the possibilities of politics and with the instincts of man" seems premature. Flathman (2002, 21) notes that Hobbes's deep skepticism exists alongside purposive self-assertion. Skepticism may chasten self-assertion (170) but self-assertion may convert skepticism into willfulness. Martel's (2007, 176) parallel between Hobbesian politics and Arendtian democracy (is Arendt a democrat?) marginalizes philosophy as a political resource.

82. Which Ahrensdorf (2000, 290) interprets as a half-conscious Periclean piety.

83. Slomp's (2000, 57, 76, 115–116) contrasting Hobbesian optimism with Thucydidean pessimism may conceal a side of the comparison (recognized by Ahrensdorf, 2000, 592; Johnson, 1993) less favorable to Hobbes. Agreeing with Flathman (2002, 112) that Hobbes's ambitions for closure are ill-considered, but for different reasons.

84. "Would it not in us . . . be great baseness and cowardice, if we should not encounter anything whatever rather than suffer ourselves to be brought into bondage?" (5.100; Hobbes trans. 1975, 380).

85. In Hobbes's translation, the Athenians tell the Melians "your enmity doth not so much hurt us, as your friendship will be an argument of our weakness" (5.95; Hobbes trans. 1975, 379–380).

86. Going beyond Kavka (1986, 438) who sees Hobbes's social theory limited by its near silence on international politics.

87. Where equality and inequality are measured by quantities of power rather than by constitutional standing (as implied by Michael Williams, 2006, 271). The influence of the latter standard presumes an alternative to the material inequalities that mark anarchic international politics.

88. Evrigenis (2014, 195) notes this possibility as fomenting domestic disorder, but this threat can be intensified within unequal international politics. Like Ahrensdorf (2000, 587–589), Evrigenis finds the source of this insight in Thucydides. I take the Thucydidean contribution in a somewhat different direction by pointing to the persistence of fear.

89. Paralleling Gauthier's (1969, 207–208) "dreadful equality" of nuclear deterrence.

90. Translations of Kant generally follow these editions: *Toward Perpetual Peace (TPP); Theory and Practice (TP); Idea of a Universal History with a Cosmopolitan Intent (UH)*; and *Speculative Beginning of Human History (SB)*, Humphrey, 1983; *Groundwork for the Metaphysics of Morals (Gr)*, Ellington, 1981; *Critique of the Power of Judgment (CJ)*, Guyer and Mathews, 2000; *Contest of the Faculties (CF)*, Reiss, 1970; *Critique of Practical Reason, (CPrR)*, Beck, 1956. References are to those editions. I have made small changes. The German texts are *Werke*, Bande 2, 4 and 5, Weischedel, 1960. References to other texts use these editions: *Critique of Pure Reason, (CpuR)* Smith, trans. 2003; *Anthropology from a Pragmatic Point of View (AnP)*, Louden, 2006; *Metaphysical Elements of the Theory of Right (METR)*, Reiss, 1970.

91. O'Neill (2015, 204–206) believes that this prospect requires less alteration of Kant's framework than Habermas suggests.

92. Interpretations of Kant's significance thus go beyond the debate over whether his project requires a transnational authority rather than the continuation of nation states (Bohman and Lutz-Bachmann, 1997, 13).

93. Bohman and Lutz-Bachmann (1997, 2); Doyle (1983, 205–235; 323–353); Ellis (2005, 79); Shell (2009, 211).

94. Tuck comments (1999, 221), "the central aspect of [Kant's] claim was that the rules governing the relations of modern states would be minimal in character, thicker . . . than those of a Hobbesian state of nature, but much thinner than those of civil society." Ellis (2005, 95) disputes this minimalist reading and O'Neill (2015, 208–209) and Smith (2016, 139) see Kant's cosmopolitanism as a resource for substantive change.

95. Shell (2009, 215); Riley (1983, chapter 6); Bohman and Lutz-Bachmann (1997, 1–22); Benhabib (2004, 25–48); MacMillan (2006, 58–59).

96. Habermas (1998, 170); Hassner (1972, 608); Bohman (1997, 180–181). O'Neill (2015, 202) disagrees.

97. Shell (1980, 127–152; 2009, 236–237) notes similarities and differences. For Riley (1983, 156–158) this reading underappreciates the importance of political activity within Kant's practical philosophy.

98. Riley's (1983, 78) interpretation of the culture of skill's outcomes is more sympathetic.

99. *CF*, 188–189, *What is Enlightenment?*, 41–42; though see *CPrR*, Part II, 151–163). Arendt (1982, 17) and Galston (1975, 180–188, 243) note differences between Kant and Aristotle but interpret them differently.

100. Galston (1975, 239), Riley (1983, 95), and Smith (2016, 139) see the achievement of peace as a cultural condition for morality and thus not itself as "the goal or end of history" (Galston). Yet peace can be an outcome of as well as a basis for morality.

101. Seeing war's significance within Kant's project as more than a puzzling anomaly (Shell, 2009, 172), more in concert with Galston's (1975, 235–236) and Smith's (2016, 147) readings.

102. Reading *CJ* 83 and 84 as reflecting complications and not simply incoherences (Ellis, 2005, 67) within Kant's political theory.

103. Galston (1975, 240); Shell (2009, 104).

104. Differing from *CPrR* 158–159.

105. For Shell (2009, 199, 295) Kant presents this heroism as available to all rational adults not just to warriors. Yet such heroism is always ambiguously related to morality. Has dutiful action originated from a nonmoral self-regard (*Gr*, 19), a pride outshining rather than reinforcing duty? Satkunanandan (2015, 126, 137–138), on the other hand, emphasizes that awe before rationality is Kant's (quite literal) call to duty.

106. Zammito's judgment that the "foundation of Kant's philosophy of history and politics" is starkly Hobbesian (1992, 328) is incomplete. If Kant envisages solving the problem of political organization for a race of devils (*TPP*, 366), he entertains a more negative view of human dispositions than Hobbes, whose natural men are more fearful than devilish. Yet Kant also represents the violent journey of the inclinations toward unsocial sociability as creating conditions enabling the kingdom of ends (*SB*, 119). See Galston (1975, 234); Riley (1983, 121).

107. Galston (1975, 63–65); McCarthy (2009, 135); Smith (2016, 143).

108. Shell (2009, 321–322).

109. For Galston (1975, 213) the binaries, despair and hope, obscure the indeterminacies of politics.

110. Differing from O'Neill (2015, 197–198).

111. For Galston (1975, 223–224) Kantian natural science seems to leave no place for chance. See also Shell (2009, 280).

112. In seeing these directions as potentially diverging I differ from Ellis (2005, 61), Galston (1975, 203–204), Riley (1983, 78), and Shell (2009, 213–235), who see more continuity.

113. Differing from Smith (2016, 144).

114. Complicating both of what Hassner (1972, 612–613) reads as Kant's alternative paths to peace, "radical revolution and regeneration" versus "gradual and indefinite progress."

115. Seeing more differences than Smith (2016, 142). Guyer (2000, xxxviii) suggests that separating the two perspectives even in the investigation of nature is not straightforward.

116. Noted by Smith (2016, 132–133). For Shell (2009, 286), this enables a prediction of perpetual peace not dependent on providence. Yet she also acknowledges (300, 342) Kant's controversial if not arbitrary reading of the revolution's politics. For Ellis (2005, 167–168) Kant is less interested in the revolution itself than in the moral quality of the responses elicited. Galston (1979, 29) underscores the ambiguity of Kant's assessment.

117. Argued by Taylor (2010) and downplayed by Smith (2016).

118. For Shell (2009, 174) "neither nature nor human history can be grasped as a systematic whole without appealing to an end beyond it, an end whose realization rests, finally, with us."

119. In characterizing the posture as politically aloof, I adopt Sallis's (2005, 52) epistemological assessment.

120. Ellis (2005, 102–103); Shell (2009, 223).

121. A claim developed variously by Ellis (2005, 63), Galston (1975, 184–185), Korsgaard (1996, 102), O'Neill (2015, 119–120), and Riley (1983, 42–45). Differences aside, all reject the Hegelian critique that Kantian morality is exclusively formal.

122. Apel (1997, 102–108); Galston (1975, 265–256); Habermas (1997, 125–126); McCarthy (2009, 64–65); Hassner (1972, 619–620). A more sympathetic examination is Korsgaard's (1996, chapter 6).

123. Agreeing with Geuss's (2008) general assessment but taking it in a different direction.

124. Thanks to Christian Golden.

125. As in *CPrR*, 122. "For inclinations . . . are consequently always troubling to a rational being and, though he cannot get rid of them, they nevertheless force from him the wish to be released from them."

126. Sherman (1997, 141–148).

127. Sherman (1997, 153) separates sentiment from sentimentality. Shell argues (2009, 287) that Kant's reliance on moral enthusiasm draws on reason rather than on affect. If so, downplaying the role of emotions in truly moral practice may be less inconsistency within than shortcoming of Kant's practical philosophy.

128. Noting Arendt's comments (1982, 69–72) on the role of sociality in *Critique of Judgment*. Conversely, Satkunanandan's (2015, 126) focus on awe as call to duty reinforces the first person singular character of Kant's conversion narrative.

129. Here, Kant anticipates Franceschet's reservations (2006, 86–93) about the "liberal enforcement" of international justice.

130. O'Neill's comments (2015, 98): "the combination of lawlike form and universal scope . . . [is one] that at least some reprehensible laws and principles cannot meet."

131. Shell (2009, 184) cautions against tracing the proceduralism of deliberative democratic theory back to Kant. Yet one of her critiques of Kant (232, 342) is his being incompletely procedural.

132. Kant may be less successful in separating rules from virtues than Franceschet (2006, 75) suggests. McCarthy (2009, 57) also finds a necessary attention to moral character in *TPP*. Galston (1975, 240–243) agrees that Kant's political aspirations require a resource that his philosophical framework blocks.

133. Recognized by Kant in *SB*, 54–55.

134. Shell observes (2009, 235, 246, 342) that Kant fails to provide principles or rules that would assist the moral politician in moving from general parameters to specific judgments. Can this problem be dealt with simply by adding another layer of rules? Ellis (2005, 170–171, 174, 180) sees this indeterminacy as one of Kant's strengths, though this judgment would seem to require a kind of faith in the progressive capacity of human reason even if not in a progressive (or providential) teleology.

135. Differing somewhat from McCarthy (2009, 140).

136. See Walzer (1977, 86–108). This constraint is hardly uncontroversial among contemporary Kantians, as in McCarthy's critique of Rawls (1997, 215–216). See also MacMillan (2006, 69) and Franceschet (2006, 87).

137. In this respect, Kant may radicalize Aquinas's privileging of right intention in assessments of war's justice. Ellis (2005, 152); Galston (1975, 183, 251–252).

138. For Shell, Kant's moral agent can experience "a sense of moral certitude comparable to the logical certitude secured by science" (2009, 63, 126; cf. 210).

139. Ellis (2005, 141). This holds even though the continuation of the human species cannot be assured. *CF*, 7. 175: cf. Galston (1975, 249).

140. Shell (2009, 234) and McCarthy (2009, 150).

141. Noted by Ellis (2005, 142, 146–147), though with different conclusions.

142. Chong's (2000) otherwise fine work narrowly equates a rational life with one capable of calculating the costs and benefits of alternative decisions.

143. Hardin's focus on the logic of group conflict emphasizes that "you act rationally when you if you do you believe serves your interest" (1995, 46). Notably, this neutrality about purposes is not shared by Hobbes.

Chapter 4

1. References to the *Introduction to the Philosophy of History* are to the Rauch (1988) translation. Other citations of the *Lectures* refer to Sibree's edition (1956). References from the *Phenomenology of Spirit* and *Elements of the Philosophy of Right* are by paragraph (*PhG*) or section (*PhR*) numbers. For these works, I have largely relied on Miller (*Phen*, 1997) and Nisbet (*PhR*, Wood, ed., 1991). Quoted passages from these works start from these translations but all have been compared to Hegel's German and some changes have been made. The German texts are the editions published by Suhrkamp (Bande 3, 7, and 12). English editions of Nietzsche are generally the Kaufmann translations, though I have also consulted Clark's and Swenson's *On the Genealogy of Morality. The Use and Disadvantages of History for Life* relies on the Preuss translation. Discussions of *The*

Greek State and *Homer's Contest* rely on the Ansell-Peterson and Diethe edition. All quotations have been compared with the German editions of Walter de Gruyter and have been slightly revised when needed.

2. Noting Avineri (1972, 56–57, 177); Cortella (2015, xxi); Franco (1999, 122, 265); Neuhouser (2008, 227); Pinkard (1994, 325); Pippin (2008, 243); Smith (1989, 112, 135); and Wood (1991, ix–xi). Habermas (1973, 193–194) and Marcuse (1960, 169, 218) differ.

3. Re Hegel; Pinkard (1992, 323; 1994, 48, 335) and Pippin (2008, 194, 272). Re Nietzsche: Hatab (1995, 12, 73–74, 91, 145, 150) and Nehamas (1985, 64–65, 70). There is the objection that the displacement of metaphysics constructs its own metaphysical perspective. Traditional metaphysics (whatever that may mean) is not simply historically outmoded; it is, so the argument goes, false in the face of an alternative taken to be true.

4. Pinkard (1994, 53, 291–294); Franco (1999, 20, 52, 57); Pippin (2008, 241); Bykova (2009, 281, 285); Cortella (2015, xxii, 88. 93, 100); Williams (1997, 2, 103, 240, 262); Wood (1991, xxiv–xxv).

5. Emphasized by (among others) Franco (1999), Pinkard (1994), Smith (1989), and Williams (1997).

6. Markell (2003, 92–93) distinguishes between Hegel's diagnostic and reconciliatory voices and interprets the diagnostic voice as, for us, more valuable (120). I agree, but argue that the synoptic, reconciliatory voice is, for Hegel, the stronger.

7. For a critique of "nonmetaphysical" interpretations as incomplete see Houlgate (2008, 117–118) as well as the comments of Cortella (2015, xiv) and Franco (1999, 186).

8. Pinkard (1994, 300, 326) disagrees though still noting (341) that political self-understandings must be more partial than philosophical ones. While Smith reads *PhR* as a book for citizens and argues that Hegel presents understanding the world as one way of changing it (1989, 13, 193), he needs to say more about what Hegelian civic understanding entails. Pippin (2008, 267–268) separates the intellectual activities of philosophers from the pragmatic concerns of historical agents. And for Franco (1999, 125) the representations of political agents need to be conceptualized by philosophy to be fully understood; civic activity in the modern state is largely unreflective (86, 229, 232).

9. Pippin (1989, 159; 2011, 32); cf. Kelly (1978, 36); Markell (2003, 103); Redding (2008, 103).

10. Noted by Pippin (2011, 11). Williams (1997, 4, 10–11, 368) argues that Kojeve's focus on struggle elevates a primitive form of recognition into an unchanging normative standard.

11. Agreeing with Barba-Kay (2017, 35–36) and Pippin (2011, 14).

12. Agreeing with Franco (1999, 92–93) and Kelly (1978, 34–35).

13. Rosen (1974, 178) suggests that "the transition from city-states to empire [within Hegel's historical narrative of the classical world] exhibits the struggle for recognition of the master-slave dialectic" and Smith (1989, 162) reads the lord/bondsman narrative as prototypically political.

14. Harris sees the deadly combats of Achilles/Hector and Eteocles/Polyneices as emblematic (1997, 352). Kalkavage (2007, 116) reads chapter 4's struggle as "an *affaire d'honneur* like that between Achilles and Hector," wherein "each claims . . . to be the one and only glorious Self" (114). Shklar (1976, 28, 59) compares the struggle to a duel between epic heroes. For Rosen (1974, 158) and Hyppolite (1974, 164), this is a struggle to

prove one's manhood. Berns (1984, 336) comments that "it is superior spiritedness that most characterizes the political man."

15. Disputing interpretations of the struggle as a battle over honor (2011, 83). Pinkard (1994, 53) also reads the narrative as anticipating "that the standards for what counts as authoritative reasons should be seen as the outcome of a process of a community's coming to take certain kinds of claims as counting *for them* as authoritative," a process that is completed within modernity (62). Cortella (2015, 157–158) offers a democratic reconstruction of Hegel that starts with the dynamic of recognition (149), though it largely ignores the life and death aspect.

16. Though his focus on care and sacrifice (2017, 56) may be one sided. Commitment implies both steadfastness and aggression, willingness to kill as well as to die.

17. Noting Harris (1997, 370).

18. Harris (1997, 350); Hyppolite (1974, 172); Pinkard (1994, 60); Williams (1997, 61–62).

19. See Franco (1999, 90); Kelly (1978, 51); Williams (1997, 77, 79, 88, 90). Butler's (1997b, 31) characterization of the outcome as "dystopic" may go too far.

20. Noting Pippin (2008, 202–203). Kojeve's account of these changes (1968, 29–30) emphasizes their revolutionary character, downplaying the extent to which institutions initiated by revolutionary activity stabilize and enable. In claiming that the narrative signals the overcoming of the "warlike Master" by the "working Slave" Kojeve's more than vaguely Nietzschean reading ignores mediating institutions that would transform this relation into one of governing and being governed (see *PhH*, 47).

21. In commenting on the conclusion of chapter 6 (Spirit—*Phen*, 666, 669–670), Kalkavage (2007, 335, 354) notes the "great arch" extending from the fight to the death to the recognition achieved through "mutual forgiveness and communal self knowledge." Williams finds (1997, 79) this arch completed in the *Encyclopedia*. Markell on the other hand (2003, 96, 126) interprets the drive toward recognition as laying the groundwork for injustices that the more critically diagnostic Hegel should recognize.

22. As in Franco (1999, 299); Shklar (1976, 49).

23. Kelly (1978, 38), on the other hand, resists reading the *Phenomenology* and the *Lectures* in parallel.

24. Since the *Lectures* were not published in final form by Hegel, questions about their completeness or accuracy can be raised. Their pedagogical context makes them less systematic than *Phen* or *PhR*. What is clear and consistent, however, is the tone. The *Lectures'* perspective of one who claims to have seen the whole (*PhH*, 13) is continuous with those of *Phen* and *PhR*.

25. For Pinkard (1994, 136–137), Hegel argues that his contemporaries' veneration for Greek culture ignores fundamental contradictions. Nonetheless, Hegel reworks "the ancient Greek ideal . . . into a modern form of *Sittlichkeit*" (2008, 31, 270–271). There seems broad agreement: Avineri (1972, 20–21, 32–33, 51, 84–85, 103–4, 111–112, 162–163, 171, 179–180, 191–192, 226); Church (2012, 76, 79–80); Cortella (2015, 8, 10, 93–94); Franco (1999, 189, 228, 292); Smith (1989, 31, 242–243); Williams (1997, 18–19).

26. Agreeing with Pinkard (1994, 136–137, 146) and seeing the limitations of Kalkavage's (2007, 269) calling the polis Eden before the fall and Shklar's (1976, 12) judgment that Periclean Athens stands as a beacon within an otherwise demoralizing narrative of the West's spiritual ills.

27. Markell (2003, 114) notes that Hegel's concern in the last sections moves away from the details of *Antigone*, though the city's use of war for its own internal purposes may parallel the "technological" rule of Creon (cf. Nussbaum, 2001, 54–63).

28. Underscored by Ahrensdorf and Pangle (2014, 146).

29. Differing from Shklar (1976, 76–77).

30. Perhaps the conclusions of Pinkard (1994, 141) and Robert Williams (1997, 347–348).

31. For Shklar (1976, 149) this is more than an example. "The gladiatorial stadium is [the Roman] model of the world." Other comparisons: *PhH*, 277, 279, 283, 286–287, 289, 312, 317–318.

32. Bykova (2009, 281, 285); Pippin (2008, 249, 252).

33. Mara (2008, 24–25; 2009, 104–105).

34. Noting Henderson (1998, 16–19); Zumbrunnen (2012, 128–130).

35. Schlosser (2014, 11–19).

36. *Protagoras* (361a).

37. So, the audience witnessing the performed tragedy may not simply have its sense of the eventual equilibrium of Greek ethical life reinforced, though this might well be Hegel's verdict (Pinkard 1994, 145).

38. *Republic* (442d–443a; 612 d) and *Gorgias* (488e–489e). This dissents from Hegel's series of judgments in *PhH*, 270.

39. For Pinkard (1994, 270), "[completing] the *Phenomenology* therefore required [Hegel] to ask whether there were within the practices of modern life a set of social institutions that . . .would support a more determinate conception of practical agency." Cortella argues (2015, 47, 135, 156) that this completion requires a democratic correction of Hegelian categories. Shklar (1976, 101, 140–141, 205ff.) is skeptical that *Phen* offers positive prospects, reading it as a bittersweet memory of the Greek ethical world, setting itself significantly apart from *PhR*.

40. Franco (1999, 333).

41. Avineri 1(972, 46–47, 51, 77–78, 85, 87, 99, 104–105, 142, 155, 161, 165); Cortella (2015, 75, 89); Neuhouser (2008, 204–229); Pinkard (1994, chapter 7); Smith (1989, 122, 130, 141–149); Williams (1997, 201, 268, 294–295).

42. Prompting Smith (1989, 6) and Williams (1997, 3, 112) to suggest that Hegel attempts to reconcile Kant with Aristotle. However, Smith observes that there is no obvious Hegelian parallel to Aristotelian judgment. Cortella (2015), Church (2012, 65, 80) and Shklar (1976, 205) may overemphasize Hegelian parallels to Aristotle. Pippin (2008, 194, 199) is skeptical.

43. On the extended meaning of *Polizie* see Franco (1999, 266). Avineri (1972, 102) notes that *Polizei* is linguistically traceable to *politeia*, prompting us to ask how the two conceptions of politics might differ.

44. See, e.g., Smith (1989, 49, 129, 238). Frank calls Aristotle's ruling and judging the work of citizens (2005, 12).

45. Franco (1999, 323); Neuhouser (2008, 205); Pinkard (1994, 326–331); Smith (1989, 112, 145–146).

46. Not the *Second Treatise*'s "freedom" or "happiness."

47. Wood's characterization of liberalism (1991, xvi–xvii) is reductive. Neuhouser's reading (2009, 204) of Hegel's engagement with "the best aspects of liberal social thought" is more sympathetic. See also Smith (1989, 133, 144) and Franco (1999, 220–221, 345).

48. Differing from Wood (1991 xxvii) and coming closer to Franco (1999, 299), Neuhouser (2008, 226), Pippin (2008, 238), and Pinkard (1994, 299, 315, 327).

49. Avineri (1972); Cortella (2015); Franco (1999); Neuhouser (2008); Pinkard (1994); Smith (1989; 2016); Williams (1997).

50. Neuhouser (2008, 221) connects Hegel's social philosophy with his logical exploration of the concept (*der Begriff*), "Hegel's term for the basic structure that reason in general must attribute to its objects if they are to satisfy its demand that the world be intelligible to it." See also Cortella (2015, xiv); Franco (1999, 125).

51. Smith (1989, 157) and Franco (1999, 331) argue that Hegel's treatment of war diagnoses a basic weakness in liberal theories of political obligation.

52. Avineri (1972, 158) notes that Hegel's war-making class and Plato's guardians exhibit different degrees of separation from the rest of the community.

53. Franco (1999, 229–230).

54. Marcuse's concern (1960, 221).

55. So, war shows the limitations of the modern state's social functions in ways that crime (Avineri, 1972, 145; Williams, 1997, 152ff.) and poverty (Cortella, 2015, xx; Franco, 1999, 268, 273; Pinkard, 1994, 317–320; Smith, 2016, 170–171; Williams, 1997, 228, 243) do not.

56. Questioning Avineri's (1972, 207) judgment that Hegel expects wars eventually to disappear. Smith (1989, 164) and Franco (1999, 333) are more cautious and Williams (1997, 361–362) openly dissents. Either way, the continued presence of war may point to deeper philosophical difficulties and not simply signal Hegel's misplaced optimism about society's future (Cortella, 2015, 135).

57. Cortella (2015, 124–125).

58. Obviously, Kant.

59. For Williams (1997, 357, 360) the persistence of international war makes Hegel's view of history tragic, but Rosen (1974, 139) contends that to read Hegelian history tragically is to read it imperfectly. Ironically, though Williams opposes Kojeve's emphasis on struggle (1997, 4, 10–11), the tragic return of war (1997, 335) implies a destabilizing reconnection. For Williams, the Hegelian historical project is tragic because it has failed, for Kojeve, because it has succeeded.

60. Franco notes (1999, 64) that the assessment of war in *PhR* largely repeats earlier judgments in the essay now known as *Natural Law* and further argues that the seminal statement on war in PhR 324 draws upon the fundamental relations between universality and particularity that structure Hegel's logic.

61. Smith comments (1989, 164) that Hegel's envisaging an end of history, marked by consensus on the appropriate ends of life, may eventually undercut his valorization of war. Conversely, that valorization of war may destabilize prospects for consensus on the ends of life.

62. Paralleling but differing from Rosen (1974, 282) and Cortella (2015, 135), who discover alienation between Hegelian philosophy and politics. My observations suggest an alienation within Hegel's philosophy itself.

63. Doubted by, among others, Ahrensdorf and Pangle (2014), Honig (2013), and Nussbaum (2001).

64. A claim that Smith (1989, 230) sees haunting Hegel's own synopticism.

65. Unlike Hegel's Plato, who moves toward the ideas in a proto-Hegelian recognition of the destructive forces undermining Greek ethics (*PhR*, Pr).

66. "Speeches were spoken, mistrusted by some of the Greeks, but they were spoken" (*Hist* 3.80). Benardete comments (2009, 84) on the significance of this statement for Herodotus's *logos*.

67. Compare Habermas's treatment of the political resources of the lifeworld (1996, 22, 354) with Hegel's critical analytic of civil society (*PhR*, 317–318). Continuities between Hegel and Habermas are noted by Cortella (2015, 157–159), Smith (1989, 222, 244–246; 2016, 161), and Williams (1997, 13). Differences are admittedly substantial. Hegel is no democrat. Habermas does not subordinate *Moralität* to *Sittlichkeit* and suspects any strongly defined ethical life as a threat to democratic pluralism and individual autonomy. While Hegel may seek to preserve what is best in the classical polis and classical political philosophy, Habermas breaks decisively with "premodernity." Still, those arguing for the significance and value of Hegelian social philosophy (Cortella, Pinkard, and Pippin) often interpret his constitutional state as anticipating the institutions and practices of deliberative democracy (Franco is more cautious). This philosophical ancestry traces the socialization of Kantian autonomy through Hegel's corrections (Cortella, 2015, xiii; Geuss, 2008, 89), into a prospective democratization via critical theory (Smith, 1989, 246).

68. Habermas (1993, 86, 98–99, 103); Rawls (1999, 121); Cortella (2015, 153). With the completed actualization of spirit perhaps displaced by theories of social evolution (Rawls, 1999, 79).

69. On Hegel's limited recognition of international law see Franco (1999, 334).

70. Generally, Geuss's (2008, 63, 85–86) and Mouffe's (1998, 167–168) judgments.

71. Made explicit by Rawls (1999, 19, 28, 46).

72. References to *Beyond Good and Evil* are to sections. Other works are cited first in full title, then abbreviation.

73. Notably Appel (1999), Detwiler (1990), Yack (1986), and Berkowitz (1995).

74. Whether these self-constructive projects require politics (and if so, what kind) gets multiple answers. Nehamas (1985, 136–137, 163, 194, 227) focuses on Nietzsche's treating life as literature, largely sidestepping political theory. For Shaw (2007, 27, 32) Nietzsche's moral stance makes him resolutely anti-political. Though reading Nietzsche's narrower political theory as reactionary elitism, Warren (1988, 209–214) argues that it can be separated from his more interesting reflections on how democratic agency is constituted (218, 232, 234). Hatab's Nietzsche is an aristocrat but Nietzschean commitments can be turned in postmodern democratic directions (1996, 2–4, 11, 224), prospects hinted also by Connolly (1990, 72–74) and Honig (1993, 73–74). Clark (2015, 174) and Church (2015, 5, 225, 227) argue that Nietzsche's aristocratic values can peacefully coexist with democratic or liberal institutions protecting freedom to be excellent. Thiele sees Nietzsche's politics as an inwardly turned "politics of the soul" (1990, 95, 164, 200, 212, 220). Strong suggests (1988, 169–170; 2000, 100, 189–191, 208) that any transfiguration of the soul requires a transformation of culture.

75. Insofar as these worlds are separable (*Schopenhauer as Educator*, 3.5; *Homer's Contest*, 174).

76. Strong (2000, 66) sees a debt to Heraclitus's ontology (as in Diels, fragment 53 in Freeman, 1983, 28. Cf. *BT* 20; *TI, Reason in Philosophy*, 2; *Philosophy in the Tragic Age of the Greeks*, 5–6). See also Gillespie (1988, 128, 144). Brann (2011, 119) is skeptical.

77. Noting very different interpretations of Nietzsche's understanding of nature. See Clark (Nietzsche, 1997, xxii; 2015, 275—genealogy), Church (2012, 115; 2015, 19, 83,

146—developmental teleology), and Shaw (2007, 82, 88—psychological and physical determinism). Warren argues that Nietzsche's cosmology is projected as a condition for critical agency (1988, 133–136); cf. Strong (2000, 67); Nehamas (1985, 231). Strauss (1996, 197) only claims that Nietzsche treats nature as a problem.

78. For Pippin, it is not the violence of war but "the psychology of love . . . [that is] a useful and broad window into Nietzsche's psychological analysis of the philosophical type" (2010, 15). Pippin interprets this eroticism as originating from an active embrace of new possibilities, "one that always anticipates the satisfactions of a possibly better life" (2010, 16). Does this origin exclude all forms of war? Perhaps not. Philosophical criticism can wage its most ruthless wars out of its love for new possibilities, straining against horizons of convention or attachments to things held personally most dear.

79. Interpreted by Church (2015, 13; 212, 114), Strong (2000, 40), and Warren (1988, 176) as constructive. Berkowitz (1995, 106), Honig (1993, 55, 62–63), and Shaw (2007, 124–125) emphasize Nietzsche's criticisms.

80. Shaw (2007, 109).

81. Differing from Berkowitz's (1995, 246) suggestion that Nietzsche believes that "massive wars will have to be waged to restore an aristocracy of spirit."

82. Cf. *TI, What the Germans Lack*, 4; Gillespie (1988, 136); Strong (2000, 289).

83. Sluga (2014, 43) reads this as suggesting that all stable politics require distinctions in rank, but the need for slavery is underplayed. Warren (1988, 225) argues that Nietzsche uncritically assumes that societies structured according to class are inevitable. Church (2015, 214) contends that Nietzsche' critique of modernity (in for example, *The Greek State*) stresses the wage slavery of the working class. These readings can be supplemented by appreciating the psychological bases and applications of Nietzsche's judgment.

84. Appel (1999, 6, 102). See also Detwiler (1990, chapter 5). Gillespie (1988, 130, 134, 147) reads Nietzsche as imagining a new great politics for a new tragic age.

85. Church (2015, 169) understands Nietzsche's national cultures as liberating their members from slavery to nature's material influences.

86. Differing from Soll (2014, 141–142) and Nehamas (1985, 209) and agreeing with Hatab (1995, 175) and Honig (1993, 42).

87. In *Zarathustra*, the last human being lives longest (*Zarathustra's Prologue*, 5).

88. Differing from Young (2014, 25–27) and Swanton (2014, 181, 193) and agreeing with Gillespie (1988, 135). This reciprocal poisonousness complicates Church's (2015, 4, 69, 122, 231) and Clark's (2015, 174) readings that Nietzsche envisages mediation between aristocratic and democratic values through a reinvented culture that allows the best to be the best. Hatab (1995, 110–111) may underemphasize differences between Nietzsche and Mill on equality. See Mara and Dovi (1995).

89. Kaufmann (1968, 298–300) makes a sustained case against ascribing anti-Semitism to Nietzsche.

90. Paralleling the comments on the "Jewish 'old testament'" as "a book of divine justice. . . . With terror and reverence one stands before these tremendous remnants of what man once was" (*BGE*, 52).

91. The latter is suggested by interpretations that point to inexorable logic at work in Nietzsche's account of modern morality (Strong, 2000, 245). This logic may be detectable only retrospectively, however, and what seems inexorable now may have been only one possibility among many.

92. Clark (2015, 25) distinguishes between Nietzsche's treatments of narrower and wider senses of morality. While Nietzsche sees some human periods as premoral (*BGE*, 32), he may be outlining the genealogies of more than one morality. Satkunanandan (2015, 30) sees Nietzsche moving beyond all narrow moralities to a higher concern for justice.

93. On language as power in Nietzsche, see Richardson (2014) and Strong (1988, 159).

94. An account that many commentators—Appel (1999, 40–42), Berkowitz (1995, 74–78), Clark (2015, 24, 31), Hatab (1995, 25–27), and Strong (2000, 241–242)—accept as Nietzsche's own. This may be premature.

95. In *Tragic Age* 1, Nietzsche comments that "everywhere the way to the beginnings leads to barbarism." See also *GM* 1.11; 2.6. Church (2015, 220–221) argues that Nietzsche's developmental teleology traces a movement away from primitive barbarism to the construction of a culture capable of challenging the modern state. Church may see the outcome of this challenge as more stable than Nietzsche does.

96. Noted by Berkowitz (1995, 98) and Strong (2000, 240), though with different forms of knowledge in mind.

97. Differing from Nehamas's suggestion (1985, 206; 215–217) that this noble morality is a personality type that Nietzsche praises.

98. Thus, Pippin, "the real genius of the slave rebellion, according to Nietzsche, lies in its going beyond a simple inversion of value types and in the creation of a new way of thinking about human beings" (2010, 70). See also Church (2015, 234).

99. And even here, perhaps only when "religions do not want to be a means of cultivation and education in the philosopher's hand but insist on having their own sovereign way" (61).

100. Seeing modern nihilism as more than the condition for postmodern human advancement (Warren, 1988, 88; Thiele, 1990, 88) and complicating the Nietzschean assessment of Christianity (Warren, 1988, 42; Honig, 1993, 61; Satkunanandan, 2015, 39, 47, 49). Both Berkowitz (1995, 113) and Strong (2000, 123) distinguish between Nietzsche's criticisms of Christianity and his representation of Christ. His account of Christianity may be similarly complex. Cf. *SE*, 3.6.

101. See also Clark and Dudrick (Clark, 2015, 272); Shaw (2007, 2).

102. Nehamas (1985, 24, 30); Gillespie (1988, 127–128); Dannhauser (1974, 183–185).

103. Possibly based on Nietzsche's reading of *Protagoras*. Strong (2000, 177–180) offers an interesting consideration of Nietzsche and this dialogue.

104. Clark's and Dudrick's (Clark, 2015, 103–109) and Shaw's (2007, 119, 151) distinctions between cognitivist and noncognitivist moralities in Nietzsche may be too binary, even if Nietzsche's noncognitivism is more complicated than on first view.

105. Differing from Thiele (1990, 161), who sees Nietzsche's truth as more personal and from Shaw (2007, 124) and Satkunanandan (2015, 40), whose Nietzschean morality seems more monologic. This interactive or intersubjective aspect of truth seems more compatible with the (different) readings of Clark and Dudrick, Pippin, Strong and Warren.

106. Paralleling Warren's insight (1988, 92) that Nietzsche's truth is his representation of a world that conditions practice, though of course there are different ways of understanding practice. Nehamas denies (1985, 53) that Nietzsche offers a pragmatist theory of truth, but this is only convincing if pragmatism is restricted to utility.

107. Satkunanandan (2015, 48).

108. On Nietzsche's musical politics see Gillespie (1988). On Nietzsche and the imagination, generally, see Czobor-Lupp (2014).

109. Differing from Church (2015, 112). These two groupings complicate Nehamas's judgment (1985, 28, 227) that Nietzsche gives literary and artistic figures pride of place. More in agreement with Gillespie (1988, 137) and Strong (1988, 156, 158).

110. Seeing *BGE*'s narrative structure differently from Strauss (1996, 190). As a performance narrative, the book may be Nietzsche's alternative to the *Phenomenology* which ends with the dawning of the science of wisdom. *BGE* concludes with Nietzsche's dissatisfaction with his own written and painted thoughts that have now become so boring, so fearfully close to becoming truths (296).

111. Differing from Young (2014) and siding more with Gemes and Sykes (2014), Clark and Wonderley (2014), and Richardson (2014).

112. Agreeing with but going beyond Honig's observation (1993, 42) that Nietzsche is recovering and restructuring traditional virtues.

113. Nietzsche's interpretation of Greek culture in *Homer's Contest* is counter-Hegelian. Though driven by "the feeling that [their] contest (*Wettkampf*) was necessary for the well being of the state" (*HC*, 178), Nietzsche's Greeks were less instinctively loyal to the common good (as in Hegel, *PhH*, 42) than instinctively competitive with one another. Greece's wars were not continuous displays of a youthfully aggressive manliness (*PhH*, 257–258); the ethic of the *Wettkampf* was an exceptional interval between pre-Homeric savagery and post-Homeric hubris (*HC*, 175, 180–181). Alexander was not the perfection of Achillean excellence (*PhH*, 223–224, 273), but a nauseating caricature (*HC*, 174). Greece's collapse was not caused by inherent dialectical contradictions (*PH*, 224, 268–269) but by a series of contingent accidents (*HC*, 179–181). Most importantly, Greek *Sittlichkeit* is not transformatively embedded within Nietzsche's higher morality.

114. See Gillespie (1988, 126) and Nehamas (1985, 221) who essentially equate Nietzschean moderation with courageous psychic mastery.

115. Satkunanandan (2015, 29) interprets a Nietzschean justice higher than morality's debt justice.

116. Nietzsche's cave imagery is compared with the Platonic position by Berkowitz (1995, 133), Higgins (2014, 90), and Strong (2000, 122, 147).

117. On the identity of this god, see, e.g., Gillespie (1988, 140–141); Kaufmann (1968, 410); Strong (1988, 115–116); Strauss (1996, 189).

118. Perhaps one reason why Strong (1988, 158) and Church (2015, 4, 69, 71, 132) read Nietzschean politics as combining aristocracy with democracy.

119. Unlike Aristotle, who criticizes the "myths [that] say the gods are of human forms" (*Metaph*, lambda, 8).

120. On Nietzsche's philosopher as hermit, generally, see Higgins (2014).

121. Though see *BGE* 66.

122. Agreeing with Honig (1993, 64).

123. As in Gillespie's (1988, 135) image of Nietzsche's great genius who imposes the higher morality of tragic culture.

124. Recalling Appel (1999); Berkowitz (1995); Detwiler (1990); Yack (1986).

125. *The Greek State* (171–172) valorizes war as the foundation of genius and the antidote to the profiteering state of "*Wer Neuen*" while Hegel embraces the ethical

significance of war for all modern political communities in *PhR* 324. Church (2015, 212) notes similarities.

126. In *Uses* Nietzsche admires "the culture of the Renaissance [that] raised itself on the shoulders of such a one-hundred man grouping," (*Uses*, 2; *TI, Skirmishes*, 37) "a nursling of more ancient times, especially the Greeks" (*Uses*, Pr). This cultural renewal will be sharply combative. "In the best case, we may bring about a conflict (*Widerstreite*) between our inherited, ancestral nature and our knowledge, as well as a battle (*Kampfe*) between a strict new discipline and ancient education and breeding" (*Uses*, 3). See Church (2015, 157).

127. This question also besets Church's (2015, 207–208, 215), Clark and Wonderley's (2014, 137), Higgins's (2014, 81, 91), and Richardson's (2014, 290–291) interpretations of Nietzsche's preferred community. Clark hypothesizes (2015, 164) that a Nietzschean endorsement of democracy emerges from his respect for science as democratic enterprise. She needs to say more about the implications and ambiguities of seeing (democratic) politics as an analogue to a scientific community. Church argues that Nietzsche's high cultural ambitions are compatible with a limited liberal state ruled by law. Yet that state seems more minimal than liberal and its ethos is one of Nietzsche's principal targets.

128. In a way, the judgment of Nehamas (1985, 224, 228), though he reads privatization as a direction within Nietzsche's texts. Rorty sees it resulting from creative rereadings.

129. Mara and Dovi (1995).

130. Connolly (1990, 73); Hatab (1995, 4, 12, 84, 86); Honig (1993, 70, 72); Strong (2000, xxviii, 100, 105–106, 189, 208).

131. Strong (2000, 278–280); Hatab (1995, 69, 132). Gillespie, however, politicizes Nietzsche's musical harmonizing of differences as a kind of imposition (1988, 135, 145).

132. Hatab's interpretation (1995, 137) raises the question of whether Nietzsche sees politics too exclusively as culture. Does agonistic democracy simply sidestep all problematic political identities (1995, 205)?

133. Suggested frequently by Butler (2010, xxii, 6, 32, 52, 105, 132, 145).

134. A binary obscuring the variety of Western philosophical voices who preceded Nietzsche, as if there were a straight line intellectual depreciation from Plato through Hegel.

135. One can agree with Berkowitz that Nietzsche's truth is not simply perspectival, but also be skeptical of any Nietzschean embrace of a bounded truth that is superperspectival. For discussions more sympathetic to Nietzsche's perspectivism see: Clark and Dudrick, 2015, 122–123, 128; Nehamas, 1985, 231; Shaw, 2007, 109–110; Strong, 2000, 295, 301; Satkunanandan, 2015, 39.

136. A more tentative version of Berkowitz's claim (1995, 252) that Nietzsche is caught on the horns of a dilemma, "the fundamental conflict between the views that the noble is made and that it is discovered." Church (2015, 19, 55, 83) resolves this by appealing to a Nietzsche who depends on a kind of vaguely Aristotelian teleology. See Mara and Dovi (1995, 21).

137. Suggested with approval by Honig (1993, 58, 72).

138. Perhaps not so whimsical. Clark (2015, 108) suggests that Nietzsche offers color as a metaphor for value. Would this mean that the most brilliant would be the best?

Chapter 5

1. Translations of passages from Thucydides rely on those of Lattimore (1998) and Smith (1962–1988), though there are some changes. Translations from the *Republic* are Bloom's (1968) with small changes.

2. Continuing some earlier work, especially Mara (2008).

3. Noting, most recently, Frank (2018, 8, 15, 31).

4. From Pericles's "recent" death (429) through the trial of the Arginusae generals (406). *Gorgias* passages are 473e–474a and 503c.

5. For Zuckert (2009, 428–430), the gathering in the *Timaeus'* could be interpreted as a conspiracy against Athens' democracy, imaging, through the presence of the Syracusan Hermocrates, the defeat in Sicily and, through that of Critias, the tyranny of the thirty. For an alternative view of this Critias's identity see Lampert and Planeaux (1998); Welliver (1977).

6. Xenophon, *Hellenica* 2.11. Also noted by Frank (2007).

7. Especially once we connect Athens' stress (7.28) with the subsequent narrative of Mycalessus' destruction (7.29–30). See Mara (2008, 201–207).

8. Making Thucydides's approach in a way democratic. See Saxonhouse (2006, 149–151) and Mara (2008, 121).

9. Translating *kinēsis* in 1.1.

10. Noted also by Orwin (1994, 179–180).

11. Differing from Orwin (1994, 177).

12. See Curley (1994, 77, n8). Hobbes's translation of 3.82 reads in part, "war, taking away the affluence of daily necessaries, is a most violent master, and conformeth most men's passions to the present occasion."

13. Price (2001) interprets internal war as the organizing theme of the narrative.

14. Kochin (1999, 413).

15. *Timaeus* 90 b–d. Noting that the beauty of the cosmos and the goodness of the *demiourgos* are likely stories (29c–d) required for Timaeus's philosophy. Zuckert (2009) offers a convincing interpretation that reads Timaeus as a philosopher whose differences from Socrates make him a Platonic character, not a spokesman for Plato.

16. Romilly (2012, 139; 1963, 336–343).

17. Agreeing with Fisher and Hoekstra (2017, 383–384).

18. Balot (2014, 118–119) offers a slightly different criticism of this "war speech."

19. Translating *prophasis* as cause (Mynott, Lattimore, Crawley) or explanation (Smith) overstates the allegedly scientific character of Thucydides's treatment. *Prophainein* can be to bring forth or to present. In calling Athenian greatness and Spartan fear the truest (*alēthestatēn*) claims brought forth, Thucydides remains with the language of political agents while also offering his own judgment about its significance. While the truest *prophaseis* were the least manifest in speech (*aphanestatēn de logō*), they may not be in contrast with more open accusations (*phaneron legoumena aitiai*). Perhaps the latter are pointedly clarified when they are read in the context of the former. Liddell and Scott's "pretext" seems misapplied here. Hobbes's "true quarrel" is more illuminating.

20. Walzer (1977, 5) reads Thucydides as a "realist" in this sense. For a critique see O'Driscoll (2015, 375–378). For a more general assessment of Thucydides and the various languages of realism in internal relations see Johnson (2015).

21. See Mara (2015, 318–320).

22. Orwin (1994, 151–153); Saxonhouse (2006, 160–163); Mara (2008, 58–59).

23. Differing from Orwin (1994, 183, 204) and Strauss (1964, 228).

24. On significance of calling Pericles's leadership an *archē*, see Morrison (2006, 148–149).

25. Strauss (1964, 231); Orwin (1994, 104–106); Saxonhouse (1996, 214); Mara (2008, 249–252).

26. Characterizing this city's wars as "expansionist" (see Frank, 2007, 449; Kochin, 1999, 405) is less straightforward than it seems.

27. In tracing the devolution of inferior regimes in Book Eight Socrates represents a timarchy driven by love of honor as giving way almost immediately to an oligarchy obsessed with wealth (*Rep*, 550 d–e). Is the designation, timarchy, simply part of a valorizing oligarchic narrative (Mara, 1997, 137–139)? Craig (1994) argues that the distinction between two kinds of timocrats, Glaucon and Adeimantus frames the conversation of the *Republic* generally.

28. Seeing this education less positively than Kochin (1999, 417).

29. The guardians of this city ignore the nuptial number and beget children out of season (546b) perhaps revealing the mistakes of confusing erotic with geometrical necessity (458d).

30. Frank (2018); Roochnik (2009); Mara (1997); Nichols (1987); Weiss (2012); Zuckert (2009).

31. While I agree with Frank that the education for war provided in *Republic* Book Five is "not a prelude to philosophy but a worrisome obstacle" (2007, 454; cf. 2018, 225–226), the dissonance may point not simply to the inadequacy of this education but to the inescapable tensions between a culture supportive of critical thinking and one faced with the (always ambiguous) challenges of warfare. In this respect, see Kochin (1999, 422–423).

32. Compare Thucydides, 3.82 with *Republic* 560e. I owe this parallel to Ryan Balot.

33. Compare *Republic*, 566a–b with Aristotle, *Athēnaiōn Politeia*, 14; *Rhetoric*, 1.2, 1357b 30–35; Herodotus, 1.59–61; Cicero *De Republica*, 1.68. Monoson (2011) sees allusions not to Athens and Peisistratus but to Sicily and Dionysius. Must we choose one over the other?

34. Noting Mara (2009, 122–123), refining Geuss (2005, 227) and Williams (2002, 154, 163).

35. A condition of peace different from that envisaged by Strauss (1964, 240).

36. Glaucon's case is less clear (Mara, 1997, 102–103).

37. See especially the discussion in Frank (2018, 16–17).

REFERENCES

Aertsen, Jan. 1993. "Aquinas's Philosophy in Its Historical Setting." In *The Cambridge Companion to Aquinas*, edited by Norman Kretzmann and Eleonore Stump, 12–37. Cambridge: Cambridge University Press.

Ahrensdorf, Peter J. 2000. "The Fear of Death and the Longing for Immortality: Hobbes and Thucydides on Human Nature and the Problem of Anarchy." *American Political Science Review* 94, no. 3: 579–593.

Ahrensdorf, Peter J., and Thomas Pangle. 2014. Trans. with Intro. *Sophocles: The Theban Plays*. Ithaca, NY: Cornell University Press.

Alter, Robert. 2004. *The Five Books of Moses: A Translation with Commentary*. New York: Norton.

Anscombe, G. E. M. 1961. "War and Murder." In *Nuclear Weapons: A Catholic Response*, edited by Walter Stein, 55–62. London: Sheed and Ward.

Apel, Karl Otto. 1997. "Kant's 'Toward Perpetual Peace' as Historical Prognosis from the Moral Point of View of Duty." In *Perpetual Peace: Essays on Kant's Cosmopolitan Ideal*, edited by James Bohman and Matthias Lutz-Bachmann, 79–110. Cambridge, MA: The MIT Press.

Appel, Frederick. 1999. *Nietzsche Contra Democracy*. Ithaca, NY: Cornell University Press.

Aquinas, Thomas. 1949. *On Kingship*. Trans. Gerard Phelan, Revised I. Thomas Aschmann. Toronto: Pontifical Institute of Medieval Studies.

Aquinas, Thomas. 1964–1972. *Summa Theologiae*. Vols. 1, 14, 18, 23, 28, 35, 37, 38, 41. Cambridge and New York: Blackfriars and McGraw Hill.

Arendt, Hannah. 1958. *The Human Condition*. Chicago: University of Chicago Press.

Arendt, Hannah. 1968. "What Is Freedom?" In *Between Past and Future*, 143–171. New York: Viking.

Arendt, Hannah. 1982. *Lectures on Kant's Political Philosophy*. Chicago: University of Chicago Press.

Aristotle. 1999. *Metaphysics*. Trans. Joe Sachs. Santa Fe, NM: Green Lion Press.

Aristotle. 2011. *Nicomachean Ethics*. Trans. Robert Bartlett and Susan Collins. Chicago: University of Chicago Press.

Aristotle. 2013. *Politics*. 2nd ed. Trans. Carnes Lord. Chicago: University of Chicago Press.

Aron, Raymond. 2003. *Peace and War: A Theory of International Relations*. Trans. Richard Howard and Annett Baker Fox. New intro. Daniel J. Mahoney and Brian C. Anderson. New Brunswick, NJ: Transaction Publishers.

Augustine, 1994. *Political Writings*. Trans. Michael Tkacz and Douglas Kries. Ed. Ernest Fortin and Douglas Kries. Indianapolis: Hackett.

Avineri, Shlomo. 1972. *Hegel's Theory of the Modern State*. Cambridge: Cambridge University Press.

Balot, Ryan. 2014. *Courage in the Democratic Polis*. Oxford: Oxford University Press.

Barba-Kay, Anton. 2017. "Locating Hegel's Struggle for Recognition." *Hegel Studien* 50: 33–61.

Barry, Brian. 1972. "Warrender and His Critics." In *Hobbes and Rousseau: A Collection of Critical Essays*, edited by Maurice Cranston and Richard Peters, 38–65. Garden City, NY: Anchor Doubleday.

Benardete, Seth. 1991. *The Rhetoric of Morality and Philosophy*. Chicago: University of Chicago Press.

Benardete, Seth. 2009. *Herodotean Inquiries*. South Bend, IN: St. Augustine Press.

Bendersky, Joseph. 1983. *Carl Schmitt: Theorist for the Reich*. Princeton, NJ: Princeton University Press.

Benhabib, Seyla. 2004. *The Rights of Others*. New York: Cambridge University Press.

Bercovitch, Sacvan. 1998. "The Function of The Literary in a Time of Cultural Studies." In *"Culture" and the Problem of the Disciplines*, edited by John Carlos Rowe, 69–87. New York: Columbia University Press.

Berkowitz, Peter. 1995. *Nietzsche: The Ethics of an Immoralist*. Cambridge, MA: Harvard University Press.

Bermeo, Nancy. 2003. *Ordinary People in Extraordinary Times*. Princeton, NJ: Princeton University Press.

Berns, Laurence. 1984. "Spiritedness in Ethics and Politics: A Sudy of Aristotelian Psychology." *Interpretation* 12, nos. 2 and 3: 335-348.

Black, Robert. 1991. "Machiavelli: Servant of the Florentine Empire." In *Machiavelli and Republicanism*, edited by Gisela Bock, Quentin Skinner, and Maurizio Viroli, 71–100. Cambridge: Cambridge University Press.

Bloom, Allan. Trans.1968. *The Republic of Plato*. New York: Basic Books.

Bohman, James. 1997. "The Public Spheres of the World Citizen." In *Perpetual Peace: Essays on Kant's Cosmopolitan Ideal*, edited by James Bohman and Matthias Lutz-Bachmann, 179–200. Cambridge, MA: The MIT Press.

Bohman, James, and Matthias Lutz-Bachmann, eds. 1997. *Perpetual Peace: Essays on Kant's Cosmopolitan Ideal*. Cambridge, MA: The MIT Press.

Boyd, Richard. 2001. "Thomas Hobbes and the Perils of Pluralism." *Journal of Politics* 63, no. 2: 392–413.

Boyle, Joseph. 1998. "Just War Thinking in Catholic Natural Law." In *The Ethics of War and Peace: Religious and Secular Perspectives*, edited by Terry Nardin, 40–53. Princeton, NJ: Princeton University Press.

Brann, Eva. 2011. *The Logos of Heraclitus*. Philadelphia: Paul Dry Books.

Bredekamp, Horst. 2007. "Thomas Hobbes's Visual Strategies." In *A Cambridge Companion to Hobbes's Leviathan*, edited by Patricia Springborg, 29–60. Cambridge: Cambridge University Press.

Brown, Alison. 2010. "Philosophy and Religion in Machiavelli." In *The Cambridge Companion to Machiavelli*, edited by John Najemy, 157–172. Cambridge: Cambridge University Press.

Burkhardt, Todd. 2017. *Just War and Human Rights*. Albany: State University of New York Press.

Butler, Judith. 1997a. *Excitable Speech*. New York: Routledge.

Butler, Judith. 1997b. *The Psychic Life of Power: Theories in Subjection*. Redwood City, CA: Stanford University Press.

Butler, Judith. 2010. *Frames of War*. London: Verso.

Bykova, Marina. 2009. "Spirit and Concrete Subjectivity in Hegel's *Phenomenology of Spirit*." In *The Blackwell Guide to Hegel's Phenomenology of Spirit*, edited by Kenneth Westphal, 265–295. Malden, MA: Wiley-Blackwell.

Cantalupo, Charles. 1991. *A Literary Leviathan*. Lewisburg, PA: Bucknell University Press.

Chong, Dennis. 2000. *Rational Lives: Norms and Values in Politics and Society*. Chicago: University of Chicago Press.

Church, Jeffrey 2012. *Infinite Autonomy: The Divided Individual in the Political Thought of G. W. F. Hegel and Friedrich Nietzsche*. University Park: Pennsylvania State University Press.

Church, Jeffrey. 2015. *Nietzsche's Culture of Humanity: Beyond Aristocracy and Democracy in the Early Period*. Cambridge: Cambridge University Press.

Clark, Maudemarie. 2015. *Nietzsche on Ethics and Politics*. With some essays co-authored by David Dudrick. Oxford: Oxford University Press.

Clark, Maudemarie, and Monique Wonderley. 2014. "The Good of Community." In *Individual and Community in Nietzsche's Philosophy*, edited by Julian Young, 118–140. Cambridge: Cambridge University Press.

Coby, Patrick. 1999. *Machiavelli's Romans*. Lanham, MD: Lexington Books.

Connolly, William. 1990. "Identity and Difference in Liberalism. In *Liberalism and the Good*, edited by R. Bruce Douglass, Gerald Mara, and Henry Richardson. New York: Routledge.

Connolly, William. 1993. *The Augustinian Imperative*. Newbury Park, CA: Sage.

Connolly, William. 1995. *The Ethos of Pluralization*. Minneapolis: University of Minnesota Press.

Connor, W. Robert. 1984. *Thucydides*. Princeton, NJ: Princeton University Press.

Cortella, Lucio. 2015. *The Ethics of Democracy: A Contemporary Reading of Hegel's Philosophy of Right*. Trans. Giacomo Donis. Albany: State University of New York Press.

Craig, Leon. 1994. *The War Lover: A Study of Plato's Republic*. Toronto: University of Toronto Press.

Crane, Gregory. 1996. *The Blinded Eye*. Lanham, MD: Rowman & Littlefield.

Crane, Gregory.1998. *The Ancient Simplicity*. Berkeley: University of California Press.

Curley, Edwin. 1994. Ed. with Intro. *Thomas Hobbes, Leviathan*. Indianapolis: Hackett.

Curley, Edwin. 2007. "Hobbes and the Cause of Religious Toleration." In *A Cambridge Companion to Hobbes's Leviathan*, edited by Patricia Springborg, 309–334. Cambridge: Cambridge University Press.

Czobor-Lupp, Mihaela. 2014. *Imagination in Politics: Freedom or Domination?* Lanham, MD: Lexington Books.

Danford, John. 2006. "Getting Our Bearings: Machiavelli and Hume." In *Machiavelli's Liberal Republican Legacy*, edited by Paul Rahe, 94–120. Cambridge: Cambridge University Press.

Dannhauser, Werner. 1974. *Nietzsche's View of Socrates*. Ithaca NY: Cornell University Press.

De Grazia, Sebastian. 1989. *Machiavelli in Hell*. Princeton, NJ: Princeton University Press.

Derrida, Jacques. 1997. *The Politics of Friendship*. Trans. George Collins. London: Verso.

Derrida, Jacques. 2005. *Rogues: Two Essays on Reason*. Trans. Pascale-Anne Brault and Michael Naas. Redwood City, CA: Stanford University Press.

Detwiler, Bruce. 1990. *Nietzsche and the Politics of Aristocratic Radicalism*. Chicago: University of Chicago Press.

Douglass, R. Bruce. 2018. *The Iron Cage Revisited: Max Weber in the Neoliberal Era*. New York: Routledge.

Doyle, Michael. 1983. "Kant, Liberal Legacies and Foreign Affairs, Parts 1 and 2." *Philosophy and Public Affairs* 12, no. 3, 4: 205–235; 323–353.

Drury, Shadia. 2008. *Aquinas and Modernity: The Lost Promise of Natural Law*. Lanham, MD: Rowman & Littlefield.

Ellis, Elisabeth. 2005. *Kant's Politics: Provisional Theory for an Uncertain World*. New Haven, CT: Yale University Press.

Elshtain, Jean Bethke. 2003. *Just War Against Terror in a Violent World*. New York: Basic Books.

Evrigenis, Ioannis. 2014. *Images of Anarchy: The Rhetoric and Science in Hobbes's State of Nature*. Cambridge: Cambridge University Press.

Farneti, Roberto. 2007. "Hobbes on Salvation." In *A Cambridge Companion to Hobbes's Leviathan*, edited by Patricia Springborg, 291–308. Cambridge: Cambridge University Press.

Ferrari, G. R. F. 2003. *City and Soul in Plato's Republic*. Chicago: University of Chicago Press.

Finnis, John. 1980. *Natural Law and Natural Rights*. Oxford: Clarendon Press.

Finnis, John. 1998a. *Aquinas: Moral, Political and Legal Theory*. Oxford: Oxford University Press.

Finnis, John. 1998b. "The Ethics of War and Peace in the Catholic Natural Law Tradition." In *The Ethics of War and Peace: Religious and Secular Perspectives*, edited by Terry Nardin, 15–39. Princeton, NJ: Princeton University Press.

Fischer, Marcus. 2006. "Prologue: Machiavelli's Rapacious Republicanism." In *Machiavelli's Liberal Republican Legacy*, edited by Paul Rahe, xxxi–lx11. Cambridge: Cambridge University Press.

Fisher, Mark, and Kinch Hoekstra. 2017. "Thucydides and the Politics of Necessity." In *The Oxford Handbook of Thucydides*, edited by Ryan Balot, Sara Forsdyke, and Edith Foster, 373–390. New York: Oxford University Press, 373–390.

Flathman, Richard. 2002. *Thomas Hobbes: Skepticism, Individuality and Chastened Politics*, New ed. Lanham, MD: Rowman & Littlefield.

Fortin, Ernest L. 1982. "The New Rights Theory and The Natural Law." *Review of Politics* 44, no. 4: 590–612.

Fortin, Ernest L. 1987. "St. Thomas Aquinas." In *History of Political Philosophy*, 3rd ed., edited by Leo Strauss and Joseph Cropsey, 241–275. Chicago: University of Chicago Press.

Franceschet, Antonio. 2006. "'One Powerful and Enlightened Nation: Kant and the Quest for a Global Rule of Law." In *Classical Theory in International Relations*, edited by Beate Jahn, 74–95. Cambridge: Cambridge University Press.

Franco, Paul. 1999. *Hegel's Philosophy of Freedom*. New Haven, CT: Yale University Press.

Frank, Jill. 2005. *A Democracy of Distinction: Aristotle and the Work of Politics*. Chicago: University of Chicago Press.

Frank, Jill. 2007. "Wages of War: Judgment in Plato's *Republic*." *Political Theory* 35, no. 4: 443–467.

Frank, Jill. 2018. *Poetic Justice: Rereading Plato's Republic*. Chicago: University of Chicago Press.

Freeman, Kathleen. 1983. *Ancilla to the Pre-Socratic Philosophers*. Cambridge, MA: Harvard University Press.

Galston, William. 1975. *Kant and the Problem of History*. Chicago. University of Chicago Press.

Garsten, Bryan. 2006. *Saving Persuasion*. Cambridge, MA: Harvard University Press.

Gauthier, David. 1969. *The Logic of Leviathan*. Oxford: Oxford University Press.

Geertz, Clifford. 1973. *The Interpretation of Cultures*, New York: Basic Books.

Geertz, Clifford. 1983. *Local Knowledge*. New York: Basic Books.

Gemes, Ken, and Chris Sykes. 2014. "The Culture of Myth and the Myth of Culture." In *Individual and Community in Nietzsche's Philosophy*, edited by Julian Young, 51–76. Cambridge: Cambridge University Press.

Geuss, Raymond. 2005. *Outside Ethics*. Princeton, NJ: Princeton University Press.

Geuss, Raymond. 2008. *Philosophy and Real Politics*. Princeton, NJ: Princeton University Press.

Gillespie, Michael Allen. 1988. "Nietzsche's Musical Politics." In *Nietzsche's New Seas*, edited by Michael Allen Gillespie and Tracy B. Strong, 117–149. Chicago: University of Chicago Press.

Habermas, Jurgen. 1973. *Theory and Practice*. Trans. John Viertel. Boston: Beacon Press.

Habermas, Jurgen. 1979. *Communication and the Evolution of Society*. Trans. Thomas McCarthy. Boston: Beacon Press.

Habermas, Jurgen. 1987. *The Philosophical Discourse of Modernity*. Trans. Frederick Lawrence. Cambridge, MA: The MIT Press.

Habermas, Jurgen. 1990. *Moral Consciousness and Communicative Action*. Trans. Sherry Weber Nicholsen and Christian Lenhardt. Cambridge, MA: The MIT Press.

Habermas, Jurgen. 1992. *Postmetaphysical Thinking*. Trans William Mark Hohengarten. Cambridge, MA: The MIT Press.

Habermas, Jurgen. 1993. *Justification and Application*. Trans. Ciaran Cronin. Cambridge, MA: The MIT Press.

Habermas, Jurgen. 1996. *Between Facts and Norms*. Trans. William Rehg. Cambridge, MA: The MIT Press.

Habermas, Jurgen. 1997. "Kant's Idea of Perpetual Peace with the Benefit of Two Hundred Years Hindsight." In *Perpetual Peace: Essays on Kant's Cosmopolitan Ideal*, edited by James Bohman and Matthias Lutz-Bachmann, 113–153. Cambridge, MA: The MIT Press.

Habermas, Jurgen. 1998. *The Inclusion of the Other*. Ed. Ciaran Cronin and Pablo de Greiff. Cambridge, MA: The MIT Press.

Habermas, Jurgen. 2006. *The Divided West*. Ed. and trans. Ciaran Cronin. Cambridge: Polity Press.

Hanson, Victor Davis. 2002. *An Autumn of War*. New York: Anchor Books.

Hardin, Russell. 1995. *One for All: The Logic of Group Conflict*. Princeton, NJ: Princeton University Press.

Hardin, Russell. 1999. "Do We Want Trust In Government?" In *Democracy and Trust*, edited by Mark Warren, 22–41. Cambridge: Cambridge University Press.

Harpham, Geoffrey. 2017. "The Essential English Department." *Chronicle of Higher Education*, October 1.

Harris, H. S. 1997. *Hegel's Ladder*. Indianapolis: Hackett.

Hassner, Pierre. 1972. "Immanuel Kant." In *The History of Political Philosophy*, 2nd ed., edited by Leo Strauss and Joseph Cropsey, 554–593. Chicago. University of Chicago Press.

Hatab, Lawrence. 1995. *A Nietzschean Defense of Democracy*. Chicago: Open Court Press.

Heath, Thomas. 1972. Trans. and Intro. *Thomas Aquinas Summa Theologiae Vol 35, Consequences of Charity*. Cambridge and New York: Blackfriars and McGraw Hill.

Hegel, G. W. F.1956. *The Philosophy of History*. Trans. J. Sibree. New York: Dover.

Hegel, G. W. F. 1969–1979. *Werke, Bande 3, 5, 7*. Frankfurt am Main: Surhkamp Verlag.

Hegel, G. W. F.1977. *Phenomenology of Spirit*. Trans. A. V. Miller. Oxford: Oxford University Press.

Hegel, G. W. F.1988. *Introduction to the Philosophy of History*. Trans. Leo Rauch. Indianapolis: Hackett.

Hegel, G. W. F.1991. *Elements of the Philosophy of Right*. Ed. Allen Wood. Trans. H. S. Nisbet. Cambridge: Cambridge University Press.

Held, David. 1997. "A Cosmopolitan Democracy and the Global Order: A New Agenda." In *Perpetual Peace: Essays on Kant's Cosmopolitan Ideal*, edited by James Bohman and Matthias Lutz-Bachmann, 235–251. Cambridge, MA: The MIT Press.

Held, David. 2004. *Global Covenant: The Social Democratic Alternative to the Washington Consensus*. Cambridge: Polity Press.

Henderson, Jeffrey. 1998. Ed. and trans. *Aristophanes: Archarnians and Knights*. Cambridge, MA: Harvard University Press.

Herzog, Don. 1989. *Happy Slaves: A Critique of Consent Theory*. Chicago: University of Chicago Press.

Higgins, Kathleen. 2014. "Festivals of Recognition." In *Individual and Community in Nietzsche's Philosophy*, edited by Julian Young, 77–92. Cambridge: Cambridge University Press.

Hobbes, Thomas. 1962. *Body, Man and Citizen*. Ed. Richard Peters. New York: Collier.

Hobbes, Thomas. 1975. *Hobbes's Thucydides*. Ed. Richard Schlatter. New Brunswick, NJ: Rutgers University Press.

Hobbes, Thomas. 1994. *Leviathan*. Ed. with an intro. E. M. Curley. Indianapolis: Hackett.

Hoekstra, Kinch. 2007. "Hobbes on the Natural Condition of Mankind." In *A Cambridge Companion to Hobbes's Leviathan*, edited by Patricia Springborg, 109–127. Cambridge: Cambridge University Press.

Honig, Bonnie. 1991. "Declarations of independence: Arendt and Derrida on the Problem of Founding a Republic." *American Political Science Review* 85, no. 1: 97–113.

Honig, Bonnie. 1993. *Political Theory and the Displacement of Politics*. Ithaca, NY: Cornell University Press.

Honig, Bonnie. 2013. *Antigone Interrupted*. Cambridge: Cambridge University Press.

Hood, Francis Campbell. 1964. *The Divine Politics of Thomas Hobbes*. Oxford: Clarendon Press.

Hornblower, Simon. 2008. *A Commentary on Thucydides: Volume Three*. Oxford: Clarendon Press.

Hornqvist, Mikael. 2004. *Machiavelli and Empire*. Cambridge: Cambridge University Press.

Houlgate, Stephen. 2008. "Hegel's Logic." In *Cambridge Companion to Hegel and Nineteenth Century Philosophy*, edited by Frederick Beiser, 111–134. Cambridge: Cambridge University Press.

Hoy, Jocelyn B. 2007. "Hegel, *Antigone* and Feminist Critique: The Spirit of Ancient Greece." In *The Blackwell Guide to Hegel's Phenomenology of Spirit*, edited by Kenneth Westphal, 172–189. Malden, MA: Wiley-Blackwell.

Hulliung, Mark. 1983. *Citizen Machiavelli*. Princeton, NJ: Princeton University Press.

Hüning, Dieter. 2007. "Hobbes on the Right to Punish." In *A Cambridge Companion to Hobbes's Leviathan*, edited by Patricia Springborg, 217–240. Cambridge: Cambridge University Press.

Hyppolite, Jean. 1974. *Genesis and Structure of Hegel's Phenomenology of Spirit*. Trans. Samuel Cherniak and John Heckman. Evanston, IL: Northwestern University Press.

Idris, Murad. 2014. "Alternative Political Theologies: Erasmus on Peace, Speech and Necessity." *Theory and Event* 17, no.4.

Ignatieff, Michael. 2004. *The Lesser Evil: Political Ethics in an Age of Terror*. Edinburgh: Edinburgh University Press.

Jaffa, Harry. 1979. *Thomism and Aristotelianism*. Westport, CT: Greenwood Press.

Jaspers, Karl. 1961. *The Question of German Guilt*. Trans. E. B. Ashton. New York: Capricorn Books.

Johnson, James Turner. 1986. "Threats, Values and Defense: Does the Defense of Values Remain a Moral Possibility?" In *The Nuclear Dilemma and the Just War Tradition*, edited by William V. O'Brien and John Langan S. J., 31–48. Lexington, MA: Lexington Books.

Johnson, Laurie. 1993. *Thucydides, Hobbes and the Interpretation of Realism*. DeKalb: Northern Illinois University Press.

Johnson, Laurie. 2015. "Thucydides the Realist?" In *A Handbook to the Reception of Thucydides*, edited by Christine Ming-Whey Lee and Neville Morley, 391–405. Malden, MA: Wiley-Blackwell.

Johnston, David. 1986. *The Rhetoric of Leviathan: Thomas Hobbes and the Politics of Cultural Transformation*. Chicago: University of Chicago Press.

Jordan, Mark. 1993. "Philosophy and Theology," in *The Cambridge Companion to Aquinas*, edited by Norman Kretzman and Eleonore Stump, 232–251. Cambridge: Cambridge University Press.

Jordan, Mark. 1998. "Ideals of *Scientia Moralis* and the Invention of the *Summa Theologiae*." In *Aquinas's Moral Theory*, edited by Scott MacDonald and Eleonore Stump, 79–98. Ithaca, NY: Cornell University Press.

Kagan, Donald. 2009. *Thucydides: The Reinvention of History*. New York: Penguin Books.

Kahn, Charles. 1979. *The Art and Thought of Heraclitus*. Cambridge: Cambridge University Press.

Kainz, Howard. 2008. *Hegel's Phenomenology of Spirit: Not Missing the Trees for the Forest*. Lanham, MD: Lexington Books.

Kalkavage, Peter. 2007. *The Logic of Desire: An Introduction to Hegel's Phenomenology of Spirit*. Philadelphia: Paul Dry Books.

Kant, Immanuel. 1956. *Critique of Practical Reason*. Trans. Lewis White Beck. Indianapolis: Bobbs-Merrill.

Kant, Immanuel. 1960. *Werke*, Bande 2, 4 and 5. Ed. Wilhelm Weischedel. Wiesbaden: Insel-Verlag.

Kant, Immanuel. 1970. *Political Writings*. Ed. H. S. Reiss. Trans. H. B. Nisbet. Cambridge: Cambridge University Press.

Kant, Immanuel. 1981. *Groundwork for the Metaphysics of Morals*. Trans. James Ellington. Indianapolis: Hackett.

Kant, Immanuel. 1983. *Perpetual Peace and Others Essays*. Trans. Ted Humphrey. Indianapolis: Hackett.

Kant, Immanuel. 2000. *Critique of the Power of Judgment*. Trans. Paul Guyer and Eric Mathews. Cambridge: Cambridge University Press.

Kant, Immanuel. 2003. *Critique of Pure Reason*. Trans. Norman Kemp Smith. New York: Palgrave Macmillan.

Kant, Immanuel. 2006. *Anthropology from a Pragmatic Point of View*. Ed. and trans. Robert B. Louden. Cambridge: Cambridge University Press.

Kaufmann, Walter. 1968. *Nitezsche: Philosopher, Psychologist, Antichrist*. 3rd ed. Princeton NJ: Princeton University Press.

Kavka, Gregory. 1986. *Hobbesian Moral and Political Theory*. Princeton, NJ: Princeton University Press.

Kelly, George Armstrong. 1978. *Hegel's Retreat From Eleusis*. Princeton, NJ: Princeton University Press.

Kennedy, Ellen. 1998. "Hostis *Not* Inimicus: Toward a Theory of the Public in the Work of Carl Schmitt." In *Law As Politics: Carl Schmitt's Critique of Liberalism*, edited by David Dyzenhaus, 92–108. Durham, NC: Duke University Press.

Kidder, Joel. 1983. "Acknowledgment of Equals: Hobbes's Ninth Law of Nature." *Philosophical Quarterly* 33, no. 131: 133–146.

Kochin, Michael. 1999. "War, Class and Justice in Plato's *Republic*." *Review of Metaphysics* 53, no. 2: 403–423.

Kojeve, Alexandre. 1969. *Introduction to the Reading of Hegel*. Ed. Allan Bloom. Trans. James H. Nichols Jr. New York: Basic Books.

Korsgaard, Christine. 1996. *Creating the Kingdom of Ends*. Cambridge: Cambridge University Press.

Lampert, Laurence. 1996. *Leo Strauss and Nietzsche*. Chicago: University of Chicago Press.

Lambert, Laurence, and Christopher Planeaux. 1998. "Who's Who in Plato's 'Timeaus-Critias and Why." *Review of Metaphysics* 52, no. 1: 87–125.

Langan, John S. J. 1977. "Beatitude and Moral Law in St. Thomas." *Journal of Religious Ethics* 5, no. 2: 183–195.

Lattimore, Steven. Trans. 1998. *Thucydides: The Peloponnesian War*. Indianapolis: Hackett.

Lerner, Ralph. 1972. "Moses Maimonides." In *History of Political Philosophy*, 2nd ed., edited by Leo Struass and Joseph Cropseys, 203–222. Chicago: Rand McNally.

Lessay, Franck. 2007. "Hobbes's Covenant Theology and Its Political Implications." In *A Cambridge Companion to Hobbes's Leviathan*, edited by Patricia Springborg, 243–270. Cambridge: Cambridge University Press.

Lefort, Claude. 2000. "Machiavelli and the Verita Effetuale." In *Writing: The Political Test*. Trans. David Ames Curtis. Durham, NC: Duke University Press.

Livy, 1939. *Ab Urbe Condita*. Trans. B. O. Foster. Cambridge, MA: Harvard University Press.

Lucretius, *De Rerum Natura*, 1959. Trans W. H. D. Rouse. Cambridge, MA: Harvard University Press.

Machiavelli, Niccolo. 1960. *Il Principe e Discorsi*. Ed. Sergio Bertelli. Milan: Feltrinelli.

Machiavelli, Niccolo. 1988. *Florentine Histories*. Trans. Laura F. Banfield and Harvey C. Mansfield Jr. 1988. Princeton, NJ: Princeton University Press.

Machiavelli, Niccolo. 1996. *Discourses on Livy*. Trans. Harvey C. Mansfield Jr. and Nathan Tarcov. Chicago: University of Chicago Press.

Machiavelli, Niccolo. 1998. *The Prince*. 2nd ed. Trans. Harvey C. Mansfield C. Jr. Chicago: University of Chicago Press.

Machiavelli, Niccolo. 2003. *Art of* War. Trans. and ed. with commentary by Christopher Lynch. Chicago: University of Chicago Press.

MacIntyre, Alasdair. 1981. *After Virtue*. Notre Dame, IN: University of Notre Dame Press.

MacIntyre, Alasdair. 1988. *Whose Justice? Which Rationality?* Notre Dame, IN: University of Notre Dame Press.

MacIntyre, Alasdair. 2016. *Ethics in the Conflicts of Modernity*. Cambridge: Cambridge University Press.

MacMillan, John. 2006. "Immanuel Kant and the Democratic Peace." In *Classical Theory in International Relations*, edited by Beate Jahn, 52–73. Cambridge: Cambridge University Press.

Mallett, Michael. 1991. "The Theory and Practice of Warfare in Machiavelli's Republic." In *Machiavelli and Republicanism*, edited by Gisela Bock, Quentin Skinner, and Maurizio Viroli, 173–180. Cambridge: Cambridge University Press.

Mansfield, Harvey C. Jr. 1979. *Machiavelli's New Modes and Orders*. Ithaca, NY: Cornell University Press.

Mansfield, Harvey C. Jr. 2013, "Strauss on the *Prince*." *Review of Politics* 75 (Special Issue 4): 650–665.

Mapel, David R. 1998. "Realism and the Ethics of War and Peace." In *The Ethics of War and Peace: Religious and Secular Perspectives*, edited by Terry Nardin, 54–77. Princeton, NJ: Princeton University Press.

Mara, Gerald. 1985. "After Virtue, Autonomy: Jurgen Habermas and Greek Political Theory." *Journal of Politics* 47, no.4: 1036–1061.

Mara, Gerald. 1986. "Justice, War and Politics: The Problem of Supreme Emergency." In *The Nuclear Dilemma and the Just War Tradition*, edited by William V. O'Brien and John Langan S. J., 49–78. Lexington, MA: Lexington Books.

Mara, Gerald. 1989. "Virtue and Pluralism: The Problem of the One and the Many." *Polity* 22, no. 1: 25–48.

Mara, Gerald. 1997. *Socrates' Discursive Democracy*. Albany, NY: State University of New York Press.

Mara, Gerald. 1998. "Interrogating the Identities of Excellence: Liberal Education and Democratic Culture in Aristotle's *Nicomachean Ethics*." *Polity* 31, no. 2: 301–329.

Mara, Gerald. 2008. *The Civic Conversations of Thucydides and Plato*. Albany: State University of New York Press.

Mara, Gerald. 2009. "Thucydides and Political Thought." In *The Cambridge Companion to Ancient Greek Political Thought*, edited by Stephen Salkever, 96–125. Cambridge: Cambridge University Press, 96–125.

Mara, Gerald. 2013. "Possessions Forever: Thucydides and Kant on Peace, War and Politics." *Polity* 45, no. 3: 318–346.

Mara, Gerald. 2015. "Thucydides and the Problem of Citizenship." In *A Handbook to the Reception of Thucydides*, edited by Christine Ming-Whey Lee and Neville Morley, 313–331. Malden, MA: Wiley-Blackwell.

Mara, Gerald, and Suzanne Dovi. 1995. "Mill, Nietzsche and the Identity of Postmodern Liberalism." *Journal of Politics* 57, no. 1: 1–23.

Marcuse, Herbert. 1960. *Reason and Revolution: Hegel and the Rise of Social Theory*. Boston: Beacon Press.

Markell, Patchen. 2003. *Bound By Recognition*. Princeton, NJ: Princeton University Press.

Martel, James. 2007. *Subverting Leviathan*. New York: Columbia University Press.

Martinich, A. P. 2007. "The Bible and Protestantism in Leviathan." In *A Cambridge Companion to Hobbes's Leviathan*, edited by Patricia Springborg, 375–391. Cambridge: Cambridge University Press.

Masters, Roger. 1996. *Machiavelli, Leonardo and The Science of Power*. Notre Dame, IN: Notre Dame University Press.

McCarthy, Thomas. 1997. "On the Idea of a Reasonable Law of Peoples." In *Perpetual Peace: Essays on Kant's Cosmopolitan Ideal*, edited by James Bohman and Matthias Lutz-Bachmann, 201–217. Cambridge, MA: The MIT Press.

McCarthy, Thomas. 2009. *Race, Empire and the Idea of Human Development*. Cambridge: Cambridge University Press.

McCormick, John. 1997. *Carl Schmitt's Critique of Liberalism*. Cambridge: Cambridge University Press.

McCormick, John. 2011. *Machiavellian Democracy*. Princeton, NJ: Princeton University Press.

McClure, Christopher. 2011. "Hell and Anxiety in Hobbes's *Leviathan*." *Review of Politics* 73, no. 1: 1–27.

McDowell, John. 2006. "The Apperceptive I and the Empirical Self: Toward a Heterodox Reading of 'Lordship and Bondage' in Hegel's Phenomenology of Spirit." In *Hegel: New Directions*, edited by Katerina Deligiorgi, 33–48. Chesham, UK: Acumen.

McInerney, Ralph. 1993. "Ethics." In *The Cambridge Companion to Aquinas*, edited by Norman Kretzmann and Eleonore Stump, 196–216. Cambridge: Cambridge University Press.

Meier, Heinrich. 1995. *Carl Schmitt and Leo Strauss: The Hidden Dialogue*. Trans. J. Harvey Lomax. Chicago, University of Chicago Press.

Meier, Heinrich. 1998. *The Lesson of Carl Schmitt*. Trans. Marcus Brainard. Chicago: University of Chicago Press.

Mitchell, Joshua. 1993. *Not by Reason Alone: Religion, History and Identity in Early Modern Political Thought*. Chicago: University of Chicago Press.

Morrison, James. 2006. *Reading Thucydides*. Athens: Ohio State University Press.

Monoson, Sara. 2011. "Dionysius I and Sicilian Theatrical Traditions in Plato's *Republic*." In *Theatre Outside Athens*, edited by K. Bosher, 156–172. Cambridge: Cambridge University Press.

Mouffe, Chantal. 1998. "Carl Schmitt and the Paradox of Liberal Democracy." In *Law As Politics: Carl Schmitt's Critique of Liberalism*, edited by David Dyzenhaus, 159–175. Durham, NC: Duke University Press.

Mouffe, Chantal. 1999. Ed. *The Challenge of Carl Schmitt*. London: Verso.

Mouffe, Chantal. 2000. *The Democratic Paradox*. London: Verso.

Müller, Jan-Werner. 2003. *A Dangerous Mind: Carl Schmitt in Post War European Thought*. New Haven, CT: Yale University Press.

Mynott, Jeremy. Trans. 2013. *The War of the Peloponnesians and the Athenians*. Cambridge: Cambridge University Press.

Nails, Debra. 2002. *The People of Plato*. Indianapolis: Hackett.

Nehamas, Alexander. 1985. *Nietzsche, Life as Literature*. Cambridge, MA: Harvard University Press.

Neuhouser, Frederick. 2007. "Desire, Recognition and the Relation Between Bondsman and Lord." In *The Blackwell Guide to Hegel's Phenomenology of Spirit*, edited by Kenneth Westphal, 37–53. Malden, MA: Wiley-Blackwell.

Neuhouser, Frederick. 2008. "Hegel's Social Philosophy." In *Cambridge Companion to Hegel and Nineteenth Century Philosophy*, edited by Frederick Beiser, 204–229. Cambridge: Cambridge University Press.

Nichols, James H. Jr. 1976. *Epicurean Political Philosophy: The De Rerum Natura of Lucretius*. Ithaca, NY: Cornell University Press.

Nichols, Mary. 1987. *Socrates and the Political Community*. Albany: State University of New York Press.

Nichols, Mary. 2015. *Thucydides and the Pursuit of Freedom*. Ithaca, NY: Cornell University Press.

Nietzsche, Friedrich. 1954. "Twilight of the Idols." In *The Portable Nietzsche*, translated by Walter Kaufmann, 556–563. New York: Viking Press.

Nietzsche, Friedrich. 1966. *Beyond Good and Evil*. Trans Walter Kaufmann. New York: Vintage.

Nietzsche, Friedrich. 1967a. *The Birth of Tragedy* and *The Case of Wagner*. Trans. Walter Kaufmann. New York: Vintage.

Nietzsche, Friedrich. 1967b. *On the Genealogy of Morals* and *Ecce Homo*. Trans. Walter Kaufmann and R. J. Hollingdale. New York: Vintage.

Nietzsche, Friedrich. 1968. *Jenseits von Gute und Böse: Zur Genealogie der Moral*. Berlin: Walter de Gruyter.

Nietzsche, Friedrich. 1973. *Nachgelassene Schriften*. Berlin: Walter de Gruyter.

Nietzsche, Friedrich. 1974. *The Gay Science*. Trans. Walter Kaufmann. New York: Vintage.

Nietzsche, Friedrich. 1980. *On the Advantage and Disadvantage of History for Life*. Trans. Peter Preuss. Indianapolis: Hackett.

Nietzsche, Friedrich. 1998. *On the Genealogy of Morality*. Trans. Maudemarie Clark and Alan J. Swensen. Indianapolis: Hackett.

Nietzsche, Friedrich. 2007. *The Greek State; Homer's Contest* in *On the Genealogy of Morality*. Ed. Keith Ansell-Peterson. Trans. Caroline Diethe. Cambridge: Cambridge University Press.

Nussbaum, Martha. 1997. "Kant and Cosmopolitanism." In *Perpetual Peace: Essays on Kant's Cosmopolitan Ideal*, edited by James Bohman and Matthias Lutz-Bachmann, 25–57. Cambridge, MA: The MIT Press.

Nussbaum, Martha. 2001. *The Fragility of Goodness*. 2nd ed. Cambridge: Cambridge University Press.

Oakeshott, Michael. 1989. *The Voice of Liberal Learning: Michael Oakeshott on Education*. Ed. Timothy Fuller. New Haven, CT: Yale University Press.

Ober, Josiah. 1998. *Political Dissent in Democratic Athens*. Princeton, NJ: Princeton University Press.

O'Brien, William V. 1981. *The Conduct of Just and Limited War*. New York: Praeger.

O'Driscoll. Ciaran. 2015. "Thucydides and The Just War Tradition." In *A Handbook to the Reception of Thucydides*, edited by Christine Ming-Whey Lee and Neville Morley, 373–390. Malden, MA: Wiley-Blackwell.

O'Neill, Onora. 2015. *Constructing Authorities: Reason: Politics and Interpretation in Kant's Philosophy*. Cambridge: Cambridge University Press.

Orwin, Clifford. 1978. "Machiavelli's Unchristian Charity." *American Political Science Review* 72, no. 4: 1217–1228.

Orwin, Clifford.1994. *The Humanity of Thucydides*. Princeton, NJ: Princeton University Press.

Owens, Joseph. 1993. "Aristotle and Aquinas." In *The Cambridge Companion to Aquinas*, edited by Norman Kretzmann and Eleonore Stump, 38–59. Cambridge: Cambridge University Press.

Parel, Anthony. 1992. *The Machiavellian Cosmos*. New Haven, CT: Yale University Press.

Parel, Anthony. 2013. "Farewell to Fortune." *Review of Politics* 75, no. 4: 587–604.

Pinkard, Terry. 1992. "The Successor to Metaphysics: Absolute Idea and Absolute Spirit." *The Monist* 74, no. 3: 295–328.

Pinkard, Terry. 1994. *Hegel's Phenomenology: The Sociality of Reason*. Cambridge: Cambridge University Press.

Pinkard, Terry. 2008. "Hegel, A Life." In *Cambridge Companion to Hegel and Nineteenth Century Philosophy*, edited by Frederick Beiser, 15–51. Cambridge: Cambridge University Press.

Pippin, Robert. 1981. "Hegel's Political Argument and the Problem of *Verwirklichung*." *Political Theory* 9, no. 4: 509–532.

Pippin, Robert. 1989. *Hegel's Idealism: The Satisfactions of Self Consciousness*. Cambridge: Cambridge University Press.

Pippin, Robert. 2008. *Hegel's Practical Philosophy*. Cambridge: Cambridge University Press.

Pippin, Robert. 2010. *Nietzsche, Psychology and First Philosophy*. Chicago: University of Chicago Press.

Pippin, Robert. 2011. *Hegel on Self Consciousness: Death and Desire in the Phenomenology of Spirit*. Princeton, NJ: Princeton University Press.

Pitkin, Hanna. 1999. *Fortune is a Woman, With a New Afterword*. Chicago: University of Chicago Press.

Pocock, John. 2003. *The Machiavellian Moment*. 2nd ed. Princeton, NJ: Princeton University Press.

Price, Jonathan. 2001. *Thucydides and Internal War*. Cambridge: Cambridge University Press.

Pritchard, David. 2010. "The Symbiosis Between Democracy and War." In *War, Democracy and Culture in Classical Athens*, edited by David Pritchard, 1–62. Cambridge: Cambridge University Press.

Rahe, Paul. 2007. "In the Shadow of Lucretius: The Epicurean Foundations of Machiavelli's Political Thought." *History of Political Thought* 28, no. 1: 30–55.

Rawls, John. 1971. *A Theory of Justice*. Cambridge, MA: Harvard University Press.

Rawls, John. 1999. *The Law of Peoples*. Cambridge, MA: Harvard University Press.

Rawls, John. 2005. *Political Liberalism*, 2nd ed. New York: Columbia University Press.

Redding, Paul. 2008. "The Independence and Dependence of Self Consciousness: The Dialectic of Lord and Bondsman in Hegel's *Phenomenology of Spirit*." In *Cambridge Companion to Hegel and Nineteenth Century Philosophy*, edited by Frederick Beiser, 94–110. Cambridge: Cambridge University Press.

Reeve, C. D. C. 1988. *Philosopher Kings*. Princeton, NJ: Princeton University Press.

Richardson, Henry. 2002. *Democratic Autonomy*, Oxford: Oxford University Press.

Richardson, John. 2014. ""Nietzsche, Language, Community." In *Individual and Community in Nietzsche's Philosophy*, edited by Julian Young, 214–244. Cambridge: Cambridge University Press.

Riley, Patrick. 1983. *Kant's Political Philosophy*. Lanham, MD: Rowman & Littlefield.

Roochnik, David. 2009. "The Political Drama of Plato's *Republic*." In *The Cambridge Companion to Ancient Greek Political Thought*, edited by Stephen Salkever, 156–177. Cambridge: Cambridge University Press.

Romilly, Jacqueline de. 1963. *Thucydides and Athenian Imperialism*. Trans. Philip Thoddy. Oxford: Blackwell.

Romilly, Jacqueline de. 2012. *The Mind of Thucydides*. Trans. Elizabeth Trapnell Rawlings. Ed. with Intro. Hunter R. Rawlings III and Jeffrey S. Rustin. Ithaca, NY: Cornell University Press.

Rorty, Richard. 1979. *Philosophy and the Mirror of Nature*. Princeton, NJ: Princeton University Press.

Rorty, Richard. 1989. *Contingency, Irony and Solidarity*. Cambridge: Cambridge University Press.

Rosen, Stanley. 1974. *G. W. F. Hegel: An Introduction to the Science of Wisdom*. New Haven, CT: Yale University Press.

Rousseau, Jean-Jacques. 1978. *On the Social Contract with Geneva Manuscript and Political Economy*. Ed. Roger D. Masters. Trans. Judith R. Masters. New York: St Martin's Press.

Said, Edward. 1979. *Orientalism*. New York. Vintage.

Salkever, Stephen. 1990. *Finding the Mean: Theory and Practice in Aristotle's Political Philosophy*. Princeton, NJ: Princeton University Press.

Salkever, Stephen. 2002. "The Deliberative Model of Democracy and Aristotle's Ethics of Natural Questions." In *Aristotle and Modern Politics*, edited by Aristide Tessitore, 342–374. Notre Dame, IN: University of Notre Dame Press.

Salkever, Stephen. 2009. "Reading Aristotle's *Nicomachean Ethics* and *Politics* as a Single Course of Lectures." In *The Cambridge Companion to Ancient Greek Political Thought*, edited by Stephen Salkever, 209–242. Cambridge: Cambridge University Press.

Sallis, John. 2005. *The Gathering of Reason*. 2nd ed. Albany: State University of New York Press.

Satkunanandan, Shalini. 2015. *Extraordinary Responsibility: Politics Beyond the Moral Calculus*. Cambridge: Cambridge University Press.

Saxonhouse, Arlene. 1983. "An Unspoken Theme in Plato's Gorgias: War." *Interpretation* 11, no. 2: 139–169.

Saxonhouse, Arlene. 1985. *Women in the History of Political Thought: Ancient Greece to Machiavelli*. New York: Praeger.

Saxonhouse, Arlene. 1996. *Athenian Democracy: Modern Mythmakers and Ancient Theorists*. Notre Dame, IN: University of Notre Dame Press.

Saxonhouse, Arlene. 2006. *Free Speech and Democracy in Ancient Athens*. Cambridge: Cambridge University Press.

Schlosser, Joel Alden. 2014. *What Would Socrates Do?*. Cambridge: Cambridge University Press.

Schmitt, Carl. 1932. *Der Begriff des Politischen*. München: Duncker & Humblot.

Schmitt, Carl. 1996. *The Leviathan in the State Theory of Thomas Hobbes*. Trans. George Schwab and Erna Hilfstein. Westport, CT: Greenwood Press.

Schmitt, Carl. 2003. *The Nomos of the Earth in the International Law of the Jus Publicum Europaeum*. Trans G. L. Ulmen. New York: Telos Press.

Schmitt, Carl. 2005. *Political Theology*. Trans. George Schwab Foreword Tracy B. Strong. Chicago: University of Chicago Press.

Schmitt, Carl. 2007a. *The Concept of the Political*. Trans. George Schwab. Foreword Tracy B. Strong. Chicago: University of Chicago Press.

Schmitt, Carl. 2007b. *Theory of the Partisan*. Trans. G. L. Ulmen, New York: Telos Press.

Schwartz, Joel. 1985. "Hobbes and the Two Kingdoms of God." *Polity* 18, no. 1: 7–24.

Seagrave, S. Adam. 2009. "Cicero, Aquinas and Contemporary Issues in Natural Law Theory." *Review of Metaphysics* 62, no. 3: 491–523.

Seitzer, Jeffrey, and Christopher Thornhill. 2008. "An Introduction to Carl Schmitt's *Constitutional Theory*: Issues and Context." In *Constitutional Theory*, translated by Jeffrey Seitzer and edited by Carl Schmitt, 1–50. Durham, NC: Duke University Press.

Shapiro, Ian. 2003. *The State of Democratic Theory*. Princeton, NJ: Princeton University Press.

Shaw, Tamsin, 2007. *Nietzsche's Political Skepticism*. Princeton, NJ: Princeton University Press.

Shell, Susan Meld. 1980. *The Rights of Reason: A Study of Kant's Philosophy and Politics*. Toronto: University of Toronto Press.

Shell, Susan Meld. 2009. *Kant and the Limits of Autonomy*. Cambridge, MA: Harvard University Press.

Sherman, Nancy. 1997. *Making a Necessity of Virtue*. Cambridge: Cambridge University Press.

Shklar, Judith. 1976. *Freedom and Independence: A Study of the Political Ideas of Hegel's Phenomenology of Mind*. Cambridge: Cambridge University Press.

Sigmund, Paul. 1993. "Law and Politics." In *The Cambridge Companion to Aquinas*, edited by Norman Kretzmann and Eleonore Stump, 217–231. Cambridge: Cambridge University Press.

Skinner, Quentin. 1978. *The Foundations of Modern Political Thought: Vol. 1*. New York: Cambridge University Press.

Skinner, Quentin. 1991. "Machiavelli's *Discorsi* and the Pre-Humanist Origins of Republican Ideas." In *Machiavelli and Republicanism*, edited by Gisela Bock, Quentin Skinner, and Maurizio Viroli, 121–142. Cambridge: Cambridge University Press.

Skinner, Quentin. 1996. *Reason and Rhetoric in the Philosophy of Hobbes.* Cambridge: Cambridge University Press.

Stocker, Michael. 1986. "Dirty Hands in Conflicts of Values and of desires in Aristotle's Ethics." *Pacific Philosophical Quarterly* 67, no. 1: 36–61.

Slomp, Gabriella. 2000. *Thomas Hobbes and the Political Philosophy of Glory.* New York: St. Martin's.

Slomp, Gabriella. 2007. "Hobbes on Glory and Civil Strife." In *A Cambridge Companion to Hobbes's Leviathan*, edited by Patricia Springborg, 181–198. Cambridge: Cambridge University Press.

Slomp, Gabriella. 2009. *Carl Schmitt and the Politics of Hostility, Violence and Terror.* New York: Palgrave Macmillan.

Sluga, Hans. 2014. "The Time is Coming When One Will Have to Relearn About Politics." In *Individual and Community in Nietzsche's Philosophy*, edited by Julian Young, 31–50. Cambridge: Cambridge University Press.

Smith, Charles Forster. Trans. 1962–1988. *Thucydides.* 4 vols. Cambridge, MA: Harvard University Press.

Smith, Margaret Michelle Barnes. 2006. "The Philosophy of Liberty: Locke's Machiavellian Teaching." In *Machiavelli's Liberal Republican Legacy*, edited by Paul Rahe, 36–57. Cambridge: Cambridge University Press.

Smith, Steven B. 1989. *Hegel's Critique of Liberalism: Rights in Context.* Chicago: University of Chicago Press.

Smith, Steven B. 2016. *Modernity and its Discontents.* New Haven, CT: Yale University Press.

Sorell, Tom. 2007. "Hobbes's Moral Philosophy." In *A Cambridge Companion to Hobbes's Leviathan*, edited by Patricia Springborg, 128–154. Cambridge: Cambridge University Press.

Spinoza, Benedict De. 1951. *Theologico-Political Treatise: Political Treatise.* Trans. R. H. M. Elwes. New York: Dover.

Spinoza, Benedict De. 1996. *Ethics.* Ed and trans. Edwin M. Curley. Intro. Stuart Hampshire. New York: Penguin.

Soll, Ivan. 2014. "The Self Versus Society: Nietzsche's Advocacy of Egoism." In *Individual and Community in Nietzsche's Philosophy*, edited by Julian Young, 141–173. Cambridge: Cambridge University Press.

Spragens, Thomas R. Jr. 1973. *The Politics of Motion: The World of Thomas Hobbes.* Lexington: The University Press of Kentucky.

Stern, Robert. 2008. "Hegel's Idealism." In *Cambridge Companion to Hegel and Nineteenth Century Philosophy*, edited by Frederick Beiser, 135–173. Cambridge: Cambridge University Press.

Strauss, Leo. 1953. *Natural Right and History*, Chicago: University of Chicago Press.

Strauss, Leo. 1963. *The Political Philosophy of Hobbes.* Trans E. M. Sinclair. Chicago: University of Chicago Press.

Strauss, Leo. 1964. *The City and Man.* Chicago: Rand McNally.

Strauss, Leo. 1969. *Thoughts on Machiavelli.* Seattle: University of Washington Press.

Strauss, Leo. 1989. *The Rebirth of Classical Political Rationalism: An Introduction to the Thought of Leo Strauss*. Selected and introduced by Thomas L. Pangle. Chicago: University of Chicago Press.

Strauss, Leo. 1996. "Note on the Plan of Nietzsche's Beyond Good and Evil." Reprinted in Laurence Lampert, *Leo Strauss and Nietzsche*, 188–201. Chicago: University of Chicago Press.

Strauss, Leo. 1997. *Spinoza's Critique of Religion*. Trans. Elsa Sinclair. Chicago: University of Chicago Press.

Strauss, Leo. 2007. "Notes on 'The Concept of the Political.'" In *The Concept of the Political*, edited by Carl Schmitt, translated by George Schwab, Foreword by Tracy B. Strong, 99–122. Chicago: University of Chicago Press.

Strong, Tracy B. 1988. "Nietzsche's Political Aesthetics." In *Nietzsche's New Seas*, edited by Michael Allen Gillespie and Tracy B. Strong, 153–174. Chicago: University of Chicago Press.

Strong, Tracy B. 2000. *Friedrich Nietzsche and the Politics of Transfiguration*. Expanded ed. Urbana: University of Illinois Press.

Strong, Tracy B. 2005. *Political Theology*. Trans. George Schwab. Foreword Carl Schmitt. Chicago: University of Chicago Press.

Strong, Tracy B. 2007. *The Concept of the Political*. Expanded ed. Trans. George Schwab. Foreword Carl Schmitt. Chicago: University of Chicago Press.

Sullivan, Vickie. 1996. *Machiavelli's Three Romes*. De Kalb: Northern Illinois University Press.

Sullivan, Vickie. 2004. *Machiavelli, Hobbes and the Formation of a Liberal Republicanism in England*. Cambridge: Cambridge University Press.

Sullivan, Vickie. 2013. "Alexander the Great as 'Lord of Asia' and Rome as His Successor in Machiavelli's 'Prince'," *Review of Politics* 75, 4: 515–537.

Swanton, Christine. 2014. "Nietzsche and the Collective Individual." in *Individual and Community in Nietzsche's Philosophy*, edited by Julian Young, 174–194. Cambridge: Cambridge University Press.

Tarcov, Nathan. 2013. "Belief and Opinion in Machiavelli's *Prince*." *Review of Politics* 75 (Special Issue 4): 573–586.

Taylor, Charles. 1979. *Hegel and Modern Society*. Cambridge: Cambridge University Press.

Taylor, Robert. 2010. "Kant's Political Religion: The Transparency of Political Peace and the Highest Good." *Review of Politics* 72, no. 1: 1–24.

Tessitore, Aristide. 1996. *Reading Aristotle's Ethics*. Albany: State University of New York Press.

Thiele, Leslie Paul. 1990. *Friedrich Nietzsche and the Politics of the Soul*. Princeton, NJ: Princeton University Press.

Thomas, Rosalind. 2017. "Thucydides and His Intellectual Milieu." In *The Oxford Handbook of Thucydides*, edited by Ryan Balot, Sara Forsdyke, and Edith Foster, 567–586. New York: Oxford University Press.

Tuck, Richard. 1999. *The Rights of War and Peace: Political Thought and the International Order from Grotius to Kant* Oxford: Oxford University Press.

Vatter, Miguel. 2013. "Machiavelli and the Republican Conception of Providence." *Review of Politics* 75 (Special Issue 4): 605–623.

Villa, Dana. 1996. *Arendt and Heidegger: The Fate of the Political*. Princeton, NJ: Princeton University Press.

Viroli, Maurizio. 1991. "Machiavelli and the Republican Idea of Politics." In *Machiavelli and Republicanism*, edited by Gisela Bock, Quentin Skinner, and Maurizio Viroli, 143–172. Cambridge: Cambridge University Press.

Viroli, Maurizio. 2010. *Machiavelli's God*. Princeton, NJ: Princeton University Press.

Wallach, John. 2005. "Human Rights as an Ethics of Power." In *Human Rights in the "War on Terror,"* edited by Richard A. Wilson, 108–136. Cambridge: Cambridge University Press.

Walzer, Michael. 1977. *Just and Unjust Wars*. New York: Basic Books.

Warren, Mark. 1988. *Nietzsche and Political Thought*. Cambridge, MA: The MIT Press.

Warren, Mark. 2001. *Democracy and Association*. Princeton, NJ: Princeton University Press.

Warrender, Howard. 1957. *The Political Philosophy of Hobbes: His Theory of Obligation*. Oxford: Clarendon Press.

Watkins, J. W. N. 1973. *Hobbes's System of Ideas*. 2nd ed. London: Hutchinson.

Weber, Max. 1949. "The Meaning of Ethical Neutrality on Sociology and Economics." In *The Methodology of the Social Sciences*, edited by Edward A. Shils and translated by Henry A. Finch, 1–47. New York, The Free Press, 1949.

Weber, Max. 2001. *The Protestant Ethic and the Spirit of Capitalism*. Trans. Talcott Parsons. London: Routledge.

Weiner, Gregory S. 2016. "Machiavelli's Inflationary Economy of Violence." *Interpretation* 42, no. 2: 217–233.

Weiss, Roslyn. 2006. *The Socratic Paradox and Its Enemies*. Chicago: University of Chicago Press.

Weiss, Roslyn. 2012. *Philosophers in Plato's Republic*. Ithaca, NY: Cornell University Press.

Welliver, Warman. 1977. *Character, Plot and Thought in Plato's Timeaus-Critias*. Leiden: Brill.

White, James Boyd.1984. *When Words Lose Their Meaning*. Chicago: University of Chicago Press.

Williams, Bernard. 1993. *Shame and Necessity*, Berkeley: University of California Press.

Williams, Bernard. 2002. *Truth and Truthfulness: An Essay in Genealogy*. Princeton, NJ: Princeton University Press.

Williams, Bernard. 2005. *In the Beginning Was The Deed: Realism and Moralism in Political Argument*. Princeton, NJ: Princeton University Press.

Williams, Howard. 2003. *Kant's Critique of Hobbes*. Cardiff: University of Wales Press.

Williams, Michael. 2006. "The Hobbesian Theory of International Relations: Three Traditions." In *Classical Theory in International Relations*, edited by Beate Jahn, 253–276. Cambridge: Cambridge University Press.

Williams, Robert E. 1997. *Hegel's Ethics of Recognition*. Berkeley: University of California Press.

Wolin, Richard. 1992. "Carl Schmitt, The Conservative Revolutionary: Habitus and the Aesthetics of Horror." *Political Theory* 20, no. 3: 424–447.

Wolin, Sheldon. 1960. *Politics and Vision*. Boston: Little Brown.

Wood, Allen W. Ed. 1991. *Hegel Elements of the Philosophy of Right*. Trans. H. S. Nisbet. Cambridge: Cambridge University Press.

Yack, Bernard.1986. *The Longing for Total Revolution*. Princeton, NJ: Princeton University Press.

Young, Julian. 2014. "Nietzsche: The Long View." In *Individual and Community in Nietzsche's Philosophy*, edited by Julian Young, 7–10. Cambridge: Cambridge University Press.

Zammito, John. 1992. *The Genesis of Kant's Critique of Judgment*. Chicago: University of Chicago Press.

Zeitlin, Froma I. 2009. *Under the Sign of the Shield: Semiotics and Aeschylus' Seven Against Thebes*. Lanham, MD: Lexington Books.

Zuckert, Catherine. 2009. *Plato's Philosophers*. Chicago: University of Chicago Press.

Zuckert, Catherine. 2017. *Machiavelli's Politics*. Chicago: University of Chicago Press.

Zumbrunnen, John. 2008. *The Silence of Democracy: Athenian Politics in Thucydides' History*. University Park: Pennsylvania State University Press.

Zumbrunnen, John. 2012. Aristophanic Comedy and the Challenge of Democratic Citizenship. Rochester, NY: University of Rochester Press.

INDEX

Aaron, 212n80

Achilles, 137–38, 225–26n14, 232n113

Aertsen, Jan, 209n39

Aeschylus, 139–40, 143

Ahrensdorf, Peter, 89–90, 216n5, 220n71, 221n82, 221n83, 221n88, 227n28, 228n63

Ajax, 196

al-Assad, Bashar, 51

al-Qaeda, 1–2

Alcibiades, 139–40, 167, 202–4

Alexander the Great, 55–56, 137–38, 232n113

Alter, Robert, 206n16, 212n80, 213n109, 220n68

Anscombe, G.E.M., 50–51, 209n28, 209n31

Antigone/*Antigone*, 130–31, 138–39, 143, 144, 150, 151, 227n27

Apel, Karl-Otto, 117, 223n122

Appel, Frederick, 229n73, 230n84, 231n94, 232n124

Aquinas, Thomas, 5, 177–78, 199–200, 201

   and Aristotle, 39–40, 41, 43–44, 48–49, 53–54, 59, 208n8, 208n10, 209n39, 209n40, 209n41

   and Augustine, 45–46, 48, 207n1, 208n19, 214n124

   charity, 41, 44, 47–48, 169–70, 177–78

   civitas, 41, 44, 55–56, 60

   common good, 41, 42–44, 48, 49, 55–56

   conscience, 40, 43–44

dissent, 44–45, 208n17

divine law, 37–38, 40–41, 177–78

eternal law, 40, 43–44

faith, 39, 40

free will, 40

Hebrew law, 39–40

and Hegel, 39

human law, 37–38, 40, 41, 44, 177–78

and international constitutionalism, 38, 39, 54–55, 56–58, 59, 83–84, 209n47

just wars, 37–38, 41, 42–43, 44–46, 47–48, 49–50, 51–53, 54–55, 56–57

   competent authority, 42–45, 48, 51–52, 57–58, 199–200

   just cause, 42–43, 45–48, 49–50, 51, 57–58, 199–200

   right intention, 42–43, 45, 48–50, 51, 52–53, 57–58, 199–200

just war theory, development of, 7, 39, 45, 51–53, 55, 207n1, 208n5, 208n24, 209n34

   discrimination, 49–50

   double effect, 49–52

   proportion, 49, 51–52

and Kant, 39, 111, 122

and liberalism, 44, 208n15

and Machiavelli, 7, 37–38, 79–80, 81, 83–84

metaphysics, 207n3

multivocality, 39–40, 208n5

natural law/natural order, 7, 40, 43–44, 55, 111

Aquinas, Thomas (*cont.*)
  and philosophy, 7, 43, 53–55,
    59, 83–84
  and political order, 7, 37–38, 41,
    42–43, 45, 55–56
  rationality, 40, 48–49
  revealed religion/revelation, 39, 40,
    41–42, 43, 53, 81–82, 83–84
  salvation, 41–42, 44, 47–48
  and Schmitt, 42–43, 51
  teleology, 37–38, 41–42, 43–44, 208n9
  and Thucydides, 47
  and tragic politics, 42, 51–52, 178,
    208n12, 209n35
  on tyranny, 43–44, 45, 55–56
  virtues in, 7, 41–42, 44, 169–70
  works (full title references only)
    De Regno, 41, 55–56
    Summa Theologiae, 39
Archidamus, 141, 192–93
Arendt, Hannah, 3–4, 23–24, 37–38, 82,
    133, 216n142, 221n81, 222n99,
    223n128
Arginusae, 234n4
Aristophanes, 142–43
Aristotle, 22–23, 30–31, 39–40, 41,
    43–44, 48–49, 53–54, 59, 71–72,
    77–78, 110–11, 145, 169–70,
    171–72, 211–12n78, 235n33
Assyria, 74–75
Athens/Athenians, 29, 31–32, 34, 47,
    105–7, 136–38, 142–44, 150–51,
    162–63, 180–82, 184, 185–86,
    187–88, 190–94, 196–97, 199,
    202–3, 209n26, 221n85, 226n26,
    234n5, 234n7, 235n33
Averroes, 211–12n78
Avineri, Shlomo, 225n2, 226n25, 227n41,
    227n43, 228n49, 228n52, 228n55,
    228n56

Balot, Ryan, 192–93, 234n18, 235n32
Barba-Kay, Anton, 133, 225n11
Benardete, Seth, 181, 229n66
Bendersky, Joseph, 205n1
Benhabib, Seyla, 2–4, 12, 108, 222n95
Bercovitch, Sacvan, 179–80
Berkowitz, Peter, 229n73, 230n79,
    230n81, 231n94, 231n96,
    231n100, 232n116, 232n124,
    233n135, 233n136

Bermeo, Nancy, 220n76
Berns, Laurence, 133–34, 225–26n14
Bertelli, Sergio, 212n80
Bloom, Allen, 181, 185, 208n20
Bohman, James, 108, 221n92, 222n93,
    222n95, 222n96
Boyle, Joseph, 52–53, 208n17, 209n34
Brann, Eva, 229n76
Bredekamp, Horst, 219n51
Brown, Alison, 72–73, 211n70, 213n102,
    213n103, 214n112
Brutus, 218n46
Burkhardt, Todd, 49–50, 51–52
Butler, Judith, 1–3, 12, 13, 33, 36–202,
    204, 207n33, 209n32, 226n19,
    233n133
Bykova, Marina, 225n4, 227n32

Caesar, 167, 218n46
China, 4
Chong, Dennis, 209n25, 224n142
Christ, 64–65, 100, 101, 231n97, 231n100
Church, Jeffrey, 129, 152–53, 159,
    226n25, 227n42, 229n74,
    229–30n77, 230n79, 230n83,
    230n85, 230n88, 231n95, 231n98,
    232n109, 232n118, 232–33n125,
    233n126, 233n127, 233n136
Cicero, 39–40, 208n8, 214n114, 235n33
Cincinnatus, 78–79, 214n121
Clark, Maudemarie, 169, 229n74,
    229–30n77, 230n88, 231n92,
    231n94, 231n104, 231n105,
    232n111, 233n127, 233n135,
    233n138
Coby, Patrick, 61–62, 209–10n51,
    210n52, 210n57, 210n58, 210n59,
    210n60, 211n66, 214n111,
    214n120, 214n121, 215n128,
    215n134, 215n139
Connolly, William, 2–3, 12, 13, 174–75,
    229n74, 233n130
Connor, W. Robert, 187–88
Corcyra/Corcyrean, 34, 183–84, 186–87,
    198–99, 207n36
Cortella, Lucio, 132, 146–47, 149–50,
    152–53, 225n2, 225n4, 225n7,
    226n15, 226n25, 227n39, 227n41,
    227n42, 228n49, 228n50, 228n55,
    228n56, 228n57, 228n62, 229n67,
    229n68

Craig, Leon, 235n27
Crane, Gregory, 178–79
Crawley, Richard, 193–94, 234n19
Creon, 138–39, 150, 227n27
Curley, E. M. 216n1, 219n53, 219n58,
219n61, 220n64, 220n65, 220n71,
234n12
Czobor-Lupp, Mihaela, 232n108

Dannhauser, Werner, 231n102
Daubler, Theodore, 206n24
David, 66, 212n81
De Grazia, Sebastian, 64, 65–66,
209n50, 210n54, 210n56,
210n62, 211n73, 211n74,
212n90, 212n91, 212n94,
213n98, 213n101, 214n113,
214n116, 214n, 215n129
democratic political theory, 1, 8, 10, 12,
13–14, 57–58, 152–53, 174,
206–7n27, 224n131
agonistic, 12, 13, 30–31, 82, 129–30,
144–45, 174, 175, 233n132
deliberative, 7–8, 12–14, 56–57, 59,
83–84, 85, 108, 133, 152–53,
229n67
democratization, 168, 229n67
Derrida, Jacques, 5, 177–78
on androcentrism, 24, 29, 30–31, 35,
178, 207n37
on Aristotle, 30–31
and deconstruction, 25–26, 29–31,
32–34, 178
and deliberative democracy, 30–31, 37
democracy that might be, 24, 29–30,
32, 33, 35, 177–78, 207n33
depoliticization, 34
enmity, persistence of, 6–7, 11,
33–34, 178
fraternity/fraternal politics, 28–29,
207n34
on history of political philosophy, 6–7,
11, 24, 31, 35
and Machiavelli, 80–81
and Nietzsche, 30–31
on the other, 30–31, 33
and Plato, 24–25, 28–29, 35, 186–87
Schmitt, critique of, 24, 25, 28, 30–31,
32, 35
Socrates, 25
the state, 24, 27–28

texts, significance of, 31–33
and Thucydides, 31–32, 34, 183–84,
207n35, 207n36
works (full title references only)
The Politics of Friendship, 24, 35
Rogues, 30, 33
Descartes, 164–65, 169–70
Detwiler, Bruce, 229n73, 230n84,
232n124
dialogic political theory, 3–4, 10, 180,
199, 202–4
Douglass, R. Bruce, 21
Dovi, Suzanne, 230n88, 233n129,
233n136
Drury, Shadia, 208n21, 211n75
Dudrick, David, 169, 231n101, 231n104,
231n105, 233n135

Eigler, Friederike, 205n5
Ellis, Elisabeth, 108–9, 111–12, 117,
119–20, 122–23, 124, 222n93,
222n94, 222n102, 223n112,
223n116, 223n120, 223n121,
224n134, 224n137, 224n139,
224n141
Elshtain, Jean Bethke, 49–50, 207n1,
209n27, 209n28, 209n30
Eteocles, 139, 225–26n14
Euripides, 143
Evrigenis, Ioannis, 93–94, 216n7, 216n8,
216n10, 216n11, 216n13, 216n14,
217n27, 218n33, 218n34, 218n47,
219n51, 219–20n63, 220n72,
220n78, 221n88

Farneti, Roberto, 219n62
Ferrari, G.R.F., 196–97
Finnis, John, 39–40, 42, 43–44, 45–46,
47, 48–49, 52–53, 54–55, 59,
208n15, 208n24, 209n30, 209n34
Fischer, Markus, 210n56, 214n120
Fisher, Mark, 234n17
Flathman, Richard, 104, 216n6, 216n9,
216n12, 217n19, 217n25,
217n28, 217–18n32, 218n34,
218n48, 218–19n49, 220n72,
220n76, 220n79, 221n80,
221n81, 221n83
Fortin, Ernest P., 208n8, 208n19, 209n41,
209n43
Foucault, Michel, 174

Franceschet, Antonio, 223n129, 224n132, 224n136
Franco, Paul, 149–50, 225n2, 225n4, 225n5, 225n7, 225n8, 225n12, 226n19, 226n22, 226n25, 227n40, 227n43, 227n45, 227n47, 228n48, 228n49, 228n50, 228n51, 228n53, 228n55, 228n56, 228n60, 229n67, 229n69
Frank, Jill, 181, 186–87, 196–97, 209n42, 227n44, 234n3, 234n, 235n26, 235n30, 235n31, 235n37
Frederick II, 167
French Revolution, 29, 116, 160–61, 223n116

Galston, William, 222n99, 222n100, 222n101, 222n103, 222n106, 222n107, 222n109, 223n111, 223n112, 223n116, 223n121, 223n122, 224n132, 224n137, 224n139
Garsten, Brian, 120, 216n8, 216n9, 216n10, 216n13, 217–18n32, 218n36, 218n40, 220n72, 220n76, 220n79
Gauthier, David, 97, 104, 216n, 216n6, 216n7, 216n12, 216n14, 216n15, 217n16, 217n19, 217n20, 217n23, 217n28, 217n30, 218n45, 219n52, 219n53, 219n57, 220n74, 221n89
Gaza, 50–51
Geertz, Clifford, 18–19, 20–21
Gemes, Ken, 232n111
Geuss, Raymond, 2–3, 4, 53, 57–58, 157, 175, 178–79, 195, 198, 199–201, 202–3, 223n123, 229n67, 229n70, 235n34
Gillespie, Michael, 229n76, 230n82, 230n84, 230n88, 231n102, 232n108, 232n109, 232n114, 232n117, 232n123, 233n131
Godolphin, Sydney, 103
Gorgias, 31–32, 33
Greece/Greeks (classical), 1–2, 4–5, 9, 24–25, 28–29, 105–6, 133, 136–38, 140–41, 142–43, 149–50, 151, 162–63, 186–87, 188–89, 199, 229n66, 232n113, 233n126
Guyer, Paul, 223n115

Habermas, Jürgen, 2–4, 12–14, 15, 17, 30–31, 37, 38, 55, 56–58, 59, 79–80, 83–84, 108, 126, 133, 152–53, 165–66, 205n2, 206n13, 209n46, 209n47, 209n48, 216n2, 221n91, 222n96, 223n122, 225n2, 229n67, 229n68
Hanson, Victor Davis, 1–3, 9, 36, 204
Hardin, Russell, 93–94, 209n25, 216n1, 224n143
Harpham, Geoffrey, 6, 202–3
Harris, H.S., 133, 225–26n14, 226n17, 226n18
Hassner, Pierre, 222n96, 223n114, 223n122
Hatab, Lawrence, 174–75, 225n3, 229n74, 230n86, 230n88, 231n94, 233n130, 233n131, 233n132
Heath, Thomas, 208n19
Hebrew Bible/Hebrews, 18, 39–40, 64–65, 66, 73–74, 100, 101, 159–60
  Deuteronomy, 206n17, 209n26
  Exodus, 212n80
  Genesis, 213n109, 219–20n63
  Kings, 209n26
  Numbers, 212n80, 220n68
Hegel, G.W.F., 5, 177–78, 199–200
  on *Antigone*, 130–31, 138–39, 143, 144, 150, 151, 227n27
  and Aristophanes, 142–43
  and Aristotle, 144–45, 227n42, 227n44
  civil society, 144–45
  classical Greece, culture and wars of, 131–32, 136–44, 145, 147, 150–51, 226n25, 226n26, 227n37
  consciousness/self-consciousness, 132–33, 134–35, 145, 147–48
  courage, 131–32, 144, 147, 148, 228n52
  and democratic theory, 152, 229n67
  equality, 133–34
  ethical life, 8–9, 129–30, 136–39, 143, 144, 145, 146–50
  freedom, 128, 130, 131, 132, 133–35, 136–37, 140–41, 144–45, 146–48
  and Herodotus, 150, 151, 229n66
  historical dialectic/immanent critique, 130–31, 133–34, 149–50, 176
  historical spiritual activity, 128, 129, 130, 134, 177–78

history, meanings of, 129, 135–36,
141–43, 150, 176
and Hobbes, 133–34, 146–47
and the individual/individuality, 136,
138, 140, 141–42, 147
institutions/structures, 130, 134–35,
144–45, 148
international law, 149–50, 152, 229n69
intersubjectivity, 132
and Kant, 128, 130–31, 135–36, 146,
147, 227n42, 228n58
and liberalism, 144–45, 227n47,
228n51
lord and bondsman, 131–34, 137,
144–45, 147, 149–50, 225n13,
225–26n14, 226n15, 226n16,
226n19, 226n20
and Machiavelli, 135–36, 149–50
and metaphysics, 129–30, 225n3, 225n7
and modernity, 8–9, 128, 130–31,
134–35, 136–37, 139–40,
142–44, 146–48
and Nietzsche, 128, 152–53, 156,
157, 162–63, 164, 173, 174, 176,
232n113, 232–33n125, 233n134
and particulars, 146–49, 150–51, 152,
199–200, 228n60
on peoples, 129, 146–48
Pericles, 141, 142–43, 192–93
philosophy, 9, 129, 130–31, 134–35,
136, 140–41, 147–50, 176, 225n8,
228n50, 228n62, 228n64
and Plato, 142–43, 150, 176, 227n38,
228n52, 228n65
progress, 140–41, 147–48
providence, 135–36
recognition, 132–33, 225n10, 226n21
religion, 130–31, 134–35
Rome, 139–41, 227n31
and Schmitt, 135–36
and social theory, 145, 152
and Socrates, 130–31, 138,
143–44, 150
and Sophocles, 130–31, 138–39,
142–43, 150, 151
spirit (*Geist*), 8–9, 128, 129, 130–38,
139–41, 142–43, 144–45, 146–50,
151, 152, 176, 177–78, 225n8
spiritedness, 133–34, 137, 144, 148,
177–78, 225–26n14

state, as spiritual achievement,
8–9, 128, 144–47, 148–49,
177–78, 225n2
and Thucydides, 141, 142–43, 144,
150, 151, 176, 188–89, 193
war
as persistent problem, 136, 138–39,
144, 146, 147, 148–50, 152–53,
173, 176, 228n55, 228n56,
228n59, 228n61
as spiritual activity, 8–9, 129,
131–32, 134–36, 146–50, 228n51
wisdom, 134–35, 149–51
women, 139–40
works (full title references only)
Elements of the Philosophy of Right,
131–32, 134–35, 144
Encyclopedia, 226n21
*Lectures on the Philosophy of
History*, 128, 131–32, 134–37,
138, 139–40, 142–43, 144–45,
226n23, 226n24
Natural Law, 228n60
The Phenomenology of Spirit,
131–32, 133, 134–35, 136–37,
138–40, 142, 148–50, 226n23,
227n39, 232n110
Heidegger, Martin, 23–24
Henderson, Jeffrey, 227n34
Heraclitus, 229n76
Herodotus, 150, 151, 229n66, 235n33
Herzog, Don, 104, 217n28, 218n43
Higgins, Kathleen, 232n116, 232n120,
233n127
Hiroshima, 208n23
history of political philosophy, varying
approaches, 3–4, 10, 11, 35–36,
180, 199
Hobbes, Thomas, 4, 5, 177–78, 199–200
and Aquinas, 86, 90–91, 102, 104–5,
220n69
and Arendt, 221n81
civic education, 97–99, 218n48
commodious living, 88, 89–90, 92,
106–7, 184, 199
commonwealth, 92, 94–97, 99, 100,
101, 102, 126–27, 217n27, 217n30
counsel, 95–96, 97, 103–4, 105–6,
218n34, 218n35, 218n36,
218n37

courage, 103
darkness, kingdom of, 98–99, 219n59
deliberation, 104
desire, 89–90
emotions, 87, 89–90, 105–7
English Civil War, 87, 103, 218n33
equality, 86, 90–91, 95, 102–3, 106–7,
    217n25, 221n88
faith, 99, 100–1
fear, 88, 89–91, 92, 103, 105–6,
    221n88, 221n89
freedom, 86, 102–3
glory/honor, 87–88, 97, 218n47,
    220n77
on God, 93–94, 95–96, 98–99,
    100, 101–2
good and evil, 89–90
happiness, 89–90
and history, 126–27
human distinctiveness, 88, 216n15
and international politics, 106–7,
    221n86, 221n88
and Kant, 89, 106–8, 109–11,
    113–14, 125–27
laws, civil, 95–97, 100–1, 218n43
laws, natural, 86, 90–91, 93, 95–97,
    100–1, 102, 105–6, 217n23
and Machiavelli, 86, 87–88, 93–94,
    101, 104–5
on madness, 89–90, 93–94, 102–3,
    217n20
materialism, 87–88, 89–91, 102–3
on Melian dialogue, 106–7, 221n85
natural rights, 86, 216n6, 217n25
nature, state of, 86, 87–88, 89–92,
    93–94, 97, 99–100, 106–7, 184,
    216n5, 217n18, 221n80
and Nietzsche, 155–56, 159
obedience, 91–92, 93–95, 100–1, 199
peace, as epistemic category, 8,
    86–87, 89–90, 91, 99–100,
    102–3, 220n72, 220n73
    as pragmatic project, 102, 104–5,
    177–78, 217n27, 221n81
    as social infrastructure, 95–96,
    97–98, 100, 218n45, 218–19n49
philosophy, 86–87, 98–99, 102–3, 104,
    218n41, 220n79, 221n81
and Plato, 199
power, 86, 88, 89–92, 94–98, 100, 101,
    102–3, 104–7

pride, 88, 89–90, 91, 93–94, 95–96,
    103–4, 105–6
punishments
    civil, 96–97, 218n44
    natural, 93–94, 95–96, 103, 218n33
and rational choice theory, 7–8, 85,
    126, 216n1, 217n31, 217–18n32,
    224n143
rationality, 7–8, 51, 85, 98–99, 101,
    105–6, 200
and Rawls, 89, 217n19
religion/scriptural interpretation,
    86–87, 98–102, 219n53, 219n56,
    219n58, 219n60, 219n62,
    219–20n63, 220n64, 220n66,
    220n71
rhetoric/narrative, 85–86, 87–88,
    91–92, 93–94, 98–99, 216n11,
    216n13
salvation/damnation, 87–88, 89, 99,
    100–1, 219n61
and Schmitt, 86, 106–7
science/political science, 85–86, 87–88,
    89–90, 94, 102–3, 125–27, 178,
    216n11, 216n12, 216n13
security/safety, 86–87, 91, 92, 94, 184,
    200, 219n51
sovereign, 86–87, 91–93, 94–98, 99,
    100–1, 103–4, 105–7, 217n16,
    217n26, 217n31, 218n47, 219n51,
    219n52, 219n60, 220n77
and Thucydides, 105–6, 183–84,
    221n83, 221n88
war, evils of, 86, 93–94, 177–78
works (full title references only)
    De Corpore, 87
    Leviathan, 85–86, 87, 92–93,
    94–95, 97–99, 102, 103, 105–6,
    133–34, 184
Hoekstra, Kinch, 216n1, 217n25, 234n17
Homer/Homeric, 169–70, 187–88,
    192–93, 232n113
Honig, Bonnie, 2–3, 12, 13, 37–38, 82,
    207n34, 216n141, 216n142,
    228n63, 229n74, 230n79, 230n86,
    231n100, 232n112, 232n122,
    233n130, 233n137
Hornblower, Simon, 196–97
Hornqvist, Mikael, 62, 81–82,
    209–10n51, 210n54, 210n56,
    210n59, 210n60, 211n64, 211n68,

211n70, 212n96, 214n119, 214n120, 215n139
Houlgate, Stephen, 225n7
Hoy, Jocelyn, 139–40
Hulliung, Mark, 209–10n51, 210n57, 210n59, 210n60, 213n98, 214n111, 214n120
human rights, 8, 12–13, 37, 56–57, 85, 201–2
Hüning, Dieter, 218n44
Hyppolite, Jean, 225–26n14, 226n18

ideal theory/idealism/idealist, 4, 83, 148, 178–79, 188–89
Idris, Murad, 206n16
Ignatieff, Michael 209n32, 209n35, 209n37
interpretation, 5, 201–2
  and citizenship, 6, 10, 202–4
Iraq, 50–51
Isidore of Seville, 41
Islamic State, 50–51
Israel, 50–51

Jaffa, Harry, 54, 208n8, 208n14, 209n41
Japan, 50–51, 208n23
Johnson, James Turner, 207n1, 208n22, 208n24, 209n28
Johnson, Laurie, 194, 221n83, 234n20
Jordan, Mark, 53, 208n11, 209n36, 209n41
Joshua, 73–74

Kagan, Donald, 181–82
Kahn, Charles, 211–12n78
Kalkavage, Peter, 133–34, 225–26n14, 226n21, 226n26
Kant, Immanuel, 5, 177–78, 199–200, 201–2, 203–4
  and Aquinas, 111, 122, 224n137
  and Aristotle, 110–11, 222n99
  autonomy, 108, 109–10, 111–12, 117–18, 119, 128
  commerce/trade, 109–10, 114–15, 222n97
  cosmopolitanism, 108, 222n94
  culture, 107–8, 109, 110–12, 113–14, 115, 123, 222n98
  and deliberative democracy, 7–8, 85, 108, 216n2, 221n91, 221n92, 224n131
desire, 110–11, 112, 113–14
  duty, 107–8, 111, 121–22, 124–27
  and emotion, 119–20, 121–22, 223n125, 223n127
  epistemology, 119–20, 223n119, 223n122, 223n123, 223n124
  freedom, moral, 119
  freedom, political, 112–14
  God, 116–17
  and Habermas, 108, 126
  happiness, 119
  heteronomy, 118–19, 123, 128
  history, 108–9, 111–12, 114, 115–17, 124–25, 126–27, 222n100, 223n112, 224n138
  and Hobbes, 89, 106–8, 109–11, 113–14, 125–27, 222n106
  international politics, 7–8, 85, 107–8, 223n129, 224n136
  kingdom of ends, 111, 112, 113–14, 118, 223n121
  and Machiavelli, 111, 118
  moral heroism, 113–14, 120, 124–25, 222n105
  moral politician, 8, 85–86, 108–9, 117–18, 119–22, 123–25, 194, 200, 201–2, 203–4, 224n130, 224n134
  moral rationality, 7–8, 85, 107–8, 117–19, 120, 125–26, 130, 178, 200–1
  morality/right, 85–86, 109–10, 111, 112–13, 118, 119–20, 121–25
  nature/natural science, 111–12, 113–15, 117, 118–19, 125, 223n111, 223n112
  and Nietzsche, 128, 155–56, 165–66, 174, 230n79
  peace, as moral imperative, 107–8, 111, 114, 177–78, 223n113
  philosophers, 108–9, 120, 121–22
  and Plato, 110–11
  political expedience, critique of, 118, 121
  procedural fairness, 119, 122–23, 224n132, 224n134
  progress, 114–16, 117, 118, 119–20, 124–25, 224n139
  providence, 114–15, 116–17, 118–19, 125–27, 223n117, 223n118
  and Rawls, 118–19, 126

Kant, Immanuel (*cont.*)
  republic/republican politics, 108,
    109–10, 112–13, 114–15, 118–19,
    121–22, 123, 223n128
  and Schmitt, 114, 123
  teleology, 115–16, 117, 223n115
  tragic politics, 119–20, 124, 178,
    222n109
  war, ambiguity of, 8, 109, 111–13,
    114–15, 222n101, 222n102
  will, 110–12, 120
  works (full title references only)
    Contest of the Faculties, 109–10
    Critique of Judgment, 107–8
    *Groundwork for the Metaphysics of
      Morals,* 107–8
    *Idea for a Universal History with a
      Cosmopolitan Intent,* 107–8
    *Metaphysical Elements of the Theory
      of Right,* 107–8
    Theory and Practice, 107–8, 114–15
    Toward Perpetual Peace,
      107–8, 201–2
    What is Enlightenment, 222n99
Kaufmann, Walter, 230n89, 232n117
Kavka, Gregory, 89–90, 104, 216n1,
    216n6, 216n12, 216n13, 217n18,
    217n19, 217n25, 217n28, 217n29,
    217n31, 217–18n32, 218n38,
    218n47, 218–19n49, 219n52,
    219n53, 220n74, 221n86
Kelly, George Armstrong, 225n9, 225n11,
    226n19, 226n23
Kennedy, Ellen, 205n12
Kochin, Michael, 186–87, 234n14,
    235n26, 235n28, 235n31
Kojeve, Alexandre, 133, 148, 225n10,
    226n20, 228n59
Korsgaard, Christine, 3–4, 108, 216n2,
    223n121, 223n122

Lampert, Laurence, 234n5
Langan, John, 48–49, 208n9, 208n11
Lattimore, Steven, 187–88, 198, 234n1,
    234n19
law of peoples, 1, 12–13, 54–55, 56–58,
    108, 152–53
Lefort, Claude, 210n53, 210n57, 211n64,
    212n89, 214n115, 214n116,
    214n117, 215n135, 216n143
Lenin, 26–28

Leonardo da Vinci, 167
Lerner, Ralph, 66
Lessay, Franck, 100–1, 219n62, 220n67
Lincoln, Abraham, 47
Locke, John, 91–92, 144–45
Lucretius, 63–64, 72–73, 74, 213n104
Luke, evangelist, 66, 212n81
Lutz-Bachmann, Matthias, 108, 221n92,
    222n93, 222n95

Machiavelli, Niccolo, 4, 5,
    199–200, 202–3
  accidents, 71–72
  agency, 62, 63–64, 66–67, 68–71,
    75–76, 81–82, 83, 177–78,
    215n137
  and Aquinas, 7, 37–38, 59, 60, 64,
    65–66, 68–70, 71–72, 79–80,
    83–84, 211–12n78, 212n81,
    214n124
  and Aristotle, 71–72, 77–78, 81–82,
    211–12n78, 214n119, 215n134,
    215n140
  autonomy, 69, 80–82
  and Christianity, 64–66, 68–69, 79–80
  citizenship, 60, 76–79, 215n130
  common good, 60, 61, 76–79, 81,
    210n56, 214n118
  corruption, 60
  and Derrida, 80–81
  desire, 60–61, 63, 71–72, 74–75,
    80–82, 104–5
  disunion, civic, 71–72, 210n53, 210n57
  dominion/empire, 77–78, 80, 81–82,
    214n120
  Florence/Florentine, 62, 69–70, 78–79,
    215n139
  fortune/*fortuna,* 63–64, 66–72, 74–75,
    76–77, 81–82, 93–94, 212n86,
    212n92, 212n93, 213n99
  free will, 67, 68–71, 212n95, 214n112
  gender in, 67–68, 80–81
  God, 68–69, 71
  heaven, 64–66, 68, 71, 72–74
  and Hegel, 135–36, 149–50
  and Hobbes, 75, 86, 87–88, 93–94,
    101, 104–5
  honor/glory/reputation, 62–63, 69,
    71–72, 74–76, 78–79, 80, 81–82,
    88, 211n69, 213n100, 214n111,
    215n128

human science of, 72–73, 74–75,
76–77, 81
impetuosity, 67–68, 69–70, 212n89
inundation, 67–68, 71, 72–74,
213n105
Italy, 62, 69–70, 74–75, 210n54,
211n68, 213n107
and Judaism, 64
judgment, 80–81, 82–83, 215n139
justice, 60, 79, 208n13, 210n54
and Kant, 81–82, 111, 118, 215n140
Latium, 215n139
Lentulus, Lucius, 214n126
and Livy, 78–79, 210n54, 214n121,
214n123, 214n126, 215n132
and Lucretius, 63–64, 72–73, 74,
213n104, 213n108, 214n112
Manlius Torquatus, Titus, 78–80,
214n124, 215n132
nature, 63–64, 67, 71–74, 75, 81–82
and Nietzsche, 154–56, 166
and philosophy, 7, 38, 62, 63–64, 67,
68–69, 74, 75–76, 77, 82–83, 178,
211n70, 211n72, 211–12n78,
216n143
and Plato, 212n90, 215n134
political order/politics, 7, 60–61, 62,
69–70, 76–77, 82, 83, 199–200,
210n52, 212n84
and Polybius, 71–72, 212n97
providence, 63–64, 66, 74–75, 81–82,
211n73, 211n75, 211n76, 211n77,
211–12n78
prudence/prudent, 68–72, 76–77,
211n65, 215n139
realism in, 7
religion, 62, 65–66
rhetoric of, 62–63, 78–79, 80, 82,
211n64, 211n67, 211n68
Rome/Roman empire/Roman republic,
61–62, 69, 73–75, 77, 78–79,
210n59, 210n60, 210n62, 211n66,
212n79, 214n111, 215n139
and Schmitt, 78, 80–81
Sforza, Madonna Caterina, 215n132
teleology, rejection of, 71–73, 76,
214n115, 215n129
and Thucydides, 183–84
truth, 68–69, 75–76, 83–84, 214n113
virtu/virtues, 67–68, 69–70, 74–75,
77–80, 215n128, 215n129

war, significance of, 60–64, 67, 79,
80, 81–82, 83, 177–78, 210n58,
210n63
works (full title references only)
Discourses on Livy, 60, 61, 62–63,
64–66, 69, 70–74, 75–76,
77–79, 202–3
Florentine Histories, 60, 78–79,
210n55
Letter to Vettori, 202–3
The Prince, 61–62, 64, 66, 67, 68–
70, 71–72, 75–76, 83, 118, 202–3
MacIntyre, Alasdair, 39–40, 44–45,
158–59, 207n3, 208n10, 208n12,
208n15, 209n25, 209n40
MacMillan, John, 224n136
Maimonides, 66
Mallett, Michael, 62
Mansfield, Harvey, 63–64, 67, 209n50,
210n55, 210n56, 210n58, 210n59,
210n60, 210n62, 211n64, 211n72,
211–12n78, 212n79, 212n80,
212n81, 212n84, 212n95, 213n98,
213n104, 213n105, 213n110,
214n113, 214n114, 214n116,
214n121, 215n139
Mapel, David, 50–51
Mara, Gerald, 179, 190–91, 192,
197–98, 207n36, 209n38,
209n42, 209n45, 209n47,
218n34, 227n33, 230n88,
233n129, 233n136, 234n,
234n7, 234n8, 234n21, 235n22,
235n25, 235n27, 235n30,
235n34, 235n36
Marcuse, Herbert, 225n2, 228n54
Markell, Patchen, 133, 134–35, 139–41,
151, 225n6, 225n9, 226n21,
227n27
Martel, James, 104, 216n8, 216n10,
216n11, 217n16, 217n23, 217n26,
217n28, 217–18n32, 218n34,
218n35, 218n36, 218n38, 218n48,
218–19n49, 219n51, 219n54,
219–20n63, 220n67, 220n71,
220n75, 220n79, 221n81
Martinich, A.P, 219n54, 219n61, 219n62
Masters, Roger, 67–68, 76–77, 210n58,
211n64, 211n65, 212n84, 212n87
Matthew, evangelist, 44–46, 99
Maurusians, 73–74

McCarthy, Thomas, 222n107, 223n122, 224n132, 224n135, 224n136, 224n140

McCormick, John, 16–17, 21–23, 206n14, 206n25, 206n26, 206–7n27, 207n30, 210n53, 210n56, 210n57, 210n59, 211n64, 213n100, 214n118, 214n119, 214n120, 215n130, 215n139, 216n143

McDowell, John, 133

McInerney, Ralph, 209n40

Media, 74–75

Meier, Heinrich, 17–18, 205n10, 206n14, 206n15, 206n18, 206n20, 206n21, 206n24, 207n32

Mill, John Stuart, 159, 174, 230n88

Mitchell, Joshua, 91, 219n50, 219n54, 219n60, 220n64, 220n67

modernity, 2–5, 8–9, 16, 21, 31, 39, 55, 56–57, 66, 128, 130–31, 134–35, 136–37, 139–40, 142, 143–44, 146–47, 148, 152–53, 154, 155, 158–59, 163–64, 165, 166–67, 169–70, 175, 176, 206–7n27, 226n15, 230n83

Monoson, Sara, 235n33

Morrison, James, 235n24

Moses, 64–65, 66, 73–74, 101, 212n80

Mosul, 50–51

Mouffe, Chantal, 12, 13–14, 30–31, 229n70

Müller, Jan-Werner, 18, 22, 33, 205n2, 205n3, 206n18, 206n19, 206–7n27

Mynott, Jeremy, 183, 187–88, 234n19

Nagasaki, 208n23

Nails, Debra, 181

Napoleon, 130–31, 159, 167

Nazi Germany, 13–14, 47–48, 50–51, 208n23

Nehamas, Alexander, 172–73, 225n3, 229n74, 229–30n77, 230n85, 230n86, 231n97, 231n102, 231n106, 232n109, 232n114, 233n128, 233n135

Netanyahu, Benjamin, 51

Neuhouser, Frederick, 225n2, 227n41, 227n45, 227n47, 228n48, 228n49, 228n50

Nichols, James, 213n102, 213n104

Nichols, Mary, 181–82, 192, 235n30

Nietzsche, Friedrich, 5, 18, 30–31, 55–56, 177–79, 199, 200–1

and agonistic democracy, 8–9, 129–30, 174, 175

and Aquinas, 169–70

aristocracy/aristocratic society, 154–55, 156–58, 160–61, 173–74, 230n84, 232n118

and Aristotle/Aristotelianism, 163–64, 169–70, 171–72, 232n119

and Christianity, 155, 159, 163–65, 231n100

and classical/Homeric Greece, 162–63, 169–70, 232n113, 232–33n125

community, 169–70

culture, 128, 129, 156, 158–59, 161–62, 164, 166, 167, 168, 172–74, 230n85, 232n109, 232–33n125, 233n131, 233n132

and democracy/democratic theory, 154, 155, 162, 164–65, 168, 169, 171, 174, 175, 229n74, 232n118, 233n127, 233n133

Dionysius, god, 171–72, 232n117

Europe/Europeans, 157–58, 159–60, 163–64, 166, 168

genealogy/genealogies, 8–9, 129, 157–58, 172–73, 174, 200–1, 230n90

Germany, politics and culture, 167, 168

good/bad, 161–63

good/evil, 159, 161–62, 166, 172–73

and Hegel, 128, 156, 157, 162–63, 164, 173, 174, 176, 232n113, 232–33n125, 233n134

and history/histories, 128, 157–58, 172–73, 176

and Hobbes, 155–56, 159, 174

and the individual/individuality, 129, 169, 173–74

instinct/emotion, 164–66, 169

and the Jews, 159–60, 230n89, 230n90

and Kant, 128, 155–56, 165–66, 174, 230n79

knowledge, 163–65, 169, 175, 231n96

language, 161–62, 231n93

last human being, 155

life, affirmation of, 154–55, 156, 158, 160–61, 169, 172–73, 233n128

and Machiavelli, 154–56, 166

mass society, 155, 159

and metaphysics, 129–30
and Mill, 159, 230n88
and modernity, 128, 154, 155, 158–60,
    163–64, 166, 168, 175
moralities/morality. 154–55,
    157–60, 161, 164–66, 169,
    231n92, 231n104, 232n123
  master morality, 156, 161–64, 169–70
  slave morality, 156, 159, 161–64,
    169, 172
nature, 154–55, 157–59, 229–30n77
and nihilism, 154, 163–64, 169,
    231n100
nobility/the noble, 157–58, 160–62,
    169–70, 172, 173–74, 231n97,
    233n136
overman (*Ubermensch*), 171–72
philosophy/philosophers, 129, 154,
    155–56, 163–64, 166, 170–71,
    172–74, 175, 176, 232n120
and Plato, 164–65, 176, 199, 232n116,
    233n134
and politics, 153, 156, 164, 166, 167,
    168–69, 172–75, 176
power/will to power, 154–56,
    160–62, 175
rationality/reason, 164–65, 169–70
religion, 158, 163–64, 231n99
Roman, 159–60
and Schmitt, 156
self-overcoming/self-creation, 8–9,
    128, 129, 154, 156–57, 166,
    169–70, 172–75, 176, 177–78
slave rebellion in morals, 157, 159–60,
    162–64, 172–73, 231n98
slavery/slaves, 156–57, 160–61, 168,
    169–70, 173, 230n83, 231n94
and Socrates, 164–65, 166,
    170–71, 172–73
on the soul, 156–58, 161–62, 169–70,
    171–72, 173–74, 229n74
spirit/spiritual, 157, 163–64, 165, 166,
    168, 169, 173
spiritedness, 157–58, 173
Stoics, 169
suffering, 169–70
teleology, 154–56, 231n95
and Thucydides, 162–63, 178–79, 199
truth/truthfulness, 155–56, 165–66,
    169–70, 172, 175, 178, 231n105,
    231n106, 232n110, 233n135

Utilitarianism/utility, 159, 162, 164–65
values, 129, 154, 155, 156–57, 158,
    159–60, 162, 166, 169, 172–73,
    233n138
virtues, 159–60, 162, 168, 169–70, 172,
    232n112, 232n114, 232n115
war, significance of, 129, 154–55,
    171, 172–73, 174–75, 230n81,
    232–33n125
  and philosophy, 154, 155–56,
    230n78
  and politics, 154, 167, 172–73
  within the self, 153, 154–55, 156,
    165, 166, 167, 170–71
works (full title references only)
  Beyond Good and Evil, 128, 153, 169
  The Birth of Tragedy, 155
  The Gay Science, 154
  Homer's Contest, 229n75
  Human, All too Human, 30–31
  On the Genealogy of Morals, 18,
    55–56, 128, 158
  *Philosophy in the Tragic Age of the
    Greeks,* 229n76
  Schopenhauer as Educator, 229n75
  Thus Spoke Zarathustra, 155,
    230n87
  Twilight of the Idols, 178–79
  *The Uses and Disadvantages of
    History for Life,* 129, 154
Nussbaum, Martha, 117, 151, 179, 181,
    209n47, 216n2, 227n27, 228n63

O'Brien, William V., 207n1
O'Driscoll, Ciaran, 51, 209n32, 234n20
O'Neill, Onora, 119–20, 124, 221n91,
    222n94, 222n96, 222n110,
    223n121, 224n130
Oakeshott, Michael, 202–3
Ober, Josiah, 198
origins, political, 55–56, 60, 83
Orwin, Clifford, 187–88, 190–91,
    207n36, 209n50, 210n56, 210n63,
    214n119, 215n131, 234n10,
    234n11, 235n22, 235n23, 235n25
Owens, Joseph, 37–38, 53

Parel, Anthony, 63–64, 66, 67, 69–70, 71,
    210n57, 212n82, 212n86, 212n93,
    212n95, 213n101
Peisistratus, 196–97, 235n33

Peloponnesians/Peloponnesian war, 31–32,
    106–7, 137–38, 142–44, 151,
    180–81, 184, 185–86, 190, 196
Pericles/Periclean, 89, 105–6, 141,
    142–43, 162–63, 181–82, 186–89,
    190, 192–93, 194–95, 198,
    221n82, 226n26, 234n4, 235n24
Persia/Persians, 74–75, 137–38, 141, 151,
    184, 191
Pinkard, Terry, 3–131, 225n2, 225n3,
    225n4, 225n5, 225n8, 226n15,
    226n18, 226n25, 226n26, 227n30,
    227n37, 227n39, 227n41, 227n45,
    228n48, 228n49, 228n55, 229n67
Pippin, Robert, 131, 132–33, 148–49,
    164, 225n2, 225n3, 225n4, 225n8,
    225n9, 225n10, 225n11, 226n20,
    227n32, 227n42, 228n48, 229n67,
    230n78, 231n98, 231n105
Pitkin, Hannah, 37–38, 67, 76–78, 80–81,
    82, 210n56, 210n57, 214n117,
    214n118, 214n119, 215n132,
    215n135, 215n136, 215n137,
    215n140
Planeaux, Christopher, 234n5
Plato, 9, 10, 24–25, 31–32, 40, 46–47,
    59, 110–11, 130–31, 142–43, 150,
    151, 164–65, 170–71, 176,
    178–79, 201–2, 204
  Adeimantus, 186, 197–98, 200, 235n27
  Anytus, 181
  Athens/Athenian, 180–81, 185–86,
    194–95, 196–97, 199
  barbarians, 186–87
  Cleitophon
  and Corcyrean narrative, 186–87,
    188–89, 198, 200
  Critias, 181, 234n5
  democracy, 181, 189, 196–97
  and Derrida, 186–87
  and desire, 184–86
  dialogue form of writing, 9–10,
    40, 180–81
  Dionysius, tyrant, 235n33
  and extremes, 9–10, 183, 185–86
  factional conflict (stasis), 185–86, 196–97
  funeral oration, 187
  Glaucon, 46–47, 181, 186–87, 194–95,
    196–98, 200, 235n27, 235n36
  Greeks, 186–87
  and Hegel, 142–43, 150, 151,
    188–89, 196–97

Hermocrates, 234n5
  and history, 184–85
  and Hobbes, 199
  honor, 194–96
  judgment, 189–90
  justice/injustice, 185, 186, 189–90,
    194–95, 197–98
  and Kant, 196–97
  Leontius, 185–86
  Logos/logoi, 189–90, 194–95, 196
  and Machiavelli, 194–95, 202–3
  nature, 187
  Niceratus
  and Nietzsche, 164–65,
    170–71, 176, 196–98, 199
  and Peloponnesian war, 9–10, 180–81,
    196, 199
  and Pericles/Periclean, 186–87,
    188–89, 194–95, 198
  and philosophy, 178–79, 184–85,
    187, 195–97
  and plague narrative, 186–87
  rationality, 185–86
  and Schmitt, 186–87
  soul, 184–86, 189, 196–97
  Sparta/Spartans, 181
  spiritedness, 195–96
  the thirty, 181, 185–86,
    196–98, 234n5
  Thrasymachus
  and Thucydides, 9–10, 178–80, 183,
    185–88, 189–90, 194–95, 196–99,
    200, 201–4
  Timaeus, 181, 187, 234n15
  Tyranny, 196–97
  war
    origin of, 9–10, 183, 194–96
    significance of, 185–87
  works (full title references only)
    Apology, 197–98
    Protagoras, 181, 227n36, 231n103
    Gorgias, 77–78, 181, 189–90, 203–4,
      227n38, 234n4
    Menexenus, 24–25, 28–29
    Meno, 181
    Republic, 24–25, 28–29, 35,
      46–47, 77–78, 147, 150,
      170–71, 172–73, 181, 183,
      184–86, 187–90, 191, 194–96,
      197–99, 202–4, 227n38, 235n31,
      235n32, 235n33
    Timaeus, 181, 211–12n78, 234n5

Pocock, John, 64, 210n56, 210n58, 210n60, 210n62, 211n66, 211n70, 211n73, 212n85, 212n95, 212n96, 212n97, 214n116, 214n118, 214n120, 215n129, 215n130, 216n142, 216n143
Polemarchus, 197–98, 200
Polyneices, 138–39, 225–26n14
Pomponazzi, Pietro 214n114
postmodernism/postmodernity, 2–3, 4–5, 54–55, 76–77, 129–30, 154, 174, 176, 206–7n27, 229n74, 231n100
power, 200–3
Price, Jonathan, 234n13
Pritchard, David, 196
progress, moral and political, 3–4, 17, 56–57
Protestant theology, 114, 219n62
providence, 41–42, 63–64, 66, 81–82, 93–94, 114–15, 116–17, 118–19, 125–26, 135–36, 223n116
Puritans, 89
Putin, Vladimir, 4, 51

Rahe, Paul, 72–73, 212n83, 213n103, 215n129
rational choice theory, 7–8, 48–49, 126, 208n24, 224n142
Rawlings, Hunter, 198
Rawls, John, 1, 2–3, 4, 12–13, 15–16, 30–31, 37–38, 46–48, 55, 56–58, 59, 79–80, 83–84, 89, 108, 118–19, 126, 152–53, 201–2, 205n11, 206–7n27, 207n29, 207n3, 208n5, 208n23, 209n31, 209n46, 209n47, 209n48, 216n2, 217n19, 224n136, 229n68, 229n71
realism/realist theory, 4, 7, 14, 16–17, 24, 31, 38, 119–20, 152–53, 178–79, 188–89, 191, 199–200, 204, 205n3, 234n20
Redding, Paul, 225n9
Reeve, C.D.C., 179, 185
Richardson, Henry, 12
Richardson, John, 231n93, 232n111, 233n127
Riley, Patrick, 222n95, 222n97, 222n98, 222n100, 222n106, 223n112, 223n121
Robespierre, 130–31
Romans, Paul's epistle to, 45–46

Romilly, Jacqueline de, 178–79, 184–85, 190–91, 198, 234n16
Romulus, 55–56
Roochnik, David, 186–87, 235n30
Rorty, Richard, 174, 202–3, 233n128
Rosen, Stanley, 131–32, 225n13, 225–26n14, 228n59, 228n62
Rousseau, 86, 123, 130–31
Russia, 4, 51
Rusten, Jeffrey, 198

Said, Edward, 207n28
Salkever, Stephen, 209n41, 209n42, 209n47
Sallis, John, 223n119
Satkunanandan, Shalini, 49–50, 56–57, 171, 209n34, 222n105, 223n128, 231n92, 231n100, 231n105, 232n107, 232n115, 233n135
Savonarola, 64
Saxonhouse, Arlene, 181, 212n88, 212n91, 215n132, 234n8, 235n22, 235n25
Schlosser, Joel, 227n35
Schmitt, Carl, 5, 177–78
  and agonism, 205n10
  and classical political philosophy, 15–16, 22–23, 24–25
  and democratic theory, 11, 13–14
  on extremes, 14–15, 16–17, 26, 207n30
  on Greek wars, 24–25
  on history of political philosophy, 6–7, 11, 22–23, 35
  and Hobbes, 19–20, 28–29
  and just war theory, 51
  and Leo Strauss, 17–18, 19–20, 206n15, 206n17, 206n21, 206n26
  and liberalism, 15–16, 37, 205n10, 205n11, 206n20
  limited war, 15, 23–24, 26–27, 33, 205n9
  and Machiavelli, 78, 80–81
  and meaning, 18–21, 26–27, 206n22, 206n23
  and nationalism, 17, 206n13, 206n14
  Nazi past, 13–14
  and Plato, 24–25
  political anthropology, 11, 18–19, 20–21, 22–23, 206n18

Schmitt, Carl (*cont.*)
  political enmity
    significance, 6, 11, 14–15, 16–17,
      18–21, 34, 177–78, 205n7, 205n8,
      207n32
    limits, 6–7, 11, 21–22, 23–24, 178
  political theology, 17–18, 206n16,
    206n17, 206n20, 206n21
  and realism, 14, 16–17, 24, 205n3,
    205n12
  and revealed theology, 17–18, 206n16
  and Socrates, 24–25
  and the state, 15–16, 19, 24, 26–28,
    30–31, 207n31
  technology/technicity, 14, 16, 21–22,
    206n25
  and Thucydides, 183–84
  and Weber, 21, 206n26
  works (full title references only)
    *The Age of Neutralizations and
      Depoliticizations,* 205n4
    The Concept of the Political, 6, 11,
      13–14, 26–27, 34
    The Nomos of the Earth, 51
    Political Theology, 19
    Theory of the Partisan, 20–21,
      22–23, 26–27, 34
Schwab, George, 205n5
Seagrave, Adam, 208n6, 208n7, 208n8,
    209n40
Seitzer, Jeffrey, 205n1, 206–7n27
Shapiro, Ian, 1, 12, 209n44
Shaw, Tamsin, 168, 173–74, 229n74,
    229–30n77, 230n79, 230n80,
    231n101, 231n104, 231n105,
    233n135
Shell, Susan Meld, 111–12, 222n93,
    222n95, 222n97, 222n101, 222n103,
    222n105, 222n108, 223n111,
    223n112, 223n116, 223n118,
    223n120, 223n127, 224n131,
    224n134, 224n138, 224n140
Sherman, Nancy, 223n126, 223n127
Shklar, Judith, 136–37, 226n22, 226n26,
    227n29, 227n31, 227n39, 227n42
Sigmund, Paul, 207n1
Skinner, Quentin, 3–4, 87–88, 210n54,
    210n56, 210n59, 210n62,
    214n116, 214n118, 216n8,
    216n13, 218n33, 218n34, 218n36,
    218n37, 219n53

Slomp, Gabriella, 14–15, 16, 19, 86–87,
    205n1, 205n3, 205n6, 205n7,
    205n8, 205n9, 206n18, 206n19,
    206n22, 207n31, 207n37, 216n1,
    216n5, 216n9, 216n15, 217n21,
    217–18n32, 218n45, 218n47,
    220n72, 220n73, 220n77, 221n83
Sluga, Hans, 175, 230n83
Smith, Margaret Michelle Barnes,
    212n81, 213n109
Smith, Steven B., 3–4, 108, 116, 136,
    206n18, 219n55, 219n56, 220n64,
    220n66, 222n94, 222n100,
    222n101, 222n107, 223n113,
    223n115, 223n116, 223n117,
    225n2, 225n5, 225n8, 225n13,
    226n25, 227n41, 227n42, 227n44,
    227n45, 227n47, 228n49, 228n51,
    228n55, 228n56, 228n61, 228n64,
    229n67
Socrates/Socratic, 24–25, 40, 130–31,
    133, 138, 144, 150, 151, 164–65,
    166, 171, 172–73, 181, 184–87,
    188–90, 192, 194–98, 199,
    200, 202–4
Soll, Ivan, 230n86
Solomon, 212n81
sophists, 138, 144
Sophocles, 130–31, 138–39, 142–43,
    150, 151
Sparta/Spartans/Lacedaemonians, 34,
    106, 137–38, 141, 190–91, 192,
    193–94, 214n111, 215n134,
    234n19
Spinoza, 211n77, 214n122, 220n71
St. Dominic, 64–65, 74–75, 80
St. Francis, 64–65, 74–75, 80
Stocker, Michael, 209n35
Strauss, Leo, 3–4, 17–18, 19, 20–22, 61,
    62, 66–67, 71–72, 82–83, 97,
    103, 206n15, 206n17, 206n21,
    206n26, 208n8, 209–10n51,
    210n56, 210n58, 210n59, 210n60,
    210n62, 211n64, 211n66, 211–
    12n78, 212n81, 212n82, 212n91,
    213n98, 213n102, 213n110,
    214n119, 214n121, 215n130,
    215n133, 216n5, 217n16, 219n53,
    229–30n77, 232n110, 232n117,
    235n23, 235n25, 235n35
Swanton, Christine, 230n88

Sykes, Chris, 232n111
Syria, 4, 51, 73–74

Tarcov, Nathan, 63–64, 210n55, 210n58,
        210n59, 212n80, 212n81, 212n84,
        212n95, 214n114, 214n116
Taylor, Charles, 131
Taylor, Robert, 223n117
Thebes, 138–40, 143, 192
theory
    and practice, 5, 53, 201–59
    as discourse, 24, 28–29, 207n28
    and resolution/closure, 5, 23–24,
        32–33, 175, 178, 198
Thiele, Leslie Paul, 173–74, 229n74,
        231n100, 231n105
Thomas, Rosalind, 192
Thornhill, Christopher, 205n1, 206–7n27
Thucydides, 4, 9–10, 31–32, 34, 47,
        105–6, 141, 142–43, 144, 150,
        151, 162–63, 176, 178, 200–3, 204
    Archidamus, 192–93
    Athens/Athenians, 140, 179, 181–83,
        184, 185–86, 190–91, 192–94,
        196–97, 202–3
    barbarians, 188–89
    Brasidas, 193–94
    Chalkidike, 193–94
    Corcyra/Corcyrean narrative, 183–84,
        187–89, 198, 234n12
    and democracy, 193, 234n8
    and Derrida, 177–78, 183–84
    Diodotus, 178–79, 184, 191–92, 193,
        194, 199, 203–4
    equality, 191–92
    extremes, 9–10, 183, 187–88
    on factional conflict (*stasis*), 183,
        184, 187–88
    on fear, 190–91
    funeral oration, 181–82,
        187–88, 192–93
    the gods/the divine, 182–83
    greatness, 190–91
    Greeks/Hellenes, 186–87, 188–89
    and Hegel, 141, 142–43, 144, 150, 151,
        176, 188–89, 192–93
    and Hobbes, 105–6, 183–84, 234n12
    Homer/Homeric, 187–88, 192–93
    honor, 190–91, 192–93
    human affairs (*ta anthropeia*),
        182–84, 187–88

Ionians, 187–88
judgment, 189–90
justice, 191–92
logos/logoi, 177–78, 181–82, 189–90,
        191–94, 198
    and Machiavelli, 183–84, 202–3
    Melos/Melians/ Melian Dialogue, 47,
        179, 182–83, 194, 199, 203–4
    motion, 188–89
    Mycalessus, 199, 234n7
    Mytilene debate, 178–79, 191–92,
        194, 203–4
    nature, 182–83, 187–88
    necessity, 9–10, 183, 189–91
    Nicias, 185–86
    and Nietzsche, 162–63, 178–79, 199
    Peloponnesians/Peloponnesian war,
        180, 184, 185–86
    Pericles/Periclean, 27–193, 194–95,
        235n24
    Persians, 184, 191
    and philosophy, 9–10, 178–79, 180–81
    plague narrative, 181–82, 185–86
    Plataea, 192
    and Plato, 9–10, 178–80, 183, 187–88,
        198–99, 201–4
    Potideia, 185–86, 209n26
    and realism, 191, 234n20
    and Schmitt, 183
    Sicily, 199
    Sparta/Spartans (Lacedaemonians),
        184, 187–88, 190–91, 192–94
    suffering, 188–89, 201–2
    Syracuse/Syracusans, 182–83, 185–86
    Thebes/Thebans, 192
    war, significance of, 9–10, 183,
        188–90, 198
    and women, 187–88
    work
        *War Between the Peloponnesians and
        the Athenians*, 202–3
Tocqueville, 168
Truman administration, 208n23
Trump, Donald, 51
Tuck, Richard, 216n4, 222n94

Ulmen, G.L., 28–29, 207n32
United States, 47, 50–51

Vatter, Miguel, 64–65, 66
Virgil/*Aeneid*, 121

Viroli, Maurizio, 64–65, 71, 209n50, 210n54, 210n56, 210n61, 211n66, 211n70, 211n74, 212n91, 212n97, 214n114, 214n116, 214n118, 214n120, 214n122, 214n126, 215n131, 215n132, 215n137

Wagner, Richard, 167
Walzer, Michael, 44–45, 46–48, 49–50, 53, 208n23, 208n24, 209n28, 209n29, 209n31, 224n136, 234n20
war and peace, varying meanings of, 5, 7, 175, 177–78
Warren, Mark, 1, 2–3, 12, 229n74, 229–30n77, 230n79, 230n83, 231n100, 231n105, 231n106
Weiner, Gregory, 211n69
Weiss, Roslyn, 185, 218n39, 235n30
Welliver, Warman, 234n5
White, Jame Boyd, 194
Williams, Bernard, 178, 235n34
Williams, Howard, 216n3
Williams, Michael, 86–87, 221n87
Williams, Robert, 131, 132–33, 149–50, 152, 225n4, 225n5, 225n10, 226n18, 226n19, 226n21, 226n25, 227n30, 227n41, 227n42, 228n49, 228n55, 228n56, 228n59, 229n67

Wolin, Richard, 17, 206n13
Wolin, Sheldon, 3–4, 37–38, 79–80, 210n56, 211n70, 211n71, 215n129
Wonderley, Monique, 232n111, 233n127
Wood, Allen, 146–47, 225n2, 225n4, 227n47, 228n48

Xenophon, 185–86, 209n26, 234n6
Xi, Jinping, 4

Yack, Bernard, 229n73, 232n124
Young, Julian, 230n88, 232n111

Zammito, John, 222n
Zeitlin, Froma. 143
Zuckert, Catherine, 62, 67, 76–77, 209n50, 210n53, 210n56, 210n59, 210n62, 211n64, 211n68, 212n81, 212n84, 212n89, 212n97, 213n100, 214n116, 214n119, 214n121, 214n122, 215n128, 215n130, 215n132, 215n138, 234n5, 234n15, 235n30
Zumbrunnen, John, 194, 227n34